Changing Higher Education in East Asia

Bloomsbury Higher Education Research

Series Editor: Simon Marginson

The Bloomsbury Higher Education Research series provides the evidence-based academic output of the world's leading research centre on higher education, the ESRC/HEFCE Centre for Global Higher Education (CGHE) in the UK. The core focus of CGHE's work and of the Bloomsbury Higher Education Research series is higher education, especially the future of higher education in the changing global landscape. The emergence of CGHE reflects the remarkable growth in the role and importance of universities and other higher education institutions, and research and science, across the world. Corresponding to CGHE's projects, monographs in the series will consist of social science research on global, international, national and local aspects of higher education, drawing on methodologies in education, learning theory, sociology, economics, political science and policy studies. Monographs will be prepared so as to maximise worldwide readership and selected on the basis of their relevance to one or more of higher education policy, management, practice and theory. Topics will range from teaching and learning and technologies, to research and research impact in industry, national system design, the public good role of universities, social stratification and equity, institutional governance and management, and the cross-border mobility of people, institutions, programmes, ideas and knowledge. The Bloomsbury Higher Education Research series is at the cutting edge of world research on higher education.

Advisory Board:
Paul Blackmore, King's College London, UK; Brendan Cantwell, Michigan State University, USA; Gwilym Croucher, University of Melbourne, Australia; Carolina Guzman-Valenzuela, Universidad de Tarapacá, Chile; Glen Jones, University of Toronto, Canada; Barbara Kehm, University of Glasgow, UK; Jenny Lee, University of Arizona, USA; Ye Liu, King's College London, UK; Christine Musselin, Sciences Po, France; Alis Oancea, University of Oxford, UK; Imanol Ordorika, Universidad Nacional Autónoma de México, Mexico; Laura Perna, University of Pennsylvania, USA; Gary Rhoades, University of Arizona, USA; Susan Robertson, University of Cambridge, UK; Yang Rui,

University of Hong Kong, Hong Kong; Pedro Teixeira, University of Porto, Portugal; Jussi Valimaa, University of Jyvaskyla, Finland; N. V. Varghese, National Institute of Educational Planning and Administration, India; Marijk van der Wende, University of Utrecht, The Netherlands; Po Yang, Peking University, China; Akiyoshi Yonezawa, Tohoku University, Japan

Also available in the series:
The Governance of British Higher Education: The Impact of Governmental, Financial and Market Pressures, Michael Shattock and Aniko Horvath
Changing Higher Education for a Changing World, edited by Claire Callender, William Locke and Simon Marginson
Changing Higher Education in India, edited by Saumen Chattopadhyay, Simon Marginson and N. V. Varghese

Changing Higher Education in East Asia

Edited by
Simon Marginson and Xin Xu

BLOOMSBURY ACADEMIC
LONDON • NEW YORK • OXFORD • NEW DELHI • SYDNEY

BLOOMSBURY ACADEMIC
Bloomsbury Publishing Plc
50 Bedford Square, London, WC1B 3DP, UK
1385 Broadway, New York, NY 10018, USA
29 Earlsfort Terrace, Dublin 2, Ireland

BLOOMSBURY, BLOOMSBURY ACADEMIC and the Diana logo are
trademarks of Bloomsbury Publishing Plc

First published in Great Britain, 2022
This paperback edition published 2023

Copyright © Simon Marginson, Xin Xu and Bloomsbury, 2022

Simon Marginson, Xin Xu and Bloomsbury have asserted their right under the Copyright,
Designs and Patents Act, 1988, to be identified as Author of this work.

For legal purposes the Acknowledgements on pp. xix–xx constitute an
extension of this copyright page.

Series design by Adriana Brioso

Cover image © Setthasith Wansuksri/EyeEm/Getty Images

All rights reserved. No part of this publication may be reproduced or transmitted
in any form or by any means, electronic or mechanical, including photocopying,
recording, or any information storage or retrieval system, without prior
permission in writing from the publishers.

Bloomsbury Publishing Plc does not have any control over, or responsibility for, any
third-party websites referred to or in this book. All internet addresses given in this
book were correct at the time of going to press. The author and publisher regret any
inconvenience caused if addresses have changed or sites have ceased to exist, but
can accept no responsibility for any such changes.

A catalogue record for this book is available from the British Library.

Library of Congress Cataloging-in-Publication Data
Names: Marginson, Simon, 1951-editor. | Xu, Xin, 1991-editor.
Title: Changing higher education in East Asia / edited by Simon Marginson and Xin Xu.
Description: London; New York: Bloomsbury Academic, 2022. |
Series: Bloomsbury higher education research |
Includes bibliographical references and index.
Identifiers: LCCN 2021035351 (print) | LCCN 2021035352 (ebook) |
ISBN 9781350216242 (hardback) | ISBN 9781350216259 (pdf) |
ISBN 9781350216266 (ebook)
Subjects: LCSH: Education, Higher–East Asia. | Educational change–East Asia. |
Education and globalization–East Asia.
Classification: LCC LA1143.C464 2022 (print) |
LCC LA1143 (ebook) | DDC 378.5–dc23
LC record available at https://lccn.loc.gov/2021035351
LC ebook record available at https://lccn.loc.gov/2021035352

ISBN: HB: 978-1-3502-1624-2
PB: 978-1-3502-1628-0
ePDF: 978-1-3502-1625-9
eBook: 978-1-3502-1626-6

Series: Bloomsbury Higher Education Research

Typeset by Newgen KnowledgeWorks Pvt. Ltd., Chennai, India

To find out more about our authors and books visit
www.bloomsbury.com and sign up for our newsletters.

Contents

List of Figures	ix
List of Tables	x
Notes on Contributors	xi
Series Editor's Foreword	xiv
Preface and Acknowledgements	xix
List of Abbreviations	xxi

1 'The Ensemble of Diverse Music': Internationalization Strategies and Endogenous Agendas 1
   Simon Marginson and Xin Xu

Part 1   Higher Education and the Global Common Good

2 Global Public Good in Korea as *Jeong* 33
   Olga Mun and Yunkyung Min
3 *Tianxia Weigong* as a Chinese Approach to Global Public Good 51
   Lili Yang
4 Global and World Citizenship in Chinese Education 69
   Arzhia Habibi
5 World-Class Universities and Global Common Good 85
   Lin Tian and Nian Cai Liu

Part 2   Internationalization and Endogenization, Regionalization and Globalization

6 Regional Higher Education Cooperation in Japan 107
   Christopher D. Hammond
7 Internationalization of Chinese Humanities and Social Sciences 129
   Xin Xu
8 Internationalization of Higher Education in Taiwan 147
   Julie Chia-Yi Lin
9 Geopolitics and Internationalization of Higher Education in Vietnam 165
   Ly Thi Tran, Huong Le Thanh Phan and Huyen Bui

Part 3 International Mobility and Academic Migration

10 Agency of International Student-Migrants in Japan 185
    Thomas Brotherhood
11 Motivations and Work Roles of International Faculty in China 203
    Futao Huang
12 The Covid-19 Pandemic and International Higher Education in
    East Asia 225
    Ka Ho Mok

References 247
Index 287

Figures

1.1	Gross Tertiary Enrolment Ratio in East Asian Education Systems, 1990–2019	13
1.2	Number of Papers in Scopus in (1) Physical Sciences STEM, (2) Biological and Health Sciences, (3) Planetary Sciences and (4) Social Sciences and Psychology from the United States, EU, China and Other East Asian countries, 2018	17
3.1	The Escalating Entities from the Individual to All Under Heaven	53
11.1	Changes in Foreign Teachers at Chinese Higher Education Institutions	209
12.1	Total Number of Chinese Tertiary Students Studying Overseas, 2000–20	227
12.2	Chinese Students' Preferred Destinations for Studying Abroad, 2010–20	229
12.3	Sources of Information about Covid-19	234
12.4	Knowledge of Covid-19	235

Tables

1.1	East Asian Nations and Education Systems, Selected Indicators, 2019 or Nearest Year	7
1.2	Twelve Leading Countries/regions in Mathematics, Science and Reading According to the 2018 OECD PISA Survey	9
1.3	Enrolment in Doctoral Education in Selected East Asian Systems	14
1.4	Papers in the Top 5 Per Cent of their Research Field by Citation Rate, Selected Asian Universities, 2006–9 to 2016–19	19
1.5	Top Science Collaborators for East Asian and World Top-Performing Systems, 2019	24
1.6	Mobility Patterns of Outbound and Inbound Students of East Asian Education Systems	25
3.1	The Private/Smaller Self and the Public/Larger Self	53
5.1	A Comparison between (Global) Public Good and (Global) Common Good	88
5.2	Basic Information about the Study Interviewees in World-Class Universities in Three Countries/Regions	91
6.1	Discursive Institutionalism: Levels and Types of Ideas	112
11.1	Characteristics of International Faculty Survey Respondents	212
11.2	Profiles of International Faculty Interviewees	213
11.3	International Faculty's Motivation to Work in Chinese Universities	215
11.4	Factors Affecting International Faculty's Work Life in China	216
11.5	International Faculty's Expected Roles in their University	219
12.1	Top Five Sources of International Students in Australian Higher Education, 2013–19	228
12.2	Wilcoxon Signed Ranks Test of the Differences Among the Various Knowledge Areas of Covid-19	235
12.3	The Most Popular Study Destinations for Chinese Students (Two-Round Comparison)	240

Contributors

Thomas Brotherhood received a DPhil from the Department of Education at the University of Oxford, UK, in 2020 and is currently Assistant Professor at Rikkyo University, Japan. His research is concerned with the internationalization of higher education, with a particular emphasis on the roles and experiences of mobile actors such as international students and foreign-born faculty.

Huyen Bui is Postdoctoral Research Fellow in the School of Education at Deakin University, Australia. Her research interests include the internationalization of higher education, international student acculturation, student mobility and international graduate employability.

Arzhia Habibi is a doctoral candidate in the Department of Education at the University of Oxford, UK. She uses Mandarin to conduct her research in the Chinese higher education context, with a specific focus on exploring the rooted and local expressions of global and world citizenship education. Her fieldwork is generously funded by the Sino-British Fellowship Trust and Universities' China Committee in London, UK.

Christopher D. Hammond received a DPhil from the Department of Education at the University of Oxford, UK, in 2020 and is currently Associate Professor in the College of Arts and Sciences at the University of Tokyo, Japan. His research focuses on studies of higher education internationalization and regionalism in the context of East Asian international relations.

Futao Huang is Professor in the Research Institute for Higher Education at Hiroshima University, Japan. Before he came to Japan in 1999, he taught and conducted research in several Chinese universities. His research interests include internationalization of higher education, the academic profession and higher education in East Asia, focused on China and Japan.

Julie Chia-Yi Lin is reading for her DPhil at the University of Oxford, UK. She has eight years of experience working in higher education and has been an administrator in international affairs at National Taiwan University, Taiwan, and an academic publisher. Her current research focus is on the internationalization of higher education, and university strategy and governance in East Asia.

Nian Cai Liu is Director of the Center for World-Class Universities and Dean of the Graduate School of Education at Shanghai Jiao Tong University, China. His research interests include world-class universities and research universities, university evaluation and academic ranking, globalization and internationalization of higher education. His recent books include *World-Class Universities: Towards a Global Common Good and Seeking National and Institutional Contributions* and *Matching Visibility and Performance: A Standing Challenge for World-Class Universities*.

Simon Marginson is Professor of Higher Education at the University of Oxford, UK, director of the ESRC/OFSRE Centre for Global Higher Education, joint editor-in-chief of the journal *Higher Education*, a lead researcher with the Institute of Education at the Higher School of Economics in Moscow, Russia, and a professorial fellow of the University of Melbourne, Australia. His work is mostly focused on international and global aspects of higher education, the global science system, the contributions of higher education and higher education and social equality.

Yunkyung Min completed her PhD project in educational administration and policy studies for her research on the governance policy of national universities in South Korea and is currently Programme Coordinator at the College of Liberal Studies, Seoul National University, Seoul, South Korea.

Ka Ho Mok is Vice President and concurrently Chair Professor of Comparative Policy of Lingnan University, Hong Kong. He researches and publishes on higher education policy and governance, comparative development and policy studies, and social development in contemporary China and East Asia. Ka Ho was named Changjiang Chair Professor of Comparative Education and East Asian Studies by the Ministry of Education in China in 2010.

Olga Mun is working on her doctoral dissertation on internationalization of research at the Department of Education, University of Oxford, UK. She is a co-convenor of the Comparative and International Education Special Interest Group at British Educational Research Association (BERA) and was previously a teaching fellow at the UCL Institute of Education, University College London, UK.

Huong Le Thanh Phan is Research Fellow in the School of Education at Deakin University, Australia. She obtained her PhD in education at Deakin University, Australia, in 2020. Her research interests include language and cultural issues, graduate employability and international education with a specialisation in the internationalization of the curriculum.

Lin Tian is Assistant Professor in the Research Institute of Education Science at Hunan University, China. Her research interests include the functions of world-class universities, and the globalization and internationalization of higher education.

Ly Thi Tran is Professor in the School of Education at Deakin University, Australia, and an Australian Research Council Future Fellow. Her research focuses on internationalization of education, international students, international graduate employability, learning abroad and Vietnamese higher education.

Xin Xu is Research Fellow in the ESRC/OFSRE Centre for Global Higher Education in the Department of Education at the University of Oxford, UK. Her research focuses on the academic research, internationalization and globalization of higher education, and Chinese higher education.

Lili Yang received a DPhil from the Department of Education at the University of Oxford, UK, in 2021. Her postdoctoral work in the ESRC/OFSRE Centre for Global Higher Education is focused on higher education and the public good. In her doctoral thesis, she explored the similarities and differences between notions of 'public' in Sinic and liberal Anglo-American traditions, and the implications for higher education.

Series Editor's Foreword

Changing Higher Education in East Asia is the fourth book to be published in the Bloomsbury Higher Education Research book series. This series brings to the public, government and universities across the world the new ideas and research evidence being generated by researchers from the ESRC/OFSRE Centre for Global Higher Education.[1] The Centre for Global Higher Education (CGHE), a partnership of researchers from ten UK and international universities, is the world's largest concentration of expertise in relation to higher education and its social contributions. The core focus of CGHE's work, and of the Bloomsbury Higher Education Research Series, is higher education, especially the future of higher education in the changing global landscape.

Each year this mega-topic of 'higher education' seems to take on greater importance for governments, business, civil organizations, students, families and the public at large. In higher education much is at stake. The role and impact of the sector is growing everywhere. More than 220 million students enrol at tertiary level across the world, four-fifths of them in degree programmes. Almost 40 per cent of school leavers now enter some kind of tertiary education each year, though resources and quality vary significantly. In North America and Europe, this ratio rises to four young people in every five. Universities and colleges are seen as the primary medium for personal opportunity, social mobility and the development of whole communities. About 2.5 million new science papers are published worldwide each year, and the role of research in industry and government continues to expand everywhere.

In short, there is much at stake in higher education. It has become central to social, economic and political life. One reason is that even while serving local society and national policy, the higher education and research sectors are especially globalized in character. Each year 6 million students change countries in order to enrol in their chosen study programme, and more than a quarter of

---

[1] The initials ESRC/OFSRE stand for the Economic and Social Research Council/Office for Students and Research England. Part of the ESRC funding that supports the Centre for Global Higher Education's research work was sourced from the Higher Education Funding Council for England, the ancestor body to the OFS and RE.

all published research papers involve joint authorship across national borders. In some countries, fee-based international education is a major source of export revenues, while this results in some other countries losing talent in net terms each year. Routine cross-border movements of students, academics and researchers, knowledge, information and money help to shape not only nations but the international order itself.

At the same time, the global higher education landscape is changing with compelling speed, reflecting larger economic, political and cultural shifts in the geostrategic setting. Though research universities in the United States (especially) and UK remain strong in comparative terms, the worldwide map of power in higher education is becoming more plural. A larger range of higher education practices, including models of teaching/learning, delivery, institutional organization and system, will shape higher education in future. Anglo-American (and Western) norms and models will be less dominant, and will themselves evolve. Rising universities and emerging science systems in East Asia and Singapore are already reshaping the flow of knowledge and higher education. Latin America, Southeast Asia, India, Central Asia and the Arab nations have a growing global importance. The trajectories of education and research in Sub-Saharan Africa are crucial to state-building and community development.

All of this has led to a more intensive focus on how higher education systems and institutions function and their value, performance, effectiveness, openness and sustainability. This in turn has made research on higher education more significant – both because it provides us with insights into one important facet of the human condition and because it informs evidenced-based government policies and professional practices.

CGHE opened in late 2015 and is currently funded until October 2023. The centre investigates higher education using a range of social science disciplines, including economics, sociology, political science and policy studies, psychology and anthropology, and it uses a portfolio of quantitative, qualitative and synthetic-historical research techniques. It currently maintains ten research projects, variously of between eighteen months and eight years' duration, as well as smaller projects, and involves about forty active affiliated individual researchers. Over its eight-year span, it is financed by about £10 million in funding from the UK Economic and Social Research Council, partner universities and other sources. Its UK researchers are drawn from the Universities of Oxford, Lancaster, Surrey, Bath and University College London (UCL). The headquarters of the centre are located at Oxford, and there are large concentrations of researchers at both Oxford and UCL. The current affiliated international researchers are from Hiroshima University in Japan, Shanghai Jiao Tong University in China, Lingnan University in Hong Kong, Cape Town University in South Africa, Virginia Tech in the United States and Technological University Dublin. CGHE also collaborates with researchers from many other universities across the world through seminars, conferences and exchange of papers. It runs an active programme of global webinars.

The centre has a full agenda. The unprecedented growth of mass higher education, the striving for excellence and innovation in the research university sector, as well as the changing global landscape pose many researchable problems for governments, societies and higher education institutions themselves. Some of these questions already figure in CGHE research projects. For example: What are the formative effects on societies and economies of the now much wider distribution of advanced levels of learning? How does it change individual graduates as people – and what does it mean when half or more of the workforce is higher educated and much more mobile, and when confident human agency has become widely distributed across civil and political society in nations with little state tradition, or where the main experience has been colonial or authoritarian rule? What does it mean when many more people are becoming steeped in the sciences, many others understand the world through the lenses of the social sciences or humanities while a third group is engaged in neither? What happens to those parts of the population left outside the formative effects of higher education? What is the larger public role and contribution of higher education, as distinct from the private benefits for and private effects on individual graduates? What does it mean when large and growing higher education institutions have become the major employers in many locations and help to sustain community and cultural life, almost like branches of local government while also being linked to global cities across the world? And what is the contribution of higher education, beyond helping to form the attributes of individual graduates, to the development of the emerging global society?

Likewise, the many practical problems associated with building higher education and science take on greater importance. How can scarce public budgets provide for the public role of higher education institutions, for a socially equitable system of individual access and for research excellence, all at the same time? What is the role for and limits of family financing and tuition loans systems? What is the potential contribution of private institutions, including for-profit colleges? In national systems, what is the best balance between research-intensive and primarily teaching institutions, and between academic and vocational education? What are the potentials for technological delivery in extending access? What is happening in graduate labour markets, where returns to degrees are becoming more dispersed between families with differing levels of income, and graduates from different kinds of universities and different fields of study? Do larger education systems provide better for social mobility and income equality? How does the internationalization of universities contribute to national policy and local societies? Does mobile international education expand opportunity or further stratify societies? What are the implications of populist tensions between national and global goals – as manifest, for example, in the tensions over Brexit in the UK and the politics of the Trump era in the United States – for higher education and research? And always, what can national systems of higher education and science learn from each other, and how can they build stronger common ground?

In tackling these research challenges and bringing the research to all, we are very grateful to have the opportunity to work with such a high-quality publisher as Bloomsbury. In the book series, monographs are selected on the basis of their relevance to one or more themes of higher education policy, management, practice and theory. Topics range from teaching and learning and technologies to research and its organization; the design parameters of national higher education systems; the public good role of higher education; social stratification and equity; institutional governance and management; and the cross-border mobility of people, programmes and ideas. Much of CGHE's work is global and comparative in scale, drawing lessons from higher education in many different countries, and the centre's cross-country and multi-project structure allows it to tap into the more plural higher education and research landscape that has emerged. The book series draws on authors from across the world and is prepared for relevance across the world.

CGHE places special emphasis on the relevance of its research, on communicating its findings and on maximizing the usefulness and impacts of those findings in higher education policy and practice. It has a relatively high public profile for an academic research centre and reaches out to engage higher education stakeholders, national and international organizations, policy-makers, regulators and the broader public in the UK and across the world. These objectives are also central to the book series. Recognizing that the translation from research outputs to high-quality scholarly monographs is not always straightforward – while achieving impact in both academic and policy/practice circles is crucial – monographs in the book series are scrutinized critically before publication, for readability as well as quality. Texts are carefully written and edited to ensure that they have achieved the right combination of, on one hand, intellectual depth and originality and, on the other, full accessibility for public, higher education and policy circles across the world.

Simon Marginson
Professor of Higher Education, University of Oxford
Director, ESRC/OFSRE Centre for Global Higher Education.

Preface and Acknowledgements

It is exciting to be working on higher education and knowledge in East Asia at this time because rapid developments are taking place, agency and capability are advancing and much is being achieved in the different countries. East Asian systems are also becoming more proactive at the global level. We sense it is early days yet in the formation of a more plural higher education world, where many cultural strands will mingle on the basis of equality of respect in *he er bu tong* (和而不同, meaning 'harmony without uniformity'). Nevertheless, if that happy outcome is to be achieved, the continuing local, national and global evolution of higher education in East Asia will be central to the process – in conjunction with the development of higher education, science and dialogic scholarship throughout the world.

In developing a more plural and constructive global conversation about higher education and knowledge, there are formidable obstacles to overcome. First, we are all constrained by the fact that higher education and science at the global level are still largely practiced as a Euro-American English-only monoculture, something we seek to problematize and challenge with this book, and in all our work. Second, there is the geopolitical dimension. *Changing Higher Education in East Asia* was prepared in and around the ESRC/OFSRE Centre for Global Higher Education and the Department of Education at Oxford University where the spirit of East/West engagement is mutually humanist, positive and intellectually stimulating. Yet the book was also prepared in 2020–1, at a time of sharply worsening relations between the United States and its closer allies, on one hand, and China, on the other. Signs of a new cold war were beginning to impact the UK where we are based. The determination of the US government to 'contain' China so as to maintain American global primacy as an end in itself, as if the United States has all the answers to humanity's problems and Chinese civilization has little to contribute, and the active pressures to decouple China and the United States in science and technology, including the stigmatizing of Chinese scholars and students in the West as 'spies' and 'dupes', are unlikely to be realized as intended. But these moves could do formidable damage to global cooperation and make mutual learning and global problem-solving much more difficult to achieve. *Changing Higher Education in East Asia* has been prepared in the conviction that no single culture, civilization or country has all of the answers and the world does not need a single hegemon. Both Chinese civilization (with its deep influence and various manifestations across East Asia) and Euro-American civilization have profound strengths. Each provides certain things that the other lacks. Other traditions also have vital contributions to make. Global West, East, North and South (terms all too simplistic to capture the complexity) have much to learn from each other. Unless that process of engaged and mutual learning takes place in higher education and science, it will not take place anywhere, and if it does not take place, there will be no viable global solutions to the existential global problems that we all face. Deep global cooperation: simple and obvious in conception, yet we inch towards it so very slowly.

In preparing this book, we have benefited from the generous and speedy responses of our authors throughout the process and have been enriched by their original insights and fine writing. Critical feedback and revisions have significantly improved the book. We thank them all most sincerely. We thank Ly Tran, Soyoung Lee and Ikuya Aizawa for their help with the information about the characters opening each part of this volume. We are grateful for the reviewers' helpful feedback. We also thank each other for the happy and enriching experience of working together on this book and on the concurrent teaching and scholarly writing. The planning, administration, editing and writing of Chapter 1 were shared equally. The order of the authors' names reflects the alphabetical convention used in books and papers related to the work of the ESRC/OFSRE Centre for Global Higher Education.

At Bloomsbury, we benefited from the wise guidance of academic editor Alison Baker and the help of Evangeline Stanford. We also appreciated the work of production editor Zeba Talkhani and designer Charlotte James.

Abbreviations

A&HCI	Arts and Humanities Citation Index
AEARU	Association of East Asian Research Universities
AIMS	ASEAN International Mobility for Students
AIT	Asian Institute of Technology (Thailand)
ARWU	Academic Ranking of World Universities
ASEAN	Association of Southeast Asian Nations
ATUP	Aim for the Top University Program
BRI	BRI Belt and Road Initiative
CAMPUS Asia	Collective Action for the Mobility Program of University Students in Asia
CCIP	Chamber of Commerce and Industry of Paris
CCP	Chinese Communist Party
Covid-19	Coronavirus Disease 2019
CSSCI	Chinese Social Sciences Citation Index
CSTI	Council for Science, Technology and Innovation (Japan)
DPP	Democratic Progressive Party
ESI	Essential Science Indicators
ESRC	Economic and Social Research Council
FICHET	Foundation for International Cooperation in Higher Education of Taiwan
GATS	General Agreement on Trade in Services
GBA	Greater Bay Area
GDP	Gross Domestic Product
HEIs	Higher Education Institutions
JSPS	Japan Society for the Promotion of Science
KAIST	Korea Advanced Institute of Science and Technology
KEDI	Korean Educational Development Institute
KMT	Kuomintang
LDP	Liberal Democratic Party
MEXT	Ministry of Education, Culture, Sports, Science and Technology (Japan)
MIT	Massachusetts Institute of Technology

MOE	Ministry of Education
MOET	Ministry of Education and Training
NIAD-QE	National Institution for Academic Degrees and Quality Enhancement of Higher Education
NRF	National Research Foundation (Korea)
NSB	National Science Board (United States)
NSFC	National Natural Science Foundation of China
NSR	New Silk Road
NTD	New Taiwan Dollar
OECD	Organisation for Economic Cooperation and Development
OFSRE	Office for Students Research England
OKAS	Oxford Korean Academic Society
PISA	Programme for International Student Assessment
PPP	Purchasing Power Parity
PRC	People's Republic of China
QS	Quacquarelli Symonds
RCEP	Regional Comprehensive Economic Partnership
REF	Research Excellence Framework
RMIT	Royal Melbourne Institute of Technology
RU	Research University
SAR	Special Administrative Region
SCI	Science Citation Index
SPROUT	Sustained Progress and Rise of Universities in Taiwan
SSCI	Social Sciences Citation Index
STEM	Science, Technology, Engineering and Mathematics
STI	Science, Technology and Innovation
TCS	Trilateral Cooperation Secretariat
THE	Times Higher Education
TPP	Trans-Pacific Partnership
UASR	University Alliance of the Silk Road
UCL	University College London
UNESCO	United Nations Educational, Social and Cultural Organization
UNNC	University of Nottingham Ningbo China
VND	Vietnamese Dong
WCU	World-Class University
WoS	Web of Science
WTO	World Trade Organization

1

'The Ensemble of Diverse Music': Internationalization Strategies and Endogenous Agendas

Simon Marginson and Xin Xu

When the second Sino-Japanese War broke out in 1937, three prestigious universities in China, Peking University, Tsinghua University and Nankai University, moved from northern to southern China for protection, merging as the National Southwestern Associated University (西南联合大学, *xi nan lian he da xue*). The multi-university flourished during the war period and was home to many prominent academics. In an essay (Feng 1946/2020) for the commemorative stele of the university, Chinese philosopher Feng Youlan (冯友兰) wrote thus:

同无妨异，异不害同。五色交辉，相得益彰。八音合奏，终和且平。

Commonalities do not obstruct differences;

Differences do not harm commonalities.

The matching of different colours leads to greater beauty;

The ensemble of diverse music brings peace and harmony.

Introduction

If the twenty-first century is the Asian century, it is partly the East Asian century. By 'East Asia' we mean not just a geographical zone but a cultural and geopolitical zone, the part of the world shaped by Chinese (Sinic) civilization. After a long period of eclipse for much of the nineteenth and twentieth centuries, except in Japan, East Asia has become as globally important as the modern West, the zone of Western Europe and North America.

For the past four hundred years, the West has dominated the world, first through acquisitive colonization and trading power and then through the industrial revolution, military supremacy, technological edge and cultural institutions, including universities and science. In the past two hundred years, Western domination has been Anglo-American domination. In the past two decades, a blink of time by historical standards, the era of Western domination has passed. The East is not replacing the West. The United States remains strong. Rather, the East is rising alongside the West, and along with other countries and regions such as India, Indonesia and Southeast Asia, Iran, Brazil and Latin America. The economic transition is already apparent. Eventually the cultural transition will have equal impact. The more multipolar world now emerging is disrupting the old Western cultural hegemony (Pieterse 2018), which is a racialized English-speaking white supremacy (Shahjahan and Edwards 2021) that subordinated all other economies, polities and cultures, all other agency, as obstacles to overcome or resources to use. In the emerging world, the Sinic role will be immense.

What Is East Asia?

East Asia is not just China, although China is now the largest economy in the world if purchasing power parity (PPP) measures are used. 'East Asia' extends from the mainland of China to include the 'Greater China', the Hong Kong Special Administrative Region (SAR), the Macau Special Administrative Region (SAR) and Taiwan, which was carved out of the mainland by the retreating Kuomintang, with American support, when the Communist Party of China took power in 1949. More controversially, East Asia includes Korea, Japan, Vietnam and Mongolia. These nations are entirely independent of China in the political sense and distinct in cultural and linguistic terms. In a constantly changing world, each is evolving with its own mix of global and national elements. Japan was never territorially incorporated into China; Korea was never conquered for long; and China's province of Annam in North Vietnam threw off the imperial yoke in 939 CE. Mongolia housed nomad polities on the northern border that alternately conquered China and was conquered by it. However, there are deep common traditions (Holcombe 2011) that unite East Asian nations in the same manner that Western Europe has a common heritage. The other countries share with China the influence of classical Chinese language, Confucianism and Buddhism, which moved from India to China, to Korea and then Japan during the high point of regional cultural sharing, the Sui and Tang dynasties in China (581–907 CE). Both Korea and Japan share China's comprehensive and centralizing form of state, which began as comprehensive in the statecraft of the Western Zhou (1046–771 BCE) and momentously took centralising shape in the Qin (221–207 BCE) and Han (202 BCE–220 CE) dynasties that have patterned all Sinic polities ever since.

More controversially still, the cultural zone of East Asia might be expanded to include the dynamic city-state of Singapore, with a majority Chinese population, Confucian educational tradition in the family and a Chinese style state; though many in Singapore emphasize that their nation is multicultural and multi-ethnic, and argue that Singapore's identity is defined more by its modern global role than by its cultural or regional lineage. *Changing Higher Education in East Asia* includes chapters on China (here referring to mainland China, as with all uses of 'China' that follow in the chapter), Hong Kong SAR, Taiwan, South Korea, Japan and Vietnam, though Macau SAR, Mongolia and Singapore are not covered here. Closed North Korea is not included either, because there are no data on its higher education.

The rise of East Asia is apparent not only in political economy but in higher education, research and science, and here deeply rooted cultural commonalities are apparent. All countries except Mongolia share the Confucian norm of self-cultivation through learning, cognitive and ethical formation in the lifelong work of the self on the self, first in the family from a very early age and then in education (Li 2012). The key moment is the formation in every child, typically at six or seven years, of *lizhi*, the reflexive commitment or 'will' to learn (163). In higher education, the East Asian systems are moving to, and in South Korea and Taiwan have surpassed, the levels of social participation in Western countries. China has overtaken the United States to become the world's largest producer of new published scientific knowledge, with Japan being the fourth largest and South Korea the ninth largest. The number of 'world-class universities' (WCUs) in the region is increasing each year, and in research in the physical sciences and related fields (though not in other fields), the top universities in China and Singapore now generate as much high citation science as do the top US universities. The system-building achievements of East Asian higher education and science – first in Japan in the nineteenth century and again after the Second World War, and then in South Korea, Taiwan, Singapore from the 1980s and China from the 1990s – are quite extraordinary. East Asian nations share a mode of state-led, centrally focused, accelerated development, grounded in high investment and performance targets, and resting on an ethic of self-improvement that is shared by individuals and institutions. This again suggests a common culture.

The building of these dynamic higher education systems, and the close parallels from case to case, especially in temporality, dramatically confirm that modern China, Taiwan, the Koreas and even Singapore continue to be partly patterned by the Zhou-Qin-Han inheritance of state-led political culture and the traditional Sinic capacity of populations to work collectively for ends shared by local communities and the state (Marginson and Yang 2021). These same capacities for effective state policy, combined with shared social responsibility from below, have been apparent during the Covid-19 pandemic, in which the death tolls in China, Taiwan, South Korea and Singapore have been relatively very low, and casualties in Japan and Vietnam have also been small in comparison to Western countries and the global South (Marginson 2020). During the pandemic, East Asian polities and societies have given priority to human well-being, grounded in Confucian humanism (*ren*), and demonstrated commitment to the public realm and community, and willingness to surrender personal interests for the larger collective good. As a result, the pandemic has scarred East Asian countries less than other countries. It seems certain that one outcome of the pandemic period will be to elevate these countries in global terms, in economy, politics, society and culture. The pandemic might also lead to enhanced regional mobility in higher education, as Chapter 12 suggests. With journeying to the West more hazardous and constrained, countries, universities, faculties, and students in East Asia may travel more within the region itself.

At the same time as endogenous cultural influences have been playing out, the East Asian systems have been strongly influenced by Western and especially US templates in building higher education and research. In every higher education system in the region, Western norms and practices are in tension with both traditional and modern endogenous thinking. But the relation between Westernization and endogenization is not zero sum; it is more complicated. In higher education, internationalization is selective and driven by national 'catch-up' agendas, not imposed from outside in a neo-imperial fashion as it once was by the Western powers, and endogenous cultural contents are becoming more important. Adapting the point made by Jacques (2012) about China, as East Asian countries become stronger they become more distinctively East Asian. The relationship, tension and synergies between isomorphic internationalization and national-cultural agendas and contents is a significant theme through the chapters of *Changing Higher Education in East Asia*.

Deep cultural roots are one thing, while contemporary agreement is another. Although East Asian countries face a shared 'rival' – the West – the struggle against an external rival does not lead to an internally integrated region in the political sense. East Asia's cultural commonalities have not led to the formation of a consensual regional identity and machinery of intergovernmental cooperation, with commitment to growing integration over time, in the manner of the European Union – East Asian nations are no closer to political regionalization than was Europe before the Second World War. There is a successful regional grouping in Asia; however, it is not in East Asia but in Southeast Asia. The Association of Southeast Asian Nations (ASEAN) is a free trade zone of ten nations that collaborate effectively in education and many other areas. ASEAN includes Vietnam and Singapore but not the nations and systems of Northeast Asia. China, Japan and South Korea attend some ASEAN meetings and by this backdoor mechanism deal with each other diplomatically. Mostly, these three nations are politically estranged, especially at the public level, while the smaller countries and SARs in East Asia are often on the defensive, minnows that navigate a changing course between the bigger fish. Each country in East Asia typically retreats to its national container and emphasizes nationalism, which is demonstrated variously not only by de-Westernization, but also by the assertion of de-Chinalization and de-Japanization within the region.

The historical wounds inflicted by Japan's aggression in the first half of the twentieth century have not healed, and both South Korea and Japan are wary of the growing strength of the much larger China. During China's long imperial period, Korea paid tribute to China while Japan refused to do so. Given their own successful modernization in the contemporary era, neither country wants to adopt a subordinate relationship now, but it seems difficult to devise a relationship of equals, and China is not impelled to do so. Relations are worsened by the positioning of Korea and Japan as US allies in American strategies designed to block China's rise and confine it through military means, with a half circle of US bases and deployments around its Pacific shore. Vietnam and China have a separate 2,200-year history of conflict. Hong Kong SAR returned to China in 1997 but its political culture has been shaped by the years in which it was an outlier of the West as a British colony, and there are tensions between many people in the SAR and the mainland polity led by the Communist Party of China. If it was a united region, East Asia would be a great powerhouse, but it is bedevilled by these questions of history, decoloniality, equality, respect, balance and primacy as well as the geopolitics of the America/China standoff. Media are often xenophobic, and routine cooperation at official levels is fraught.

East Asian higher education is not – and never has been – a unity itself. Though East Asia is a region in the cultural sense, it is not a region in other ways, especially given the internal political tensions. The region lacks top-level structure of coordination for interregional higher education cooperation. None of the handful of university-initiated or government-initiated programmes, such as Association of East Asian Research Universities (AEARU) and Collective Action for the Mobility Program of University Students in Asia (CAMPUS Asia), is on anything like the scale of the Erasmus and Horizon programmes in European Union. China's Belt and Road Initiative and the subsequent University Alliance of the Silk Road (UASR) includes a small number of universities in Hong Kong SAR, South Korea and Japan, but it primarily extends to partners outside East Asia in Eurasia, Africa and Latin America (UASR 2021). The regionalization of East Asian higher education manifests not in system-wide cooperation, but in the shared cultural base (despite resistance to this idea, when systems are determined to assert national identity) and, often more promisingly, in the bottom-up cooperation between universities and between individual scholars, scientists and students who work across the borders.

In this introductory chapter, we provide a brief summary of economy, demography, society and higher education and science in East Asia, and we trace the building of mass higher education systems as well as the concurrent building of science systems in the region. We also explore East Asian higher education between the antinomies of Western modernization and East Asian identity and strategy. Finally, we foreground the chapters in the book.

Diversity and Commonality

Size, Economy, Education

Table 1.1 sets down features of the economy, demography, society and education in East Asia. At first sight the differences stand out, particularly in size, language and wealth. In population, economy and surface area, mainland China towers over the region. In 2019, its GDP of USD23.5 trillion constituted 17.2 per cent of world GDP, with East Asia as a whole constituting one-quarter of world GDP. In 2019, China's per capita income was just below the world average, but the processes of modernization and the movement from the countryside to the cities are still unfolding and GDP per capita is highly uneven by region, with

Table 1.1 East Asian Nations and Education Systems, Selected Indicators, 2019 or Nearest Year

Country/Region[a]	Main use language	Population 2019 millions	Surface area 2019 sq. km. ('000s)	Total GDP PPP 2019 USD billion	GDP PPP per capita 2019 USD	Gross tertiary enrolment ratio	
						1990 %	2019 %
China (mainland)	Mandarin	1,397.7	9,600	23,488	16,804	3	54
Japan	Japanese	126.3	378	5,504	43,594	n.a.	n.a.
Vietnam	Vietnamese	96.5	331	810	8,397	3	29
South Korea	Korean	51.7	100	2,276	44,011	37	96
Taiwan	Mandarin	23.6	36	1,143	49,800	n.a.	n.a.
Hong Kong SAR	Cantonese	7.5	1.0	469	62,496	18	81
Singapore	English	5.7	0.7	580	101,649	n.a.	89
Mongolia	Mongol	3.2	1,564	42	12,862	18	66
Macau SAR	Cantonese	0.6	0.03	83	129,451	33	100
World	–	7,673.5	134,543	136,678	17,201	14	39

[a] See text for discussion of which countries and regions are included in 'East Asia'. n.a. = data not available. GDP = gross domestic product. PPP = purchasing power parity. US = United States. SAR = special administrative region. US dollar amounts are current 2019 prices. Gross tertiary enrolment data for Hong Kong SAR is for the year 1992 not 1990; for Singapore and Mongolia, it is 2018 not 2019.

Source: Authors, original data from World Bank (2021); UNESCO (2021); United States Central Intelligence Agency (CIA) for Taiwan data.

the urbanized Eastern parts of the country much wealthier than the Western provinces.

Leaving aside thinly populated Mongolia, East Asia divides into (1) China, a region in itself, (2) medium-sized Japan, South Korea and Vietnam, with the last much poorer than the others; and (3) the small densely populated high capitalist enclaves of Taiwan, the largest of these, Hong Kong SAR, Macau SAR and Singapore. Japan, South Korea and the countries/regions in group 3 now have per capita incomes akin to those of Western Europe. On this measure, Singapore has become significantly wealthier than even Switzerland.

In the past four decades, the whole region, with the exception of Mongolia, has been energized and transformed by accelerated economic development led by state policies. Japan became the world's second largest economy by the 1980s; however, its economy entered a long period of stagnation in the early 1990s. China has experienced high annual economic growth since the mid-1980s, and the other countries in the region have also seen rapid growth by world standards, albeit less consistently than in China. Economic transformation has underpinned the advance of participation in higher education. Table 1.1 compares the gross tertiary enrolment ratio in 1990 with that in 2019. In China the ratio advanced from 3 per cent to 54 per cent, and in South Korea it was close to 100 per cent in 2019.

Table 1.1 also indicates the diverse languages in use. There are two primary groupings: the Chinese languages Mandarin, the national language, and Cantonese, and the languages Mongol, Korean and Japanese, which are not mutually intelligible but have common roots in the Altaic zone in central Asia. Mongol is spoken in Eastern Mongolia with various Chinese languages used elsewhere in the country. Vietnamese is the largest Austroasiatic language. It has been significantly influenced by successive borrowings from Chinese and like Chinese, but unlike the Altaic derivatives, it uses tonal forms in speech. However, while the region is linguistically diverse, China, the SARs and Taiwan, South Korea, Japan and Vietnam have for long shared written Chinese. The written forms of Korean Hanja and Japanese Kanji derive from classical Chinese. This is one key to the underlying cultural similarities.

As noted, another important cultural similarity is the common commitment to Confucian self-cultivation (Tu 1985), manifest in the priority given to education by families and the state. All countries in the region that are tested perform exceptionally well in the Organisation for Economic Cooperation and Development's (OECD) periodic comparison of learning achievement at age fifteen, the Programme for International Student Assessment (PISA),

Table 1.2 Twelve Leading Countries/Regions in Mathematics, Science and Reading According to the 2018 OECD PISA Survey

Mathematics		Science		Reading	
China (four provinces)	591	China (four provinces)	590	China (four provinces)	555
Singapore	569	Singapore	551	Singapore	549
Macau SAR	558	Macau SAR	544	Macau SAR	525
Hong Kong SAR	551	Estonia	530	Hong Kong SAR	524
Taiwan	531	Japan	529	Estonia	523
Japan	527	Finland	522	Canada	520
South Korea	526	South Korea	519	Finland	520
Estonia	523	Canada	518	Ireland	518
Netherlands	519	Hong Kong SAR	517	South Korea	514
Poland	516	Taiwan	516	Poland	512
Switzerland	519	Poland	511	Sweden	506
Canada	512	New Zealand	508	New Zealand	506

Note: The four Chinese provinces are Beijing, Shanghai, Jiangsu and Zhejiang.
Source: Authors, original data from OECD (2019: 17–18).

as Table 1.2 shows. East Asian schooling systems occupy the first seven places in the PISA mathematics comparison and seven of the first ten places in science. They are slightly less strong as a group in reading, but all are in the top seventeen out of the seventy-eight education systems in that comparison. The performance of the four Chinese provinces can be noted. While these are in affluent parts of the country, and scores in poorer parts of China are lower, a reasonable comparison to city-provinces such as Beijing and Shanghai is the wealthy urbanized communities of Singapore or Hong Kong SAR which are richer than the Chinese cities. As Table 1.2 shows, the Chinese provinces are way ahead of even Singapore and Hong Kong in mathematics and science, and also first in the world in reading (OECD 2019: 17–18). The OECD notes:

> Around one in six 15-year-old students in Beijing, Shanghai, Jiangsu and Zhejiang (China) (16.5%), and about one in seven students in Singapore (13.8%), scored at Level 6 in mathematics, the highest level of proficiency that PISA describes. These students are capable of advanced mathematical thinking and reasoning. On average across OECD countries, only 2.4% of students scored at this level. (OECD 2019: 15)

This concentration of well-formed talent is highly significant, but equally important is the fact that the proportion of the age group in the Chinese provinces that achieve below level 2 in all three disciplines is exceptionally low (1.1 per cent). This compares with the OECD average of 13.4 per cent. The low achiever group is also relatively small (2.3 to 7.5 per cent) in the other East Asian systems (OECD 2019: 17–18). This is much the strongest region in the world in terms of student learning achievement, and it is a levelling up achievement in which almost no child is left behind. Other countries talk about it; East Asian countries do it. It is an exceptional social-cultural platform for fostering the capability of populations and the development of higher education.

A Common Dynamic of Educational Development?

As the chapters in this book demonstrate, East Asian state strategies and policies in higher education are nationally nuanced. The political systems and cultures vary. The economic and social challenges are different. The inherited resources for education, and the capacity of states and families to invest in education, are uneven. Nevertheless, at the outset of this book, we want to expand on the dynamism common to all of the East Asian education systems where the national wealth approaches or exceeds world average GDP per capita. This common dynamic rests on two elements derived from the heritage of Chinese civilization. First, as noted, there is the classical Chinese state, which assumes a comprehensive responsibility for order, stability and prosperity, and intervenes at will. It is not a limited liberal state of the Anglo-American kind (Marginson and Yang 2021). Compared to most states outside East Asia, the East Asian state operates at a relatively high level of competence, especially in matters of designated national priority, which in the past thirty years (earlier in Japan) have included higher education and science. Second, there is the Confucian educational family.

Ten years ago, one of us published a paper arguing that the Sinic education systems can be understood in terms of a distinctive 'Confucian model' of higher education development (Marginson 2011). Later the term was amended to 'post-Confucian model' to acknowledge the impact of Western modernization in East Asia, and the resulting hybridity, but the argument about the distinctive features of the model was unchanged (Marginson 2013). In summary, the post-Confucian model of higher education system is embodied by the following:

- Focused state policies with a long-term horizon, supported by monitoring of measured performance, animated by the drive to lift educational

participation, scientific output and the leading universities to Western (especially US) levels;
- Deep and universal Confucian aspiration for education and the embedded family commitment to education, including a willingness to share the national cost through both normal schooling and shadow schooling, releasing additional state resources for institution-building, research and quality improvement;
- A shared perception concerning higher education's contribution to both individual cultivation and the public good; hence the common focus on quality education, respect for teachers and commitment to continuously developing and improving education among government, university, faculty, families and students;
- Advanced levels of national investment, continually increasing as a proportion of GDP, especially in China and Singapore. National investment is crucial to the post-Confucian model. In the two systems where the growth of investment has stopped, Japan and Taiwan, educational development has lost most of its dynamism, and until now Vietnam and Mongolia have been too poor to pursue advanced investment;
- The growth of educational infrastructure in both the public and private sectors, enabling the rapid expansion of participation in a range of institutions, with the state carrying only part of the cost of infrastructure but regulating private sector quality as a public good. This includes private sector policy in Japan and South Korea, where those institutions house the majority of students;
- The focused development of a layer of leading research-intensive universities or WCUs, a strategy vigorously pursued by all East Asian systems;
- The mediation of participation and access to institutions of hierarchical value on the basis of social consensus by the universal examination systems inherited from the imperial tradition. This instrument allows participation to be expanded to any level without changing systemic structures or destabilizing system norms;
- Systematic strategies of internationalization to drive improvement (e.g. Wang, Wang and Liu 2011), including partnership building, benchmarking of disciplines and institutions, selective adaptation of systemic and organizational templates, offshore doctoral study and researcher experience, and inward people mobility.

Among scholars there has been some push-back against the notion of a post-Confucian model, on the grounds of differences of national identity between

East Asian countries, or on the grounds that national development should be understood in universal terms, governed by a single political economy, rather than varying on the basis of historical-cultural context. However, there has been no critique, empirical or philosophical, of the identified East Asian commonalities in education and in the related political culture, nor of the argument that these commonalities derive from the potent Sinic heritage of state and family. Western modernization has not displaced Sinic tradition; it has combined with it. The countries in the Chinese civilizational zone pursue modernization paths that are different from those of North America or Europe, and in higher education and research (though not in all fields of social development), this path seems to be broadly similar across the whole region.

Governance, Growth and Talent Pools

In joining in the worldwide tendency towards adoption of neoliberal system design and neo-managerial frameworks of university administration, East Asian governments stepped back to steer higher education from the middle distance. The partial devolution is apparent in different forms, such as rendering local governments and universities with more autonomy, or allowing more room for private providers of higher education. In Macau SAR, the proportion of the enrolment in private tertiary education rose from 34.6 to 55.2 per cent between 2000 and 2019; in Hong Kong SAR, it grew from 3.3 to 17.7 per cent from 2003 to 2019. Private sectors dominate South Korean and Japanese higher education, with 70–80 per cent gross enrolment rates in private higher education institutions (UNESCO 2021).

Nevertheless, devolution and diversification has not been pursued to the point of losing control, and central governments in East Asia orchestrate higher education more closely than Western states, often investing more vigorously as well. Governmental expenditure on education expanded in all East Asian systems in the past three decades (UNESCO 2021), and in China it remains the main funding source (Han and Xu 2019). As noted, post-Confucian system strategies are characterized by long-term vision, growing resource inputs and focus on leading research-intensive universities. Centrally initiated schemes that set out to develop WCUs often become the most influential schemes in each system: the Double First-Class Programme and previous Projects 985 and 211 in China, the Top Global University Project in Japan, Brain Korea 21 Project in South Korea,

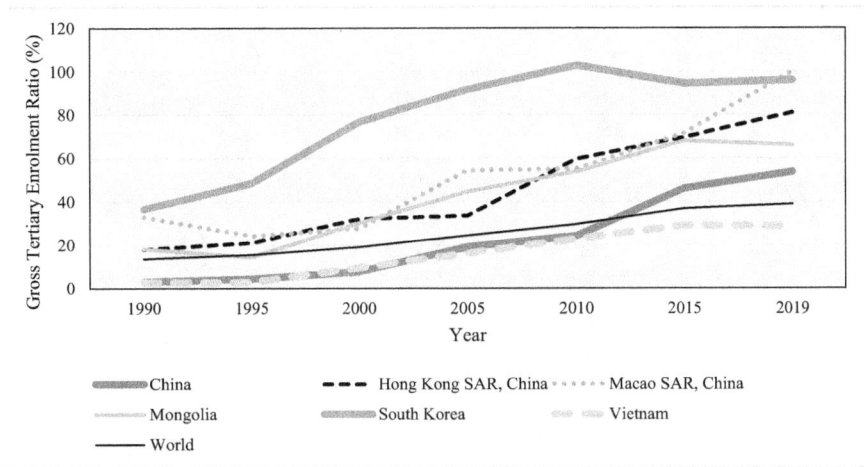

Figure 1.1 Gross Tertiary Enrolment Ratio in East Asian Education Systems, 1990–2019.
Note: Data not available for Japan, Taiwan, Singapore. Figure based on data in year 1990, 1995, 2000, 2005, 2010, 2015 and 2019. Data for South Korea and Mongolia in 2018 not 2019; for Hong Kong SAR, 1992 not 1990, 1994 not 1995, 2003 not 2000; for Macau SAR, 1994 not 1995.
Source: Authors, original data from World Bank (2021).

Higher Education Sprout Project in Taiwan, and Project 911 and Project 322 in Vietnam. Hong Kong SAR and Macau SAR are included in the Greater Bay Area development plan led by mainland China. In Mongolia, parallel top-down schemes have appeared in broader-scale policies like Mongolia Sustainable Development Vision 2030.

Higher education systems in East Asia have experienced explosive growth (shown in Table 1.1 and Figure 1.1). In 1990, all systems except for China and Vietnam had a gross enrolment ratio in tertiary education above the world's overall level. With continuous growth over the past thirty years, all except Vietnam have now achieved a gross enrolment ratio well above the world's level of 39 per cent and above Martin Trow's (1973) 50 per cent threshold for universal education. Note that despite a comparatively low enrolment rate in Vietnam, the ratio increased around ten-fold in the period. The features of the post-Confucian model noted in the previous section have enabled a relatively orderly massification of higher education. Universal education poses questions about quality assurance, thus shifting the governance's focus to accountability and efficiency (Mok 2003). Other major impacts of massification have been the increasingly competitive graduate job market, devalued credentials and intensified equity issues within widening participation (Tight 2019).

Table 1.3 Enrolment in Doctoral Education in Selected East Asian Systems

Systems	2010	2014	2018	Growth from 2010 to 2018 (%)
China	290,853	306,651	380,444	31
Hong Kong SAR	7,953	8,426	10,286	29
Macau SAR	583	1,013	2,245	285
Japan	73,734	74,093	80,767	10
Mongolia	2,190	3,407	4,295	96
South Korea	53,533	69,975	74,750	40
Vietnam	4,683	8,870	14,686	214
World	2,607,763	2,778,267	3,109,787	19

Note: Data not available for Taiwan and incomplete for Singapore. Data for China is for the year 2013 not 2010; for Vietnam, the year is 2011 not 2010.
Source: Authors, original data from UNESCO (2021).

Massification has also been associated with the snowballing expansion of postgraduate education – as the job market becomes more competitive, a postgraduate qualification becomes both an alternative pathway and additional credential. The transition to the knowledge society – where high-level skills, often associated with a doctorate, bear more significance – also facilitates the growth of doctoral education (Shin, Kehm and Jones 2018). Table 1.3 shows the growth of doctoral education in East Asia. All systems except for Japan experienced a growth rate higher than the world level, with Macau SAR and Vietnam experiencing more than 200 per cent growth rates. (Note Japan already had a large doctoral education base in 2010, which has been sustained with slow growth.) As of 2018, China hosts the largest number of doctoral students in the world, followed by the United States, Germany, India, Iran, Brazil, UK, Turkey, Russia, Spain, Japan and South Korea (UNESCO 2021).

Doctoral education concentrates in science and engineering disciplines (Shin, Kehm and Jones 2018), and it has generated a larger pool of skilful qualified scientific researchers and labourers. South Korea, Japan and Singapore are among the countries with the highest rate of researchers per 1000 total employment – nineteen in South Korea in 2018, fourteen in Japan in 2018, thirteen in Singapore in 2017; across the world, the recent highest ratio was twenty-two in Denmark in 2017 (UNESCO 2021). Domestic doctoral researchers contribute to scientific publications, as in China when doctoral students needed certain number of Science Citation Index (SCI) publications to graduate (Li 2016). In addition to locally trained doctoral researchers, East Asian systems share talent pipelines in the form of educated returnees and diasporas from the West. The most popular overseas destinations for East Asian students are countries in the West (Table 1.6 below). As East Asian economies, higher education and research advance, an increasing number of outbound students return to East Asia upon graduation or soon after. Diaspora researchers staying in the West also maintain positive links with their home country for scientific collaborations (e.g. Welch and Hao 2013). Furthermore, an increasing number of international students and academics are journeying to the East for education and career opportunities. This traffic was previously concentrated in Hong Kong SAR and Singapore, but China has become a growing magnet. All of these people flows converge to form an ever-expanding talent pool for scientific research in East Asia.

Research and Science

Prior to the mid-1980s, East Asia made a negligible contribution to published world science, except in Japan. Going by present trends, by 2030 East Asia's output of science papers in the main bibliometric collections, Web of Science (WoS) and Scopus, will exceed the combined output of North America and Europe. While China's size dominates the picture, Japan remains a strong science system despite lack of growth while Singapore, especially, and South Korea have impressive achievements in both academic and industry science. In terms of the proportion of national GDP spent on R&D, South Korea is second highest in the world, behind only Israel (OECD 2021).

Bibliometric collections do not provide a full picture of the knowledge generated in universities and research institutes in East Asia. Few non-English language papers are included – which particularly affects the social sciences, where many problems investigated are local or national not global, and the humanities, where the main conversation is in national languages. Nevertheless, the trends in global science indicate the dynamism of the region.

Funding and Output in Research

In the year 2000, East, Southeast and South Asia together comprised 25.3 per cent of worldwide R&D investment. By 2017, that proportion was 41.7 per cent, mostly in East Asia, while the US share fell from 37.2 to 25.5 per cent (NSB 2020: figure 14). Most published science is from universities. A crucial funding indicator is R&D investment in research in higher education. Between

2000 and 2019, this metric rose from USD3.4 to USD41.8 billion in China, in constant 2015 prices. Resources multiplied by 12.25 in real terms in less than a generation. In Japan, South Korea, Singapore and Taiwan together, funding for university science rose from USD24.3 to USD34.8 billion. There was little change in Japan, but funding rose from USD2.5 to USD8.3 billion in South Korea, multiplying by 3.27 times. In Singapore, between 2000 and 2018, it rose from USD1.0 to USD3.6 billion, 3.80 times. This compares with the doubling of funding in the United States and near doubling in the EU-15 over the period (OECD 2021).

The trajectory in published science has followed funding. Between 2000 and 2018, the number papers multiplied by 9.96 in China and by 4.17 in South Korea, with a more modest growth in Singapore (2.39) and Taiwan (2.12). China's share of published global science rose from 5.0 to 20.7 per cent over this time period, though Japan's share fell from 9.1 to 3.9 per cent (NSB 2020: figure 5A-3). In Japan, both funding and outputs showed almost no change, a suggestive correlation, while science grew markedly across the world as a whole.

However, the role of East Asia in science is uneven by discipline. Figure 1.2 indicates not one global science system but several, with the weight of China and East Asia varying markedly between them. In 2018, China was much the largest producer in physical sciences STEM (science, technology, engineering and mathematics), having grown its world share of Scopus papers in this cluster from 8.5 to 27.7 per cent since 2000, much more than each of the United States and Europe. The combined East Asia share of physical sciences STEM papers was over 40 per cent. China's share of world science in biological, biomedical and health disciplines grew from 2.3 to 13.3 per cent over 2000–18 period. The priority given to biomedical sciences, health-related research and adjunct life science was higher in both the United States – where these disciplines constituted 48.0 per cent of all 2018 US papers – and EU (39.1 per cent) than in China (23.0 per cent). China had 22.9 per cent of papers in planetary science, but a minor presence in Scopus social sciences. Because many papers in social science and psychology are in national languages (Figure 1.2), and English language papers often focus on local or nation-bound English-speaking country issues, this cluster does not really constitute a global field of knowledge. China had 613 papers in Scopus in social science in 2000, 1.1 per cent of the world total, and 4.4 per cent in 2018 (NSB 2020: table S5-A). East Asia outside China was stronger in producing social science papers in the English language. Liu et al. (2015) examine China's publications in the WoS Social Science Citation Index (SSCI) for 1978–2013 period. Hong Kong SAR, where universities have

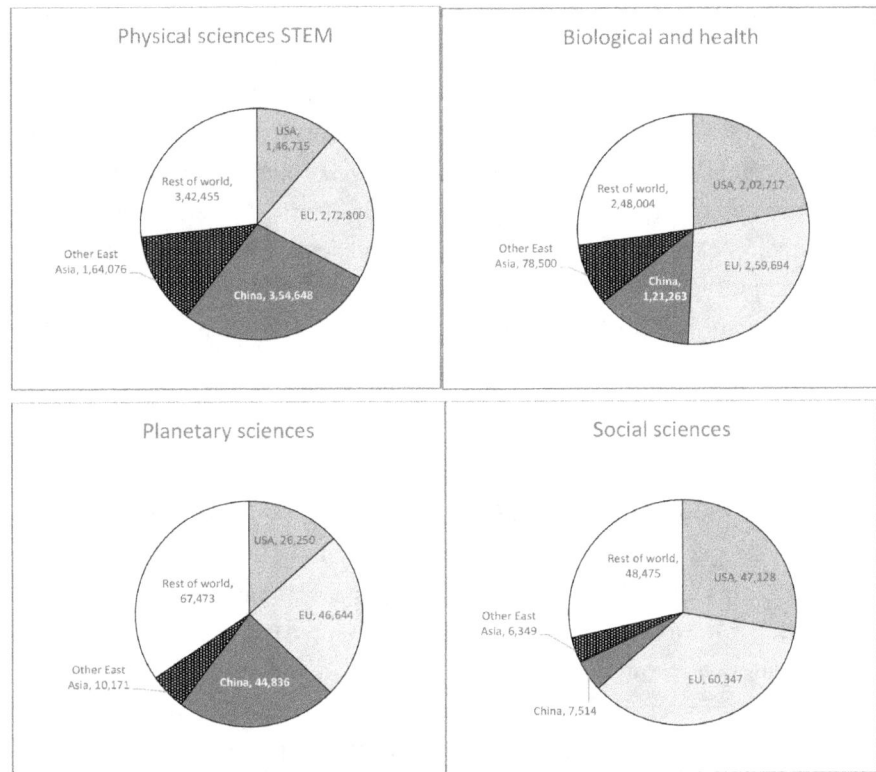

Figure 1.2 Number of Papers in Scopus in (1) Physical Sciences STEM, (2) Biological and Health Sciences, (3) Planetary Sciences and (4) Social Sciences and Psychology from the United States, EU, China and Other East Asian Systems, 2018.

Note: Physical sciences STEM (science, technology, engineering and mathematics) include astronomy and astrophysics, chemistry, computer and information sciences, engineering, materials science, mathematics and statistics, and physics. Biological and health sciences include biological and biomedical sciences as well as health sciences. Planetary sciences include agriculture, geosciences, atmospheric and ocean science as well as natural resources and conservation. Social sciences include social sciences and psychology. Most social science and humanities, and most non-English papers, are excluded from Scopus.

Other East Asia systems: Japan, Singapore, South Korea and Taiwan; Vietnam is excluded; Hong Kong and Macau SARs included in China.

Source: Authors, from NSB (2020: table S5A), originally sourced from Scopus.

an Anglo-American discipline profile, published almost twice as many social science papers in WoS as the Beijing region (559).

In China, the skew to physical sciences STEM is partly explained by the funding priority for projects in construction, communications, energy, transport and other developmental domains, including engineering and computer science. Between 2000 and 2018, there was rapid growth in computer science (multiple of 17.57), engineering (9.77), materials science (8.78) and chemistry (7.51). For the year 2018, China had a long lead over the world's other countries in the number of published papers in chemistry, materials and engineering and was first also in computer science and more narrowly, physics. Papers in engineering rose from 13,777 in 2000 to 134,542 in 2018, in chemistry from 6,762 to 50,753 and in computing from 3981 to 69,932. The US share of physical sciences STEM papers fell from 23.7 to 11.5 per cent in 2000–18 (NSB 2020: tables S5A-2 to S5A-16).

High Citation Science and WCUs

However, the proportion of US papers located in the top 1 per cent of the field in 2016 (1.88 per cent) was higher than in China (1.12 per cent). Using this indicator, China outperformed the United States only in mathematics, though it was moving towards US citation performance in a second discipline, computer science. The two research universities in Singapore had an exceptionally high 2.97 per cent of papers in the top 1 per cent. The proportion in South Korea was 1.02 per cent, in Taiwan 1.00 per cent and in Japan 0.88 per cent (NSB 2020: table S5A-35).

When comparing science citation performance between countries, China does better in its leading WCUs than in national science as a whole. Table 1.4 lists the leading East Asian universities on the basis of publications in 2016–19 inclusive in the top 5 per cent of their field. China overwhelmingly dominates the list, with Singapore's universities also doing very well. Both national science systems exhibit remarkable rates of annual increase in the number of high citation papers in the last column, when compared with the other countries in the table. Table 1.4 also includes selected comparators from North America and Europe. In 2015–18, Tsinghua University was sixth in the world in top 5 per cent papers, its 1451 exceeded only by Harvard, Stanford and MIT (Massachusetts Institute of Technology) in the United States, Toronto in Canada as well as Oxford in the UK. Most of these universities, especially Harvard and Toronto, were sustained by paper volume in biomedicine and related fields. However, the top Chinese universities were weaker than the Euro-American comparators in the proportion of all their papers that were in the top 5 per cent. Using this indicator, Hunan University (10.1 per cent) was the strongest in China (Leiden University 2020).

'The Ensemble of Diverse Music'   19

Table 1.4 Papers in the Top 5 Per Cent of Their Research Field by Citation Rate, Selected Asian Universities, 2006–9 to 2016–19

University	System	Top 5% papers 2016–19	Top 5% papers 2006–9	Annual growth top 5% papers over ten years (%)	Proportion of papers top 5% 2016–19 (%)	Number of international papers in 2016–19
Universities producing 600 or more papers in top 5% of their disciplinary field in 2015–18						
Tsinghua U	China	1,574	402	14.62	7.4	15,137
Zhejiang U	China	1,427	316	16.27	5.5	13,588
Shanghai Jiao Tong U	China	1,211	296	15.13	4.6	14,311
National U Singapore	Singapore	1,072	521	7.48	8.3	19,575
Huazhong U S&T	China	1,057	117	24.62	5.6	8,391
Peking U	China	1,051	313	12.88	5.7	14,041
Nanyang Technological U	Singapore	928	278	12.81	9.2	14,769
Harbin IT	China	927	171	18.42	5.7	6,811
Central South U	China	899	86	26.45	5.3	6,989
Xi'an Jiaotong U	China	849	109	22.79	4.9	8,407
Sun Yat-sen U	China	819	153	18.27	4.8	9,975
U Science and Technology	China	780	246	12.23	6.6	7,903
U Chinese Academy of Sci	China	775	6	62.60	5.7	16,400
Sichuan U	China	760	124	19.88	4.1	6,405
Wuhan U	China	622	114	18.49	5.3	6,515
Fudan U	China	737	222	12.75	4.4	9,261
Hunan U	China	709	69	26.23	10.1	3,567
South China U Technology	China	700	84	23.62	6.2	4,565
Nanjing U	China	694	185	14.13	5.7	8,022

(Continued)

Table 1.4 Continued

University	System	Top 5% papers 2016–19	Top 5% papers 2006–9	Annual growth top 5% papers over ten years (%)	Proportion of papers top 5% 2016–19 (%)	Number of international papers in 2016–19
Tianjin U	China	679	93	21.99	5.1	5,832
U Tokyo	Japan	653	676	-0.35	4.4	14,333
Beihang U	China	607	42	30.62	5.8	5,473
Shandong U	China	605	132	16.44	3.8	6,727
Jilin U	China	605	115	18.06	3.4	5,631
East Asian universities leading their systems with less than 600 top 5% papers in 2015–18						
Seoul National U	South Korea	588	339	5.66	3.4	10,116
U Hong Kong	Hong Kong SAR	511	314	4.99	6.6	7,773
National Taiwan U	Taiwan	293	280	0.45	3.3	7,375
Selected comparators from outside East Asia and Singapore						
Harvard U	USA	4,230	3,626	1.52	12.4	44,071
U Oxford	UK	1,696	1,045	4.96	10.5	28,903
U Toronto	Canada	1,691	1,221	3.31	7.2	27,583
MIT	USA	1,586	1,210	2.74	15.1	17,129
U Cambridge	UK	1,117	1,440	2.57	10.2	24,954
ETH Zurich	Switzerland	640	940	3.92	9.9	16,599
U Melbourne	Australia	546	941	5.59	6.9	19,143
U Utrecht	Netherlands	577	758	2.77	8.0	15,430

Note: Data does not include Israel. All universities with 600 papers published in 2016–19 and in the top 5 per cent of their field on the basis of citations, plus selected East Asian systems not otherwise included. International denotes proportion of all papers (not just top 5%) that were co-authored outside the country.

Source: Authors, from Leiden University (2020).

China's WCUs do exceptionally well in the STEM disciplines. In the number of top 5 per cent 2016–19 papers in the domain of mathematics and computing, Tsinghua was the world leader and the first six universities on the list were all from China. In the list for physical sciences and engineering, Tsinghua was again number one, well ahead of MIT in second place. Tsinghua, Zhejiang, Harbin Institute of Technology, Shanghai Jiao Tong, Xi'an Jiao Tong, Huazhong University of Science and Technology, South China University of Technology, National University of Singapore and Nanyang Technological University in Singapore were all in the world top twenty in the both lists. None of the universities from Japan, South Korea and Taiwan is in either list (Leiden University 2020). They have fine science systems but catch-up to the US peak has not occurred, though Tokyo and Seoul National are strong. Hong Kong does better in mathematics than in physical sciences/engineering. Arguably, China's superior performance in STEM derives not just from its exceptional and focused investment, but its double strategy of building endogenous national capacity while fostering improvement through internationalization, achieving a mutually enhancing synergy between each of global and national research collaboration (Marginson 2018, 2021).

East Asia and the West: Internationalization, Endogenization, and Regionalization

Along with its remarkable development, East Asian higher education is embedded in constant tensions between endogenization, internationalization, and regionalization. Tensions arise both from the East-West relationship and internal dynamics within East Asia. Both 'the East' and 'the West' are constructed based on a differentiation against 'the other' or 'the rest' – see, for example, Edward Said (1977) on 'the Orient' or Stuart Hall (1992) on 'the West'. In East Asia, 'the West' is a frequently used reference point, which is more culturally related than geographically specific. 'The West' can include countries and regions sharing occidental cultures, such as Australia and New Zealand, not geographically located in Europe or North America. In response to Bertrand Russell's book *The Problem of China* (1922), Spanish philosopher José Ortega y Gasset suggested that East and West could 'fall in love':

> Today, the struggle between East and West has the whole demeanour of falling in love. Europe, touched by the deepest spiritual crisis that it has ever suffered, has

just discovered Asia sentimentally and is experiencing a phase of enthusiasm. At the same time, the East, especially its most profound manifestation, China, has discovered Europe and fallen in love in equal proportion. The finest Westerners of the present time would like to be a little Chinese, in the same way that astute Chinese would like to be people of London, Berlin, or Paris. (Ortega y Gasset 1949, from Lu and Jover 2019)

However, the East and the West have developed a love-hate relationship. In East Asia, the West is perceived as both a friend and foe. In the continued colonial imaginary, the West is symbol of modernity and model of democracy. The West is also a potential political and military ally. Incessant internal conflicts within East Asia makes the continuing external presence of Western power welcome in some countries (Holcombe 2011). According to the colonial perception, the East is still inferior to the West and needs to catch up. Such perceptions feed into the continuing white supremacy and Anglo-Euro hegemony in East Asian higher education, where the 'the foreign moon is fuller' (a Chinese saying, meaning the foreign is always considered better) and where Western knowledge, ideas, models, publications, universities, students and academics are given more privilege than the local equivalents. At the same time, the West is seen as a conqueror, colonizer, competitor, oppressor and exploiter who should be cautioned against. This conflicted mindset has deep roots in colonial history – in the Western colonization of Hong Kong SAR, Macau SAR, Vietnam, Singapore and parts of China since the nineteenth century as well as in Meiji Japan's 'leaving Asia to enter Europe' and the subsequent colonization by Japan of South Korea, Taiwan, Singapore and parts of China. To uproot the colonial aftermath, East Asian systems push back against the persisting Western influences, some to a larger degree than others. China's vigilance towards the West is doubled by Cold War memories and recurring ideological conflicts.

The dual perception of the West is never fully resolved in East Asia and its higher education. The modern higher education systems in East Asia bear Western influences, be it the liberal arts paradigm, the Humboldtian model of universities or the contemporary WCU templates and rankings that apply indicators rooted in Western reality that not surprisingly reproduce Western dominance. Western influences are particularly evident in both the models and practices of the internationalization of higher education. In this chapter, we use 'internationalization' with a neutral normative sense to mean interactions, cooperation, mobilization and communications between nations ('international') but internationalization practice must always be interrogated in terms of the models, norms and behaviours it fosters.

Internationalization approaches differ across the East Asian systems. Here, geography and contextualized cultures matter. Island states can be restricted by their limited resources and face potential dangers of isolation from the continental world. Island systems like Japan, Singapore, Taiwan, Hong Kong SAR, Macau SAR and South Korea (a peninsular state separated by North Korea from the continent) are actively outward-looking, keen to develop external links and maintain a strong presence in the world, to be a nexus of mobilities and to avoid insular status. In comparison, as quasi-continental states, China and Vietnam have resources within the nation, tensions with bordering nations and a more open choice about external engagement. Such states oscillate between times of extensive internationality and times of self-sufficiency and even isolation as the histories of the United States and Russia show. Mongolia is a landlocked country between China and Russia, mostly restricted in resources, vision and engagement with the outside. While the world is connected via the Internet, geographically shaped mindsets persist in the system orientations to internationalization.

Western supremacy could entrench internationalization approaches: national WCU schemes which follow Western models, international partnerships and branch campus mostly developed with Western universities, asymmetrical mobility of students and academics, asymmetrical cross-border research collaborations, the reform of teaching and curriculum to incorporate Anglo-American elements like English-medium instruction, and promotion of Anglo-American elements in research such as prioritizing English-language publications. Although East Asian systems are rising in global science in the bibliometric sense, as outlined, the epistemologies, discourses, methodologies, evaluative criteria bear Western imprints. Internationalization easily becomes a synonym of Westernization.

Despite an immerse local knowledge pool, countries and regions in East Asia prioritize publications in internationally recognized journals, mostly Anglophone and Western (Chou 2014; Shin 2007; Xu 2020). Table 1.5 illustrates strong but unbalanced research collaboration ties between East Asia and the West. Academics in almost all East Asian systems work most closely with researchers from the United States, though Singapore and Mongolia are exceptions. In East Asian systems, the top five collaborators always include China and Japan but the rest are all Western, and while other East Asian systems appear in the top ten collaborators, Western systems have much stronger presence, despite the total weight of East Asian papers in science output. Obversely, in the Western countries that rank high in the volume of science publications, only China from East Asia

Table 1.5 Top Science Collaborators for East Asian and World Top-Performing Systems, 2019

System	World share rank	Top ten collaborators (listed in rank order)
East Asian systems		
China	2	USA, Germany, UK, Australia, **Japan, Singapore**, Canada, France, **South Korea**, Sweden
Japan	5	USA, **China**, Germany, UK, France, **South Korea**, Australia, Switzerland, Canada, **Taiwan**
South Korea	8	USA, **China, Japan**, Germany, UK, Switzerland, France, Canada, Australia, Italy
Singapore	16	**China**, USA, UK, **Japan**, Australia, Germany, France, **South Korea**, India, Canada
Taiwan	19	USA, **China, Japan**, Germany, UK, France, Italy, Australia, Switzerland, **South Korea**
Vietnam	44	USA, **Japan**, Germany, **China**, UK, France, Switzerland, **South Korea**, Australia, Italy
Mongolia	108	**China**, Germany, USA, Russia, Italy, UK, **South Korea**, Sweden, Hungary, **Japan**
Other systems among top ten world share of scientific publications		
USA	1	**China**, UK, Germany, Canada, France, **Japan**, Australia, Switzerland, **South Korea**, Italy
UK	4	USA, Germany, **China**, France, Australia, Switzerland, Italy, Netherlands, Spain, Canada
Germany	3	USA, UK, **China**, France, Switzerland, Netherlands, Italy, Spain, **Japan**, Australia
France	6	USA, Germany, UK, **China**, Switzerland, Italy, Spain, **Japan**, Netherlands, Canada
Canada	7	USA, **China**, UK, Germany, France, **Japan**, Australia, Switzerland, Italy, Netherlands
Switzerland	9	USA, Germany, UK, France, Italy, **China**, Spain, **Japan**, Netherlands, Canada
Australia	10	USA, **China**, UK, Germany, **Japan**, France, Canada, Netherlands, Switzerland, Italy

Note: East Asian systems in bold; no data for Hong Kong and Macau SARs.
Source: Authors, original data from Nature Index (2021).

figures in the top five collaborators; all the rest are Western countries, except in Australia where Japan is fifth collaborator. Furthermore, not all collaborations are conducted on an equal basis. Some retain colonial and exploitive features.

Patterns in international student mobility between the East and the West are more asymmetrical than the relations in research. As Table 1.6 shows,

Table 1.6 Mobility Patterns of Outbound and Inbound Students of East Asian Education Systems

Systems	Top ten outgoing student destination systems[a]	Top ten systems of incoming student systems
China	USA, Australia, UK, **Japan**, Canada, **South Korea**, **Hong Kong SAR**, Germany, France, New Zealand	n.a.
Hong Kong SAR	USA, Canada, **Macau SAR**, **South Korea**, Germany, Ireland, Switzerland, Brazil, Norway, Malaysia	**China**, **South Korea**, India, Indonesia, Malaysia, Pakistan, **Macau SAR**, Kazakhstan, USA, Bangladesh
Macau SAR	**Hong Kong SAR**, Portugal, Canada, **South Korea**, Morocco, Germany	**China**, **Hong Kong SAR**, Cabo Verde, Portugal, Malaysia, Brazil, Philippines, **Japan**, **South Korea**, Guinea-Bissau
Japan	USA, UK, Australia, Germany, Canada, **South Korea**, Brazil, France, Malaysia, Hungary	**China**, **Vietnam**, Nepal, **South Korea**, Indonesia, Thailand, Sri Lanka, Myanmar, Malaysia, USA
Mongolia	**South Korea**, **Japan**, USA, Australia, Kazakhstan, Turkey, Germany, Hungary, Austria, UK	**China**, Russia, **South Korea**, **Japan**, Turkey, Vietnam, Laos, **North Korea**, Poland, Afghanistan
Singapore	Australia, UK, USA, Malaysia, Germany, Canada, Ireland, New Zealand, **Japan**, Switzerland	n.a.
South Korea	USA, **Japan**, Australia, Canada, UK, Germany, France, **Hong Kong SAR**, New Zealand, Netherlands	**China**, **Vietnam**, **Mongolia**, Uzbekistan, **Japan**, Pakistan, Nepal, USA, Indonesia, Bangladesh
Vietnam	**Japan**, USA, Australia, **South Korea**, France, UK, Germany, Canada, Finland, New Zealand	Laos, Cambodia, **South Korea**, **China**, France, Myanmar, Mozambique, Timor-Leste, Thailand, Nigeria

Note: n.a. indicates data not available.

[a] Data not available for Taiwan; for China and Singapore's inbound students' origins; for Macau SAR's destination country after Germany; East Asian systems are in bold.

Source: Authors, original data from UNESCO (2021).

while Western countries are the top destinations for students moving out of most East Asian systems, Western students do not dominate the lists of students moving to East Asian countries. East Asian countries mostly attract students from East Asia, Southeast Asia and Central Asia – another example of bottom-up regionalization. Only Hong Kong SAR, Macau SAR, Japan, South Korea and Vietnam attract Western students from the United States, France and Portugal (note that in each case there is a historical imperial or neo-imperial relationship). This indicates persisting perceptions of the Western countries as old acquaintances through coloniality, as bearers of modern knowledge and cutting-edge research, as providers of quality education and valued accreditation, and as guarantors of better life and employment opportunities. The 'Western Dream' (especially the 'American Dream') is still alive and well. But the landscape is changing, with Singapore, Hong Kong SAR and then China rising as regional educational hubs, offering familiar cultural magnets and rising prospects for better futures (Lee 2015).

East Asia is never fully Westernized. The fundamental cultural differences between the East and the West make it impossible to fully assimilate each other. East Asian higher education systems are resilient and are increasingly active in shaping their own agendas, working with not only global benchmarks but also national-cultural models. There are push-backs from academics, institutions and governments against the reproduction of Western supremacy into national higher education systems. National policies issued in 2020 by the Chinese government firmly asserted the importance of domestic publications in the Chinese language and rejected the previous '(S)SCI supremacy' (MOE 2020; MOE and Ministry of Science and Technology 2020). The constant emphasis on 'Chinese characteristics' and 'Chinalization' of higher education and research again indicates endogenization efforts (Xu 2021a). De-Westernization also happens in scholarly investigation on (East) Asia. The 'inter-referencing' approach proposed by Chen Kuan-Hsing (2010) in the book *Asia as Method* raised a possibility of comparing Asia with Asian characteristics, not against Western standards. Similarly, Japanese Sinologist Yoshimi Takeuchi expresses the idea of replacing the East-West dichotomy with a broader framework:

> It is important in analysing Japan to refer to the United States and Western Europe, for they represent the advanced nations of modernisation. Nevertheless, we must also look elsewhere. In studying China, for example, we should not limit ourselves to seeing this nation only vis-à-vis the West. It was at this time that I realized the importance of conceiving of modernisation on the basis of

a more complex framework than that of simple binary oppositions. (Takeuchi 1961: 156–7)

The Book

The book by no means exhausts the issues relevant to higher education development in East Asia. No chapter specifically examines the massification of higher education in East Asia (though see Yonezawa and Huang 2018 for a discussion of Japan in global context); none discusses collaborations in Eurasia or East-South cooperation, both of which have growing significance in East Asian and global higher education. Those are themes for future research.

The contents of *Changing Higher Education in East Asia* exemplify the *he er bu tong* (和而不同) idea of 'harmony without uniformity'[1] suggested in the opening of this chapter. Each chapter is different in scope and focus, but we trust that they share commonality and complementarity. Common strands of discussion include how the Sinic tradition (evident not only in China but also in the South Korean *jeong* perspective which has Sinic roots) intersects with the up to now primarily Anglo-American globalization of higher education, how Eastern universities engage with Western ideas, how individual and institutional agency plays out in the East Asian higher education context, and how geopolitics has shaped and continues to shape the higher education landscape in East Asia. All chapters showcase the uniqueness of East Asian higher education as individual national/regional systems and as a cultural region.

Another recurring theme is the integration of 'Eastern' and 'Western' knowledges, and realities. East Asia is inseparable from the West. The contents of this book reflect the interplay between the two. Equal dialogues across cultures can foster hybridization and greater common understandings. Furthermore, valuing, articulating and engaging with Eastern knowledge in the Western dominated research space contribute to epistemic diversity and justice (Xu 2021b). In general, Western concepts, methodologies, epistemologies and language are evident in all chapters: not least because the book is written and published in English. Western models of universities, such as the WCU model

---

[1] The Chinese phrase *he er bu tong* (和而不同) have various English translations. Three translations exist in this book: 'harmony without uniformity' in the Preface and Chapter 1, 'harmony without conformity' in Chapter 3, and 'unity in diversity' in Chapter 4. While we all engage with this term, interpretations differ and the choices of translations differ. This exemplifies the *he er bu tong* idea. In line with *he er bu tong*, we as editors respect authors' choices and have kept their chosen translations in respective chapters.

discussed in Chapter 5, and Western discourses about higher education, such as 'global public/common good' and 'global citizenship education' discussed in Chapters 2–5, and the Western-origin concept of student agency, as detailed in Chapter 10, are highlighted in the book. Nonetheless, these are not discussions that use a Western lens to examine Eastern reality, a pitfall postcolonial and decolonial scholarships rightly warns against (Yang 2019). It is almost the reverse. For example, in Chapters 2–4 the Western notions are interrogated in the light of Eastern ideas, scholarship and practices. In all chapters, the question of Western models and their applicability or not is a continuing reflexive theme. All chapters engage with the local and endogenous tradition, knowledge, epistemologies, expressions, discourses, practices, reality and culture, some more vigorously than others. Their explorations do not merely transplant Western ontological, epistemological or methodological assumptions to the East Asian reality. All have roots in East Asian knowledge and reality. All articulate the uniqueness of the East while achieving at least some synthesis across local, national, regional and global (including Western) knowledges. All, in their various ways, are working in an indeterminate and exciting cultural zone in which new perspectives, insights and hybrids constantly appear.

Both editors have rich experiences with and profound academic interests in both 'Eastern' and 'Western' traditions, cultures and higher education. All the non-Asia-based authors have long-standing academic experiences and scholarly interests in East Asian higher education. All of the Asia-based authors have rich experiences with and comprehensive understandings of Western higher education and research. We believe that our contributors have navigated through Western and Eastern perspectives without privileging any of them, and have achieved meaningful dialogues through complementarity. In sum, although this book does not directly address decolonial issues, we hope that it testifies that epistemic diversity, mutual understandings and equal cross-cultural dialogues are not only desirable but also viable in the ecology of global knowledge (Santos 2014; Marginson and Xu 2021).

Chapter Contents

The chapters that follow address different aspects of East Asian higher education provision, development, originality and the tensions inherent in internationalization and identity. They come in three parts. Each part opens with a word that exists in written languages of Chinese, Japanese, Korean, and

Vietnamese. Each word foregrounds the theme of each part: 和 (mainly means 'harmony and peace') for Part 1 on global public good; 天下 (mainly means 'the world') for Part 2 on internationalization and endogenization, regionalization and globalization; 人 (mainly means 'human') for Part 3 on international mobility and academic migration. The three words also embody philosophical traditions and ontological understandings from East Asia about relationships, the world and humanity. Meanings of each word are largely common across the languages, but differences exist. These characters were chosen to exhibit the beauty of East Asian cultures, highlight their philosophical value, illustrate the cultural commonalities within the region and demonstrate nuances across them.

Part 1 on 'Higher Education and the Global Common Good' locates the largely Western origin discourses of global public good and global citizenship in the East Asian higher education context. Chapter 2 by Olga Mun and Yunkyung Min, working with interviews in South Korea, applies the endogenous lens of *jeong* to explore the global public role of higher education. Lili Yang's Chapter 3 proposes the Chinese idea *tianxia weigong* as an arguably richer approach to understanding global public/common good in general and in higher education, and discusses the implications in higher education practices. In Chapter 4, Arzhia Habibi reviews the literature on global and world citizenship education in Chinese and English languages, with a special focus on their articulation in Chinese higher education. Chapter 5 by Lin Tian and Nian Cai Liu reports on seventy-four interviews conducted in China, Western Europe and the United States which discussed the education, research and service functions of WCUs, enabling a regional comparison of how they understand their contributions to the global common good.

Part 2 on 'Internationalization and Endogenization, Regionalization and Globalization' explores the interplay, synergies, dynamics and differences between various ways in higher education of seeing and practising the self and the world: forming the nation, imitating the West, focusing on the East Asian region, reaching out to influence the global. Chapter 6 by Christopher D. Hammond, drawing on sixty-seven interviews in Japan, examines the current state and possible futures of regional cooperation in Northeast Asian higher education, with focus on government-initiated programmes in student mobility and science. In Chapter 7, Xin Xu discusses tensions in internationalizing Chinese humanities and social sciences research, with a contextual agency framework developed from English and Chinese discourses. Chapter 8 by Julie Chia-Yi Lin explores the internationalization of higher education in Taiwan, in the context of the ongoing contests and ambiguities of the Taiwan project, drawing on analysis of governmental policies and interviews with senior university administrators. In Chapter 9, Ly Thi Tran, Huong Le Thanh Phan and Huyen Bui locate the internationalization of higher education in Vietnam in the changing national and geopolitical contexts before and after the watershed Đổi Mới social and economic reform in Vietnam.

The final section is on 'International Mobility and Academic Migration' in East Asian higher education. Chapter 10 by Thomas Brotherhood explores the role of individual agency in the education-migration nexus, with evidence from biographical-narrative interviews with international student-migrants in Japan. Futao Huang's Chapter 11 investigates the characteristics, motivation and work roles of non-language-teaching international faculty in Chinese higher education, drawing on survey and interview data. Chapter 12 by Ka Ho Mok examines the impact of the Covid-19 pandemic on the internationalization of higher education, student mobility and regional collaboration in East Asia. Also drawing on empirical survey data, and while noting the fast changing and fracturing geopolitics of the US-China relationship, the chapter suggests implications of the pandemic period for the future development of higher education in East Asia and the rest of the world.

Part One

Higher Education and the Global Common Good

和

Chinese meaning:

Harmony (harmonious, to harmonize), peace (peaceful, to make peace), calm(ness), gentle(ness), warm, happy, Japanese, to echo, to mix, to reconcile, to end in a draw, to win a mah-jong game, sum, and, with

Japanese meaning:

Harmony (harmonious), peace (peaceful), calm(ness), sum, Japanese

Korean meaning:

Harmony, peace (peaceful), calm(ness), warm, to echo, to gather, to mix, sum, to allow, to reconcile, Japanese, to season

Vietnamese meaning:

Harmony (to harmonize), peace (to make peace), to mix, to end in a draw

2

Global Public Good in Korea as *Jeong*

Olga Mun and Yunkyung Min

Introduction: Setting the Scene

In the past four decades, Korea's higher education has experienced a dramatic increase in participation. The rate of college matriculation grew from 27.2 per cent in 1980 to 70.4 per cent in 2019, making Korea the first ranked country in terms of student enrolment among the Organisation for Economic Cooperation and Development (OECD) countries for the past ten years (KEDI Statistics 2020). The growth might be partially attributed to the strong value of education by individuals and the society at large and, possibly, by the flourishing of private universities. As of 2019, out of the total 191 universities, 156 are private, 34 national and 1 public. Not only the majority of the universities are private, 62.4 per cent of higher education funding comes from private sector investments in contrast to 37.6 per cent support from the government. The Korean government's investment in higher education is low compared to the OECD average of 66.1 per cent.

Despite most of the financing coming from private sources, the government takes an active role in shaping the higher education policy for all universities in the spheres of autonomy, tuition fees, student recruitment and internationalization. Private universities cannot set their own tuition fees as these are defined by government guidelines. All universities are required to follow strict government-set standards and policies in order to retain state funding. The lack of autonomy and close state regulation of higher education attracted academic criticism that the government interference hinders change and development rather than drives it (Park 2015; Shin and Park 2007; Jeong 2018).

Meanwhile, like many higher education institutions around the world, Korean universities are also facing commercialization and marketization pressures.

With the spread of neoliberalism since the mid-1990s, Korean universities have been striving for change and reform in order to become globally and regionally competitive and attractive to international students. While commercialization of higher education is embraced by some academics and policymakers as inevitable, there is no consensus on the role of the market in higher education. Furthermore, not many studies exist on the perception of the public good role of higher education of both private and public universities. We aim to contribute to the existing literature by analysing the interpretations of the public good role of higher education by policymakers and academics that are based at a private and a public university. Hence, the goal of our project is to understand how different higher education stakeholders in South Korea see the social and public role of the increasingly marketized universities and whether *jeong* might be a useful lens for understanding the public good role of Korean higher education. *Jeong* is a term which has several associations, as will be discussed, but important among them are kindness and deep care.

The chapter consists of the following subsections. Before describing the design of the case study and the conceptual framework, we will briefly comment on the existing global research on the topic of the public good role of higher education. The brief review of the literature will be followed by the explanation of the concept of *jeong*, methodological elaborations, the findings, discussion and final thoughts. We conclude our chapter by highlighting the relevance of Korean indigenous philosophy in interrogating global trends in higher education in East Asia and beyond.

Jeong and Higher Education

On the Public Good Role of Higher Education

The debates on the social role of higher education are usually framed in response to a narrower view of the economic role of higher education (Zajda 2020). Proponents of the human capital theory tend to focus on the individual gains of the university degree or the role of the university in relation to the local or national economies, and criticism of such approaches exist in the literature (Marginson 2019). Furthermore, critical scholars of higher education see a wider social role of the universities in terms of educating responsible global citizens (Marginson 2011; Stein 2020). In a wider sense of the public good, higher education might contribute to social justice, peace, local and regional development, global cooperation, international knowledge exchange. New scholarship highlights interpretations of the mixed notions and divisions of the public/private good discussion in Russia (Marginson 2017), and further differences between the role of the individual and state power in the Anglo-American tradition and Chinese tradition in conceptualizing the public good (Marginson and Yang 2020). Scholars also make the point that definitions of the 'public' depend on the country context (Hazelkorn and Gibson 2019).

The discussions on the wider embeddedness of higher education are not new and many studies exist that compare country case studies in Europe, North America and Asia and the role of world-class universities (Marginson 2020; Rider et al. 2020). While multiple studies discuss the public role of research universities (Owen-Smith 2018) and case studies of social responsibility of higher education internationally (Papadimitriou and Boboc 2021), rarely do such studies analyse the international trends through non-Western epistemologies or the Korean concept of *jeong*. Furthermore, there is a trend in the academic literature to focus on research and research-intensive universities, while the role of teaching is seen as separate and/or supplementary. Indeed, in the current chapter we are unable to fully discuss the rich debates that exist on what is the public or public common good in higher education literature and the research versus teaching dichotomy. Our intention is rather to see how the public good is understood by academics in South Korea and whether this relationship could be conceptualized through a concept of *jeong*.

Despite the criticism and limitations, the trend to analyse international education reforms in Eurocentric onto-epistemological ways is prevalent in the comparative and international education literature (Silova, Rappleye and Auld 2020). Even when the analysis of East Asian education trends or philosophies exist, it tends to focus predominantly on selected thought traditions or the most well-known ones, for instance Confucianism (Liu and Ma 2018). To that end, as indicated, the 'public' in this chapter is intentionally analysed through the South Korean lens of *jeong*, which is considered to be one of the main indigenous philosophical concepts for South Koreans (Choi and Lee 1999; Lim 1993).

This book chapter aims to contribute to emerging literature in higher education that highlights indigenous beliefs and values in creating socially and environmentally sustainable higher education institutions. Also, it aims to underline the importance of embedding diverse epistemologies in academic research and methodologies. We agree with Mignolo (2011: 39) that 'the multiplication of options, rather than the elimination of them, is … the road to global futures'.

There are many approaches that could be relevant in conceptualizing beyond Western philosophies in higher education research. Some studies that are relevant to the current book chapter highlight the role of kindness exemplified in the Māori concept of relatedness and humility, *manaaki* (Buissink et al. 2017), and the notion of togetherness, social responsibility and ethics of care as in African thought, *ubuntu* (Waghid 2020) in creating a more just and epistemically diverse global higher education system. The concepts of *manaaki* and *ubuntu* resemble the notions of *ren* (kindness) and *li* (respect) in Confucianism. However, since the purpose of this chapter is to understand the public good discussion in South Korean context, let us elaborate on the concept of *jeong* underpinning this chapter, which also speaks to the notions of *manaaki* and *ubuntu*. The motivation behind using this approach is to highlight the rich epistemic traditions of East Asia, and it is also an invitation to conceptualize global higher education trends through multiple epistemic traditions. We further join critical scholars of comparative education research in their aspirations to include diverse epistemologies in designing research methodologically and epistemically:

> We need not only to recognise the global plurality of comparative education knowledge projects, but also to deploy them for examining tensions and contradictions within the globalised field of comparative education. (Takayama, Sriprakash and Connell 2017: S7)

Indeed, it has been historically important and is timely nowadays to develop comparative research and analytical frameworks that conceptualize education processes through diverse epistemic lenses. In this chapter, *jeong* is embraced methodologically and as a conceptual framework in relation to higher education research. Below we proceed with elaboration of *jeong* in Korean higher education.

Main *Jeong* Characteristics

Jeong is not unique to South Korea and is present in other East Asian contexts, such as in China, Japan and Vietnam. While scholars locate the meaning of *jeong* in multiple East Asian contexts, the working definition in this chapter is grounded in South Korean literature as, arguably, *jeong* in Korean culture contains more extensive meanings than the original meaning of the Chinese character (Chung and Cho 1997).

The concept of *jeong* comes from the Chinese character *jeong* (情), which refers to the mind or emotion (Yoon 2016). More specifically Lee (1994a) also argues that the character *jeong* (情) represents a combination of heart (心) and pure (青), which means unspoilt and unmanipulated human mind. The concept of *jeong* is similar to that of 'affection' and 'attachment', but rather than including strong feelings such as love, it is a more passive form of 'emotional bonding' (Choi, Kim and Kim 2000). To be more specific, (1) *jeong* is a type of emotion; (2) it arises from nurturing human relationships that embody understanding, inclusion and assistance; and (3) it lasts for a long period of time (Choi and Lee 1999).

Jeong is formed under the following conditions (Choi and Lee 1999): (1) when we struggle together and share tight-knit experiences; (2) when we care for another and even consider the other person to be an extension of ourselves; (3) when there are no walls or secrets to divide one from another; and (4) when we go beyond our self-interests. Indeed, in an ideal setting, deep *jeong* should be developed over time. In this chapter, we do not have an opportunity to elaborate more on the breadth and the depth of *jeong*. However, we would like to point out that deep *jeong* is seen as more desirable as it is more lasting. Deep *jeong* might include the stages of disagreement, debate, blame and forgiveness.

There are five thematic strands that correspond to key *jeong* characteristics that might help explain the definition, concept and generative conditions of *jeong* in more detail (Ko 2010; Mayumi 2018). First, it is a relationship. One might argue that in Korean society *jeong* is widely used not only in family relations but also in teacher-student relations and at workplaces. Furthermore, *jeong* can be developed towards plants, hometowns, dogs and even stones (Ko 2014). In other words, *jeong* is a fundamental and important means of establishing a relationship in Korean culture, and many Koreans maintain their relationship with others by putting the other person in the category of 'We' – 'in which "I" and "You" exist as an inseparable unit' (Lee 1994b: 122). In Korea, it is considered that *jeong* makes human relations more human (Ko 2010). From this perspective, the sociality of Koreans based on *jeong* can be contrasted with the human relations of Western society based on individualism (Yoon 2016).

Second, while it is formed spontaneously, it is persistent. *Jeong* is not created through trying, rather it is created naturally. It is formed over a long period of time through the acts of worrying, caring and helping another person and considering the other person's position (Mayumi 2018). One might put forward an argument that a classroom or a university environment at large might be a potential setting for the formation of *jeong* among classmates, the community and between students and faculty. Third, the value of authenticity of the other person's intentions, sincerity and reciprocity are important (Ko 2010). The Korean proverb says: 'There must be a give and take in *jeong* (scratch my back and I will scratch yours).' Fourth, it is a sense of bonding and a sense of community (we-ness). People who understand and help others are viewed as human and compassionate, while those who do not are thought of as cold and heartless. *Jeong* culture creates a sense of community that is Us (we-ness), and Koreans value we-ness (Mayumi 2018). For example, when Koreans introduce themselves, rather than 'my parents', 'my friends' and 'my school', they use the expressions 'our parents', 'our friends' and 'our school' (Cho 2002).

The final, fifth, characteristic that is described in the literature is ambivalence. *Jeong* is not necessarily always a positive feeling, nor does it always happen reciprocally. People who feel that they are close to another will have *jeong*, even if those feelings are not reciprocated (Yang 2006). Thus, South Koreans also commonly use the term 'bitter *jeong*'. It means that during a long relationship, the parties involved will inevitably face both agreements and disagreements. That said, it is possible to overcome challenges and disagreements and maintain deep *jeong*. It seems developing deep *jeong* might be especially important in order to teach students and professors to learn from each other, overcome disagreements over political divides or other contested experiences and topics.

However, *jeong* might also have negative attributes (Ko 2014; Yu 2015). First of all, the sense of community, which is formed through *jeong*, does not fully tolerate individual space and life. Participants beyond the relationship or group bound by *jeong* might be seen as outsiders and, hence, excluded from this special relationship (Mayumi 2018). In this way, *jeong* also has shown negative characteristics such as invading personal domains, distinguishing between insiders and outsiders, and sometimes even discriminating against outsiders (Yoon 2016). Indeed, the negative aspects could be present in the higher education sector as well, for example, by excluding international students who are not closely aware of the *jeong* culture or other outgroup members. Given the negative characteristics, it can be said that *jeong* is an ideal-type value that Koreans have pursued beyond everyday emotions (Ko 2014).

The intertwined nature of human relationships represented by *jeong* can also be found in higher education. For instance, it is common knowledge that in Korean universities students from the same department and student clubs hold an event titled 'MT' every year. Participation in the MT event includes travelling into nature or visiting another city for two days and one night, and engagement in the prepared 'relationship building' programmes, which help deepen friendships and build bonds. Professors often accompany student gatherings to build a teacher-student bond.

Before we move to the findings section of our study that addresses the role of Korean philosophy of *jeong* in developing professor-student and university-public relationships in more detail, below we turn to describing the methodological steps on how we collected and analysed data and ensured rigour throughout the research process.

Methodology and Research Questions

The research design for this project mainly consisted of three steps. During the initial phase and the first step of the research process, research questions were designed by senior research members who also communicated with the prospective participants via e-mail. The second step included nine semi-structured interviews that lasted for fifty to sixty minutes. Five were conducted in a public university, two in a private university and two with ex-government officials. The interviews were conducted in Korean and English languages, as chosen by the participants. The transcription was completed by a third party. The final third step of the research process included data analysis. The co-authors of this book chapter contributed to the second and third stages as we joined in the middle of the research process and worked collaboratively in conducting and scheduling interviews during the fieldwork in Seoul. The fieldwork took place in 2019, and most of the interviews were conducted in person. Two supplementary interviews were conducted in 2020.

Thematic analysis was chosen as the primary method to analyse the collected data in order to discern the main interpretations of the role of *jeong* in the way participants reflected on the notion of the public good role of higher education. Overall the six-step process of the reflexive thematic analysis was followed, including familiarization, generating codes, constructing themes, revising and defining themes, and producing the report (Braun et al. 2018). The co-authors collaboratively discussed the main themes in the interviews and codes via online meetings and the exchange of e-mails and notes. The initial set of codes was developed individually and calibrated during the process of follow up meetings. The rigour was ensured through iterative analysis of data and through a close collaborative work that included both individual and joint data analysis. Through analysing the empirical material multiple times, attempts were made to minimize individual interpretive bias. Finally, in November 2020, preliminary findings were presented at the Oxford Korean Academic Society (OKAS) and feedback was received from scholars of *jeong* based in South Korea, United

States and the UK. Participation in the OKAS seminar and positive feedback received from the attendees reassured the co-authors of the importance of the research development on *jeong* as a concept and methodology.

Reflections on Positionality, Fieldwork and *Jeong*

In addition to the higher education literature, the second contribution of this book chapter is to the methodological literature on higher education research. The co-authors maintain that the Korean concept of *jeong* might be used not only as a concept and philosophy, but also as *methodology* in conducting research. For instance, it might seem that the process of data collection and fieldwork is a formality during which a researcher is collecting empirical material for the project. However, comparative and international education as an academic field has a complex history ridden with the colonial and neocolonial practices (Takayama, Sriprakash and Connell 2017), some of which might entail Western-based scholars researching international contexts with limited linguistic capabilities, with no contextual knowledge and by instrumentally working with 'local' research assistants in order to gain short-term 'local' expertise.

In the current project, both collaborators contributed to the data collection, writing up and the design of the book chapter. Moreover, both participants had diverse and hybrid positionalities. For example, Olga is an ethnic Korean from Kazakhstan. She has a basic understanding of the Korean language and an experience of living in Seoul. Yunkyung, in turn, speaks fluent Korean and was largely seen as an insider when conducting the interviews. Joint participation in the fieldwork as well as listening to one another carefully allowed the researchers to collect rich data in multiple languages, minimize biases and co-create a book chapter. A feeling of *jeong* emerged overtime as they shared food together, travelled in Seoul and, despite the pandemic, work and childcare responsibilities, persevered and finished the analysis and documentation.

At times it was challenging working on the book chapter as initially the interviews with government officials were not secured. However, Yunkyung was able to conduct the missing interviews. Furthermore, during the initial fieldwork in 2019, Olga had a birthday and it was a bit lonely. Despite knowing Olga only for a brief period of time, Yunkyung brought her flowers. By overcoming the challenges of the fieldwork and blurring the boundaries of a research trip and sharing a personal celebration, an opportunity arose to further nourish *jeong*. At the writing up stage, co-authors were based in different time zones. The pandemic has been raging at different rhythms in the UK and South Korea. During numerous calls, Olga saw Yunkyung's son, whom she first met in person during the fieldwork, and the boundaries of the personal and professional were further mixed as the authors were working from home. However, in new research on higher education blurring the personal and professional is not always seen in a negative light, as 'unprofessional'. Quite the opposite; it is grasped as a politics of kindness and care – a helpful condition in developing the cultures of recognition in a neoliberal academia (Aquarone et al. 2020). By truly working together, getting to know each other over time, listening to each other, and treating the research collaboration as a continuous joint endeavour, we were able to develop a sense of *jeong* within the research collective. *Jeong* allowed to not simply work on a 'project' together but turn the occasional feelings of loneliness and despair into a respair through joint writing at the time of a global pandemic.

Jeong's Characteristics in Korean Higher Education

Based on the literature review in the previous sections, the formation of *jeong* might take place on the individual micro-level in formations of friendship groups and on a wider institutional level, for example, in the classroom or at an organization. Since *jeong* is not widely theorized in higher education literature, we operationalize the concept based on the interview responses from the participants and propose initial thoughts on the role of *jeong* in understanding the public good in Korean higher education.

Through the initial analysis of the interviews, the stage that is typically called *familiarization* in the thematic analysis literature (Braun et al. 2018), we palpated that the *jeong* culture is foundational in realizing the public good role in Korean higher education. The theme of caring for the local, regional and global community, and nature, as well as developing professor-student relationships, emerged in numerous interviews. Through constructing and revising themes individually and collectively and in relation to the *jeong* classification described in the literature, we finalized the following themes: (1) *Jeong* as a humanistic pedagogy (relationship-orientedness and humanity in higher education); (2) *Jeong* as community development (a culture of helping and sharing); (3) *Jeong* as the culture of togetherness and we-ness; and a final category of (4) *Jeong* as beyond human pedagogy (nature-human nexus in higher education). These categories may be seen as independent or interrelated. They might happen on their own or be parts of a larger process. For instance, the individual pursuit of relationship-orientedness and humanity might lead to community development (a culture of helping and sharing), which in turn might result in the culture of togetherness and we-ness. Alternatively, each step might be happening independently of the others. In the following section, let us describe the first category of *jeong* as a humanistic pedagogy in more details.

Jeong as a Humanistic Pedagogy (Relationship-Orientedness and Humanity in Higher Education)

In the traditional perception of the role of higher education, three roles are usually defined: teaching, research and public service. Interestingly, in the analysed interviews, academics from diverse disciplines including education studies and engineering highlighted the important role of teaching and not research in the formation of positive social relations in and beyond the classroom. Such public engagement might take shape in the form of summer schools or winter schools. The interviewees shared their experiences of organizing such seminars, summer and winter schools in order to foster a humanistic pedagogy among their students and departments. One participant shared that he was engaged in outreach activities related to peace building in Asia for two decades in order to build bridges and develop humanistic values:

> It means that forty times, for four or five days, the Korean university, the four universities and two universities in Japan, the students are gathering to study, to have fieldwork, to talk with each other. (Interviewee DPU, public university)

Since his engagement lasted for decades (sustained engagement is a criterion for deep *jeong* development) and he organized it not in the self-interest for career promotion or research impact, the participant's response was categorized in relation to *jeong* as a humanistic pedagogy. Another academic highlighted that though in his discipline public engagement is not considered to be very important and international publications are seen as the main goal, he still participated in pedagogic summer camps and outreach activities:

> Sometimes I have a course for like high school students about introducing ergonomics in my discipline, we have an academic society and in our department we have a summer camp once a year. (Interviewee CPU, public university)

In the quotes above we extracted some of the examples as expressed by the participants in relation to the importance of the development of humanistic values through higher education. Other examples of *jeong* as a humanistic pedagogy included stories about satellite teaching across different countries, campuses and student exchange programmes. Professors emphasized that it was important for them to help students learn about other cultures, so that they could become better professionals and contribute to society through work.

Indeed, it is important to recognize that some social bond formation in South Korea may happen as a result of blood ties, school ties and region ties. To this end, developing *jeong* as a humanistic pedagogy might be a possibility that warm compassion might be extended beyond one group and into society as a whole or the world. This possibility can be seen in the following interview:

> I am doing it for humanitarian purpose, to help these people. So, that kind of criteria cannot be quantified but I am doing this because I like it even though I do not get any credit from them. (Interviewee BPU, private university)

In the example above, an interviewee sought to realize the public value of the university by pursuing humanitarian purposes through unconditional sharing and helping without the wish for compensation, which is precisely a characteristic of *jeong* formation.

To sum up, selected quotes from the interviews resemble wider trends in South Korean universities that aim to help build meaningful professor-student and student-student relationships through inclusive university life, rituals as eating together and spending time together running various summer and winter schools, outreach programmes for students and the public. However, some professors indicated that these public good initiatives are rare, and they are not institutionalized and widespread. Nevertheless, we maintain that given that many of such educational and volunteering engagements are happening over long period of time, decades even, and are often intrinsically motivated, it might be argued that at the basis of such relationships and initiatives lies the feelings of *jeong* as a humanistic pedagogy.

Jeong as Community Development (a Culture of Helping and Sharing)

Another characteristic of *jeong* is that people help others and share what they have. South Korea was one of the poorest countries in the world during the Japanese occupation and the Korean War in the 1950s, but since then it has achieved substantial economic growth and development. One of the driving forces behind the economic growth is considered to be education (Kwak et al. 2010). Many representatives of the Korean political, business and social elites went to study abroad with government scholarships and returned to South Korea, which arguably supported the country's development. Therefore, an argument exists in the society which is reflected in the quote from the participant below that now it is Korea's turn to help countries in the global South:

> In Korean culture, when we are poor we receive so much help from outside. So, nowadays we should pay back, it's a political agenda, it's a cultural agenda in Korean society and in Korean Government. (Interviewee DPU, public university)

The participant further elaborated that community is seen not only in the immediate terms of the local community but also on national and international levels. An internationalist perspective is interesting and particularly important, especially in the light of increasing populist, divisive and nationalist movements around the world. The participant maintained:

> And in Korean culture from a long time ago, during summer vacation, students go to the rural society to develop some of the environmental conditions and some medical school or some dental school, students tried to go there and to, contribute, I think there were one or two weeks. And nowadays so many, many students go abroad, to other countries, Mongolia, Cambodia, and they give a medical service or a dental service and social work service. (Interviewee DPU, public university)

There was no consensus in terms of how interviewees saw the level of global engagement of Korean universities. Some think that it is still largely driven by national interests, while others highlighted that increasingly the universities are becoming more globally engaged, especially in Asia:

> Yeah, they have a dream to assist more and more big size to North Korea, all of the faculty members, I think even the students … In academic level some people argue the young generation, young faculty members in poor countries can be given to study the opportunity in this university but I think that is not sufficient, the size is not sufficient for me. (Interviewee DPU, public university)

> Like helping some East Asian countries, like Vietnam and Laos, and something like those countries. That's one area. And the other one is publish the papers in international journals, this, those are two trends that we have. (Interviewee APU, public university)

Overall, the shared sentiment among many interviewees was that South Korea is now in a position to help other countries through developing student mobility programmes, joint research initiatives and international development programmes. In less than half a century, Korea managed to transition from a donor-receiving country to becoming an aid-giving country. It is beyond the scope of this book chapter to analyse relevant literature on international development, neocolonialism and voluntourism. However, it is worth mentioning that South Korea, indeed, presents an interesting case of an East Asian player in the field of international development. Furthermore, if Korean volunteer students and academics truly embraced deep *jeong*, then this could be in fact a reassuring step in actually building epistemically just and respectful development and collaboration projects.

In addition, one interviewee expressed deep concerns about the access problems to higher education on a national level, particularly for low-income students: 'sometimes I see students, they are very good and then they cannot get a good education because they are poor. I think that's just very absurd' (Interviewee CPU, public university). He stressed that the government and universities need to be open to all students regardless of their background, but at the moment, government regulates student admissions policies and there is a quota system, so the departments can't define how many students to accept and according to which criteria. The same interviewee also highlighted the importance of the role of higher education in helping both local and global communities. The participant reflected on one case when an external commission was evaluating the performance of their department and the reviewer asked about the department's public contribution. But the researchers tended to focus on narrow research metrics indicators, and they could not address fully the reviewer's question and were embarrassed:

> So, we had this big meeting and then presented, our dean presented how many papers we published, our QS ranking is this good, and things like that and this question was very similar, we were very embarrassed because he said 'what are some stories you as professors or the graduates contributed to society, what did you do?' and we did not prepare for that. (Interviewee CPU, public university)

The quote above shows the tensions between the pressure of being a world-class university and produce global research, while contributing to the local, regional and global public good initiatives. However, to a large extent, most of the interviewees agreed that the public good role and community development is important for South Korean universities.

In summary, in this part of the book chapter we presented an analysis of the interviews that described the public good role of higher education at the local, regional and global levels. Academics highlighted the role of higher education in class mobility and the need to support low-income students nationally. Some of the interviewees highlighted that students are self-motivated to enrol in public service programmes to help in rural areas and internationally. Due to the fact that students participated in such programmes regularly on a voluntary basis, it might be concluded that the sense of *jeong* as community development permeated such public volunteering activities.

Jeong as the Culture of Togetherness and We-ness

A widespread argument is present in the literature on neoliberalism in global higher education that it promotes the ideas of individualism and competition (Zajda 2020). Furthermore, new literature emerges on the themes of loneliness, overwhelming workloads and student alienation in marketized universities (Aquarone et al. 2020). On the contrary, feelings of togetherness and we-ness, which are defined as the relational integration with other people (Reid et al. 2006), are the characteristics of *jeong*. One of the most vivid examples of the *jeong* as the culture of togetherness and we-ness was found in a communal garden initiative.

A small garden was created on the roof of a university building where local residents, students and alumni with children could plant and grow vegetables. The professor who designed the garden envisioned everyone enjoying the space and cultivating a sense of a close-knit community. The culture of we-ness could be found in the way that everyone nurtured and enjoyed the precious space together, which exemplified the public value of the university. The professor behind the initiative shared that after all what could be more important than smiling together. He also highlighted the importance of intergenerational learning and public pedagogy:

> Let's involve civil engineering alumni. They have some in their department and they have grandchildren. They come with the grandchildren and enjoy the weekend here and they will like it, and they love it, so we can make sustainable roof. (Interviewee BPU, public university)

The importance of intergenerational learning came up in another interview as well when a participant explained that more dialogues are necessary to build a culture of peace and human rights globally:

> So, the human rights and peace is such an important agenda for me and I try to have the opportunity and all of my experience should be shared with the young generation. (Interviewee DPU, public university)

The example of a communal garden is a successful case of how a university space could be used to build meaningful relationships between the local community, students, faculty and alumni. Contrary to the practices in some Western universities where alumni are frequented with e-mails related to fundraising and where university e-mails are cut off once students graduate, the South Korean case of a communal garden creating an inviting space 'to smile together' exemplifies a more humane alternative to building relationships and a culture of care. We classify such approaches as being inspired by *jeong* as the culture of togetherness and we-ness.

Jeong as Beyond Human Pedagogy (Nature-Human Nexus in Higher Education)

Finally, the last theme that we will briefly highlight in the current book chapter is in relation to the respect for nature, flora and fauna. While the posthuman theme featured less prominently in the interviews, the same participant who cultivated the culture of togetherness and we-ness also developed a beyond human space on a rooftop garden situated on a university campus. More specifically, in the public garden that he created, he designed a place for bees and humans. Furthermore, the building relied on rainwater to maintain the essential sewage systems. In many ways, the roof was a fundamental piece of the building infrastructure that drew on sustainable water sources and also created a successful space for people to socially interact with each other as well as with the animals visiting and inhabiting the space. Since the building was located against the backdrop of mountains, the roof provided a place of calmness and an opportunity to interact with nature in a busy Seoul city. The lead professor and designer of the rooftop project shared the following thought:

> We grow vegetables together, we have this potato and give it to the public people and also in Korea we have Chuseok full moon festival because there are many foreign students, they want to know the Korean customs so we go together here and make a special moon cake, and eat and enjoy, and distribute to the other people. One more thing we make kimchi here. We grow vegetables and make kimchi. How can students know, we have our community, a very good community. They come here and help us make kimchi together and make some cultural experience with the foreign students and donate something to other people. So, it is a special atmosphere. (Interviewee BPU, public university)

The example above of a beyond human space that was designed and built in a sustainable way was unique. It also created space to integrate international students into a local community. The sustainable rooftop initiative attracted a lot of attention in the media and the professor behind it contributed to many sustainability initiatives around the world. To conclude, by embracing *jeong* as beyond human pedagogy, the rooftop garden with bees in Seoul is a unique example demonstrating how a university could become a space to foster meaningful social and beyond human relationships with nature, plants, insects and animals.

Discussion

While most of the interviewees described the public role of higher education – locally, nationally and globally – mostly in positive terms, one interviewee from a private university voiced an opinion that private universities and their students are not necessarily interested in public engagement. The participant stated that the universities need to make money, and students are mostly interested in receiving an education in order to get a good job after graduation. The interviewee maintained that private universities do not necessarily have to participate in public engagement, as they are not the government:

> Well, that's unanimously no because especially public institutions, probably you are familiar with our situation right now, only 20 per cent of public institutions, 80 per cent of the private ones, so it's a private dominant market in our country but for the private institutions we are getting financial support from the Government about five to ten so that's very limited. So, given that why should we do what the Government asks us to do? So, we have to do whatever we want to make money. So it's money making activities. It's less relevant than with the public mission of higher education I think. (Interviewee BPU, private university)

Another interviewee from a private institution added that most of the Korean funding applications do not have a component requiring researchers to engage in outreach activities. An interviewee from the public university added that to many researchers their primary engagement is academic scholarship and not public engagement:

> Well, to be honest I'm not quite sure whether other faculty members are interested in a social engagement, the public good missions, but basically what they are mostly interested in is mostly research activities, doing research whether or not there is public good or private good but that's what they do. (Interviewee BPU, private university)

A former government official, in turn, criticized that Korean universities are becoming commercialized, and that they are pursuing private profit rather than serving the public good, resembling some of the sentiments that neoliberal globalization is negatively impacting *jeong*:

> The current university is becoming an enterprise due to many factors such as the government's higher education policy, financial pressure, and private academia foundations' demand for capital. The corporatization of universities has an ideological character that keeps the capitalist system firm. Universities are being swept into a very wrong direction. To prevent this, we have to go back to the questions 'What is a university?' and 'What is a good university?' A university is basically an educational institution and a place to learn something. However, the separation of capitalism and the function of research and education leads to fewer and fewer knowledge that can be learned, leaving a bad habit that should not be learned. (Ex-government official interview)

The concern about commercialization of higher education and education as a private commodity was also voiced by other participants:

> As I said before 1998, or 2008, in 1998 there was a financial crisis in Korea. In 2008 is a global financial crisis. Before that as I said we had a very strong social orientated, public good orientated culture but after that the students became more and more individual with a private goal. More higher mobility orientated, more stable job. (Interviewee DPU, public university)

In other words, it is possible to see from the sample of this study that there are tensions in how academics at private universities and public universities conceptualize the public role of universities. However, as our case study was exploratory, it is not possible to make strong and definitive generalized conclusions. A more detailed study might evince richer findings on the public good role of private and public higher education institutions as the majority of the interviews in our sample were from the public university and only two interviews were conducted at a private university.

Concluding Thoughts

This book chapter, to the best of our knowledge, is the first attempt in the academic literature, both in English and Korean languages, to suggest looking at the public good role of higher education through a Korean concept of *jeong*. Based on the *jeong* concept discussed earlier, four ways to conceptualize *jeong* in higher education were put forward: *jeong* as a humanistic pedagogy (relationship-orientedness and humanity in higher education), as community development (a culture of helping and sharing), as the culture of togetherness and we-ness, and as beyond human pedagogy (nature-human nexus in higher education). While the pursuit of *jeong* does not necessarily occur in all research partnerships or relationships in higher education and there are tensions between the commercialization and marketization of higher education trends and some perceptions of the global public good role of the universities, we argued that it is possible to include *jeong* not only in our everyday life or in the way students and professors interact with each other in higher education but also in producing academic research. Hence, we shared how we incorporated *jeong* in our research and suggested *jeong* as both a conceptual frame and as a methodology.

3

Tianxia Weigong as a Chinese Approach to Global Public Good

Lili Yang

Introduction

This chapter conceptually explores the Chinese idea of *tianxia weigong*, meaning all under heaven belongs to and is for all. As the chapter will show, this idea provides an alternative approach to understanding higher education's cross-border activities and global collective outcomes in addition to the Anglo-American concepts of global public goods.

There is a common trope that higher education produces public goods including global public goods. Nevertheless, while higher education's production of national public goods is widely discussed and relatively better supported, that of global public goods is still under-recognized, studied and provided (Marginson 2018a). On the one hand, it remains unclear what global public goods means. On the other hand, higher education is in short of resources and support for producing global public goods (Deneulin and Townsend 2007; UNESCO 2015).

The idea of higher education's global public goods is closely related to the world view and state/society/education assemblage of the context in which higher education is embedded (Marginson and Yang 2020b). The state/society/education assemblage is understood as the scope of, and relationship between, the state, society and education. The world view is essential in how 'global' is understood in the context, whereas the state/society/education assemblage, to a large extent, shapes the connotations of the public (good) of higher education. However, the existing discussions concerning higher education's global public goods mainly assume the Anglo-American world view and state/

society/education assemblages, which are marked by a dualistic world view and methodological nationalism (Beck 2016), and the prioritization of the private (good) over the public (good) (see also below; Marginson and Yang 2020a). As will be shown later in this chapter, problems may arise when using the Anglo-American concepts of global public goods to explain the higher education phenomena in non-Anglo-American contexts.

The chapter argues that the Chinese idea of *tianxia weigong* provides an alternative approach to understanding and explaining higher education's global public goods. It starts with an examination of the Chinese interpretations of the public (good) in higher education with a special focus on a pair of terms: the larger self, representing the public, and the smaller self, representing the private. It then investigates the Confucian way of understanding the world – the Confucian anthropocosmic world view – and the idea of *tianxia weigong*, used to describe the Chinese approach to global public goods. Further, there is a critique of the Anglo-American concepts of global public goods in higher education. Taking into account the problems of the Anglo-American concepts in higher education, the chapter discusses the implications of *tianxia weigong* for global public goods of higher education. Finally, the chapter ends with a critical reflection of the limitations of the idea of *tianxia weigong*, including concerns of employing the idea in realpolitik.

The *Gong* (Public) and *Si* (Private) in China: The Collectivist Tradition

'Self' is a key term in seeking to understand the *gong* (public) and *si* (private) in the Chinese context. The absolute 'self' in the Western sense does not exist in China (Cheng and Yang 2015: 127). Instead, there is coexistence of *dawo* (the larger self) and *xiaowo* (the smaller self), and the 'individual' is always a relative concept. Based on the interaction of the 'smaller self' and 'larger self', people's conceptions in terms of public and private change.

The smaller and larger selves are relative concepts that operate simultaneously at multiple scales (see Figure 3.1 and Table 3.1). Additional circles/entities can be added between any two nested circles that are illustrated in Figure 3.1. For example, there are local communities between the family and the state. As will be discussed in the next section, the series of nested circles demonstrates the Confucian way of understanding the world, from the smallest entity – individual/self – to the largest entity – *tianxia* (all under heaven)/the world.

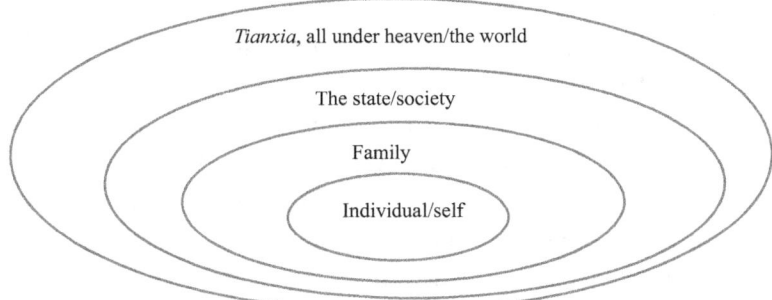

Figure 3.1 The Escalating Entities from the Individual to All under Heaven.
Source: Author, after Huang (2010).

Table 3.1 The Private/Smaller Self and the Public/Larger Self

The private/smaller self	The public/larger self
The individual/self in family	The family
The family	The state/society
The state/society	*Tianxia* (all under heaven)/the world

Source: Author, after Huang (2010).

The individual may be conceptualized as a version of the smaller self, and, in this instance, the family can be understood to be the larger self that operates around it. However, this type of relationship also exists at larger scales. The family unit may be understood as a smaller self in relation to the larger self that is the broader society or the state. Further, the state represents the smaller self in relation to the larger self of *tianxia*, all under heaven. In a pair of the smaller self and the larger self, the smaller self is the private whereas the larger self is the public.

According to the relationship between the private/smaller self and the public/larger self, not only the private is nested within the public, private interests are subordinate to public interests. The Confucian moral principle requires the smaller self and the private interests to be sacrificed for the larger self and the public interests when necessary. For example, in neo-Confucian master Zhu Xi's (1130–200) views, the public is legal whereas the private is illegal (Zhu and Lv [1175] 2001). This demonstrates a collectivist tradition in China – the collective's interests and goals should be primary (Earley and Gibson 1998; Marginson and Yang 2020a). This collectivist tradition is still salient in China, though connotations of the primary collectives have changed over time (see more in Marginson and Yang 2020a).

The importance of collectivism is paradoxically enhanced by the Confucian individualism in the Chinese context, which refers to 'the fullest development by the individual of [their] creative potentialities – not, however, merely for the sake of self-expression but because [they] can thus best fulfil that particular role which is within [their] social nexus' (Bodde 1957: 66). The connotation of the individual in imperial China were far from the Western sense. The individual in imperial Chinese sense had no relation to Western individuality or individualism. Rather, the individual was regarded as the starting point of the expanding entities (i.e., the self, the family, the state and all under heaven), and the importance of the individual lay in its identity with the larger entities (Xu 2017). As Rosemont Jr (2015: 4) states, 'human beings can only be understood relationally, never as isolates, and are thus best accounted for as the sum of the roles they live, with no remainder or consequence'. In imperial China, and arguably to a certain extent today, individuals were not regarded as independent agents in society, but were tagged as members of the family (or other social nexuses today). However, there has been a trend of the expansion of individual autonomy and the phenomenon of individuals disembedding from collective entities in contemporary China (Marginson and Yang 2020a).

In addition, the overlap between the state and society shows the ambiguity of the state and society and implies a tradition of having a comprehensive state rather than a limited liberal state in the Chinese context (Marginson and Yang 2020a). The state enjoys a central status and has the potential to intervene in any social domain for the sake of maintaining social order and promoting prosperity, although in imperial times, the state as an entity was not as solid as *tianxia* and gained its central status as the legitimate representative of *tianxia* with the responsibility to advance the good of *tianxia* (Liang 1990).

The normative preference of the public over the private and the comprehensive state continues to make a difference in the contemporary Chinese higher education, despite the impact from Western individualism and (neo)liberalism in the past century. For example, the primary missions of higher education today are state-oriented, which is reflective of the central status of the state. According to Gernet (1996) and Collins (2016), the higher education system in China is structured as an extension of the state, and it has been deliberately designed and guided to support the state's pursuit of modernization. On the one hand, higher education is designed to achieve the objectives of contributing to public goods. In imperial times, such public goods primarily referred to goods of *tianxia*, indicating the idea of global public goods in the traditional Chinese sense. On the other hand, China's efforts of modernization have consolidated the state but marginalized *tianxia*. National public goods rather than global public goods have become the central concern in contemporary Chinese higher education. Nevertheless, the Belt and Road Initiative indicates the increasing importance of *tianxia* idea in China (see also below; Marginson and Yang 2020a).

Notably, there is a need to distinguish conceptual discussions and policy manifestations. Although global public goods are relatively less emphasized in contemporary Chinese higher education compared to national public goods, the Confucian anthropocosmic world view and the traditional Chinese ideas about *tianxia* and *tianxia weigong* (all under heaven belongs to/is for all) remain important, and they have the potential to shed new light on discussions of global public goods of higher education.

The Confucian Anthropocosmic World View and the Idea of *Tianxia Weigong*

The Concept of *Tianxia*

Tian, meaning heaven, is a core concept in the Chinese political culture and is an essential character that further constitutes many other core concepts including *tianxia*, all under heaven. In addition to being the material 'heaven', *tian* is also closely related to Chinese people's notions of worship, referring to the highest supernatural force.

Building on the term *tian*, *tianxia* literally means all human beings, creatures and things under heaven – in other words, everything in the world. Meanwhile, *tianxia* contains abstract connotations, reflecting the belief that heaven is above all and controls all. As will be discussed later, among all of the entities illustrated in Figure 3.1, *tianxia* is the largest entity in scope in the Confucian social imaginary. It contains all other smaller entities, and it represents the idea of the entire world of shared values and cultures, including nature as well as humanity (Zhao 2006, 2009). Ideally, all contained smaller entities are in an equilibrium status and collectively constitute a harmonious world.

Scholars/researchers today often interpret *tianxia* in two ways – one is *tianxia* as a normative appeal and the other is *tianxia* in realpolitik (Wang 2017: 5, 12). While *tianxia* as a normative appeal concerns the abstract and discursive Confucian idea of *tianxia*, *tianxia* in realpolitik focuses on designing a world governance system in realpolitik based on the *tianxia* idea (see more in Callahan 2004, 2008; Wang 2017).

Tianxia as Normative

As a normative appeal, *tianxia* is a symbolic ideal, and it suggests the idea of 'no other' and a universal civilizational order (J. Xu 2017; Z. Xu 2018). In this universal civilizational order, all component units are nested within the largest entity *tianxi*a, all under heaven. The ultimate aim of human beings is to bring harmony and peace to *tianxia*. This, according to Confucianism, can be realized by emphasizing on culture, value and mutual acceptance and recognition. For example, there is the idea of harmony without conformity (*heer butong*) that highlights heterogeneity and requires mutual understanding and respect, flexibility and dialogue (Fang 2003). In Fei Xiaotong's words, 'value your own value, and that of others. With the shared value, we will share the world peacefully.'[1] Arguably, the idea of *tianxia* partly parallels with the cosmopolitan thought that all humanity belongs non-exclusively to a single community (Duara 2017: 67).

To interpret *tianxia* in the contemporary context, Zhao (2011: 3) argues that *tianxia* as a normative appeal calls for thinking through the world rather than thinking of the world. Thinking through the world is to understand the world not as an aggregation of nation states, as methodological nationalism does (see below), but as a world per se. As *tianxia*, the world is a collective entity, comprising sub-collective agents that are in harmonious and positive-sum relationships. In this case, *tianxia* is the larger self, and all other sub-collective agents are the smaller selves. The subordination of the smaller self to the larger self suggests prioritizing the interests of *tianxia* over the other parochial interests, including national interests. In addition, by thinking through the world, human beings' belongingness to humanity and the world is stressed, and further their responsibility to serve the world is consolidated.

Tianxia in Realpolitik

How might the normative idea of *tianxia* be implemented in realpolitik? Zhao (2011) argues for a political sovereignty at the *tianxia* level, and lower-level entities below *tianxia*/the world. These lower-level entities are not nation states. In Zhao's (2011) view, a distinctive example of *tianxia* in realpolitik is the Zhou Dynasty (1100–256 BCE). In Zhao's view, the contemporary extension of the *tianxia* model would involve a world government controlling a larger territory

---

[1] 各美其美，美人之美，美美与共，天下大同。- Xiaotong Fei, Speech titled "Research on humans in China – A personal experience (*Ren de yanjiu zai zhongguo: Geren de jingli*)".

and military force than that controlled by the autonomous substates. These substates would be independent in most respects, except in their legitimacy and obligations, for which they would depend on the recognition of world government. Rather than being based on force and self-interest, the cultural empire would use ritual as a means to limit the self and its interests. *Tianxia* is a hierarchical world view that prioritizes order over freedom, elite governance over democracy, and the superior political institution over the lower level. (Duara 2017: 70)

As Duara (2017) suggests, *tianxia* in realpolitik diverges from the dominant Western views concerning the characteristics of states, interstate relations and ways to organize the state and the world. For example, the state in a *tianxia* system is not self-interested, as the case with nation states, but follows rituals to limit its own interests. The relationship between states is not always equal. In the *tianxia* system, at least in scholarly discussion, it is acceptable to have hierarchy between states (Yan 2011: 97, 104; see also below). With regard to organizing the state and the world, *tianxia* idea's emphases on harmony over diversity, stability over liberty and meritocracy over democracy are major divergences from the Anglo-American world view (Wang 2017: 13). Further, the Confucian notion of solving practical problems of statecraft through norms, values, behaviours and accepted rituals rather than law, contract and the final backing of state coercion also diverges from the dominant narratives today.

These divergences make the *tianxia* idea in realpolitik seemingly unacceptable in modern times, especially given the existence of various political cultures throughout the world. For example, hierarchical relationships between states are critiqued because of the potential for major countries to influence and even dominate weaker ones (Callahan and Barabantseva 2011; Chirot and Hall 1982; Fairbank 1968; Wang 2003).

The Confucian Anthropocosmic World View and the Anglo-American Dualistic World View

The Confucian anthropocosmic world view is embodied in the idea of the 'one body' and 'the unity of heaven and humanity', and it has played a fundamental role in moulding Chinese people's understandings of the world. Lu and Jover (2019: 428) assert that the Confucian anthropocosmic world view is arguably one of the biggest contributions of the Chinese tradition to a balanced and sustainable development of the world in the twenty-first century.

In line with the connotations of *tianxia*, all things on earth, despite their multitude, compose one body (Zhang 1996: 81). This describes a state where human beings and nature reach a harmonious equilibrium, and all component units of the world constitute an organic whole. The 'one body' and 'unity' idea originated in Daoism and was later adopted and reinterpreted by Confucianism. It was initially proposed by Hui Shi (around 370–310 BCE) and his friend Zhuangzi (around 369–286 BCE). All under heaven, according to Zhuangzi, constitutes a whole body – 'May love flood over the myriad things: heaven and earth are one body.'[2] Ideally, people are expected to work collectively and in a harmonious way with each other, and other creatures and nature, for the collective welfare of the world. This idea is embodied in *tianxia weigong* (all under heaven belongs to all and is for all). I shall come back to this later.

This anthropocosmic world view differs from the Anglo-American dualistic world view, which epistemologically understands the world through an opposed duality: I and non-I (Kivelä 2012: 60). The duality of I and non-I reflects a long-lasting tension, that between individual and community. There is the mindset of Hobbesian zero-sum competition, assuming a zero-sum relationship between I and other. The dualistic world view and the zero-sum assumption constitute foundational pillars of the current world order that subsumes the world under self-interested and mutually competitive nation states – this understanding of the world is also known as methodological nationalism (Chernilo 2006: 7; Wang 2017). It is the methodological nationalist depiction of the world that explains the notion of 'global' in the Anglo-American notion of global public goods. Here 'global' refers to beyond nation states.

Certain ideas are indicated by the methodological nationalist approach of 'global' in global public goods. First, global public goods are those goods that transcend national borders. In the current world order, nation states primarily respond to domestic needs and prioritize their own interests. Thus, global public goods are often de facto subordinate to national goods. Second, the zero-sum assumption of the relationship between nation states may imply a non-positive-sum relationship between national goods and global public goods. The two aspects, in addition to the problems of the concept of public goods per se, at least partly account for the problems of the general under-provision and under-awareness of the importance of global public goods, including in higher education (see below).

---

[2] 泛爱万物，天地一体也。 – *Zhuangzi, Tianxia.*

Methodological nationalism is in contrast with the Confucian anthropocosmic world view. Further, the notion of global public goods in the traditional Chinese sense that follows a collectivist tradition and the Confucian anthropocosmic world view would diverge from the Anglo-American notion of global public goods.

Tianxia Weigong and Global Public Goods in the Traditional Chinese Sense

The concept of global public goods in the traditional Chinese sense needs to be interpreted through the perspective of *tianxia weigong*. Building on the idea of *tianxia* as a normative appeal, *tianxia weigong* claims that all under heaven belongs to all and is for all, implying that there is 'no other' and 'no private' in the world.

> When the Way (*da dao*) prevails, all under heaven is for and belongs to all, in which the selection criteria are wisdom and ability. Mutual confidence is promoted and good neighbourliness is cultivated. People do not regard as parents only their own parents, nor do they treat as children only their own children ... They despise indolence, yet they do not use their energies for their own interests. In this way selfish scheming are repressed ... This is called the Great Harmony (*da tong*).[3]

As the *Book of Rites* states, *tianxia weigong* reflects human beings' pursuit for universal love and welfare, which entails the contents of fairness between oneself and others. It is also a situation where people are able to realize harmony without conformity.

There are at least two important attributes in association with global public goods in the traditional Chinese sense. First, values are essential. As noted, though there are value-relevant assumptions underlying the Anglo-American concept of global public goods (i.e. the limited liberal state and the private takes precedence over the public), the concept per se does not pay particular attention to values concerning the connotations of goodness. Rather, the traditional Chinese concept of global public goods regards certain values as essential to the normative judgements of what the collective goodness of the world means and who decides that. Important values in Confucianism include diversity, fairness, harmony and peace. Second, contrary to the Anglo-American idea of global

---

[3] 大道之行也，天下为公。选贤与能，讲信修睦；故人不独亲其亲，不独子其子……力恶其不出於身也，不必为己……是谓大同。 – Liyun, *Book of Rites*

public goods, *tianxia weigong* imagines the world as a public realm, rather than as an aggregation of nation states, and argues that all humans are responsible to contribute to the good of the world. The Chinese concept of global public goods therefore is interpreted as goods collectively shared and produced by all humanity. Not only all human beings are responsible for contributing to global public goods, they need to have access to consuming global public goods too.

Global public goods in the traditional Chinese sense to a certain extent echoes United Nations Educational, Social and Cultural Organization's (UNESCO) global common goods (UNESCO 2015). As Tian and Liu argue:

> In China, the meaning of 'public good' goes far beyond the idea of 'good' or 'wealth' … They are goods for public benefit, which are produced on the basis of public demands, relying on public power and through consensus and cooperation … In this sense, the meaning of public goods in China is more related to common goods, which are collective in nature, beneficial to all, and perhaps fostering social inclusion, integration, tolerance, equality, and human rights, with a distinct feature of intrinsic value and shared participation. (Tian and Liu 2018: 10)

The problems of the Anglo-American interpretation of global public goods as economic public goods that transcend national borders have been pointed out by many scholars/researchers (see, for example, Deneulin and Townsend 2007; Locatelli 2017). In response, UNESCO (2015) and many others, including Deneulin and Townsend (2007) and Szadkowski (2019), advocate using global common goods instead in discussing global collective welfare. According to UNESCO (2015), the notion of global common goods implies the cooperative operation of a wide range of stakeholders worldwide who are interested in both defining and producing common goods shared by humanity, acknowledge the possibility to interpret connotations of the concept in various ways across cultural contexts, and have a normative orientation in favour of mutual welfare. In addition, for global common goods, all agents in the world, including grassroots agents, collectively communicate and act for the universal interests. Governments and grassroots society also play important roles in the production of global common goods. This is a wholly inclusive and bottom-up process.

Nevertheless, global common goods and global public goods in the traditional Chinese sense have differences. To begin with, the primary distinction between global common goods and the Anglo-American concept of global public goods lies in varied interpretations of common goods and public goods. But the two concepts understand the notion of 'global' in a similar way. The concept of global common goods also understands the world through a perspective of methodological nationalism, though it encourages the participation from non-governmental international agents in supporting the production of global common goods including in higher education. As non-governmental agents are often vulnerable compared to national governments, global common goods can be de facto subordinate to national pursuits. For example, consider the US withdrawal from the Paris climate agreement (McGrath 2020). This partly explains the underproduction of global common goods in higher education. Thus, global common goods may not be the approach to addressing the problem of the under-provision of goods collectively shared by humanity.

Meanwhile, the concept of common goods deliberately avoids the discussion of the public/private dualism, especially the boundary and relationship between the public and the private (Marginson 2018a). The long-standing dilemma regarding the public/private dualism is not addressed, but deliberately ignored. This is different from the idea of *tianxia weigong*, which avers that the public/larger self is normatively more important than the private/smaller self – for example, global public goods take precedence over national private goods.

Critiques of the Anglo-American Concepts of Global Public Goods

The Anglo-American framework can be subjected to critique when applied in other contexts.

First, the Anglo-American concepts of global public goods do not work well in non-Anglo-American contexts with different political cultures, including in China. Connotations of public goods are important in unpacking that of global public goods. According to Marginson (2018a), there are primarily two approaches to public/private (good) in the Anglo-American political culture. At the risk of over-simplification, one is the political approach that identifies the public with the state. In this case, public goods refer to the governmental-produced or -owned goods. The other is the economic approach that views the market as the private. Samuelson's notion of public goods, referring to goods that are non-rivalrous and non-excludable, is one of the most widely used concepts in this sense (Samuelson 1954). The two approaches to a certain extent are interrelated – the government is responsible for producing public goods (non-rivalrous and non-excludable goods) as these goods are usually under-provided following the market mechanism (Bayer and Urpelainen 2013; Carnoy et al. 2014). However, the two approaches are based on the Anglo-American imaginary of capitalist societies composing of two parts. The two parts are the market sector where the exchange of goods follows the law of market, and the non-market sector with governmental intervention. Samuelson's formula, for instance, assumes a minimal state that takes action only when the market fails, reflecting the Anglo-American tradition of having a limited liberal state (Marginson and Yang 2020a). This assumption is in conflict with the state/society/market relations as described in Chinese socialist society (Carnoy et al. 2014; Marginson and Yang 2020a). In addition to the Anglo-American approach imaginary of capitalist societies, the normative preference of the private (good) over the public (good) is also at odds with the Chinese context.

Second, although the concepts cannot work well in non-Anglo-American contexts, as the previous point demonstrates, the Anglo-American concepts of global public goods (sometimes global common goods) are often used as a universal theory in explaining higher education phenomena across the world (for critiques of this, see, for example, UNESCO 2015). Further, considering the existence of a wide array of political and educational cultures worldwide, whether there exists a universal theory that can work across cultures invites discussions and debates.

Third, the Anglo-American concepts of global public goods have problems in its own terms. For example, scholars/researchers have pointed out the problems caused by the Anglo-American interpretations of public goods in higher education, including the shortage of public funding for higher education, too much emphasis on individual pecuniary returns of higher education and the overlooking of non-pecuniary goods produced by higher education (Deneulin and Townsend 2007; Locatelli 2017; UNESCO 2015). They therefore call for investigations of alternative concepts in discussing higher education's collective contributions. The concept of common goods, as argued by UNESCO (2015), is one possible alternative. Here the notion of common goods suggests joint activity by a wide array of agents engaged in both defining and producing common goods, respects the potential for diverse interpretations in practice based on differing cultural contexts and has a normative orientation in favour of collective welfare (UNESCO 2015). Notably, the concept of public goods in the traditional Chinese sense seems to partly overlap with UNESCO's common goods (Tian and Liu 2018).

The concept of global public goods is often interpreted as those public goods (in the Anglo-American sense) that extend beyond national borders and are shared by people from different countries. For example, global public goods are defined as goods whose 'benefits are sufficiently widely dispersed across the globe' (Taylor 2014: 13). Here 'global' is interpreted following the idea of methodological nationalism – which equates society with nation-state societies and the globe with a group of nation states (Beck 2016; Han, Shim and Park 2016). In part, the problems caused by the concept of public goods persist when using the above concept of global public goods to explain the higher education phenomena in the Chinese context. In part, there are additional problems caused by the way 'global' is understood as 'beyond national borders'.

Implications for Global Public/Common Goods of Higher Education: National and Global Perspectives

Higher Education and Global Public/Common Goods

Building on the previous discussions of the collectivist tradition and the ideas of *tianxia weigong*, this section focuses on implications for global public/common goods in higher education, especially regarding possible ways to sustain the production of global public/common goods in higher education practices. In this section, notions of global public goods and global common goods are used in a combined way to refer to goods that are collectively shared by all humanity, as enlightened by the idea of *tianxia weigong*.

Higher education systems are routinely connected in a global common space (Marginson 2018b). Many of higher education's outcomes are collectively shared by all humanity. Higher education contributes to global public/common goods by educating students. For example, students' acquisition of skills and knowledge further promotes economic prosperity worldwide (Griffiths and Arnove 2015); global citizenship education programmes in higher education can play important roles in forming students as global citizens (Davies and Pike 2010); students also enhance their capability in higher education, which is crucial to promoting the well-being of the individual and humanity (Boni and Walker 2013; Sen 1999); and higher education graduates are more capable of international mobility (Verbik and Lasanowski 2007).

Higher education also promotes global equity. For example, universities may serve the role of a consultant to international agencies whose missions are promoting global equity as well as to those national governments in need (Woodfield et al. 2009). Some university projects are designed to help tackle specific problems faced by low-income countries – consider research on dengue fever and malaria and research designed to assist with food security and urban water supply. Universities also educate students from across the world, including those from low-income countries (Viggiano et al. 2018). However, it should be noted that higher education may have negative effects on global equity too. For example, with continuous outflow and low returning rates of talents, low-income countries often face the problem of brain drain (Beine, Docquier and Rapoport 2008). Nevertheless, when compared to the objective of promoting national equity, there is arguably a lack of commitment to promoting global equity in higher education.

Higher education also contributes to global public/common goods by producing knowledge (Stiglitz 1999). Ideally, knowledge is collectively shared by and available to all humanity. In addition to being a global public/common good, knowledge can further lead to many other global public/common goods, such as ways to tackle global climate change, providing consultation with regard to policies, human flourishing of arts and the like.

However, in higher education practice, global public/common goods are often less aware-of and underproduced. Specifically, in the production of global public/common goods, higher education faces at least the following four problems.

First, as the main financial supporters of higher education, national and local governments tend to invest in higher education activities that are conducive to their own interests. For example, a national government may focus on increasing the country's international competitiveness through higher education's contributions to the improvement of human capital and knowledge production and transfer (Fougner 2006). Correspondingly, practices of a certain national higher education system may show a tendency of recruiting and educating more students in areas that are regarded as important to the country's development, and of conducting research according to national governments' needs. Further, the orientation of educating students can be largely leaning towards skills training, and as a result, there is less attention to the development of individual students' capability and individuality (Marginson 2019). Governments' investment in research may target specific research topics and areas of national priority (Bayer and Urpelainen 2013; Reisen, Soto and Weithöner 2008). As a result, those activities that can contribute to global public/common goods are less supported. Taking East Asian countries as an example, there is a strong preference for developing applied sciences related to construction, transport, communication and other facets of national development (Marginson 2020). These areas are viewed as essential for the countries' modernization. In comparison, areas that are less relevant to national development but are critical to the collective welfare of the world are less stressed and supported. For example, there is often a lack of support for humanities and arts, which are important aspects of human flourishing.

Second, related to the first point, global citizenship education in higher education also faces difficulties, largely due to national governments' strong focus on preparing students as national citizens (Calhoun 2006; Qi and Shen 2015). According to Davies and Pike (2010) and Jarvis (2002), universities tend to centre their moral and citizenship education around a nationalist strand. The nationalist elements, for example those embodied in patriotism, may be at odds with core values held by global citizenship education.

Third, national governments can employ policies that negatively influence the production of certain global public/common goods in higher education. For example, in many countries, immigration and visa regulations discourage international mobility of students and faculty. International mobility is not only beneficial to mutual understanding and collaboration, but also individuals' formation as global citizens. In addition, governmental regulations relevant to national security considerations and public accountability requirements can impede academic freedom and international collaboration in higher education (Palfreyman 2007; Traianou 2015).

Fourth, in higher education systems where the neoliberal idea of competition is particularly pursued, universities tend to draw much attention to competition, including in higher education admission, knowledge production and dissemination, and application of funding. These higher education systems often have steep horizontal stratifications. The emphasis on competition is harmful not only to national higher education equity, but to global higher education equity as a global public/common good. Further, there is less concern about working collectively for the sake of global public/common goods when competition is much emphasized. For example, there is a trend towards privatization of knowledge in higher education across the world, and this can hamper the global dissemination and reproduction of knowledge produced in higher education.

Implications of *Tianxia Weigong*

Enlightened by the idea of *tianxia weigong*, the chapter proposes the following suggestions in response to the aforementioned problems with the objective of effectively sustaining higher education's production of global public/common goods.

If the world is understood not as an aggregation of nation states but as *tianxia*, global public/common goods become the larger self, which, normatively speaking, has a more important status than national goods. It is imperative for national governments to stress and support the production of global public/

common goods in higher education. Efforts can be made in various aspects. In allocating financial support for research in higher education, more support is needed for research that focuses on addressing global common challenges and issues, and promoting the global welfare. The Confucian anthropocosmic world view that centres on achieving a harmonious balance between humanity and nature may provide a framework for global ecological research grounded in the idea of *tianxia*.

In addition to financial support, changes of policy orientation are also important. For example, according to the idea of 'no other', regulations limiting international mobility and international collaboration in higher education rarely have an intrinsic justification. Thus, immigration and visa regulations need to be more accommodating of the international mobility of students and academics as well as international collaboration in higher education. Meanwhile, academic freedom, which is commonly regarded as an essential value in higher education and therefore an important global public/common good value, needs to be genuinely protected by not only academia, but also by governments and society.

Tianxia also provides a foundation for the idea of individuals being global citizens. In *tianxia*, individuals are not naturally imagined as citizens of certain countries, but members of *tianxia*. Their recognition with *tianxia* is the primary. The national identity of the individual is secondary to being a member of *tianxia*. This reverses the dictum of the former British prime minister Theresa May who said: 'If you believe you're a citizen of the world, you're a citizen of nowhere.' The *tianxia* viewpoint is not a mere abstraction. It may not exist for Theresa May, but it already exists in China. As Liang (1990: 163) states, 'in the minds of the Chinese people, what is close to them is family, and what is far from them is *tianxia*. The rest [including the state] they more or less ignore.' Therefore, including global citizenship components into higher education becomes critical.

Further, as higher education contributes to the welfare shared by all under heaven, the production of global public/common goods deserve collective contributions from not only governments but also grassroots society, through a bottom-up democratic process. All human beings, as members of *tianxia*, are responsible for contributing to the production of global public/common goods. This leads to an inclusive, democratic and bottom-up process of producing global public/common goods. There are many aspects that grassroots society can contribute, including financial investment, collective efforts in balancing the relationship between knowledge available for humanity and protecting intellectual property rights, and the establishment of mutual trust between higher education and society.

Concluding Remarks

The prevalence of global challenges, conflicts and struggles over power points to the under-provision of global public/common goods. Higher education contributes to global public/common goods. However, higher education institutions worldwide are also facing challenges and limitations that negatively influence their contributions to global public/common goods.

Scholars/researchers seek solutions to the under-provision of global public/common goods. Some call for active participation and contribution from the non-governmental sector and communities, as the idea of global common goods suggests. Some point to the intrinsic problems inherent in the existing nation-state and interstate system. Scholars/researchers familiar with the Chinese *tianxia* and *tianxia weigong* critique methodological nationalism and propose to think through the world, not of the world. Certain values are emphasized, including harmony and diversity. When the central concern is the world/*tianxia*, parochial goods are subordinate to global public/common goods. The practical issue is to develop mechanisms guaranteeing the sustainable provision of global public/common goods. In higher education, activities based on the perspective of *tianxia* offer the potential means of overcoming the obstacles that confine higher education's production of global public/common goods.

However, it remains a question of to what extent the *tianxia* idea can be employed in realpolitik. As the chapter has demonstrated, the divergences between the *tianxia* idea and the dominant world views today, including hierarchy versus equality, meritocracy versus democracy, and using norms and rituals to rule versus rule by law, indicate the difficulties in employing the idea in realpolitik. This has arguably become even more difficult in the contemporary world with the increasing tensions between China and the United States, and the critiques about China as potential hegemon, for example, as reflected in its promotion of the Belt and Road Initiative (see, for example, Callahan 2008; Callahan and Barabantseva 2011). Perhaps the Chinese idea of 'harmony without conformity (*heer butong*)' suggests a possible way forward. In Fei's (2015: 50) words, 'an appreciation of one's own culture, an understanding and appreciation of other cultures, and mutual respect, would result in people's living together harmoniously, which then leads to the status of harmony without conformity'.

4

Global and World Citizenship in Chinese Education

Arzhia Habibi

Introduction

For some, it may come as a surprise to consider the concept of global and world citizenship education (世界和全球公民教育, *shijie he quanqiu gongmin jiaoyu*) as it relates to and is practiced within China's higher education landscape. With a strong educational focus on patriotism, as well as national and cultural rejuvenation, it may at the outset seem as though there could be no conceptual or empirical space for the practice, exploration and development of global and world citizenship education in China. However, a closer look at the history, cultural symbols, civilizational dynamics, grassroots movements, societal relationships and philosophical underpinnings of the country – and how such social forces have shaped the contours of practices and perspectives among students and academics in Chinese educational settings – challenges this assumption. Indeed, attentiveness to the Chinese scholarship context on the topic yields insight into novel, rich, complex and layered conceptualizations of global and world citizenship education, which exist on the peripheries of Anglophone discourses that often have little breathing space for non-dominant conceptualizations of the term.

As such, the purpose of this literature review is to take readers into the heart of the burgeoning scholarship concerning global and world citizenship education in the Chinese context through highlighting the contemporary debates and key scholars that are working in the field, their philosophical orientations, as well as the few empirical studies that are being advanced in educational settings. The literature review thus responds to increasing calls within the English language literatures (e.g. Parmenter 2011; Davies et al. 2018; Hayhoe 2020; Yang 2020;

Alviar-Martin and Baildon 2021) to encounter and engage with the perspectives generated in East Asian educational contexts, as well as Mandarin discourses (Song 2018; Wu 2020) which are looking to construct a localized and culturally sensitive global and world citizenship education body of knowledge.

With this purpose in mind, I hope to contribute to efforts toward global cognitive justice (Davies et al. 2018) in which many different voices are heard, and a more diverse contribution of thought and voice are offered to discourses on global and world citizenship education. I adopt the concept of polyvocality in which 'two or more simultaneous melodic lines are perceived as independent even though they are related' (DeVoto 2017: 1). I do this in order to harmonize the voices of the Chinese context with my own particular understanding and positioning in relation to global and world citizenship education. I thus use this chapter as a communicative bridge and a shelter for these multiple voices to be expressed, albeit not in their native tongue, but in a register that nonetheless honours and respects the lived realities and theoretical orientations in the Chinese scholarship context, which I privilege in this chapter.

Working Definitions of Global and World Citizenship Education

Firstly, it is necessary to unpack the notion of global and world citizenship education and offer some working definitions to the reader. There is both tentativeness and mistrust around the term global and world citizenship education in the Chinese scholarship context with particular trepidation around the term 'citizenship' (公民, *gongmin*) which, among certain scholarship circles, is perceived as a Western concept (Song 2018). Nonetheless, the term citizenship has become part of official political rhetoric since the 2001 adoption of the *Action Plan for the Development of Civic Morality* (公民道德建设实施纲要, *gongmin daode jianshe shishi gangyao*) (Zhao 2013; Song 2018). Song (2018, 2020) braids together political, philosophical and spiritual (in the form of Daoist cosmologies) discourses in Mandarin to offer a definition that is culturally sensitive, attentive to the socialist proclivities and thus attuned to the Chinese context:

> Education must embrace the notion of humanity as a shared community with a common destiny; –it must foster in young people a deep respect of 'all living things, never seeking to do harm'.[1] It must help the young recognise that

---

[1] Here, Song draws upon a phrase found in the Confucian Analects, 礼记 (*liji*) in the chapter Doctrine of the Mean 中庸 (*zhongyong*). In Mandarin, it is written thus: 万物并育而不相害，道并行而不相悖 (*wanwu bing yu er bu xiang hai, dao bingxing er bu xiang bei*).

regardless of country or belief, or even the willingness of some to believe the world is a whole, we are already fused as members of one community and bound by the same fate. That we live in interdependency… and 'the prosperity of one is the prosperity of all, the sufferings of one, are the suffering of all, where all share in the honours, disgraces, joys and pains of life'. (Song 2020)[2]

This can be contrasted with UNESCO's definition of global citizenship education, which defines it as

a sense of belonging to a broader community and common humanity. It emphasises political, economic, social and cultural interdependency and interconnectedness between the local, the national and the global. (UNESCO 2015: 14)

At present, the definitions offered by supranational organizations, such as UNESCO, on global citizenship education hold sway in its popular conceptualizations and mainstream discussions in global North (defined here as political systems, educational institutions, organizations and news agencies situated within Anglo-American traditions of thought and assumptions on liberalism, freedom and democracy) literatures. Thus, in surfacing the definitions offered by Chinese scholars, as well as their philosophical orientations, we can glimpse at another rooted vision of global and world citizenship education, which, while still deeply normative in its emphases on moral conduct, offers alternative visions into its embodied practices and perspectives in educational settings.

Organization of the Literature Review

The review will first begin with a look at the question of language, and how meanings embedded in Mandarin and English are not easily translated, but nonetheless shape the contours of the discourses of global and world citizenship education. This will inform the next section on citizenship education in the Chinese context and its philosophical underpinnings and historical legacies. The review will then explore recent developments of global and world citizenship education in moral education (德育, *deyu*) research. Building on this will be an exploration into the frictions and prevalent themes in Chinese citizenship education, with a focus on negotiations between the imaginaries of local, national

---

[2] With thanks to Lili Yang for her guidance and suggestions on translation, origins and interpretation of this quote, which in Mandarin reads as follows: '一荣俱荣、一损俱损，休戚与共、唇齿相依' (*yirong jurong, yi sun ju sun, xiuqi yugong, chunchixiangyi*).

and global as they relate to both empirical and theoretical discussions of global and world citizenship education. Finally, the chapter will look at current relevant empirical studies of global and world citizenship education in Chinese higher education, and conclude with an indication for future research.

A Question of Language and (Re)interpretation

The Chinese discourses on global and world citizenship education contain multiple, layered and textured meanings. Thus, to unfold these terms as they relate to the Chinese context will no doubt be 'partial, controversial and unfinished' (Parmenter 2011: 370), and will require further thought and sensitivity to evolve and deepen the discourse. Still, it is important to note that dependent on the social and intellectual positioning of the scholar writing on global and world citizenship education, and their creative usages of political, social and philosophical vocabularies, there nonetheless remains continued emphasis on the following terms: unity in diversity (和而不同, *heer butong*); all under heaven is for all (天下为公, *tianxia weigong*); seeking common ground while holding differences (求同存异, *qiutong cunyi*); and building a community for the shared future of mankind (构建人类命运共同体, *goujian renlei mingyun gongtongti*).

The imprint of these vocabularies in writings of global and world citizenship education in Mandarin points to the spiritual, moral and philosophical undertones of the discourses, which may be described as a synergy of Daoist, Confucian and Buddhist teachings (Wan 2019), which are also entangled with political discourses. These philosophical resonances operate as a musical hum in the background to the day-to-day educational activities among diverse agents in Chinese higher education, and are more explicitly and consciously used by scholars dedicated to writing and teaching in Mandarin on global and world citizenship education. To be attentive to this background musical hum, I now turn to a discussion of the philosophical particularities of global and world citizenship education in the Chinese context.

Citizenship Education in the Chinese Context and Its Philosophical Underpinnings

Chinese educational institutions' expressions of 'citizenship' education emphasize moral, political and ideological education, and they are so deeply enmeshed with one another that they transform into terms ideo-political education and ideo-moral education (Zhong and Lee 2008). L. P. Wang's (2019) study in China, explored possibilities for the implementation of global and world citizenship education in secondary schools from the perspective of curriculum and state policy. She highlighted how the emphasis in both curriculum materials and educational state policy continues to be placed upon 'political and social education, moral education and values education' (L. P. Wang 2019: 137). This emphasis on the cultivation of moral qualities as the basis for citizenship education in the Chinese context has led some scholars to take a historical perspective, arguing that moral education is another form of paternalistic control exerted by the state (e.g. Fairbrother 2014). Zhao (2013) and Fairbrother (2014) thus surmised that this emphasis is due to the state's desire for social order and stability, and for patriotic subjects who are loyal and uphold proper socialist values.

Such critical explorations into educational practices can yield essential insights regarding the political and sociocultural dynamics which shape the Chinese citizenship education (中国公民教育, *zhongguo gongmin jiaoyu*) landscape. However, it is important not only to ascribe political motivations towards the present pedagogies and discourses in Chinese institutions, but to consider the cultural and philosophical roots of such emphases. A philosophical and cultural perspective may suggest that the importance placed on morals and values in citizenship education discourses, policies and practices also has Confucian and cultural underpinnings (L. P. Wang 2019). Such underpinnings include, for example, the cultivation of self as the starting point for one's relationships with the family, the community and wider Chinese society (Shi 2018; Print and Tan 2015) as well as a focus on 'social harmony by observing rites and practicing self-control over mind, word and deed' (Law 2013: 603; Law 2011). Thus, the Chinese Communist Party's (CCP) emphases on moral education cannot be entirely subsumed into a nationalist agenda for the sole purpose of maintaining control under the guise of 'harmony'. Indeed, different agents within the complex nexus of citizenship and moral education exert creative agencies and innovative practices that often exist on the periphery of formalized educational activities and curriculum. These agents, particularly those that are formally affiliated with an institution, such as academics, may in a certain regard have to 'dance with chains' in negotiating their academic autonomy and agency (戴着镣铐跳舞, *daizhe liaokao tiaowu*) (Han and Xu 2019). However, they still hold power to choreograph profoundly meaningful intellectual and relational movements, within their own particular social context and circumstances as well as the educational institution they may be affiliated with.

The expression of these meaningful intellectual and relational movements that are in part informed by certain philosophies is further explored in the ethnographic work of Veg (2019), Ning and Palmer (2020) who inquire into the practices behind the term 'grassroots' (民间, *minjian*), in different educational volunteering programmes, and among Chinese grassroots intellectuals. They refer to *minjian* as a relational, emotional, autonomous and intimate space that is often consciously operating beyond, or below, the radar of CCP rhetoric and interventions. These are local, lived, practical spaces where it may be possible to be 'inside the system' (体制内, *tizhi nei*) by virtue of a university teaching position but nonetheless work 'outside the system' (体制外, *tizhi wai*) with disenfranchised communities (Veg 2019: 8). Similarly, Ning and Palmer (2020) discuss how volunteers in educational programmes related to the support of migrant workers' children are caught between the 'moral imperatives of altruistic sacrifice derived from China's socialist revolutionary tradition and "neoliberal" utilitarianism derived from market rationality' (395). Yet as these volunteers refuse to commit their allegiance to either the socialist revolutionary tradition or the utilitarian approach, they remain 'at a loss for words and produce an ethics of emotional authenticity that resists incorporation into any discursive ethical system' (395). Such ethnographic work thus demonstrates how relationships and practices can exist beyond or on the periphery of state rhetoric, ideals and practices.

In addition, in C. Wang's (2019) anthropological investigations into service learning programmes in rural China, she discusses how volunteers reimagine a rooted global condition in which they had to learn how to 'connect to the soil' (接地气, *jie di qi*) and thus with their students. Here, she suggests that the volunteers were able to question the instrumentalized approaches in Chinese education and spark a self-reflexive process in which *jie di qi* extended beyond glorifying differences through service learning as a decoration for one's CV, but served as a deeply relational and moral exercise through engagement with students in the rural community (C. Wang 2019). These anthropological discussions on embodied ethical actions in the context of grassroots movements and educational service learning programmes thus indicate that tracing the choreographies of morality among differing agents often requires looking through the veils of political rhetoric and grand slogans in order to bear witness to such 'intimate utopias' (Ning and Palmer 2020) that exist *between people*. Such embodied movements can thus bridge the nebulous relationship between philosophical writings and day-to-day practices as they relate to global and world citizenship education actions and ideals.

The Fusion of State Rhetoric and Philosophical Underpinnings

To pay attention to the background musical hum of Chinese philosophical underpinnings, and how they are incorporated into theoretical debates concerning global and world citizenship education, allows us to see how scholars fuse state rhetoric with Chinese philosophical perspectives in order to explore and express global and world citizenship education ideals in a manner that is culturally responsive, historically aware and conscientious of political boundaries and limitations. For example, the concept of 'unity in diversity' (和而不同, *heer butong*) is foregrounded by some scholars (e.g. Wan 2005; Wang and Wu 2011; Wang and Wang 2016) as an important component to Chinese expressions of global and world citizenship education in the context of the nation's ethnic minority diversities. Moreover, other Confucian philosophies such as 天下 (*tianxia*) and 大同 (*datong*) also envisioned the Chinese empire as transcending geographical and racial boundaries (Wang 2017) and have been elaborated on by some scholars who discuss resonances of these philosophical underpinnings with global and world citizenship education in a Chinese context (Qi and Shen 2015).

Furthermore, in discussions of '天下' (*tianxia*), Wang (2017: 5) highlights that 'as a body of thought and practice, *tianxia* has wavered between the normative claim to values and culture on the one hand, and coercive mechanisms of domination on the other'. He argues that, in its usage, there are tensions between a moral urge for universal principles which, at times, can become an ideological veil for 'power politics' and that 'in its modern avatars', it hinges between 'cosmopolitanism and interstate geopolitics' (5). It is therefore evident that the contemporary adoption of the term is suffused with both political impulses and moral urges for world unity. Wan (2019) further describes the notion of world unity '大同' (*datong*) by historically contextualizing the concept. He suggests that the term 'refers to the ideal state of society depicted in *the Rites*,[3] a concept that was traditionally understood to have denoted the conditions of a "lost paradise" which had prevailed under the legendary sage-kings who had reigned long before the birth of Confucius' (2019: 124). However, similar to the notion of all under heaven, the concept has been reinterpreted by political institutions and intellectuals. One of the most prominent of these intellectuals Kang Youwei sought to 'recast' the notion of *datong* (大同) as 'Confucius's prophetic anticipation of a future ideal world that was to be realized in the Age of Universal Peace' (Wan 2019) and which Yan (2017) describes as a longing for

---

[3] 'Rites' refer to the Confucius Book of Rites '礼记' (*Liji*) which described the dynamics, practices and systems of the Zhou Dynasty.

'a reimagined human community' (254). The rearranging and reinterpretation of these philosophical concepts into a 'new constellation' (255) for a reimagined world unity is a pattern of scholarly behaviour among many authors coming from or speaking of the Chinese context. Indeed, to acknowledge these impulses to reinterpret philosophical concepts among scholars is important in order to understand the nature, usages and contours of the philosophical variants of global and world citizenship in the Chinese scholarship context.

In addition, L. P. Wang (2019) reinterprets Confucian ideals on diversity in order to discuss multicultural education and the relational self, dedicated to finding a point of harmony which does not refer to *sameness* but alludes to the generation of something new, 'the connections between individuals' (9). Jiang (2017) also explores education for international understanding, a term often related to global and world citizenship education in the Chinese context (Song 2018), and emphasizes *understanding* as opposed to *international* in relation to China's ethnic minorities. Here, she suggests that there is a need to integrate conversation around ethnic minorities within the landscape of education for international understanding and the call for unity in diversity (Jiang 2017: 173). Yet the debates around ethnic minorities, their positioning, voice, perspectives and practices in the context of global and world citizenship education is still embryonic and requires further exploration, acknowledgement and collaboration with these voices in both theoretical and empirical endeavours (Song 2018).

Variations of these philosophical sayings are also incorporated into political rhetoric, and they are part of different international policies and agendas which include the Belt and Road Initiative. This enmeshment between political and philosophical sayings is captured in the commonly used term 'building a community for the shared future of mankind' (构建人类命运共同体, *goujian renlei mingyun gongtongti*) used by President Xi Jinping on various international platforms. While this political rhetoric cannot be a catchall for these philosophical underpinnings, it is important to note that Chinese scholars will actively use this political language to communicate a culturally attuned and sensitive discussion of global citizenship education, attentive to the political realities of the country. For example, Zhou (2019), Yang (2017) and Liu and Zhang (2018) draw upon this language of building a community to depict the contemporary landscape of interconnectivity and friction in China and the global community, and weave this language into calls for further development of global and world citizenship education. Others such as Xu (2020) focus a critique on the underpinning philosophies of liberalism in global North discourses, offering an alternative perspective of 'self-cultivation' (修身, *xiushen*), which they describe as the foundation for 'building a community', with focused self-reflection on moral conduct, which extends to the family, society, state and the whole world (Xu 2020: 62).

To delve into these philosophical resonances, and their enmeshment with political rhetoric, further aids our understanding that moral education is central to debates of global and world citizenship education. As such, in order to understand the relationship between global and world citizenship education and moral education, I now turn to tracing the connections, frictions and dialogues between both bodies of scholarship.

Recent Developments of Global and World Citizenship Education in Moral Education Research

Chinese philosophical underpinnings are increasingly being drawn into theoretical debates, in both English and Mandarin languages, of global and world citizenship education, and discussed in relation to moral education research trends. The primary focus on moral education research in the context of global and world citizenship education highlights both the state policy emphasis on moral education for all educational institutions in China, and the socially constructed educational spaces that draw upon, and are informed by, culturally and philosophically rooted perspectives.

These theoretical debates often emphasize the importance of cultivating the emotional and moral lifeworlds of students. Tan (2019), for example, advocates for a more robust moral narrative on global and world citizenship education practices, coalescing and reinterpreting the vocabularies and principles of the philosopher Wang Yangming to speak of humanity's shared oneness predicated on an innate knowledge (良知, *liangzhi*) that humans can express their own moral agency in the world. Building on this further, Huineng Lu, Wang and Ivanhoe (2009) interpret Wang's philosophies of *liangzhi* to suggest that these principles are essentially metaphysical and lead humanity to realize their oneness with the world and all its diverse social, ecological, material, spiritual and relational expressions.

> If gentlemen [exemplary persons] of the world merely devote their effort to extending their liangzhi [innate knowledge], they will ... regard other people as their own persons, regard the people of other countries as their own family, and look upon Heaven, Earth, and all things as one body. (translated by Chan 1963:166, as cited in Tan 2019: 5)

Drawing upon Wang Yangming's cosmology of oneness, Tan (2019) posits that Wang's notion of *liangzhi* affirms 'human dignity equality and potential' and 'underpins and constitutes the vision of shared humanity in global citizenship' (6), but that the realization of such shared humanity and dignity must come through the elimination of selfish desires. It is thus evident that polishing of the mirror of the heart (Tan 2019), and all the moral imperatives this entails, is foregrounded as the foundation and starting point for a global and world citizenship education that is resonant with these Chinese philosophical ideals.

However, certain developments in moral education research do not satisfy the critical questions being asked by some theorists, for example Cheng (2019) and Wu (2020). Cheng suggests that some theorists can fall prey to grand narratives that favour an unquestioned moral universalism with little attentiveness paid to 'hidden gender bias, discrimination, repression, and inequality behind moral discourse or discover power when it is intended to impose unified and homogenous discipline under the mask of moral universality' (Cheng 2019: 570). Similarly, Wu (2020) engages with postcolonial theory to critique the dominance of Western paradigms in global and world citizenship education, and the unquestioned philosophical assumptions embedded within global ethics. Yet both scholars also pay heed to the tension between being critically aware of dominant and grand narratives, and this leading to an insular Chinese conservativism and nationalism (Cheng 2019; Wu 2020).

The anxiety around grand narratives, and the frictions therein, further becomes evident when the term citizenship is used in the Chinese educational context. As mentioned previously, there has been trepidation around the usage of 'citizenship' and its relation with certain constructed Western concepts of civil society, freedom and activism. In certain scholarship circles, there is concern that the advancing of moral education theories in China has become a process which replicates mainstream theories from international discourses (Cheng 2019). This echoes Zhao's (2013) explorations of the employment of the concept citizenship education in China, which she posits is transfigured into the language and practices of Chinese educational contexts. Thus, in the context of this 'colonial modernity' (Wan and Palmer 2019) which shapes much of what is valued, listened to and honoured in international discourses, there remains a desire among moral education researchers to 'reconstruct and expand consensus on values and – at the same time – to be aware of the homogenization and Westernization brought about by globalization' (Cheng 2019: 568). It is evident there exists a friction in the discourse and practices of moral education and the burgeoning debates of global and world citizenship education in the

Chinese context. On the one hand, there is a longing among scholars to explore, unravel and advance the theory and practice of moral education in Chinese educational contexts, and to trace its connections with global discourses. Yet, conversely, there can remain an unquestioned allegiance to grand narratives which, at times, can lead to oppressive behaviours and paternalistic control in educational institutions.

To a certain extent, these frictions and longings in moral education research point to the present state and scholarly focus on a *rooted* and *patriotic* morality in conceptualizations of global and world citizenship education, along with a scepticism of hegemony within certain global discourses which may be experienced as oppressive grand narratives. In order to further trace the prevailing themes of global and world citizenship education, I now move to highlight the local, national and global dynamics within the Chinese citizenship education landscape.

Negotiation of the Local, National and Global in Chinese Citizenship Education

Based on the multiple and converging layers of context in the Chinese citizenship education landscape, Pan (2011), Law (2006), Song (2016) and L. P. Wang (2019) emphasize the importance of understanding Chinese citizenship from a multidimensional perspective. This multidimensional perspective acknowledges the tensions and synergies between the local, national and global dynamics at the level of individuals as well as within state educational policy. For example, these versatile tensions are highlighted in Sriprakash, Singh and Qi's (2014) study, which looks at conceptualizations of international mindedness[4] in international baccalaureate programmes in Australia, India and China among parents, students and educators. In Beijing schools, they found an emphasis on patriotic and national allegiance which shaped their participants' 'experience, perception and conceptualisation of international mindedness' (66). This further brought about layered tensions between, for example, loving the motherland and honouring one's 'local rootedness' and understanding and appreciating other cultures (Sriprakash, Sing and Qi 2014: 67). The emphasis on moral righteousness at all school levels in Chinese society was therefore painted

---

[4] International Mindedness, while involving another body of literature closely connected to the development and criticism of the international baccalaureate curriculum in multiple educational contexts, is a term related to global citizenship and global citizenship education (Singh and Qi 2013).

as inherent to patriotic education.⁵ Moral education is thus also connected to a sensibility of rootedness and patriotic love for China, in which a cultural consciousness is fostered in the project of building a 'common spiritual home for the Chinese nation' (Li 2011: 166, as cited in Cheng 2019: 568). This emphasis on *family* and *home* in the vocabulary of patriotic education points to culturally nested and socially situated expressions of global and world citizenship in Chinese educational institutions, which also follows the rhetoric of current state policies.⁶

To elaborate on the negotiations between the local, national and global, Fu (2019) explores the alternative online practices related to citizenship education in a Chinese school setting, suggesting that authentic citizenship learning for Chinese students occurred through 'everyday engagement with other individuals, families, sociocultural communities, and political communities' (3). In other words, citizenship education was experienced in grounded participation through social and cultural activities that were meaningful to young people. Thus, the acknowledgement of the importance of non-formal activities for young people in China is necessary in order to understand grounded expressions of global and world citizenship education beyond solely capitalistic, pragmatic and dominant framings of the term, which often depicts young people as solely interested in global experiences for personal accumulation (Reddy 2018). The significance of non-formal activities will be further elaborated on in the following section dedicated to Chinese higher education.

In light of some of these empirical studies that have highlighted the local, national and global dynamic, there is thus some consensus (L. P. Wang 2019) concerning the multidimensional nature of citizenship in a Chinese educational context. Yet questions remain around whether a local, national and global theoretical framework can sensitively capture the hushed practices of global and world citizenship in Chinese educational settings, due to the socially nested and often non-formal movements and relationships of students,

---

⁵ The Chinese expression for patriotism 爱国主义 (*aiguo zhuyi*) translates to an ideology of love of country. In Sriprakash, Singh and Qi's (2014) study, they foregrounded how the expressions of patriotism was found in the local, national and global dialect among international baccalaureate programmes at schools in Beijing. One school had, for example, the motto 'cherish the motherland, aspire to become a global citizen' [胸怀祖国心, 志做世界人, *xionghuai zuguo xin, zhi zuo shijie ren*] (Sriprakash, Sing and Qi 2014: 67).
⁶ In January 2020, the Ministry of Education issued an outline discussing the implementation of patriotic education in the new era (新时代爱国主义教育实施纲要, *xin shidai aiguo zhuyi jiaoyu shishi gangyao*), guidelines which apply to all educational institutions in China: moe.gov.cn/srcsite/A12/moe_1416/s255/202002/t20200219_422378.html.

as delineated by Fu (2019) as well as the anthropological discussions of C. Wang (2019) and Ning and Palmer (2020).

The studies cited above took place in Chinese schools, and they highlight important conceptualizations of multilayered and entangled visions of citizenship. Thus, I now turn to a focus on empirical studies of global and world citizenship education in Chinese higher education institutions, which have distinctly different contextual dynamics to Chinese schools. However, the discussion will again highlight the common theme of negotiation between the local, national and global for different actors exploring global and world citizenship education, and the prevalence of non-formal educational activities for students on global and world citizenship education relevant courses.

Empirical Studies of Global and World Citizenship Education in Chinese Higher Education

The institutional tensions and synergies between the creation of an international university, and the emphasis on cultivation of patriotic sensibilities among its Chinese students through compulsory ideological courses (Han and Xu 2019), are present as Chinese higher education institutions and their actors begin to wrestle more specifically with global and world citizenship education perspectives and practices (Peng 2009). These dynamics are explored by Jiang and Xu (2014) who interviewed both academics and students regarding their perspectives of compulsory university-run political, ideological and moral education courses. Interviews with one professor highlighted how 'certain popular concepts' like 'human rights, democracy, rule of law, and environmental protection' were perceived as aligning 'with the international community' (Jiang and Xu 2014: 81–2). Yet another educator they interviewed spoke of the concept of global and world citizenship education as 'unreal without any actual significance. What is overridingly important is to build up the strength of the nation' (Jiang and Xu 2014: 79). There are thus diversities among educators' understandings with some looking to embrace popular concepts (e.g. human rights and democracy) and others focused on 'national rejuvenation'.

Furthermore, Yan's (2017) study of Sino-foreign universities, which she proposes have the goal of cultivating international talents and, as a corollary, global and world citizenship among their student population, emphasizes the importance of awareness towards the exigencies of the local higher education context. She concluded that the awakening of a form of global and world citizenship consciousness among different higher education stakeholders is intimately connected to one's local consciousness, and global citizenship should not mean neglecting local and national circumstances (Yan 2017). These notions of local, national and global are echoed in Song and Rao's (2018) theoretical discussion of global and world citizenship education in the Chinese context, emphasizing the cultivation of 'good citizens'[7] within the nation as the foundation for global and world citizenship education development. Without such a foundation, they suggest that a learner on world citizenship education programmes would become a 'rootless wanderer' with extremist attitudes focused entirely on abstract ideals of the global common good (Song and Rao 2018). Thus, implicit within these discussions is the notion that to neglect one's local and national context is contrary to the love and commitment needed for the development of the Chinese nation, which echoes previous discussions regarding the moral emphasis on patriotism as a virtue, cultivated through education.

A look at citizenship practices and perspectives on the periphery of Chinese higher education courses brings to the fore scholars such as Zhang and Fagan (2016), Jiang and Xu (2014), Zhang (2016), Yang (2017) and Hua (2020) who acknowledge the importance of non-formal activities among student communities. For example, Zhang and Fagan explore how citizenship content was primarily experienced through interactive activities in students' day-to-day life outside of 'teacher-centred pedagogy' (2016: 137) from political and ideological education courses. Moreover, Jiang and Xu (2014) reflect on the importance of students' activities outside of the moral, political and ideological courses, as one student stated: 'My moral concepts are all formed through my own life … events held by many student societies are enlightening' (Jiang and Xu 2014: 75). In addition, Zhang (2016) discusses the civic experiences of Chinese university students in the contexts of mass media and citizenship education (ideological, political and moral education) classes and relates it to the construction of a form of cultural citizenship. In the study, Zhang (2016) highlights how participants acknowledged mass media as a platform for expression, discussion and participation, emphasizing the significance of individual life experiences and practices. He thus concluded that 'informal learning' through daily life may serve as a determining force in 'negotiating a new direction of citizenship learning' (2016: 263). Yang (2017) and Hua (2020)

---

[7] 'Good' is here translated from '良好' (*liang hao*) which may also be interpreted as 'fine'. The first character '*liang*' may also be used in combination with '*shan*' meaning kindness and thus speaks to particular virtuous qualities of an individual.

further describe how formal curriculum in Chinese higher education is often limited and narrow, particularly as it relates to discussions of global and world citizenship education, and requires students to independently quest for these concepts beyond formalized structures. It is therefore evident that potential understandings and perspectives of global and world citizenship education exist, and are constructed, in pockets of activity, community and practice outside of formal classroom activities.

In addition, Zhou's (2019) study of global and world citizenship education discourses in global North and Chinese literatures surfaces the notion of 'community' (共同体, *gong tong ti*) and posits that this concept is not founded upon common identities, nor even on morality, but rather it rests on the interconnectedness and interdependency among all members, institutions and organizations within both the wider world and the worlds of individuals (Zhou 2019: 207). This echoes the work on intimate utopias authored by Ning and Palmer (2020) as well as the relational experiences of student volunteers involved in service learning programmes (C. Wang 2019), and reflects the Confucian ideals which emphasize nested relationship. Such framings of these rooted practices may take us further into alternative expressions of citizenship, without the voices of such practices wholly subsumed into political rhetoric or materialistic ideals of questing for the global for personal accumulation.

In sum, as Chinese higher education institutions are a complex social environment, it is necessary for scholars working in the field to carefully consider the particular framework they use to interact with the space. Thus, such attentiveness to one's own epistemologies can help shape culturally sensitive descriptions and investigations of global and world citizenship education without suffocating the voices of local actors, their practices or cosmologies that may exist on the periphery of the CCP rhetoric, institutional policies or dominant neoliberal and capitalistic framings.

Conclusion

This literature review has explored the complex and burgeoning field of global and world citizenship education in the Chinese educational context. Through preliminary discussions of language and reinterpretation, as well as the philosophical underpinnings around citizenship education, the moral and ethical foundations for global and world citizenship education were highlighted.

This led to a discussion on developments in global and world citizenship education and moral education research, and the dynamic interplay between local, national and global in Chinese citizenship education studies. Finally, relevant empirical studies of global and world citizenship education in Chinese higher education were brought to the fore, with attention paid to the local, national and global dynamic and non-formal educational activities.

In writing this book chapter, I have heavily leaned on the scholarship and intellectual labours of those writing in Mandarin, particularly Song Qiang (Song and Rao 2018; Song 2018; Song 2020) who have laid essential groundwork for both the theoretical and empirical explorations of the topic in the Chinese context. As such, to further advance this burgeoning field of global and world citizenship education in China, interested scholars could look to thicken a theoretical understanding of how different Confucian, Daoist and Buddhist philosophies are reinterpreted, and may become entangled with socialist ideals to construct meanings of global and world citizenship education in Mandarin discourses. In addition, more longitudinal and ethnographic empirical work of relevant global and world citizenship education programmes could facilitate understanding of how such ideals are embodied and enacted in different higher education communities, and thus deeper an integration between research in moral educational theory and practice (Cheng 2020). Finally, collaborative and cross-cultural work could be conducted among Chinese and non-Chinese scholars in order to synthesize, compare and be attentive to prevailing theories of global and world citizenship education in the global North, and their usages or rejections in the Chinese scholarly context. In this spirit, I call upon Cheng (2019), who posits that research and writing is a process in which 'every single researcher is only a blade of grass on the mountain' (Cheng 2019: 578), a sentiment which speaks to the possibility of an ecological landscape in which every blade of grass is part of a greater functioning ecosystem of scholarship dedicated to unfolding the textured layers of global and world citizenship education in China.

5

World-Class Universities and Global Common Good

Lin Tian and Nian Cai Liu

Introduction and Purpose

World-Class Universities (WCUs) in the Context of Globalization and Internationalization

Globalization is probably both inevitable and unstoppable, and it is now widely noted that globalization is reshaping higher education worldwide. Internationalization is a key strategy of a nation and its institutions of higher education in responding to the impact of globalization from social, political, economic and academic motives (Altbach and Knight 2007). For universities, the internationalization of higher education is also considered as the process of integrating international, intercultural or global dimensions into the purposes and functions (e.g. education, research and service) of universities (Knight 2004), which has been a grand goal of many universities all over the world, albeit in different forms. Universities are laying great emphasis on internationalization, as both concept and agenda. A wide range of policies and practices related to it have been adopted and developed in universities to implement their internationalization plans, including recruiting international students, fostering students' intercultural capabilities, internationalizing the content of the curriculum and facilitating international research mobility (Soliman, Anchor and Taylor 2019).

The irresistible trend of internationalization of higher education is determined by the 'international nature' of universities themselves. As producers of knowledge that is borderless, universities themselves often act transnationally (Morrow and Torres 2000). Also, the increasing international communication and cooperation among universities in different countries and regions partly catalyse the emergence of the concept of 'world-class university' (WCU), as these universities are often more internationally connected and networked, with an international vision and the capability to function globally (Wang and Lan 2019). WCUs are indispensable and important players in the process of globalization and internationalization.

It is commonly agreed that WCUs are academic institutions committed to creating and disseminating knowledge in a range of disciplines and fields, delivering elite education at all levels, serving national needs and furthering international benefits (Altbach 2009; Liu 2009). To be more specific and from a quantitative perspective, in this chapter WCUs refer to universities ranked among the top-100 lists in ARWU, QS and THE,[1] which also see themselves as 'world-class' universities. There are certain agreed-upon features of WCUs, including: (1) talent concentration; (2) abundant resources; (3) global engagement; (4) international reputation; and (5) favourable governance (Salmi 2009; Wang, Cheng and Liu 2013).

Leaders of many WCUs describe the missions and roles of their universities in the framework of globalization and internationalization, including developing students' global competence, promoting international exchanges and cooperation, jointly coping with major global challenges and serving the global community. For instance, Richard Levin, the former president of Yale University in the United States says: 'Our goal is to become a truly global university – educating leaders and advancing the frontiers of knowledge not simply for the United States, but for the entire world' (cited in Ma 2013: 34). Also, in the 108th Anniversary Speech of Tsinghua University, the president of Tsinghua University in China, Yong Qiu, proposes that 'Tsinghua University is moving into the global world … it effectively implements the global strategy, focuses on enhancing the global competence of students, carries out excellent research to serve China and the world, and promotes in-depth international exchanges and cooperation, thereby promoting its international influence' (Qiu 2019).

WCUs in the Context of Global Common Good

According to Marginson (2019), WCUs, as 'thickly' networked institutions, are more globalized than the national-local societies in which they are

---

[1] These are mainstream world university rankings. ARWU means the Academic Ranking of World Universities, QS represents the Quacquarelli Symonds World University Ranking, and THE refers to the World University Ranking of Times Higher Education.

located, and they sustain an expanding worldwide space for research inquiry, academically codified thought and the dissemination of knowledge. Tian (2019) emphasizes WCUs' indispensable roles in societal, political, cultural and individual development at the global level. For example, WCUs have the capability and responsibility to deal with the most pressing and difficult challenges for the benefit of human society, influencing the advancement of the world and contributing to the sustainable development for the world. This again highlights the international nature or, more inclusively, the global nature of WCUs, which transcends the local and national interests. In this regard, WCUs do more than just serve social interests and contribute to the public good in a framework in which 'human well-being is framed by individualistic socio-economic theory' (UNESCO 2015: 78). They are also concerned with international perspectives, underlining the interconnectedness of the world and highlighting the well-being of the global communities that humanity forms, thereby contributing to the global common good, which is common to all people in the sense of benefits or interests (Tian 2019). A comparison between (global) public good and (global) common good can be seen in Table 5.1.

Tian and Liu's (forthcoming) study elaborates WCUs' contributions to the global common good. Specifically, (1) WCUs cultivate talents and leaders with global perspectives and future orientation, and they guide people to think about broader global interests and human well-being; (2) WCUs generate transformative and leading scholarship, ideas and practices; (3) WCUs construct global collaborative networks and then build a global academic community through global cooperation; (4) WCUs are dedicated to revealing and solving the most complex problems in the global society; (5) WCUs have a firm commitment to the sustainable development of the world; and (6) WCUs contribute to inclusive innovation and social mobility. Also, Marginson's (2019) study underpins roles of WCUs in producing global common goods. For instance, WCUs help people to form global competences which enable them to act across national and cultural boundaries; WCUs are a fecund zone of cross-border mobility and mixing of people. Apart from this, van der Wende (2019) highlights WCUs' contributions to the global common good and their roles against the backdrop of globalization that brings both opportunities and challenges for them. WCUs not only need to respond to the profitable side of globalization (i.e. global flow of talents), but also need to address the challenges of globalization (e.g. migration and social exclusion), to be more open and inclusive, and to become a truly international and intercultural learning space.

Table 5.1 A Comparison between (Global) Public Good and (Global) Common Good

	Public good	**Common good**
Principles/theories	Equity and social justice	Besides equity and social justice, also solidarity and cooperation
	Political economy theory	Philosophical and political perspective
Nature	Non-excludable and non-rivalrous in terms of consumption of a commodity	Non-excludable and non-rivalrous in terms of participation and generation of the good themselves
	The public quality is predetermined	The common quality is dynamic and not pre-existing
Governance	Public governance	Shared governance
	Result of the action of public institutions	Result of the interaction of the different components of society
	Top-down approach	Bottom-up approach
	Passive role of those who benefit	Active role of those who benefit
Value	Global public good is quasi-universal in terms of accessibility to countries, people and generations	Global common good implies the empowerment of all actors in a world society who have a right to a fully informed and critical participation
	Instrumental, can be treated as economic resources	Cannot be reduced to economic resources or to factors of production because of intrinsic social and relational value

Source: Adapted by authors from Locatelli (2018).

Obviously, these important contributions are closely related to WCUs' three functions of education, research and service, indicating that they are functioning well in the context of internationalization and global common good and making contributions to the global society.

The Basic Functions of WCUs

As global research universities, WCUs share the same three basic functions of education, research and service with other research universities, though there are differences in focus and priority when they are functioning.

Education refers to universities that use educational and teaching resources to educate students to become talented people. WCUs are committed to educating world-class talents, including global leaders with the global citizenship and interests that go beyond national boundaries, top-notch innovative talents, excellent scientific researchers and scholars, with interdisciplinary, internationalized, diversified and up-to-date educational models (Shin 2013; Kim et al. 2018).

Research refers to the systematic creative work carried out by universities to advance knowledge and to use this knowledge to invent new technologies and applications. WCUs are committed to conducting forward-looking, world-leading and diversified high-level research, aiming to solve the most severe and complex problems of global society. They focus on the frontier of basic research and high-level applied research, targeting areas that require innovation and in-depth understanding. In general, WCUs' significant research contributions create their world-renowned academic reputation. Research excellence is a vital sign that distinguishes WCUs from other research universities (Shin 2013; Tian and Liu forthcoming).

Service pays greater recognition to universities doing more to engage in the society. WCUs prioritize their services at global and national levels, and this service function is enhanced through WCUs' excellence in education and research. Specifically, WCUs' service function includes (but is not limited to) responding to global challenges, contributing to sustainable development, improving the livelihood of mankind, improving public policy-making, promoting national development and providing global alumni service (Gu and Liu 2011; Tian and Liu forthcoming).

The Purpose of This Study

Prior studies demonstrate that in their three basic functions of education, research and service WCUs play a vital role in relation to internationalization and global common good. Previous research mostly discusses WCUs as a whole as if their goals are common. This can lead to neglect of their differences and diversity. WCUs are global institutions but also based in a locality and full of national characteristics. A genuine WCU should be both globally oriented and locally rooted, and it can only be built and developed in terms of the unique geopolitics of the country and national culture and traditions (Lu and Yang 2018). This chapter focuses on the following research question:

- How (do) WCUs function differently in different countries and regions in the context of internationalization and global common good, and why?

The study focuses on WCUs in China, the United States and Europe.[2] There are significant differences among universities in the same country and among countries in the same region, but differences between large countries/regions are greater and are the issue here.

The chapter begins with the broad literature on WCUs in the context of internationalization and global common good, and WCUs' basic functions of education, research and service. It then moves to research method, procedures and empirical data, and then to the findings, before linking the findings to the previous literature.

Research Method

The research was conducted using a qualitative research framework, with semi-structured interviews. The rationale is that WCUs' functions are not abstract, but are closely related to a wide array of practices and activities influenced by various factors. Interviewing people who are knowledgeable about or directly engaged in practices and activities related to universities' functions (education, research and service) was instrumental in obtaining useful data with which to answer the research question.

Data Collection

This study is part of broader research project, which adopted a purposive sampling to identify participants. Potential participants were invited by the researchers through email. The purpose of interviewing people from different countries and regions, organizations, positions was to ensure a broader coverage of relevant groups of people who may have a good understanding of WCUs' functions and to ensure that the samples are information-rich for in-depth analysis. Between December 2016 and May 2019, a total of seventy-four in-depth interviews were conducted (see Table 5.2 for details).

---

[2] In European higher education system, there are differences between the European continental countries and the UK, and differences among European continental countries. The focus on European WCUs in this study is to summarize some points of commonality among them. When compared with Chinese and American WCUs, the common points of European WCUs are obvious. The European countries in this chapter include the UK, the Netherlands, Switzerland, Portugal and Germany. Although the researchers did not directly conduct interviews in German universities, some interviewees working in Dutch and Swiss universities were Germans or had worked in German universities before, and they provided rich information about German universities.

Table 5.2 Basic Information about the Study Interviewees in World-Class Universities in Three Countries/Regions

Groups	Country/Region	University	Interviewees
WCUs	China	3 WCUs in China	N = 14 University leaders = 2 Deans and directors = 9 Professors = 3
	United States	3 WCUs in the United States	N = 10 University leaders = 2 Deans and directors = 4 Professors = 4
	Europe	3 WCUs in Europe	N = 12 University leaders = 2 Deans and directors = 6 Professors = 4
RUs	China	3 RUs in China	N = 7 University leaders = 2 Deans and directors = 3 Professors = 2
	United States	3 RUs in the United States	N = 5 University leaders = 2 Deans and directors = 1 Professors = 2
	Europe	3 RUs in Europe	N = 12 University leaders = 4 Deans and directors = 4 Professors = 4
International experts	Global	International (academic) experts in relevant fields	N = 14 Including experts from China, the United States, Europe, Japan, Australia, etc.

Notes: (1) WCUs refer to the top 100 institutions in the major global rankings (ARWU, QS and THE), which declare themselves as WCUs; RUs refer to institutions not ranked among the top 200 list in the three rankings as mentioned above, which never declare themselves as WCUs. All data are based on major global rankings in 2018. (2) For comparative purposes, only public research universities were chosen; (3) University leaders include the (vice) president/chancellor/rector, (vice) provosts, etc. (4) European universities were located in the Netherlands, UK, Switzerland and Portugal.

Source: Authors.

Interview questions were closely related to the research question. Interviews were conducted in both Chinese and English (according to the interviewees' preferences).

Data Analysis

Interview data were coded and analysed using MAXQDA 2018 based on qualitative content analysis. Transcripts were coded according to participants' responses to each question and to the most salient categories (also called themes) emerging across the set of interviews. An initial list of main categories corresponding to the questions asked in the interview was formed deductively. As a second step, data were coded with the main categories (e.g. differences in WCUs' service function). Third, text passages were compiled in the main categories, and subcategories were formed inductively from the material. Fourth, text passages were assigned to subcategories (e.g. the degree of international engagement was a subcategory under differences in WCUs' service function). Last, all categories were refined under more general headings related to the research question and a category system was formed.

Participants in the interviews are referred to by code names[3] for the purposes of both ensuring anonymity and facilitating tracing references from the data.

Results and Findings

WCUs Function Differently in Different Countries and Regions

In total, 96 per cent of interviewees ($N = 71$) believed that WCUs in China, the United States and Europe are functioning differently in terms of education, research and service,[4] though some admitted that they were not very familiar with certain countries or region, and some interviewees gave examples related to WCUs' functions in only one or two of the three regions.

Differences in the Education Function

Ten interviewees considered that Chinese WCUs emphasize the public good aspects of their education function, highlighting their role in producing public benefits. Chinese WCUs employ a low-tuition policy and students can apply for generous scholarships through various channels. Despite that, Chinese WCUs adopt a competitive admission mechanism, using entrance examinations to emphasize education equity, with a merit-based selection. The degree of internationalization of undergraduate education in most Chinese WCUs is

---

[3] For example, WCL1 means the first participant in a Chinese WCU, who is a university leader. In the code names, each letter has its meaning, i.e. W=WCUs; R=RUs; C=China; U=the United States; E=Europe; L=Leader; D=Dean or director; P=Professor; EXP=Expert.

[4] The findings of this study are primarily related to WCUs' differences in their three functions in the context of internationalization and global common good. This does not include all aspects of their differences in the three functions.

relatively low, because most undergraduate courses are taught in Chinese, attracting fewer international students. In light of this, many Chinese WCUs have gradually increased the number of English-taught undergraduate courses to attract more international students and enhance the internationalization level of education.

American WCUs adopt a high-tuition policy at all educational levels. Six respondents noted that higher education in the United States has become a profitable global business, and the public good role of higher education is weakened. However, some interviewees pointed out that WCUs in the United States offer a transfer process that allows students studying in community colleges to successfully enter WCUs. This is an important way for unprivileged students to obtain better educational resources. In addition, education in American WCUs is highly internationalized, and these universities attract excellent undergraduates and postgraduates worldwide.

In Europe, WCUs' emphasis on the public good of education, and tuition policies, vary. Unlike WCUs in the UK, most WCUs in continental European countries adopt a modest- or low-tuition policy. Among them, Germany employs a tuition-free policy. WCUs in Germany, the Netherlands, Switzerland and Portugal adopt a non-competitive admission mechanism, which is also different from their counterparts in the UK. These countries conform to the principle of egalitarianism in undergraduate education, that is, students can choose to enter any top national universities after completing high school courses and passing graduation exams, though some popular majors, such as medicine and law, have additional entry requirements. This was explained by one of the European interviewees as follows:

> WED5: Switzerland is a very egalitarian country, so it tends to emphasize that there are no real big class differences … in Switzerland, WCUs are not elite. By contrast, in the US, if you want to study at Harvard or Princeton, you have to be part of a certain elite group in terms of financial and social background. This is completely different here. Our three top universities are open to everybody according to a merit-based system that everybody is able to have the opportunity to attend the university … I'm a German … the egalitarian orientation is much more pronounced in Germany.

Postgraduate education in European WCUs is highly internationalized, but undergraduate education is less internationalized ($N = 17$). Interviewees considered two main reasons for this situation: national policy restrictions and language barriers.

Differences in the Research Function

Five interviewees pointed out that compared with education and service functions, Chinese WCUs attach more importance to the research function, investing heavily in research and giving more weight to research activities in science, technology, engineering and mathematics (STEM) rather than in humanities and social sciences. Some interviewees assume that this may lead to an imbalance between faculty's participation in teaching and research, and it may also cause an imbalance between research activities in STEM and humanities and social sciences.

Eight interviewees argued that in American WCUs, the commercialization trend of research continues to be strengthened, which occurs in parallel with the government funding cuts. More and more American WCUs are carrying out contract research for enterprises. Interviewees believed that coupled with the continuous shrinking of government funding and universities' increasing demand for funds to maintain operation, the commercialized research activities will increase, thereby damaging the ability of WCUs to carry out genuine academic research. As one of the American WCUs' interviewees stated:

> WUD4: X University (an American WCU) is one of the best examples. It has been the site of some of the most controversial outside research contracts. It explains like, we don't have any public money, we need private money, and so we will ask corporations for money. The corporations are willing to give money, but only if the university does the corporations' research. So essentially, the department of a university becomes a research and development arm of the corporation. I don't want to say this happens in a majority of departments … but the probability is higher when WCUs want lots of money… conducting the research for the corporation is not going to win awards, and it's not going to advance basic research or fundamental knowledge … it produces a product.

Eleven interviewees believed that most European universities had inherited the German Humboldt model. Most of these universities give equal attention to education and research. Also, European WCUs place great emphasis on interdisciplinary cooperative research. Apart from this, European WCUs encourage open access of research outputs and are committed to promoting open science.

Differences in the Service Function

In China, serving national development is deeply embedded in the service function of WCUs, and the service activities of Chinese WCUs are largely consistent with national development goals ($N = 31$). This is closely related to the nature of Chinese WCUs as public universities primarily funded by the government. At the same time, Chinese WCUs have shifted to a more internationally visible direction, with an increasingly important role in serving the international community ($N = 7$). In addition, in recent years some Chinese WCUs have included service as an indicator in the faculty evaluation system. However, a small number of Chinese respondents ($N = 3$) pointed out that the alumni service and its internationalization level in Chinese WCUs still needed to be improved.

In the United States,[5] the service function of WCUs, especially those universities that are evolved from land-grant universities, had a long history ($N = 18$). Interviewees believed that the service function of land-grant universities mainly included three aspects: (1) cooperative extension, which is mainly about the agricultural assistance provided by universities in the early days; (2) outreach, which is the regular service provided by universities, for example, medical services provided by the medical centres of universities; and (3) extension programmes/continuing education. Along with the development of society, the form and content of service function in American WCUs have been enriched and have become more diversified. In addition, American WCUs highlight their important role in serving economic development and take it as a basis for obtaining government funding. As a result, most American WCUs include service as an indicator in the faculty evaluation system. Apart from this, American WCUs have long been active and key players in the international community, with a higher level of international engagement when compared with WCUs in other countries. At the same time, American WCUs attach great importance to the alumni service and its extent of internationalization ($N = 9$).

In Europe, given that most top universities in the continental European countries follow the German Humboldt model, emphasizing the integration of education and research functions, in the past the service function in European WCUs had been missing ($N = 8$). As one European interviewee explained:

> WEP1: I think European universities are more oriented to the first two functions and see service as a newer function. Europe is different in this aspect ... many universities consider it as something new ... I think this has to do with the

---

[5] Four out of the six American universities in this study had evolved from land-grant universities. Interviewees in these universities emphasized the land-grant tradition of WCUs. Not all US institutions share the service function in this form, or at least not to the same extent.

traditions in Europe, again, the traditional Humboldt model that emphasizes teaching and research, and it doesn't talk about service ... if you look at the new agenda on the modernization of European higher education ... they now emphasize a lot of community engagement and social mission ... especially since the European crisis.

The European WCUs' emphasis on service function pales in comparison with their American counterparts: (1) European WCUs often regard the service function as the 'third function/mission', implying that, in the beginning, this did not belong to the basic functions of a university, but it was gradually added over time; (2) the universities in the five European countries in this study had only taken local and international service activities into consideration in recent years, with more emphasis on serving the European community in terms of international scope. European WCUs do not include service as an indicator in the faculty evaluation system. Most European WCUs (except WCUs in the UK) pay less attention to alumni service and its internationalization level.

Major Factors Affecting the Differences between Regions

The interviewees considered that WCUs were functioning differently in China, the United States and Europe because of three factors: (1) the history and culture of different countries and regions ($N = 19$); (2) universities' funding sources ($N = 19$); and (3) governmental and political factors ($N = 19$).

Culture and History

Nineteen interviewees mentioned that the establishment and development of WCUs are influenced by the history and culture of their countries and regions. History and culture shape WCUs and also affect their functions. For example, Chinese WCUs are steeped in Confucian ideas that emphasize the public good and public nature of education, and continental European universities are affected by the egalitarian tradition. Also, taking WCUs in the German-speaking region as an example, these universities inherit the German Humboldt model of the nineteenth century. This cultural and historical tradition determines that these universities attach great importance to research and education rather than service. By contrast, world-class land-grant universities in the United States have a clear mission to serve the country and the society at the beginning of their establishment.

Funding Sources

Nineteen interviewees believed that funding sources lead to the differences in functions of WCUs in different countries and regions. The providers of funds constitute the stakeholders of WCUs. To a large extent, stakeholder expectations affect the functions of WCUs. WCUs in China, the United States and Europe have different funding schemes. According to data gathered in the interviews, about half of the funding for Chinese WCUs was from the government. The proportion of government funding in American universities was relatively low. The situation in European WCUs varied, with on average about half the funding stemming from the government. In British WCUs, tuition and fees paid by international students was also a primary funding source, but in Swiss WCUs, about 90 per cent of the funding was from the government.

On this basis, WCUs in China and Switzerland first needed to serve national and social needs. Swiss WCUs were very interesting cases. The funding sources for Swiss WCUs – funding from the federal government or cantons – determine the scope of Swiss WCUs' services. The direct democracy promoted by Switzerland naturally links the WCUs with the cantons to which they belong. Because government funding accounts for a relatively large proportion in universities' financial income, WCUs in China and most European cases placed great emphasis on the public good aspect of their functions. By contrast, as indicated previously, the trend of commercialization of research activities in American WCUs was related to the decline of government funding.

Governmental and Political Factors

Nineteen interviewees proposed that WCUs' functions are inevitably affected by the governmental policies and political factors, especially given that most public WCUs are mainly funded by governments This is especially evident in China and Europe. China's Double First-Class project is a major strategic decision made by the government, which aims to enhance China's education development and promote the country's core competitiveness, affecting all Chinese WCUs' education, research and service functions. The *Exzellenzinitiative* launched by the German government influences German top universities' research direction and specific research activities. The British government and relevant departments have introduced the Research Excellence Framework (REF) to support and ensure that British universities' research is at a world-class level.

Discussion

WCUs' Different Responses in the Broader Context of Internationalization and Global Common Good

As global research universities, WCUs are more responsive to global changes and trends (Tian and Liu 2020). In fact, differences in the three functions of the WCUs can be viewed as their different responses in the broader context of internationalization and global common good. According to Sporn and van der Wende (2020), this is an instrumental perspective, indicating that though universities are relatively resilient to changing external circumstances, they can also be seen as an instrument for achieving predetermined preferences and interests. The university is involved in a set of social, political and economic contracts.

WCUs' Different Responses to the Trend of Internationalization

The different responses of the WCUs to internationalization can be demonstrated by the internationalization level of education, the varied priorities in research as well as the internationalization level of alumni service.

The results of this study show that American WCUs are more internationalized in education than their counterparts in China and Europe, attracting excellent undergraduates and postgraduates worldwide. By contrast, the internationalization level of undergraduate education in most Chinese and European WCUs is relatively low, because most undergraduate courses are taught in their native languages, even though Europe has the Bologna Process that seeks to facilitate student mobility. Though there is a mixed feeling in Europe about international student recruitment (more related to students who are not European citizens), a growing number of Chinese WCUs have increased the number of English-taught undergraduate courses to attract more international students, thereby enhancing the internationalization level of education. This result is in tandem with Tian and Liu's (2020) study that, as uprising stars among WCUs, Chinese WCUs particularly highlight the recruitment of more international students and the diversified source countries of these students. In a broader context, this trend is enhanced by the Belt and Road Initiative (BRI) or the New Silk Road (NSR) Initiative, which seems to be gradually shaping an internationalization agenda for Chinese higher education (van der Wende et al. 2020). Tian and Liu (2020) find that in the Chinese context WCUs saw the NSR Initiative as an opportunity and responded positively to it, by establishing exchange programmes and increasing student exchanges with universities in NSR countries, and organizing (jointly) academic and cultural programmes related to the NSR Initiative. This accords with our research finding in two respects: first, in a more metaphorical sense, the NSR Initiative can be understood as a contextual factor, shaping broad directions and conditions at a macro-level (van der Wende et al. 2020), given that WCUs are often more responsive to the trends, changes and needs of the outside world, and more globally and internationally oriented; second, the NSR Initiative can also be regarded as a policy with international relevance proposed by China (Tian and Liu 2020), which particularly influences Chinese WCUs that are often responsive to national policies.

The findings of this study show that Chinese WCUs thought highly of the research function, investing heavily in research and giving more weight to research activities in STEM. This reflected the fact that the internationalization of higher education in China was no longer confined to student and faculty mobility and transnational cooperation; rather China was attempting to build its own centres of excellence to benchmark with top universities worldwide, first by enhancing its research capability and outcomes in STEM. The success of this approach is confirmed by scholars who argue that China has already established itself as a global player in STEM, though its humanities and social sciences are much less internationally visible (van der Wende et al. 2020).

Regarding the internationalization level of alumni service, though most WCUs in continental European countries paid less attention to it, both American and Chinese WCUs were making efforts in this aspect. The results of this study show that American WCUs were taking the lead in the internationalization of alumni service, being closely followed by Chinese WCUs. This is partly explained by Marginson's (2011) finding that global capacity and global connectivity are preconditions for universities to act globally. Global connectivity here is not just electronically, but through partnerships, networks and the ongoing exchange of personnel, staff and students. In this sense, the internationalized alumni network helped to improve the global connectivity of WCUs. Also, unlike American WCUs that tended to see the expansion and internationalization of the alumni network as a way of obtaining donations, most Chinese WCUs tend to see it as a tool to enhance their international influence and reputation (Li 2020).

WCUs' Different Responses to the Global Common Good

WCUs' different responses to the global common good were illustrated by their varied emphases on the public good of education, the commercialization trend in research, the promotion of open access and open science, and their international roles in providing services.

Though the public good and the common good are two different concepts in higher education, they are still closely related to each other, both emphasizing access, equity and fairness in higher education. Therefore, WCUs' varied emphases on the public good of education reflect their standings in response to the global common good. In this study, Chinese and most European WCUs attached greater importance to the public good of education, whereas American WCUs went in the other direction (though they had the transfer system that created opportunities for unprivileged students). This aligned with Lewis and Hearn's (2003) study that the higher education system in the United States is facing the growth of marketization and privatization due to the deduction or removal of state funding from higher education. This situation, along with other factors, has posed challenges to the public side of higher education in the United States. In contrast, Chinese WCUs, as important components of the Chinese higher education system, were consistent with the nature of Chinese higher education as a common good that is beneficial for all and encourages tolerance, equity, understanding and inclusion (Tian and Liu 2019).

The commercialization trend in research, the promotion of open access and open science present great contrasts in responding to the global common good. The commercialization trend in research that emphasized economic profit among American WCUs undermined the contributions based on WCUs' research to the global common good. That is to say, if WCUs' research becomes profit-oriented, their research is more likely to produce only profitable products rather than extending the boundary of human knowledge; also, their commitment to inclusive innovation is compromised. Inclusive innovation highlights solutions to important issues where innovation is needed, but there is no profit motive. In contrast, the promotion of open access and open science advocated by most European WCUs echoed with the idea of the global common good. Open access, as one of the preconditions of open science, allows scientific information, data and outputs to be more widely accessible. Open science is a movement aiming to make science more open, accessible, efficient, democratic and transparent, thereby ensuring that science truly benefits the people and the planet and leaves no one behind (UNESCO 2019).

WCUs' international roles in providing services varied among the WCUs in China, the United States and Europe. American WCUs laid great emphasis on serving the international community, but most European WCUs focused more on serving Europe, and their attention to the service function was a recent development. As more newly formed WCUs, Chinese WCUs had a clear goal to expand their international influence through serving the international community, with a strong national focus at the same time. This confirms previous findings that argue that most American WCUs have a distinctive global function (Ma 2014). At the same time, most Chinese WCUs are tasked with realizing national rejuvenation and achieving global influence (Yang 2018).

In general, based on the results of this study and the above discussion, WCUs' different responses, based on their three functions in the context of internationalization and global common good, is a complex matter affected by various factors. These responses include conflicts and tensions, but also efforts to conciliate, adapt and assemble the national features of the higher education system, and the structural and cultural features of the single institution, in relation to new external pressures (Vaira 2004). WCUs are not always and essentially global and international. As nation-builders and academic institutions, they are deeply embedded in localities and polities, being influenced by culture and history, and funding sources, as well as the governmental and political factors.

Factors Affecting WCUs' Three Functions in the Context of Internationalization and Global Common Good

Culture and History

Culture and history affect the education function of WCUs. As noted, compared with American WCUs, Chinese WCUs and most European WCUs (except WCUs in the UK) emphasized the public good of education. This was affected by Confucian traditions in China and the egalitarian tradition in the continental European countries. This finding meshes with Yang's (2017) finding that Chinese higher education, deeply influenced by Confucian culture, valued the public good and public nature of universities. This result is also supported by Wolfensberger's (2015) finding that in European countries such as the Netherlands, Germany, Austria, Switzerland, Finland and Sweden, the selectivity, competitiveness and stratification of higher education was not universal. Most of these countries used a non-competitive recruitment mechanism, with significant influence from the egalitarian tradition.

However, though both Chinese WCUs and most European WCUs attached importance to the public good of education, the former emphasizes selection and competitivity in student admission. Marginson (2013) explains this from a cultural perspective. He points out that, compared with Europe and North America, East Asian countries influenced by Confucian culture have long used examinations as a social and academic selection mechanism, which indirectly enhances the value of education. However, in this framework, competition and selection in the examinations are based on fairness and equity and designed to achieve the goal of merit-based admission.

In contrast with this, American WCUs are often labelled as elitist. The findings of this study have demonstrated that the public good of the American WCUs is in question. Marginson's (2013) study elaborates on this from a historical and cultural perspective. He notes that American educational culture emphasizes a meritocratic and competitive ideology. Marginson does not classify British and American universities in the same system. Hu (2019) believes that both of them belong to the Anglo-Saxon system. The results of the present study show that compared with other European continental universities, British WCUs, like American WCUs, pay insufficient attention to the public good of education. This is consistent with Reichert's (2009) finding that in the UK (especially in England), elite values that are often publicly denigrated are still deeply ingrained in social and political choices and networks, and sustain many institutional practices.

In addition, interviewees in this study considered that history and culture had affected the service function of WCUs. As noted, Chinese, American and European WCUs' emphases on the service function varied, and the contents of service were different. American WCUs, especially those universities based on the traditional land-grant university model, highly valued the service function and their role in promoting economic development. In Europe, many WCUs that followed the Humboldt model did not consider service to be one of the basic functions of universities. Chinese WCUs' emphasis on the service function was somewhere in between and largely guided by national policies. This finding is in line with March's (1993) study that, for universities, a crucial factor is what characterizes the era when a university was established, indicating what kind of basic norms and values were important and the impact of these on the university's later trajectory in a path-dependent process.

Funding and Polities

The findings of this study show that WCUs that were functioning differently in the context of internationalization and global common good were also affected by their funding sources as well as by governmental and political factors. WCUs mainly supported by government funding, as in China and Europe, first needed to meet national or social expectations, serve public needs and pay attention to the public good of education. For WCUs mainly supported by market income, such as the WCUs in the United States, the commercialization trend meant there was insufficient attention to the public good of education.

Based on the different roles of government and market in the allocation of higher education resources, Hu (2019) finds there are two different kinds of higher education system: the Anglo-Saxon system (British-American system) and the Roman system (continental European system). The Anglo-Saxon system follows an academic logic, which adheres to the principle of liberalism, advocating free competition for resources and talents. The continental European system follows the political logic, which adheres to the principle of nationalism, emphasizing government's control and financial support, and focusing on national needs. However, the description of the British-American system may not be entirely well-founded. According to the research findings, the British system is somewhere in between the continental European system and American system as it emphasizes both governmental control and free competition.

Nevertheless, in the present study, WCUs in China and continental European countries are strongly linked to the continental European system described above, with the government and its funding playing a dominant role, ensuring that national policy and public needs are important to those WCUs. Almost all WCUs in East Asia are set up, managed and funded directly by central or national government, on the basis of learning and imitating Western universities. From the beginning of their establishment, these universities have directly served the modernization of the country and society, with a clear mission to serve the public good (Huang 2017). The egalitarianism pursued by most WCUs in continental European countries in their education function is also related to national policies. For example, German higher education's tuition-free policy is supported by Article 5.3 of the German constitution: 'Arts and sciences, research and teaching shall be free' (Hüther and Krücken 2018: xi).

Unlike WCUs in China and continental European countries, American WCUs have developed into strongly competitive entrepreneurial universities. The United States is the world's largest exporter of higher education, and the commercialization of research activities in these universities continues to be strengthened. According to Clark (1986), the steering of the US higher education system is more market-oriented in the sense of responding mostly to the demands of the labour market, corporate needs and similar stakeholders.

American universities are organizational actors with a clear competitive spirit (Sporn and van der Wende 2020).

Conclusion

From a functional perspective focusing on differences, the present study examines WCUs' functions in different countries and regions, and factors causing these differences, in the context of internationalization and the global common good. The findings of this study contradict the homogeneous organizational model that is used to legitimize WCUs as a category. The study partly accords with the idea that 'the university is pluralistic and fragmented because of the nature of its activities' (Lockwood 2011: 126). However, these two perspectives are not in conflict, and it is possible to reconcile these opposing views by applying to universities the concept of *organizational allomorphisms* (a morphological variant of the same basic structure derived from a specific context: see Vaira 2004; Rodriguez-Pomeda and Casani 2016). In a broader context, the different responses of WCUs in China, the United States and Europe are closely related to their localities and polities.

This study may be a starting point for an investigation of how the criteria of WCUs vary according to differences in culture, history as well as national and political systems. As Mohrman (2005: 22) states: 'it would be quite interesting to learn of a new definition of a world-class university that is not simply an imitation of Harvard but a creative blend of the best of East and West'.

Part Two

Internationalization and Endogenization, Regionalization and Globalization

天下

Chinese meaning:

World, earth, all under heaven (the sky), state power, the whole country

Japanese meaning:

World, earth, all under heaven (the sky), state power, the whole country, world-top (the best in the world)

Korean meaning:

World, earth, all under heaven (the sky), state power, the whole country, world-top (the best in the world)

Vietnamese meaning:

World, earth

6

Regional Higher Education Cooperation in Japan

Christopher D. Hammond

Introduction

Cross-border research collaboration and internationalization of higher education have expanded dramatically in recent decades, supported by and contributing to widespread processes of economic, cultural and communicative globalization. Increased global competition in higher education has also facilitated increases in cross-border cooperation at the region-level, as nations and universities form tactical alliances and consortia to enhance the global competitiveness of their national systems. In Asia, regional collaboration in research and a dramatic rise in research outputs (particularly from China) has led some to suggest a tilting of the research world toward Asia and away from the West (Cummings 2014). This shift has been accompanied by a rise in intra-regional innovation and the expansion of inter-university linkages within Asia, pointing to an emerging pattern of higher education regional integration. Aligning with broader patterns of region building in the economic sphere, the higher education sector in Asia has witnessed a dramatic rise in both informal de facto regionalization (Kuroda 2016) and government-initiated forms of regionalism. Within the broader Asian region, research collaboration and exchanges between Japan, China and South Korea have also increased in recent decades. Along with a rise in informal 'bottom-up' cooperation, there have also been efforts made by the governments of the three countries to establish formalized programmes for collaborative regional research and exchange.

This chapter presents a qualitative study of two such formalized programmes aimed at fostering regional cooperation between China, Japan and South Korea. The aims of the research were to understand the cognitive and normative policy ideas about regional cooperation in Northeast Asia[1] from the perspectives of actors involved in government-initiated programmes for higher education regional cooperation at Japanese universities. This takes in an investigation of how policy ideas at the government-level were adopted, resisted and repurposed across different institutional and disciplinary contexts. To investigate these issues, two programmes for regional cooperation were selected: one representing higher education's societal role as a producer of research-based knowledge and the other representing its social function as a site for teaching and learning. The programme addressing the former role is the A3 Foresight programme, a funding scheme for scientists to engage in regional research collaboration. The programme addressing the latter role is Collective Action for the Mobility Program of University Students in Asia (CAMPUS Asia), a regional exchange programme for students at top universities in the three countries.

The research design took the form of an interpretive study underpinned by a naturalistic social constructivist epistemology (see Checkel 2006). Nine participating universities were selected as cases, and the primary source of data were the transcripts of semi-structured interviews with sixty-seven individuals involved in varying capacities in either A3 Foresight or CAMPUS Asia. These actors included academics, administrators and students (both current participants and programme alumni). A total of fifty-two documents from five key governmental organizations involved in regional cooperation were also collected and analysed, and these served as structuring elements with which to compare and illuminate the ideas of actors in the selected universities. Data analysis and interpretation involved a combination of methods, including the deductive application of an analytical framework from a political science theory known as discursive institutionalism (Schmidt 2008, 2010) along with inductive thematic analysis. Utilizing these methods, an attempt was made to construct nuanced and informed answers to the following research questions:

- What policy ideas do actors involved in the CAMPUS Asia and A3 Foresight programmes at Japanese universities have about regional cooperation between Japan, China and South Korea?
- How do these ideas compare across institutional and disciplinary contexts?
- What do actors perceive are the barriers that impede regional cooperation at the higher education and broader societal levels?

---

[1] In this chapter 'Northeast Asia' refers to mainland China, South Korea and Japan, while 'East Asia' refers to the broader region including the three countries.

- How do these ideas compare with policy ideas for higher education regionalism at the government level? How are government-level ideas adopted, adapted and resisted by actors at Japanese universities?

Literature Review

Higher education regional cooperation has been addressed in the literature, but the majority of this research focuses on European processes such as the Erasmus Programme, Bologna Process and the Lisbon Convention. While often held up as an exemplar of regional integration, scholars have increasingly begun to question the alleged influence of the European 'Bologna Process export model' in other regions, and the unquestioned assumptions that Europe should serve as model by which other regions should be compared (Cabanda, Tan and Chou 2019; Chou and Ravinet 2016, 2017). Chou and Ravinet rightly suggest that comparing various world region building projects against a particular 'model of success' limits the possibilities for comparative regionalism as a field; more can be gained from contextualized and nuanced studies that acknowledge the unique complexities that shape different regions and initiatives for regional cooperation.

Although higher education regional cooperation beyond Europe has been addressed by a number of scholars (Chou and Ravinet 2017; Robertson et al. 2016), there is a relative lack of research that has focused on the Northeast Asian context. A number of descriptive policy analyses of CAMPUS Asia (Byun and Um 2014; Sugimura 2012; Yonezawa and Meerman 2012) and empirical and conceptual work on broader processes of East Asian higher education regionalization (Chao 2014; Hawkins, Mok and Neubauer 2012; Kuroda, Yuki and Kang 2010; Mok 2012) can be found in the literature, but high-quality empirical studies of the CAMPUS Asia programme are limited (Breaden 2018; Kyung 2015), and research on the A3 Foresight programme is virtually absent (Hammond 2019). As the East Asian region is increasingly recognized as an important global player in the higher education landscape (Marginson 2011), further empirical studies of this dynamic region are warranted.

There is also space for novel theoretical interrogations of higher education region building. Theories of regional integration are prevalent in the field of International Relations (Acharya 2012; Börzel 2016; Katzenstein 2005; Rosamond 2005; Schmitter 2005), and some of these have been applied to studies of higher education, but little novel theorization has occurred in the field of Higher Education Studies itself. Exceptions include the research by Robertson, Azevedo and Dale (2016) with their 'cultural political economy' approach to the study of regionalism, and a conceptual framework for the 'regionalization' of higher education proposed by Jane Knight (Knight 2016). Knight's framework, often called the 'FOPA model', posits a continuum of intensity, characteristics and three 'approaches' to what Knight terms higher education 'regionalization', and has been applied by some scholars to the East Asian context (Chao 2014; Chen and Shimizu 2017; Hou et al. 2017). The functional approach relates to the 'practical activities of HEIs and systems' (including 'Collaborative Programmes'); the organizational approach entails the 'architecture that evolves to develop and guide the regionalisation initiatives in a more systematic (although some might call bureaucratic) manner'; and the political approach refers to the 'strategies that put higher education initiatives on the agenda of decision-making bodies' (Knight 2016: 119–20). Knight suggests that the three 'approaches' to regionalization are interrelated, ideally working in unison to complement and reinforce one another.

It is useful to conceptualize these varied elements of higher education regional cooperation and consider how they might influence processes of region building. However, a deficiency of the FOPA model is that it limits regional cooperation phenomena to seemingly static possibilities. More importantly, simply investigating these three dimensions is insufficient, because the model as it stands ignores the critical influence of the sociocultural context. In order to gain a deep understanding of the policy processes of higher education regionalism and regionalization in various contexts, it is necessary to uncover the ideas and principles informing the discursive practices of the range of actors involved in these processes. This focus on the ideational dimension of higher education regional cooperation has been put forward by Chou and Ravinet as part of a three-step approach to implement their research agenda for comparative higher education regionalism (Chou and Ravinet 2016). The first step involves a process of mapping the diversity of regional higher education initiatives in a particular area and time period, including the identification of the 'constellation of actors' involved in these processes (281). The second step entails an investigation of the institutional arrangements adopted and the ideas and principles embedded in the regional initiatives (282). The third step involves 'conceptualising higher education regionalism', which entails theory development based on the grounded, qualitative and comparative empirical work inherent in the previous steps that the two scholars argue 'has yet to be undertaken' (282).

This study aimed to undertake some of this empirical work and adopted a research design that fits within Chou and Ravinet's second step, focusing on the 'ideas and principles' of actors involved in higher education regional cooperation in Japan. Following from the work of Vivian Schmidt (discussed below), Chou and Ravinet explain that ideas and principles 'refer to the paradigms, policy ideas, and programmatic ideas guiding that region's higher education initiatives', and that gaining an inductive understanding of these varied ideas can help 'facilitate the distilling of regional models of higher education cooperation' (2016: 282).

Chou and Ravinet offer a valuable contribution to their research agenda in a paper that compares policy ideas for higher education regionalism in Europe and the Association of Southeast Asian Nations (ASEAN). They conducted 53 interviews with policy actors in a range of governmental organizations involved in higher education region building in the two regions (Chou and Ravinet 2017), and they present in their paper a number of noteworthy findings. A notable finding pointed to a commonality that reportedly emerged in both ASEAN and European forms of higher education regionalism, a phenomenon they term the 'knowledge discourse', which emphasizes 'the role of knowledge in economic growth, international competition and social cohesion' (11).

While valuable, Chou and Ravinet's methodological approach to uncover the ideas and principles driving higher education regionalism in their selected contexts is insufficient. As policy is a process that involves not only 'operational formulation' and 'implementation' at the government-level, but it also includes 'delivery on the ground' and 'consumption and evaluation' by actors at universities participating in regionalist projects (Yeatman 1990, 1998, cited in Ozga and Lingard 2007). During these later stages of the policy process, actors have the capacity to adapt policies at varying degrees to align with their own ideas, values and interests. As such, to gain a comprehensive picture of the policy process, it is necessary to include the voices of these actors. This study aimed to do just that by incorporating the voices of administrators, academics and students into the analysis.

Analytical Framework

An analytical framework was adopted to investigate the ideas of actors and those imbedded within policy documents informed by a political science theory known as discursive institutionalism. Discursive institutionalism refers to approaches concerned with the 'substantive content of ideas and the interactive processes of discourse in institutional context' (Schmidt 2015: 171), and acknowledges a 'dynamic, agent-centered approach to institutional change' (305). In addition to the importance placed on the unique characteristics of individual actors, discursive institutionalism also acknowledges the impermanent and changeable nature of institutions (Hay 2011).

Schmidt (2008) posits that the ideas of actors differ in both levels of generality and type. Levels of ideas may represent specific 'policy solutions'; encompass more general 'programmes' that define the problems, norms, ideals and goals that frame the more immediate policy ideas; or at the most basic level indicate underlying 'philosophies': the rarely contested world views 'that undergird the policies and programmes with organising ideas, values, and principles of knowledge and society' (Schmidt 2008: 306).

The three levels of ideas (policy, programmatic and philosophical) can also be distinguished by type: they can be either cognitive, suggesting 'what is and what to do', or normative, indicating 'what is good or bad about what is' with respect to 'what one ought to do' (Schmidt 2008: 306). According to Schmidt, an important question for researchers studying ideas is why some ideas become policies, programmes and philosophies while others do not. Table 6.1 presents a framework for how these levels and types are organized. This framework provided a useful tool that informed the interview questions and the approach

Table 6.1 Discursive Institutionalism: Levels and Types of Ideas

	Cognitive	Normative
Policy level	How policies are defined, and how they offer solutions to problems	How policies meet the aspirations and ideals of the actors involved
'Programmatic' level	How contexts are understood and how problems are defined, and how methods to solve them are identified	How the ideals and norms that frame the more immediate policy ideas are defined
Underlying philosophies	How policies and programmes mesh with deeper principles and norms of relevant scientific disciplines or technical practices	How policies and programmes resonate with the deeper core of principles and norms of public life, whether newly emerging values or the long-standing ones in the societal repertoire

Source: Author, adapted from Schmidt (2008: 306–7).

to data analysis of the ideational factors shaping higher education regional cooperation in Northeast Asia.

While this framework is useful for understanding and comparing the ideas of different actors, a potential downside is that parsing ideas into distinct categories threatens to reduce their complexity and nuance. Furthermore, the act of isolating ideas in practice can be difficult, especially at the deeper levels of the framework. Because underlying philosophies in particular are 'left unarticulated as background knowledge', the actors in question may themselves be unaware of them (Schmidt 2008: 308). As such, any attempt to uncover these underlying philosophies via interviewing may be a futile endeavour. Despite these concerns, the framework arguably offered a suitable means for identifying and categorizing the ideas shaping the institutions of regional cooperation at Japanese universities in a systematic way (particularly at the policy and programmatic levels), enabling for a rigorous interpretive analysis.

Case Selection

The programmes for higher education regionalism selected for analysis were the A3 Foresight and CAMPUS Asia programmes. These are introduced briefly below.

A3 Foresight

The A3 Foresight programme is run jointly between the Japan Society for the Promotion of Science (JSPS), the National Natural Science Foundation of China (NSFC) and the National Research Foundation of Korea (NRF). The programme aims 'to create world-class research hubs within the Asian region, which by advancing world-class research will contribute to the solution of common regional problems, while fostering new generations of talented young researchers' (JSPS 2015). Criteria for funding includes expectations that the collaboration between institutions will produce research of world-class academic value as well as 'contribute to the continuous development of collaboration between the core institutions in the future' (JSPS 2015). Since 2005, a number of projects have been funded for five-year intervals in a range of scientific fields. Five participants from two different universities representing three projects in the fields of chemistry, physics and biology agreed to be interviewed for this study.

CAMPUS Asia

Efforts to improve collaborative research in the higher education sector have been couched within a broader political project to realize improved relations and increased cooperation between Japan, China and South Korea. In 2010, Japanese Prime Minister Yukio Hatoyama proposed his vision of an 'East Asian Community' with the intention of shifting Japan's foreign policy position away from the influence of the United States and embracing a more Asia-focused orientation. This same year the first Japan-China-Korea Committee for Promoting Exchange and Cooperation convened and established the CAMPUS Asia programme (Yonezawa and Meerman 2012). The goals of the programme are to foster student and academic exchanges between the three countries, and establish a framework for quality assurance. The agency in Japan tasked with evaluating CAMPUS Asia describes how the programme

> aims to promote cooperation among universities and mutual understanding among students of the 3 countries through various forms of exchange programmes between universities, and ultimately contribute to strengthening the competitiveness of universities and nurturing the next generation of outstanding talents of Asia. (NIAD-QE 2019: i).

The pilot version of CAMPUS Asia was launched in 2011. At the outset, ten Japanese universities were selected to participate in exchanges with counterparts in China and Korea. In 2015, it was agreed to renew and increase the number of collaborative programmes between the three countries and attempt to expand the framework of the programme to ASEAN countries in the mid- to long term (MEXT 2016). At the First Japan-China-Korea Education Ministers' Meeting in January 2016, a commitment was made to increase financial support for the programme, and in October of the same year, the programme began its second phase with the inclusion of seventeen participating Japanese universities. From within this group of seventeen, nine universities and their respective CAMPUS Asia programmes were chosen as cases.

The various CAMPUS Asia programmes selected include disciplines such as medicine, architecture, law, education, policy studies, engineering and new media (animation), as well as cross-disciplinary social science programmes like conflict resolution and sustainable development. As such, the selected cases have a balance of natural/physical sciences, social sciences and humanities disciplines. In total, sixty interviews were conducted with academics ($n = 15$), administrators ($n = 11$) and students ($n = 34$) participating in the various CAMPUS Asia programmes, as well as two interviews with government officials involved with the programme.[2]

Findings

The constructed findings highlight a range of interconnected ideas about the current state and possible future of regional cooperation in Northeast Asia. Using the discursive institutionalist analytical framework described above, ideas about perceived realities and intended outcomes of the CAMPUS Asia and A3 Foresight programmes were designated in the analysis to the categories of cognitive and normative 'policy ideas'. Broader ideas about the roles of Japanese higher education and the international relations shaping the Northeast Asian region which contextualized and informed ideas about the two programmes were categorized as second-level 'programmatic ideas'. The 'underlying philosophies' category was also utilized in the analysis, but the nature of these often unspoken world views posed challenges for rigorous qualitative interpretation and are thus omitted from the findings presented in this chapter.

While these categories were utilized to code and organize the data, the findings below are presented based on the most dominant and salient themes that emerged from an inductive analysis of the categorized texts. In order to better understand the perspectives of actors at Japanese universities, the major themes that emerged at the government level are presented first for juxtaposition.

Government-Level Ideas

The rationale for collecting documents from the government level was to help clarify the ideas and goals of the programmes at the point where they were initially conceived as well as to provide a structural frame by which to better understand the ways universities and individual actors within them reflected, repurposed or replaced these ideas based on their own ideas of regional cooperation. A total of fifty-two documents totalling approximately 265,800

---

[2] Only five interviews from A3 foresight were conducted in comparison to sixty for CAMPUS Asia. While the hope was to have a better balance between the two programmes, issues of access and opportunities for further interviews from CAMPUS Asia gatekeepers resulted in the final distribution of participants.

words were selected and analysed. The government-level agencies from which documents were collected were and are the Trilateral Cooperation Secretariat (TCS), Japan's Council for Science, Technology and Innovation (CSTI), the Ministry of Education, Culture, Sports, Science and Technology (MEXT), the Japan Society for the Promotion of Science (JSPS) and the National Institution for Academic Degrees and Quality Enhancement of Higher Education (NIAD-QE). All of these organizations have been involved in key capacities in one or both of the programmes under study.

The five government organizations surveyed all generally espoused the common policy ideas of mutual understanding, human resource development, economic interdependence, quality assurance and competitiveness when making references to the goals of the programmes for regional cooperation, higher education more broadly and/or science, technology and innovation (STI) in the context of the Northeast Asian region. In this respect, the case of Japan aligns with the ASEAN and European forms of regionalism which emphasize the 'knowledge discourse' (i.e. 'the role of knowledge in economic growth, international competition and social cohesion') discussed above (Chou and Ravinet 2017).

However, these terms were interpreted differently and emphasized at varying degrees, and frequently evidence emerged that the different organizations embodied different philosophies. For example, the TCS, by its very nature, is focused on achieving economic, political and social cooperation among the three countries, although the underlying motives for achieving this cooperation are arguably as varied as the diverse stakeholders that comprise the organization. CSTI, by contrast, is primarily focused on Japan's competitiveness in the STI fields and sees cross-border cooperation as a tool to augment this competitiveness, not only in economic but also in political terms. Human resources must also be developed to achieve this end. CSTI made clear that it viewed STI not only as a means of producing knowledge, augmenting growth and solving global problems, but also as a form of science diplomacy:

> the international competitiveness of science and technology systems is improved by using science and technology for diplomacy and using diplomacy for science and technology promotion to contribute to solving common global issues to all mankind and at the same time to increase the wealth and power of the nation. (CSTI 2015).

This strategic approach to the steering of STI priorities highlights another, more political orientation to the notion of competitiveness. The remit of CSTI in 'overlooking' all STI policy in Japan has placed it in a powerful position with regard to the steering of higher education, a role that entails inherent tensions with MEXT. MEXT, too, sees education and regional cooperation as mechanisms to produce global human resources, while JSPS appeared to have the most unique view of government agencies surveyed, valuing knowledge creation and collaboration for its potential to advance human societies and solve global and regional problems with little reference to the 'economy' or notions of competitiveness.

Also evident from the analysis of documents spanning a twenty-year period was the potential for developments in the economic and political arenas to influence policies for regional cooperation in STI and higher education. Most notable was the de-emphasis on creating an East Asian Community which aligned with changes in power and political orientation in Japan. References to an 'East Asian Community' disappeared from the texts upon return to power of the conservative Liberal Democratic Party (LDP) in 2012, which has traditionally prioritized the US-Japan alliance over Asia-oriented foreign policy. There were also subtle shifts in the discourse of science and technology, as growing global competition (including increasing collaboration of industry with universities overseas) coincided with increased calls for the practical application of knowledge and for Japanese universities to contribute to innovation. The analysis highlighted how the ideas at the government level during the conception and implementation of A3 and CAMPUS Asia have not remained static, but have evolved over time in response to external forces and domestic political change. In addition to change over time, the 'government' is clearly not a monolithic entity with a clear consensus about its policy ideas and interests. Various organizations will have their own ideas that at times conflict with those of others. This fact became more apparent through interviewing two government officials from different agencies, and it highlighted the importance of ideas of individual actors involved in shaping processes of regional cooperation.

University-Level Ideas

Actors at Japanese universities involved in policy implementation on the ground had a range of their own ideas of regional cooperation, leading to the frequent adaptation and repurposing of the government-level 'knowledge discourse' to align with their own institutional, disciplinary and individual agendas. Some of the most salient emergent themes are presented below.

Disciplinary Variation

It was expected there would be notable differences in ideas between the categories of academics, administrators and students – and across different universities – and in many instances there were indications that these categorical distinctions did provide a means for delineating certain ideas of regional cooperation. Furthermore, the identities, experiences and distinguishing characteristics that make participants individuals undoubtedly had an influence on the ideas they presented. However, what was most apparent were the strong differences in ideas of regional cooperation across academic disciplines. There seemed to be a sharp distinction between programmes and actors that envisioned regional cooperation as involving facing head-on the historical and political issues that continue to impede peaceful diplomatic relations between the three countries, and those that felt it was better not to speak about these sensitive topics. In both cases, these groups aligned their ideas of regional cooperation closely with their subject areas: actors in humanities and STEM fields generally felt discussing political issues to be unhelpful in achieving successful cooperation, focusing instead on points of positive cultural connection and collaborative opportunities within their specialisms, while those involved in social science-oriented programmes saw addressing sensitive historical and political issues as essential for future peace and regional stability. A salient example is provided by Waseda's CAMPUS Asia programme which, while open to students of all academic disciplines, takes an approach grounded in the social sciences focused on conflict resolution and social innovation:

> We had very intensive, active discussions during our summer programme. The theme was history in East Asia and we asked students to group up, then write up one page of a fictitious common history book on the page of the 9th of August 1945.[3] So it was totally up to the students to decide what they're going to write. It was quite dynamic, because ... views of historical events among the mainland Chinese people and the Taiwanese students[4] were totally different and initially they were not talking to each other, you could sense it was very ... kind of uncomfortable, yeah? But then we deliberately mixed students of those backgrounds and put some of them in the same group and eventually they did their own conflict resolution. Like a Taiwanese student came up with tears saying that 'My group members coming from China and Korea and elsewhere were open to listen to my perspective and

---

[3] The date of the US atomic bombing of Nagasaki, Japan.
[4] Waseda's programme also makes a point to include students from Taiwan (and was the only programme to do so), although they are not allowed to study abroad in mainland China.

actually asked me to give my perspective which would never have happened in a regular setting.' And it was very emotional. But that means it had a catalyst effect. (Academic, Conflict Resolution, CAMPUS Asia, Waseda University)

Encouraging discussion of sensitive issues and making attempts to understand the different perspectives of students from the three countries (and beyond, in some cases) was an approach to regional cooperation found in the UTokyo (University of Tokyo), Waseda and Okayama University cases. In the majority of the programmes studied, however, this was not common practice. Instead of focusing on regional points of conflict, students were encouraged to work within the bounds of their academic disciplines, finding common points of collaboration and, in some cases, celebrate the shared elements of the cultures of the three countries.

Those from the STEM disciplines had their own unique ideas about regional cooperation. In some instances, discussion of controversial issues between the three countries was expressly forbidden by senior professors, and young researchers were encouraged to instead focus on their 'mutual love of science'. This idea of mutual love often entailed a transcendence of national boundaries, as many academics and students used the term borderless to describe the nature of their disciplines and their ideas of scientific collaboration. From this perspective, researchers passionate about scientific discovery could cooperate and contribute to the creation of new knowledge regardless of cultural or national background. However, when the discussion shifted to the perceived purpose of top-down programmes for regional cooperation like A3 Foresight and CAMPUS Asia, the existence and importance of borders became more tangible. A common theme that emerged echoed the ideas found in many government-level documents: the idea of regional collaboration for the purpose of augmenting global competitiveness, notably with regard to improving East Asia's standing against that of the West. For example, the Engineering CAMPUS Asia programme at Tokyo Tech was described in terms of competition with the United States and Europe:

> if we know each other, then probably we can optimize all of the situations [*sic*] together to make a big promotion among the three countries. I mean against the US and Europe. US group and Europe group. (Academic, Engineering, CAMPUS Asia, Tokyo Institute of Technology)

Similarly, A3 Foresight was described in part as

> a research programme started with the idea that it is important to work hard in Asia so that the countries are more powerful and do not lose to Europe or America. (Academic, Biology, A3 Foresight Program, UTokyo)

The idea of competition with the 'West', while seemingly contradictory to the notion of a truly borderless, global science, may provide the cognitive conditions that serve as an impetus for scientists in Northeast Asia to engage in regional cross-border collaboration.

Institutional Variation

While differences across academic disciplines emerged as a distinguishing feature of the varied policy-level ideas of regional cooperation, institutional characteristics also appeared to shape strategies for internationalization and, by extension, actors' cognitive and normative ideas about the two programmes in particular. An institutional characteristic that was often discussed was geographical location, particularly whether the respective university was located in the global city of Tokyo or in more rural and remote areas of Japan.

Both proximity to urban centres and international visibility appeared to be influential factors that shaped institutional identities, which subsequently impacted internationalization strategies and policy ideas for regional cooperation. UTokyo served as the exemplar of a globally visible and prestigious urban research university, which helped to highlight the unique features and strategies of the other case universities. As the premier flagship national university in Japan, UTokyo's international strategy includes partnerships with other world-class universities and cross-border collaborations for the pursuit of path-breaking research and knowledge production. In this capacity, UTokyo naturally partnered with its flagship counterparts in China and Korea (Peking University and Seoul National University, respectively) for its CAMPUS Asia programme, and a number of top-tier research universities for its A3 Foresight projects.

By contrast, actors at universities with lower levels of global brand recognition, generally positioned in less well-known cities and more rural parts of Japan, reported challenges with regard to pressures from the government to 'globalize', attract more international students and effectively market their mobility programmes. Without this global brand status, these universities had to devise innovative approaches to attract both funding and international actors to their campuses. One such institution was Okayama University (located 675 km from Tokyo), which devised its CAMPUS Asia programme to focus on sustainable development grounded in the idea of addressing regional and global issues from a local perspective:

Okayama University cannot compete with Tokyo University or Kyoto University. We have to take advantage of the features of the university related to the local community and local development ... And one of the features is that this city itself is sustainable development-conscious and also has strong, I would say, infrastructure, [in its] community-based learning centres ... [students] can contribute to the local community, and that can be linked with national and also regional as well as global issues. (Academic, Sustainable Development, CAMPUS Asia, Okayama University)

In addition to geographic location, an institution's vision of internationalization (or lack thereof) also appeared to have an effect in shaping actors' views toward regional cooperation. Tokyo's Waseda University stood out as an example of how an institution's ethos can have a strong influence in shaping its international activities. A number of actors interviewed at Waseda mentioned the vision of the university's founder (and former prime minister of Japan), Shigenobu Okuma, and how his legacy continues to shape Waseda's strategy. The university's approach to CAMPUS Asia in particular connected to this vision, which embodies the long tradition of the university's acceptance of international students from East Asia. Unlike Japan's national universities which were founded in the late nineteenth century for the purpose of helping the Japanese nation to modernize and catch up with the West, the founding mission of Waseda, established in the same period, was to foster a harmony of the civilisations of the West and the East, and to contribute to global society. This mission to serve as a bridge between East and West was described as being influential in the university's willingness to host international students, and its continued proactive recruitment of a diverse student body. This idea that Japanese universities can serve as a contact zone for East Asia was not limited to actors at Waseda and was identified as a broader contextual theme related to the social functions of higher education perceived by actors across a number of cases.

Commonalities across Cases

A prevalent policy-level idea that emerged, particularly among the current and former students who were interviewed, was that undertaking study abroad or research collaboration in Northeast Asia would serve to 'broaden perspectives'. For these individuals, face-to-face international communication was perceived as key to gaining alternative understandings of the varied issues confronting the three countries. This idea of face-to-face interaction was often juxtaposed with the notion of exposure to information presented through the media, which was generally considered to be lacking and biased.

The discourse of broadening perspectives aligns in some ways with the ideas of mutual understanding found in the government-level policy documents. Indeed, gaining an insight into other perspectives on regional or global issues would help individuals to better understand those who held viewpoints alternative to their own. However, the notion of 'mutual understanding' does not imply an inherent internal change of perspective on the part of the individual, nor does it imply an integration of others' viewpoints into one's own view of the world. Instead, it suggests tolerance and possibly even a strategic knowledge of the other. Broadening perspectives, by contrast, implies growth, an increase in cognitive flexibility and an expansion of one's own understanding of the world. I argue that this is an important distinction indicative of the differences between the stated goals of the government and those of many actors at the higher education level. Having said that, many of the same actors also described the perceived benefits of participation in the programmes in instrumental terms, viewing the skills and experiences gained as 'added value' that could be utilized to enhance employability.

Whether academics, administrators or students, many actors discussing their role in either CAMPUS Asia or A3 Foresight framed their narratives from normative, future-oriented perspectives. While some emphasized an envisioned future in which the three countries achieved improved levels of peace and stability, many focused on these as the ideal end-product of their own more personal-level goals, which frequently connected to ideas of employability for CAMPUS Asia and A3 graduates. In a sense, the notion of future prosperity allowed for a normative idea of regional cooperation that pushed in both the directions of regional peace and economic competitiveness simultaneously. Like other ideas mentioned above, the employability narratives were often discipline-specific.

To use the government's keyword term, a significant number of actors were interested in the capacities of their programmes for regional cooperation to produce (global) human resources. Administrators in particular often repeated the rhetoric of the government-level policy documents, discussing 'producing global leaders', or 'next generation leaders of East Asia'. However, the nature and social function of these 'resources' varied considerably in the views of participants, and as such the discourse of human resources was one that was adapted considerably on the part of actors at universities. While generally shaped by discipline, nuanced differences in the employability narratives emerged at times because of particular institutional identities.

Barriers to Regional Cooperation

While there was substantial variation in the range of policy and programmatic ideas about what regional cooperation in Northeast Asia is and should be, there was relative consistency across cases regarding a number of perceived barriers that impede the realization of these ideas in practice.

A nearly ubiquitous policy-level barrier described across all cases and by academics, administrators and students alike was the trouble recruiting Japanese students to take part in study abroad programmes in East Asia. The number of Japanese students interested in studying abroad in general was described as being low, with those who do go abroad typically choosing to study in English-speaking Western countries like the United States, UK, or Australia. While broader trends of declining participation in study abroad overall are arguably a barrier in itself, participants interviewed emphasized that it was particularly difficult to market and attract Japanese students to a study abroad programme in East Asia. The lack of interest in such programmes in China or Korea was recognized by some as indicative of a larger and more serious issue. When asked what the main barriers were to achieving regional cooperation, a student from UTokyo mentioned that the big problem was a lack of awareness and interest in the neighbouring countries of China and Korea on the part of the Japanese, which she attributed to *muchi* (ignorance):

> Whenever you go to the university library in South Korea and China they have so many books about Japan. Novels, essays, ... many things. Both written in Japanese and English, so they try to understand from many perspectives. I'd always go to the library in the two countries, and I always found my favourite authors of Japanese books, and so that was very good for me as well. But when I think about Japan how many authors, like Korean authors and Chinese authors can I name? And how many books in Chinese and Korean language do I have access to in the Tokyo University library? So I think this is a 'one-way love' from China and South Korea to the Japanese society.
>
> ...But because we developed first, and we think that we are the first Asian country to attain the successful life, I have a feeling that we have failed to learn about our neighbours in a deep sense. We know their political leaders but it's hard for us to name the other kind of leaders, we know K-Pop, ... but that's it!
>
> So I feel like Japanese people including myself should have more interest in many kinds of things in South Korea and China and I think that's the same for political issues as well; South Korean and Chinese people they know so much ... but for Japanese people we don't know anything. Right? Comfort women,

who are they? Nanjing Massacre, when is it? So like, this gap between Japanese and Chinese and Korean people is very huge and I feel like the Japanese side is 'muchi' (ignorance), including myself. (Student, International Relations and Public Policy Studies, CAMPUS Asia, UTokyo)

An official from the Japanese government expressed a similar sentiment:

I know a lot about the Germans and Europeans, their history, their culture, their everyday life. But, to my shame, I have so little idea about Chinese and Koreans and I must confess, it was, my first time in Korea was about 15 years ago and in Seoul I have to admit what I didn't know, what I had known about Korea was so little. It's really a big shame for me. And more or less the same is true of the Japanese people. (Official, CAMPUS Asia Monitoring, NIAD-QE, Japanese government)

A number of actors discussed how perceptions of Japan's national self and its relationships to other nations in the region were bound up with the country's leading role in modernizing and its subsequent economic development during the twentieth century. This coincided with the development of a national identity imbued with a sense of superiority towards its East Asian neighbours, reflective of Jeremy Breaden's descriptions of Japan's self-perception as being 'ahead and above' the rest of Asia (Breaden 2018).

While the twenty-first century has witnessed Japan experiencing prolonged economic stagnation and a range of societal challenges that pose obstacles for recovery, according to a number of actors, the (now mistaken) view that Japan is 'Number 1' in Asia has persisted, posing a number of challenges in itself:

The reason why we'd like to promote CAMPUS Asia, one of the biggest reasons, is we say that China or Korea has a very big dynamism [sic], and I should say that Japan, or Japanese universities – we have to catch up with their activities in many cases. Once Japanese or Tokyo Tech students visit KAIST or Tsinghua or Korea or China, they will be so surprised. Because students believe that Japan is the best, the highest, and the most international situation or something ... the answer is no. Once they go over there, they are so surprised to see it. (Academic, Engineering, CAMPUS Asia, Tokyo Institute of Technology)

Lack of awareness, ignorance and a misplaced sense of superiority on the part of Japanese people were described by a number of actors as reasons both for the lack of popularity of East Asian study abroad opportunities and for difficulties in attaining successful regional cooperation.

Other barriers discussed by participants included xenophobic forms of nationalism (prevalent in all three countries), biased portrayals of regional 'others' in the media and through formalized schooling as well as a range of institutional barriers inherent to the organizational culture of Japanese universities that impeded regional cooperation and efforts towards internationalization more broadly. These included a perceived insecurity imposed by funding constraints, a culture of risk avoidance among higher education administrators, a lack of vision for internationalization and the dominance of an atmosphere of competition both within universities and across the sector.

Repurposing of Government-Level Ideas

The need for funding was often given as a reason for university stakeholders to apply for the CAMPUS Asia and A3 Foresight programmes, which entailed framing the ideas actors had about regional cooperation in terms that would be met with approval by the government. One such term was the government-level idea of 'global human resources' which was frequently adopted but then reinterpreted by actors at Japanese universities. Participants at times admitted outright to using certain terms simply because they felt it was a necessary step to be awarded programme funding from the Ministry of Education:

> Well 'human resources', personally I don't like the [term] human resources, the manager's view – it's one of the resources; financial resources, natural resources, human resources … but I have to use it because it's in the application [*laughs*]. But anyway, the idea is that human resources that can lead not only in terms of employability in the private companies or government but also in the community, who can lead the sustainable development in the community. (Academic, Sustainable Development, CAMPUS Asia, Okayama University)

Another academic understood the government-level emphasis on human resources, competitiveness and quality assurance as an infusion of an economic orientation into the notion of regional cooperation, a view he described differed from his university's vision:

> I think it really depends on how we can define the term quality, or maybe competitiveness. If the government used that term only from the perspective of efficiency, or kind of the economic benefit or something like that, this is not our goal. We really want to interpret the term 'quality' or 'competitiveness' in a much broader sense. So if we are very successful in producing human-oriented practitioners who contribute to world peace, maybe social innovation all over

the world, I think it might be a different quality that the government wants but this is a kind of quality and competitiveness from our point of view that we really want to pursue. (Academic, Political Science and Economics, CAMPUS Asia, Waseda University)

The capacity of university actors to adapt and repurpose government-level ideas is illustrative of their agentic power, and it highlights how the policy process continues to evolve through the phase of implementation (and again through consumption and evaluation). But this agentic power clearly had its limits. It was expressed by many that running the exchange programmes and research projects would not be possible without funding from the government. These financial constraints entailed not only the adoption of 'knowledge discourse' terminology in CAMPUS Asia funding applications, but also a shift towards applied scientific projects (as opposed to basic research) in the A3 Foresight programme, described as necessary to satisfy the government's desire for applicable knowledge and innovation.

Discussion and Conclusion

Japan has experienced an evolving relationship with surrounding Asia that has shifted rapidly from aid to trade, to seeing the region as both a valuable resource for human capital and economic development and a collection of burgeoning economic rivals (Breaden 2018). Today, Japan and Japanese universities must reckon with interconnected developments in the global higher education landscape dominated in many respects by the neoliberal project, as well as their new roles in a rising Asia. Many in Japan have grasped this emerging reality and have become active participants in shaping a new vision for the country and its engagement with the region. Actors in government have recognized that endless disputes with important neighbouring economies are unsustainable and have worked in recent years to regionally integrate activities across a wide range of sectors. Education and scientific knowledge production are two of these important arenas, as policymakers have committed to cultivate the next generation of leaders and innovators who have developed positive networked relationships with counterparts in neighbouring countries.

Actors at Japanese universities involved in policy implementation on the ground had a range of their own ideas of regional cooperation, and frequently adapted the government-level 'knowledge discourse' to align with their own institutional, disciplinary and individual agendas. The finding of the resistance to and repurposing of certain government-level ideas echoes claims made by Jeremey Breaden, who described how CAMPUS Asia projects represent an 'ongoing negotiation of diverse, multi-tiered interests' and provide a 'convenient framework through which to actualise agendas unconnected to its stated goals of regional integration' (Breaden 2018: 51).

The stark distinctions in the policy ideas of regional cooperation across academic disciplines are suggestive of deeper, foundational beliefs that are shared by particular academic communities (Becher and Trowler 2001). Variation in ideas about higher education regional cooperation connected to the distinctive underlying philosophies of different academic disciplines, with STEM fields typically focused on 'borderless' knowledge production and competitiveness, the arts on cultural connections and creative collaboration, and social sciences on communicative action for the resolution of regional problems. Based on these findings, I argue that in order to fully conceptualize regionalism in the higher education policy sector, it is essential to engage the ideas of actors operating in various academic disciplines at universities.

While a number of the ideas of actors at Japanese universities varied across institutions, disciplines and role-types, many were commonly shared. One such idea was that through higher education regional cooperation young people can discover the means to solve the problems that current leaders cannot, and they can work together towards the achievement of collective regional goals. Many at universities in Japan – academics, administrators and students – expressed this ideational vision and were committed to realizing concrete changes in Japan's relations with its neighbours in their lifetimes.

The above ideas and the many others shared by participants in this study point to the nuanced complexity of the ideational dimension of regional cooperation in Japanese higher education and highlight how merely investigating the functional, organizational and political dimensions of regional cooperation is insufficient. Higher education regional cooperation in Northeast Asia from the perspective of Japan is a multifaceted endeavour that is bound up with the nation's political, economic and sociocultural engagement with the region spanning millennia, with modern historical developments in particular contributing to a complex range of challenges, tensions and opportunities. This study has highlighted some of the important ideas giving shape to this ongoing and dynamic process at Japanese universities.

7

Internationalization of Chinese Humanities and Social Sciences

Xin Xu

Introduction

The landscape of global research has shifted drastically over the past decades. Rising powerhouses from East Asia are challenging the previously dominant positions of Anglo-European systems. China is one noticeable example. From 1991 to 2017, China's national R&D expenditure has increased approximately thirty-fold, from USD13 billion to USD445 billion (OECD 2020). In 1986–8, China shared 0.7 per cent of the world science and engineering publications. The predominant producers in that period were the United States (38.2 per cent worldwide share), UK (8.1 per cent) and Japan (7.1 per cent) (US National Science Foundation 2020). Since 2000, China's science and engineering publications have increased nearly ten-fold. China now shares 21 per cent of global science publications, ranking first globally in total number. Comparatively, the United States now shares 17 per cent of global science publications, followed by India (around 5 per cent), and Germany, Japan, UK with around 4 per cent worldwide share of science publications (US National Science Foundation 2020).

China's rise in global science was powered by its extensive internationalization of higher education and research, the depoliticization of science and the expansion of open networks in global science (Marginson 2018). Nonetheless, such global-national synergy (Marginson 2018) did not happen to the same extent in humanities and social sciences. Chinese humanities and social sciences research, while gradually demonstrating global visibility, is still not as noticeable as the sciences disciplines. Here 'Chinese humanities and social sciences research' refers to research hosted in mainland China, not that conducted in 'Greater China' or by Chinese diaspora researchers. The social sciences publications from

China only account for 1.04 per cent of its international publications, in contrast to the high-performing science disciplines such as engineering (25.47 per cent of its international publications) (US National Science Foundation 2020).

To internationalize humanities and social sciences research is more complex than science research. In China, higher education and research sit in a convergence of heterogeneous and at points conflicting influences: imperial governance style with its emphasis on stability and unity, Sinic tradition and particularly Confucianism, Marxism-Leninism and 'socialism with Chinese characteristics', Western cultures imported by colonization and diffused through globalization. In China, science and engineering research has been delinked from – although not completely – the epistemological, cultural, ideological and political tensions created by the swirl of different influences. However, humanities and social sciences research is so culturally embedded and ideologically attached, that it can hardly escape from the tensions between endogenous knowledge, national agenda, political correctness and Western imprints (Gao and Zheng 2018; Xu 2021b; Yang, Xie and Wen 2019).

Nonetheless, this does not mean Chinese academics, universities and government do not have the agency to shape their own agenda. Departing from this point, this chapter investigates tensions in the internationalization of Chinese humanities and social sciences through an exploration of the relationship between agency and context. It first synthesizes the theoretical underpinning of 'contextual agency' based on both Chinese and English scholarships, which testifies the viability of approaching epistemic diversity in research and the value of cross-cultural dialogues (Xu 2021a). The chapter then reports findings drawing on three sets of empirical data, including national policies, institutional policies as well as interviews with academics, senior university administrators and journal editors in China.

A Framework of Contextual Agency

Discussions on 'agency' are widespread in philosophy, sociology, psychology, (political) economy and in educational studies. Each discipline approaches and articulates the concept slightly differently, but a common understanding of agency is *the capacity to take independent actions on one's free will*. Both individuals and the collective of individuals have agency. In the higher education and research context, this means students, students' families, academics, administrators, leadership, universities, industrial partners, local and national governments, international organizations, the invisible global college of academics (Wagner 2009) as well as other agents all have the agency.

A long-standing debate about the concept of agency is its relationship with the structure. 'Structure' can also be understood as 'context', 'environment' and 'system', with nuances across the terms. The structure can be social, temporal, spatial, relational and material. There are, as will be elaborated later, two different ontological understandings of agents and structure: agents and structure as separated or agents and structure as holistic. Both strands of discussions are evident in Anglo-European discourses that are rooted in the Anglo-European ontologies of the world. Nonetheless, there are also discussions in the non-Anglo-European scholarship, which is often termed as 'Southern', 'alternative', 'subaltern' or 'other' knowledge. This chapter intentionally avoids those labels, as all terms are too simplistic and derived from the 'Northern' gaze, again re-asserting the 'Northern' supremacy in global knowledge. Such scholarships often stay in their discourse circle and are not fully acknowledged in a wider knowledge pool. In the global academic space dominated by Anglo-European cultures, some other cultures often become less visible.

As just argued, academics have the agency to shape the scholarship. This chapter thereby brings in discourses rooted in the Chinese tradition, synthesized with the Anglo-European discussion, to present a broader understanding of the contextual agency. In doing so, it joins the growing body of scholarship that calls for epistemic justice and aims to pluralize global knowledge (e.g. Chen 2010; Connell 2007; Santos 2014; Tlostanova and Mignolo 2012).

Agents and Structure as Separated

In the understanding of agents and structure as separate entities, the structure is external to the agents. In Anglo-European discourses, this externalization may be traced back to the Judeo-Christian tradition (Chen and Bu 2019): Adam and Eve exhibited free will, only resulting in the expulsion from Eden and the Fall. In the development of modern sciences, particularly in subjects like biology, nature is further examined as an external biophysical object to human beings. The dichotomy of human and nature in the material sense extends to the dualism of agents and structure in social terms, where social structure is closely linked with material and resources.

When agents and structure are separated, they are often perceived as confrontational. One approach views agents as having agency *but are conditioned, embedded, framed and contextualized* by the structure. For instance, the concept of 'bounded agency' (Evans 2007: 92) 'sees actors as having a past and imagined future possibilities, which guide and shape actions in the present'. The bounded agency is socially situated, 'influenced but not determined by environments and emphasizing internalised frames of reference as well as external actions' (93). In this understanding, the context provides resources, opportunities, but also creates demands, threats and constraints on agents. The level of agency sits on a continuum, which ranges from reacting to the context, to adapting to the environment and to modifying the context the agents are situated in (Fumasoli and Huisman 2013). However, the context is omnipresent and remains the precondition.

Discussion on the bounded agency also appears in traditional Chinese philosophy. Confucian philosopher Mengzi asserted the role of self-cultivation, while emphasizing the essential influences of the context: 'In years of good harvest, young men are mostly lazy; in years of famine, young men are mostly violent. Not they were born with different characters, it is what drowns their heart and mind that leads to this consequence.'[1] The Chinese idioms *mou shi zai ren, cheng shi zai tian* (谋事在人，成事在天, 'Man proposes, God disposes') and *ting tian you ming* (听天由命, 'follow heaven['s mandate] and resign to the fate') express the similar sentiments. Note that both phrases emphasize *tian* (天) as the ultimate context. Although *tian* is translated as 'Heaven' or 'God' here, it is not a Christian or solely religious concept. The use of these terms in translation is due to a lack of equivalent concepts in English.

Tian (天) is an important concept in Chinese tradition with different layers of meanings. It is spatial, temporal and immaterial (Chen and Bu 2019; Zhao 2016). In the spatial and material sense, it means the sky, nature, the non-human world and the universe (e.g. *tian xia*, 天下, 'all under the sky or heaven'). In the temporal sense, it is associated with the rhythm of the world (e.g. *tian shi*, 天时, 'season, time, and timeliness'). In the immaterial sense, it can refer to the almighty power that rules the world, or the ritual controller of one's destiny (e.g. *tian ming*, 天命, 'God's will'), or the emperor's mandate in imperial times (e.g. *tian zi*, 天子, literal translation as 'God's son', which refers to the 'emperor'). In Chinese tradition, *tian* is the ultimate and overarching 'context' for human agents, which will appear again in the discussion that follows.

---

[1] 富岁子弟多赖，凶岁子弟多暴，非天之降才尔殊也，其所以陷溺其心者然也。(*Fu sui zi di duo lan, xiong sui zi di duo bao, fei tian zhi jiang cai er shu ye, qi suo yi xian ni qi xin zhe ran ye.*)

Another approach views agents as having agency *despite the condition, embeddedness, framing and contextualization* in the context. This approach understands agents as in the context, but able to transcend the constraints. In this understanding, the capability of agents is important, as capability is 'a kind of freedom: the substantive freedom to achieve alternative functioning combinations (or, less formally put, the freedom to achieve various life-styles)' (Sen 1999a: 75). The idea that humans can control, surpass or overcome the context is not unique in occidental tradition; similar ideas can also be found in the Chinese tradition, in phrases like *ren ding sheng tian* (人定胜天, 'humans can triumph the heaven'). Agency can be asserted via self-cultivation for self-transformation. For instance, Chinese philosopher Xunzi argued for a division between *tian* and *ren* (人, 'human'). He perceived human nature as evil by default. However, he thought humans can exert moral agency, as their mind/heart (*xin*, 心) can control the inborn human nature and decide the actions of a person: 'The mind/heart is the ruler of the body and master of its spirit. It gives commands but it is not subject to any command' (Xunzi, 21.9, translation cited from Jiang 2012: 101).

Agents and Context as Holistic

Agents and context can also be considered integral to each other. The Chinese concept *tian ren he yi* (天人合一, 'the unity of heaven and humanity') is an important concept here. It connotes a holistic anthropocosmic vision, that 'human beings are an integral part of the cosmos, which is characterised as consanguinity with heaven, earth, and myriad other aspects of nature' (Chen and Bu 2019: 1131). Although the idea of *tian ren he yi* can be interpreted as the coexistence of human and nature, its connotation is broader than the environmentalist appeal (Gao 1995). The dichotomy between agents and structure diminishes through the lens of *tian ren he yi*, as the whole world and human society are perceived as an organic and all-inclusive entity. There are various expressions about *tian ren he yi* in Chinese tradition, famously represented by Daoist Zhuangzi. Zhuangzi thinks that everything material and immaterial, including human agents, nature, environment and all creatures, coexist as one entity.[2] In this harmonious entity, agents and context work together in a balanced and mutually enriching way. 'Neither heaven nor the human defeats each other' (天与人不相胜也, *tian yu ren bu xiang sheng ye*),

---

[2] 天地与我并生，万物与我为一。(*Tian di yu wo bing sheng, wan wu yu wo wei yi.*)

said Zhuangzi. Chinese philosopher Qian Mu (1990) concluded in his final piece that the philosophy of '*tian ren he yi*' is the biggest contribution Chinese culture brings to humankind.

In the Anglo-European discourses, one cluster of arguments emphasizes the transferability, interconnectivity and interdependency between agents and structure, an idea similar but not exactly equivalent to *tian ren he yi*. For instance, in Anthony Giddens' (1984) cycle of structuration, agents and structure interact and transform each other, forming a continuous loop of changes enabled by the reflexive monitoring of agents. Coleman (1994) argued that the macro (structure) changes could interact with the micro (agents) and could in turn lead to agents' revolution of the structure. In those discourses, agents and structure are not completely separated and are attributed with equal significance, yet they do not form a holistic entity as in the idea of *tian ren he yi*.

Contextual Agency in Higher Education and a 'Glonacal' Framework

Among the different understandings of agents and structure, this chapter adopts a holistic view that agency and structure can coexist within the same entity – a *tian ren he yi* approach. It posits that agency needs to be understood as *contextual* (in relation to context) and not isolated; while at the same time, agency is not necessarily *contextualized* (embedded in the context). To operationalize this perspective in analysing higher education, this chapter builds on the 'glonacal' (global-national-local) agency heuristic (Marginson and Rhoades 2002), which also highlights agency as contextual but not fully contextualized.

The 'glonacal' (Marginson and Rhoades 2002) understanding of higher education moved beyond the organizational theory model. The latter positions universities as strategic actors but passively *embedded* in multilayered and multidimensional spaces (e.g. Fumasoli and Huisman 2013; Ma and Cai 2021). In the 'glonacal' agency heuristic, agency simultaneously exists in global, national and local scales. Agents and the structure are also interchangeable – the national, for instance, can be both the agent and the context to influence the institutional and individual. Scales are not mutually exclusive. Relations between scales are open to multiple intersections, and the direction of interactions do not confine to a hierarchical order of global-national-local (Marginson 2021; Marginson and Rhoades 2002).

Building on the 'glonacal' perspective, this chapter views higher education and research as encompassing global, regional, national, institutional and individual scales. The regional scale is added to reflect the importance of regional cooperation, which is in 'global' but not entirely global. The local scale is separated as institutional and individual, for the purpose of examining their interactions in a clearer sense. Agency is embodied in different agents at each of these scales: namely, the internationally influential science structure (e.g. citation indices and publishing industry), autonomous academic communities and transnational organizations or research groups at the global scale; regional collaboration platforms or initiatives at the regional scale; national policy and funding structure at the national scale; universities and research institutions at the institutional scale; academics and research students at the individual scale.

Zooming into the examination on Chinese humanities and social sciences, this chapter focuses on the global, national, institutional and individual scales. 'Regional' is left out as no regional framework in (East) Asia is hugely impactful to China (see Chapter 1 of this book). If examining Southeast Asian or European contexts where regional cooperation is influential, or African or Latin American contexts where a common regional identity is strong, it will be essential to include the 'regional' scale.

Methodology

This chapter draws on data collected for a larger-scale study on the impacts of incentivizing international publications in Chinese humanities and social sciences (Xu 2018), and a subsequent analysis of the national policy trajectory of internationalizing humanities and social sciences (Xu 2021b). The analysis for this chapter is based on three data sets: seventy-five interviews with academics, editors and senior university administrators in China; 172 university policy documents; and a corpus of national policy documents published between the 1960s and 2020.

Interviews were conducted at six case universities selected from the '985' and '211' programmes. The '985' and '211' programmes were national world-class university (WCU) initiatives between the 1990s and 2010s in China, which included a selected number of top-performing research-intensive universities. Three case universities were formerly '985' universities (currently 'Double First-Class Universities') and three '211' universities (currently

'Universities with Double First-Class Disciplines'). Three were humanities and social sciences-oriented and three stronger in science disciplines. The universities are located in northern China (labelled as Uni-NA and Uni-NB), eastern China (Uni-EA and Uni-EB), western China (Uni-W) and central China (Uni-C).

Humanities and social sciences academic interviewees were selected through a purposive, criterion-based sampling strategy, aiming for variation and balance across their disciplines, institutional affiliations, career stages, leadership roles, international experiences and publication records. Interviewees also included six senior administrators with policy-making experiences on humanities and social sciences research at each case university, and four Chinese editors from journals indexed by Social Sciences Citation Index (SSCI), Arts and Humanities Citation Index (A&HCI) and Chinese Social Sciences Citation Index (CSSCI). Interviews were conducted in Chinese and during September 2016 and May 2017. Seventy-one interviews were audio-recorded; note-taking was used for the other four, all upon participants' consent. The research was approved by the author's university's ethics committee and was conducted with full ethical considerations.

Institutional incentive documents were first collected via online search in the official websites of each '985' and '211' universities between March and May 2016. An additional twenty-three incentive documents were collected during fieldwork in China between September 2016 and May 2017. National policy documents were collected between 2015 and 2020 from the websites or archival databases of national government offices in China. Policy documents also included high-profile speeches of China's national leaders, which were documented on governmental websites, in books or covered by the Xinhua News Agency, the official state-run press agency of China. The collected national policies were published between the 1960s and 2020.

Interview transcripts and policy documents were analysed with NVivo. All analysis started from open coding to generate major themes, and then moved to clustering, comparing and finally building connections and categorizations (Saldaña 2013). This chapter quotes Chinese phrases that were used by interviewees or appeared in policies that are important. Chinese phrases are either translated or cited in the pinyin form, supplemented with Chinese characters and English translations. The translation was validated with the back-translation strategy, with references to English-medium government websites, press releases and academic publications.

Dynamics of Internationalizing Humanities and Social Sciences in China

Global Scale

Global humanities and social sciences are open and expanding spaces, but the rate of international collaborations is growing at a slower rate and smaller scale as compared to sciences (Larivière, Gingras and Archambault 2006). This is due to the single-author publishing habits in humanities and social sciences, and to various linguistic, cultural, epistemological, structural challenges in humanities and social sciences international collaborations (Weidemann 2010). Notably, Western ideas and cultures were diffused worldwide through the Anglo-European dominated neoliberal globalization as a continuing form of globally cultural (neo)colonization. Although global research is increasingly diversified, epistemic diversity is accompanied by epistemic inequity and injustice, particularly in the humanities and social sciences (Xu 2021a). Despite a growing number of humanities and social sciences publications from non-dominating systems, the global space is largely dominated by the hegemonic power of Anglo-European (*Northern* or *Western* in other terms) systems (Connell 2007).

For instance, the 'English imperialism' (Phillipson 1992) persists in global academia. It is more problematic in humanities and social sciences for English to become the lingua franca than in sciences. As humanities and social sciences research is deeply entangled with language and discourses, English dominance leads to the hegemony of Anglophone knowledge – after all, 'language use is closely connected to the rhythms of power' (Held et al. 1999: 346).

Chinese language, despite being spoken by the largest population in the world as the first language, does not feature in international journals, indices and communication spaces. This means that to register and communicate knowledge rooted in Chinese humanities and social sciences, Chinese academics, institutions and government need to express, deliver and communicate in English. Such a process of 'English-cization', often unduly perceived as equivalent to 'internationalization', shows many pitfalls. To name a few: the misrepresentation and misinterpretation of the original Chinese ideas, epistemic injustice towards knowers from China due to their English language proficiency or their identity of being Chinese, and the appropriation of Chinese knowledge towards Anglophone frameworks – an example in this chapter, is the unideal translation of Chinese *tian* as *God* or *Heaven*, which as explained earlier, does not capture its original meaning and undesirably introduces Western religious connotation with the concept.

System wise, the globally influential universities, research centres, publishers, citation indices, editors and scholarly associations are still dominated by Anglo-European systems. The WCU movements took roots in Anglo-European criteria, which not only recycles the unequal hierarchy in global research, but also reinforces the prioritization of science and engineering outputs, rather than humanities and social sciences research (Marginson and Xu 2021). Across interview participants from the six case universities, many observed that humanities and social sciences research is not equally valued as science disciplines, both at their institutions and in Chinese higher education.

Furthermore, in global humanities and social sciences, the research agenda, paradigms, theories and the temporalities of knowledge remain largely shaped by Anglo-European culture and reality, resulting in devastating risks of epistemicide (Alatas 2003; Santos 2014). Knowledge produced by agents from disadvantaged groups risks being wronged, marginalized, ignored or exploited (Dübgen 2020; Santos 2014). The disadvantaged groups are not limited by a single identity, such as nationality; there is a plurality of disadvantages. To name a few, non-white scholars in Anglo-European systems and outside, female scholars, scholars working with endogenous knowledge not widely acknowledged.

As each individual has plural identities (Sen 1999b, 2006); one could face double, triple or even multiple discriminations. For example, a 'Chinese' identity is multilayered, which can be related to Chinese (including the Greater China) nationality, ethnicity, ancestry, family, birth place, diaspora status or ideologies and cultures (Xu 2021a). In global academia, being a 'Chinese' humanities and social sciences academic could trigger possible discriminations based on one's nationality (China, non-Anglo-European); ethnicity or race (Chinese or Asian, non-white); assumed language (Chinese, non-English); assumed religious belief (non-Christianity); assumed ideological and political stance (communism, not capitalist); assumed knowledge (Chinese, non-Anglo-European); or assumed research agenda and paradigm (Chinese reality and tradition, not Anglo-European ones). In the current study, a few interviewees reported discriminatory experiences in international academia. Some experiences were related to the language use, demonstrated by a (self-) perceived deficiency because of their English capability. Some were related to their research agenda and paradigm, which were rejected by international (Western if known) peer reviewers or editors as they were not 'Western' enough. Some involved racial discrimination, when a Chinese interviewee reported that international faculty (from Western countries) at their institution enjoyed more privileges. Other factors, although not directly linked with a 'Chinese' identity, further constitutes the possibility of multiple discrimination. Factors identified in the study include discipline (some more prioritized than others), gender (female academics more disadvantaged than males), educational background (Western education more valued than others), work experiences (previous experiences in Western countries preferred than others) and career stage (early-career academics are more disadvantaged than the seniors).

In general, global academia does not constitute the most favourable context for the development of Chinese humanities and social sciences. However, since agents from China are integral parts of global academia, their agency is not restrained by the global academia. The following sections will further explain the dynamics with the global as well as across national, local and individual scales.

National Scale

At the national scale, humanities and social sciences research in China are conditioned by the dual influence of traditional roots and 'Western' imprints (see the discussion of the 'West' in Chapter 1 of the book). The roots of Chinese humanities and social sciences knowledge can be traced back to as far as Zhou Dynasty (1046–256 BCE, including the Spring and Autumn period and the Warring States period) (Yang, Xie and Wen 2019). Chinese philosophical, political, social and literary traditions originated then, and these were continuously shaped by thoughts like Confucianism, Daoism, Legalism and Buddhism (Tu 1999). But in contemporary China, the institutionalization of humanities and social sciences subjects bears Western imprints. Western ideology, cultures and sociopolitical ideas have been introduced to China through colonization, modernization and internationalization of Chinese humanities and social sciences (Yang, Xie and Wen 2019). As noted, 'the indigenous Chinese traditions have never become a dominant force in modern times, notwithstanding incessant clamours for the indigenisation of the Chinese knowledge system' (Liu 2018: 242).

The Chinese government has been exerting its collective agency to push back against the worldwide neoliberal capitalism agenda as well as the recycling of global hegemonic power into national space. The agency exerted at the national scale closely interacts with agents at global, institutional and individual scales.

In general, humanities and social sciences research has been getting increasing policy attention and funding allocation in China. The government has also been encouraging Chinese universities and academics to 'go out' (*zou chu qu*, 走出去) to broaden their international influence (e.g. National Planning Committee of Philosophy and Social Sciences 2006). Such an approach challenges the hegemony of Anglo-European systems noted earlier; though as the examination of national policies demonstrates, the policies oscillate between internationalization and endogenization. Endogenization is constantly highlighted in national policies, for example, by reminding universities and academics of the 'Chinalization' of humanities and social sciences (e.g. Ministry of Education 2011). As summarized in Xu (2021b), the 'Chinalization' of humanities and social sciences has triple connotations: epistemically, to respect and inherit the historical, cultural and philosophical roots of Chinese traditions; ideologically, to uphold Marxism with Chinese characteristics; and practically, to set agendas grounded in Chinese reality and bring about impacts in contemporary China. The interlinked connotations add indigenous cultural awareness, political sensitivity and pragmatic orientations to Chinese humanities and social sciences research, which makes it impossible to be fully Westernized in its internationalization process.

For global academia, China at the national scale has also proposed the sense of responsibility for humankind and advocated the development of humanities and social sciences with 'the care for humankind' (*guan huai ren lei*, 关怀人类) (Central Committee of the Chinese Communist Party 2017). This concept corresponds to previous policy discourses like 'harmonious world' (*he xie shi jie*, 和谐世界) and 'building a community with a shared future for humankind' (*gou jian ren lei ming yun gong tong ti*, 构建人类命运共同体). The proposed 'community with a shared future for humankind' goes beyond the dichotomy between China and 'the other'. It also moves away from a hegemonic and zero-sum imagination of the world system, and an orientation based on nation-states, to a broader cosmopolitan understanding of 'all under heaven as one family' (*tian xia yi jia*, 天下一家).

Institutional Scale

Chinese universities are influenced by the global landscape and national policies, but exercise their agency in various degrees. In the current study, university policies and interviews with senior administrators demonstrated a clear strategic alignment to the global WCU narratives. For instance, the senior administrator at Uni-W explained: 'We initiated our incentives for humanities and social sciences international publications because we would like to enhance our performance in the ranking of ESI (Essential Science Indicators) and to improve our impacts.' Universities also manifested influences from national policies, where the policy rhetoric on 'going out' appeared repetitively in institutional documents and in fifteen participants' interviews (including senior university administrators). Universities' policies and interviews with senior administrators also demonstrated a close focus on the national funding schemes and their growing emphasis on humanities and social sciences research. Across universities, a certain level of policy borrowing also happened, which was confirmed by senior administrators that they would 'learn from' institutions of similar type when formulating policies.

Institutions, however, were not completely bounded *in* the structure. They showcased different kinds of autonomy to internationalize humanities and social sciences research, working *with* or *beyond* the context. Some universities utilized the funding sources to formulate supportive schemes for the development of humanities and social sciences at their institution. Within each university, different departments also had room for institutional agenda-setting and decision-making. As the senior administrator at Uni-C explained, their university-level policy acted as a 'signal', just like the role national policies are playing for universities, but departments can formulate their own policies based on their own orientations. For instance, the analysis of institutional policy documents revealed a large proportion of universities were actively promoting growth in the number of international publications. Against this backdrop, a few departmental leaders interviewed articulated clear rejections to the quantity-oriented approach, and they highlighted that in research evaluations their departments valued research with good academic quality, strong impacts and genuine contributions to knowledge. Some departments also took the leadership role in establishing and hosting new international journals, and extending international partnerships not only with Western institutions, but with partners sharing similar research and strategic interests. A department at Uni-W had long-term collaborative relationships with Central Asian universities, particularly on issues related to the Silk Road. This was again a sign of national policy's influence (noticeably the national Belt and Road Initiative), but the partnership started before the national policy and showcased bottom-up autonomous features.

Individual Scale

Chinese humanities and social sciences academics (and research students, though they were not interviewed in the current study) are situated in a convergence of influences from the global, national and institutional scales.

In addition to the global influences noted in the earlier section, Chinese academics reported perceiving the national policies, funding structure and institutional evaluative policies (particularly career-related ones) as 'the conductor's baton' (*zhi hui bang*, 指挥棒), guiding and influencing their research and career. But this does not mean academic freedom was denied. Academics could tango with the agenda, particularly when that could lead to a win-win situation. For instance, academics were generally positive about the rising policy attention and funding support for humanities and social sciences research, which provided more resources for their research. In line with the national policy, a large proportion of academics highlighted the importance of international communications and 'going out', while voicing the need to balance it with local contribution and endogenous knowledge. In relation to scholarship, Chinese humanities and social sciences academics rejected the 'self-colonization' (Dang 2005: 68) of Chinese humanities and social sciences. This idea of balancing international and national-local was a consensus among both the academics and national policies, though less so across institutional policies which were more performatively oriented.

But not everyone is following the agenda set by the wider context. Among the twenty-eight academics not in favour of the incentive schemes, half of them had taken an 'adaptive' stance to reconcile or compromise with the policy orientation, while the other half reported a resistant stance. They rejected following the institutional agenda. Some academics stated that despite larger monetary and career-related benefits associated with international publications, they preferred to publish in top domestic journals. Their goals were to gain domestic reputation, generate impacts in the local community and demonstrate their influence in domestic academia. Nine academics reported taking actions to make changes to the institutional policies.

Academics also reported challenging and reshaping the Anglo-European-dominated global academia, with a sense of responsibility for being a member of the global community. They actively contributed to international journals, not only by writing for them but also as reviewers and editors. For instance, one academic in English studies was an editor of a prominent international journal. She said she would never judge if an article was written by native English speakers or not and make decisions based on their language proficiency – as a non-native English speaker, she often felt *'offended'* when seeing native speakers expressing their 'sense of superiority', in review comments like 'as far as I can tell, the paper was written by a *non-native speaker* – please find a *native speaker* to *polish* the language'.[3] Articles and knowledge should be judged based on their originality and contributions, not the language, said the academic. Participants also reported the increasingly active roles Chinese humanities and social sciences academics were playing in international scholarly associations and international collaborations with Western and non-Western academics. Some perceived the invisibility of Chinese humanities and social sciences not as a fixed situation and suggested a developing and forward-looking mindset. They thought that as there was still room and gaps in the global knowledge pool, there would then be opportunities and responsibilities to make more contributions with Chinese knowledge and language.

Conclusion

This chapter unpacks the dynamics of contextual agency at the global, national, institutional and individual scales. As the analysis shows, the internationalization of Chinese humanities and social sciences is not influenced by a single set of factors (such as the national 'going out' strategy) or determined by a single group of agents (such as by universities alone). The global academia, Chinese government, universities, humanities and social sciences academics and editors all play a role in the process. All agents navigate through various contextual conditions and act as contexts to others. The global, national, institutional and individual contexts can be restricting, enabling or restrictively enabling (or the other way around, similar to the idea of a double-edged sword). The same factors can be restricting to some agents, while enabling to others. However, agents work not only *within* the context, but also *with* and *beyond* the context. The un-separatable and inter-transferable features of agents and the context point to the possibility to understand Chinese humanities and social sciences research in a more nuanced way.

The perspective of contextual agency also points to new understandings of institutional autonomy and individual academic freedom, particularly in the

---

[3] Phrases quoted in italics here were expressed in English by the interviewee.

Chinese context. The autonomy and freedom in Chinese higher education and research do not correspond exactly with Western notions. Government, universities and individuals are not necessarily antagonistic towards each other. The institutional autonomy and individual academic freedom lie in not only the power against and freedom from structural constraints, but also the power and freedom to work with and through the context. This may be of interest to future research.

Tensions in the internationalization process, as revealed in this chapter, showcase the intrinsically 'in-between' dilemma of Chinese humanities and social sciences research (Xu 2021b): it swings between internationalization and endogenization, global connection and national agenda, international knowledge and endogenous cultures, epistemological openness and ideological vigilance. The oscillations are ever evolving and never ending. As this study reveals, in national policies, institutional strategies and individuals' activities, finding a balance in-between is a recurring and important theme to all agents. Being in-between may appear chaotic, but it is not being in limbo. Rather than being 'either-or' or 'neither-nor', the in-betweenness is a 'both-and' space that rejects dualistic perceptions. It then creates possibilities and hybridity – just like Schrödinger's cat that is both alive and dead, and like the '*zhong yong*' (中庸, 'the Golden Mean') philosophy in Chinese tradition where being in-between is most desirable.

The in-betweenness explains the ambivalence and some seemingly self-conflicting dilemmas, such as why Chinese humanities and social sciences can appear both open and closed, both free and restricted. Existing scholarships on Chinese humanities and social sciences research have depicted tensions in its development and internationalization (e.g. Gao and Zheng 2018; Hayhoe 1993; Liu 2018; Yang et al. 2019), but the in-betweenness as a whole had not been fully grasped. The paradoxical positioning may seem problematic to research grounded in non-Chinese (often Anglo-European) perspectives, or to those used to a 'black-or-white' binary thinking mode. Nonetheless, it offers a nuanced framework to comprehend the complexity of Chinese higher education and research, and it proves that local reality and subtlety can be examined from local perspectives and explained with local discourses, rather than appropriated to Anglo-European frameworks. Together with the attempt to diversify the understandings of 'contextual agency' by engaging with Chinese and English scholarships, the concept of 'in-betweenness' again highlights the importance of endogenous epistemologies and the value of pluralized knowledge.

Acknowledgements

The research leading to this work was supported by the Economic and Social Research Council (Grant number: ES/T006153/1); Clarendon Fund, University of Oxford; Santander Academic Travel Award, University of Oxford; Research Grant, Universities' China Committee in London. The author would like to thank Professor Alis Oancea, Dr Heath Rose and Professor Hubert Ertl for their invaluable support for the research project this chapter draws on.

8

Internationalization of Higher Education in Taiwan

Julie Chia-Yi Lin

Introduction

Internationalization of higher education has caused significant changes to the Taiwanese higher education system, from the specific talents that it cultivates to the core concept of higher education. To some, internationalization is a means to attain global recognition and to enhance national competitiveness in East Asia (Lo and Hou 2020; Chan and Lo 2008; Shin and Harman 2009; Mok and Yu 2013). States have engaged in a series of construction projects designed to enhance the international competitiveness of their higher education sectors. This happened in Taiwanese higher education in the early 2000s when national higher education funding projects were launched with a 'heavy emphasis on internationalisation' (Song and Tai 2007: 324). Governmental funding policies aimed at building internationalization soon followed, demonstrating Taiwan's enthusiasm to take a larger, more active role in an interconnected world.

There is a strong interrelation between sociopolitical changes and higher education reforms in Taiwan, as noted by Mok (2002) and Lin and Yang (2019). At times, these changes seem to be the primary driving factor behind the internationalization process (Law 1996; Weng 1999; Mok 2002). Papers discussing the development of internationalization in Taiwan have largely focused on governmental policies and programmes. While these are crucial to understanding internationalization in Taiwan, this near exclusive focus on the role that government has played excludes other major drivers of the process, resulting in an incomplete understanding of how Taiwan has positioned its higher education systems towards the goal of deeper international connections and competitiveness. Marginson and Rhoades (2002) argued that the literature on internationalization has not 'adequately address[ed] the local dimension' (286). Their 'glonacal agency heuristic' proposed that in order to fully understand all perspectives in the internationalization of higher education, one must consider the significance of global, national and, of course, local dimensions. Too few studies of internationalization in Taiwan have presented the institutional – that is, local – perspective on internationalization.

There were rapid and unexpected global changes in 2020. It is apparent in the interviews reported in this chapter that responses to the Covid-19 pandemic have had a large impact on Taiwanese institutions' capacity for internationalization. Restrictions on international travel and new measures limiting campus entry both created barriers to international participation and recruitment. Despite this, Taiwanese universities have developed a number of means to counteract the stifling effect of the virus and the various national responses to it. Innovations have included opening up Taiwanese university facilities to students from foreign universities, setting up virtual courses for incoming exchange students who are unable to travel to Taiwan and ensuring that students who are unable to re-enter their home countries have access to the same student activities available to Taiwanese students. These changes, each of which was made through individual institutional policy rather than through government decree, have had a net positive effect on Taiwan's overall ability to internationalize.

This chapter examines recent higher education internationalization developments in Taiwan and presents an array of Taiwanese universities' perspectives on their individual strategies in order to supplement the available research done from national policy and geopolitical angles. It also notes how discussions on the 'national identity' in Taiwan are affecting higher education. Interviews were conducted with deans, heads, and vice presidents of international affairs from five different Taiwanese universities. Interviewees explained their university's internationalization strategies, and their responses to the Covid-19 crisis, and considered the impact of the sociopolitical climate regarding national identity.

The Changing Environment of Internationalization

Developments in Higher Education Policy

As in other East Asian states, in the past two decades the internationalization of higher education in Taiwan was accelerated by government policies. It was also shaped within the larger evolution of the higher education system, which was again government led.

Taiwan's higher education system experienced substantial changes in the past half century. After the adoption of democratic governance in the 1990s, Taiwan moved from the fully government-controlled system of the 1980s to the current democratic system. The best documented reforms in Taiwanese education occurred during the 1990s, with a series of changes led by the Ministry of Education (MOE). This is often referred to as 'The Democratisation' (Law 2002). From 1993 on, the inclusion of more Taiwan-based content in textbooks brought a clear shift from the early Kuomintang (KMT) government era where the 'Republic of China identity' was the only perspective allowed in schools. In 1995, the University Law was amended and higher education institutes were granted more autonomy including the power to elect their own leaders. The MOE also reduced its funding of national universities to 80 per cent, asking higher education institutions to fund the remaining 20 per cent. This was widely considered to be an advanced move, especially among Asian governments which have a reputation for keeping strict controls over their schools. This movement, combined with the inclusion of local languages in the curriculum, was described by some as 'Taiwanization', '[a] democratic education movement [that] creates "space" for local identities, issues, and characteristics that ha[ve] been suppressed in the past' (Law 2002: 72). However, Mok argues that these changes led Taiwan to a 'state supervision model' (2002: 151) without dispensing with all state-led governance. The elected university or college presidents still required approval from the MOE before their appointment was formalized. Furthermore, the funding reduction was not aimed to lessen university dependence on the MOE, but was related more to fostering marketization.

Internationalization first became known to the broader Taiwanese society in the mid-2000s when the government launched the Aim for the Top University Program (ATUP) project in 2006. The project and its funding caught the public's attention and showed the government's determination to internationalize Taiwan's higher education. ATUP focused on two goals: advancing Taiwanese universities into the World University Ranking top 100, and founding research centres in crucial fields. ATUP ended in 2016, having distributed a total of USD1.6 billion to twelve universities and thirty-four research centres.

The ranking-centred goal of ATUP received wide criticism from the public, the media and the academic world. Besides the possibility that the funding's focus on ranking would further enlarge the stratification between leading comprehensive universities and smaller, private universities, people were also concerned that the vanity involved in chasing ranking/status improvement could become obstacles to higher education's ability to explore more important improvements, such as teaching quality and admissions equity. The government was criticized for 'committing too many public resources on international research excellence and for caring too little about local development' (Yang 2019: 17). Scholars also raised concerns that the pursuit of world university rankings would promote elitism (Hou et al. 2020: 9), and that because the rankings are 'often funded by Western standards and systems' (Shreeve 2020: 922), measures to pursue them might not fit Taiwan's needs.

At the end of the ATUP programme period, the MOE reported that seven universities had been included in the Academic Ranking of World Universities (ARWU) top 500 universities, and eleven of the twelve funded universities were included in the QS World University Ranking's top 500 in 2015, including National Taiwan University which was ranked seventy. The MOE therefore concluded that the project had shown achievement (MOE n.d.). Fu, Baker and Zhang (2020) found that between 2006 and 2010, non-funded institutions saw increases in their publications, showing that the whole system experienced improvement, and growth was not limited to funded institutions alone.

When the Democratic Progressive Party (DPP) took office in 2017, ATUP was replaced by a new national higher education project. The Tsai administration launched an all-inclusive project in 2018 called Sustained Progress and Rise of Universities in Taiwan, also known as the Higher Education Sprout Project or SPROUT. Its main objectives were to 'enhance the quality of universities and encourag[e] its multifaceted development' and to 'elevate international competitiveness and to build leading research centers' (MOE 2019). Endowed with $86.85 billion dollars (NTD) over four years, SPROUT continues to fund research centres, but has broadened its scope for improving university quality.

SPROUT defines university quality in four sections: (1) university features, (2) social responsibility, (3) teaching, and (4) transparency. University social responsibility is a new criterion in the development of higher education in Taiwan. Internationalization is listed under university features. Teaching is an individual section, broadening the emphasis in higher education institutional development from research alone. Transparency, or 'making resources more public' (MOE 2019), focuses on self-evaluation, publication and information sharing, as well as admission for less-advantaged students. After the first selection cycle, seventy-five universities, eighty-five universities of technology and junior colleges, and sixty-five research centres received SPROUT funding, and four comprehensive universities were granted whole-school programme funding.

In the transition from ATUP to SPROUT, policies for development grew more detailed with finer divisions for budget items. One of the main criticisms of ATUP had been its quantity-led focus. When higher education is simplified down to numerical indicators on world university rankings and citation indices, there is a risk of creating surface growth with no actual cultivation of students, researchers or the institution itself. SPROUT set out to build real-world connections by stressing spheres of university social responsibility and strengthening university-industry cooperation. With an emphasis on teaching, and a core mission to 'secure students' equal right to education' (MOE 2019), it demonstrated a stronger concentration on talent cultivation at home.

By addressing local needs, SPROUT attempts to fill the gap created by global competition motives that ignore the social dimension. Having moved from funding a few comprehensive, research-intensive universities, to evaluating universities, universities of technology and junior colleges within one programme, the new SPROUT approach has been described as 'egalitarianism' (Hou et al. 2020). Moving away from the ranking mindset can also be read as steering away from elitism in higher education (Lo and Hou 2020). The introduction of university social responsibility has also funded many who have deep engagement with their local communities, further combining the higher education sector with broader society. Lo and Hou (2020) pointed out that the policy shift aims to 'enhance the publicness of higher education' (503) and with the number of selected universities expanding from 12 to 158, 'all types of higher education providers are eligible for the government funding grants' (Hou et al. 2020: 6). Compared to ATUP's heavy emphasis on world rankings, SPROUT applied strategic planning 'to stop the move towards homogeneity and promote diversity' (Lo and Hou 2020: 500). It has shifted towards encouraging diversified development and is intended to cultivate uniqueness in higher education institutions. In the past, research from science, technology, engineering and medical science (STEM) fields received more financial support, leading to criticism that the policy directs all universities towards becoming research-intensive, comprehensive institutions (Hsueh 2018). SPROUT is aimed differently, and supports exploration and the development of each university's own specialties. For example, in an interview, an officer from the MOE encouraged private universities and colleges to establish research centres for social sciences or humanities (The Central News Agency 2018).

Despite these changes, there are concerns about the new national projects among both the public and scholars. President Tang from Chinese Medical University called for the list of evaluation committee members to be published (Wu 2020). However, no information regarding committee members, the quantitative and qualitative evaluation indicators, or the comparisons made between institutions was released. Announced information included only the funding distributed and the names of the schools who received it. Some have also noticed a re-emergence of government control. To better supervise universities, the government often increases quantitative and qualitative key performance indicators for projects, and it publishes increasingly detailed constraints and budgetary requirements (Fu and Chin 2020: 3). These more detailed budgetary items which gave the government greater capacity to monitor higher education institutions raised a heated discussion about academic autonomy. In 2018, the MOE rejected the appointment of a new president of National Taiwan University. The government-supervision model nominated by Mok in 2002 has become quite relevant in this new government-academic context.

Societal and Identity Changes, and Their Influence on Higher Education

The overall policy shift from ATUP to SPROUT reflects intensified local focus and can help Taiwanese identity building. This reflects broader changes in Taiwanese society.

From the democratization of the 1990s to internationalization projects of the 2000s, national identity has remained a core value for Taiwanese higher education. Different policy foci have been introduced and shifted to make room for the nation's developing understanding of itself. It is useful to look deeper into the role of national identity in higher education internationalization, how it is defined and how it has influenced internationalization in Taiwan. This has not been sufficiently discussed.

The discussion surrounding national identity often relates back to the definition of a 'nation' or 'nationalism'. For some, a nation is formed by ancestral ties, and the central feature of national identity should be ethnicity or common ancestry. Connor (1994) described a nation as a self-aware ethnic group (see also Dahbour 2002: 19). Anderson (1983) argued differently. While noting that there are some unchangeable factors including ethnicity, he asserts that the decisive elements defining a nation lean toward a mutually recognized consensus or comradeship among a group of people. He famously referred to a nation as an 'imagined community' (1983) and stressed the socially constructed aspect that it carries.

In Taiwan, identity has been a complex issue without one absolute definition. Given the number of nations that have ruled over it, from the Netherlands, to the Qing Dynasty, to Japan, until the current Republic of China, different combinations of cultural identities coexist on the island. The lack of clear identity persists today. Law (2002) noted the struggle:

> 'Taiwan has suffered from a dual identity crisis. At home, Taiwanese people have lacked consensus on their 'national' identity since the KMT's assumption of power. This is reflected by ethnic conflicts over places of origin (Taiwan or the Chinese mainland) and struggles for Taiwan's independence from, or unification with the Chinese mainland'. (Law 2002: 65)

Wu's (1996) research asked interviewees about their support for Taiwanese independence and about reunion with China. He grouped interviewees into three categories: Chinese nationalists, those who supported union with China and denied Taiwanese independence; Taiwanese nationalists, those who supported independence and denied union with China; and practicalists who supported both. He found that Taiwanese nationalists were not firm supporters of nationalism, but showed more support for general separatism and self-determination. Wu interpreted this as meaning that their values were not centred on the nation, but on liberty. Identity continued to shift in the 1990s when Taiwan's first presidential election was held. Society started to emphasize commonalities among the Taiwanese people: 'Taiwan[ese] government no longer uses people's differences in the place of origin and time of settlement in Taiwan to maintain the domination of the mainlanders over native Taiwanese' (Law 2002: 75).

The Election Study Center of National Chengchi University has conducted yearly surveys on Chinese/Taiwanese identity recognition since 1992. In 2020, support for Taiwanese identity reached a record high of 67 per cent, while those who identify themselves as both Chinese and Taiwanese dropped to 27.5 per cent. Taiwanese identity supporters first surpassed those who support both identities in 2008. The gap between the two groups widened at an accelerated pace from 2018 through 2020 (Election Study Center, National Chengchi University 2020). Muyard noted that 'a new Taiwanese national identity defined by civic nationalism and multiculturalism has emerged in the past two decades' (2018: 55). Sullivan and Lee (2018) claimed that 'although the 2016 campaigns were fought predominantly on economic issues, national identity remain[ed] the core issue and the major cleavage in Taiwanese politics' (5). This is generally recognized as being true for the Tsai government's second election in 2020.

Education is often used as a tool for government to cultivate belief or consensus in the public (Vikers 2011 cited in Hammond 2016: 555). Hammond looked closer and captured how national identity is applied in higher education. He pointed out that 'the dual policy agendas for national identity formation and HE [higher education] internationalization appear to go hand in hand' (2016: 556) when viewed from an economic standpoint. Law (1996) further narrowed the scope down, claiming that Taiwan sees 'sociopolitical tasks of higher education to be as important as economic considerations' (390).

It is also important to include cultural and philosophical factors in the discussion since Confucian values have deeply influenced Taiwanese society and have a profound effect on the Taiwanese identity (Lin and Yang 2019). In Lin and Yang's research, many interviewees noted that Confucian values were the foundation of their institutions. Highly influential though it is, the researchers also noticed that Confucianism was more of a 'cultural heritage' that remained 'as the way of life' (152) and not an identity-forging tool. Lin and Yang (2019) noted that there has been a recent de-Sinicization trend in Taiwanese higher education, where the '"new" Taiwanese cultural identity' (152) was being fostered and where Chinese cultural factors were downplayed due to the political tension with the People's Republic of China. However, Confucianism is still the main value-set in the education sector. This further demonstrates that Chinese cultural factors do not equal Confucian values in Taiwanese society.

In 2019, a protest broke out in Hong Kong against the government's attempt to amend their Extradition Law. Many in Hong Kong opposed the amendment, concerned that it 'may reduce the city's freedom and autonomy' (Lo 2020). Social movements have strengthened the changing values and identities of both the people in Hong Kong and Taiwanese citizens, bringing the two societies closer together in mutual protest 'against erosion of their democratic rights' (Lai 2020: 7). Members of Taiwan's higher education sector have evidenced their values through their responses to the Hong Kong protests. In November of 2019, universities in Hong Kong closed as a result of the ongoing civil unrest. Seeing this, seven Taiwanese universities offered special visiting student programmes allowing all students attending Hong Kong universities to study in Taiwan instead. The MOE later established a special programme to facilitate students in Hong Kong to transfer into Taiwanese universities for degree programmes. 'The internal consensus was that politics is separated from the rights to education' stated a Taiwanese scholar (Tian 2019). By this bottom-up response, Taiwan's higher education institutions demonstrated their determination to defend the rights to, and the value of, education, a central idea in Confucian thought and a value that transcends political disputes.

Institutional Strategy

Another missing core issue is institutional strategy. Given both executive power and strategy, Taiwan's internationalization of higher education can be more focused and competitive. Without strategy, project execution is scattered and lacks focus (Chiang 2008: 68). The MOE encouraged a more strategic approach and urged schools to establish methods beginning in 2015 (Lee and Fu 2017: 1), but the question remains as to whether or not Taiwanese higher education operates with a fully developed strategic framework at the local level.

Mintzberg (1987) formulated the 5Ps concept in a discussion of strategic theory: Strategy as Plan, Ploy, Pattern, Position and Perspective (11). Plan, Pattern and Position apply better in the higher education context than the other two. Plan is a 'consciously intended course of action' (12); Pattern is an action that repeats, whether intended or not, though both can entail the performance of a strategy; Position is a way to connect the organization to the environment, acting as 'a mediating force' (15). Chiang (2008) also considered strategy to be a map for action (68). Han and Zhong (2015) combined two popular methods for examining university strategy: Balanced Scorecard and Strategy Map Approach, and analysed the top 100 universities in the Times Higher ranking. Their research categorized the Strategy Maps from universities into five categories: Comprehensive, Core, Technical, Service and Special. Based on the premise that higher education institutions are 'non-profit and intelligence-based organisation[s]' (942) and have different priorities than businesses, Han and Zhong concluded that the Strategy Map approach 'can be a tool for improving university management' (949) but had some problems when used for higher education institutions, such as misuse of terms or a full method adoption without differentiation from business institutions.

Since the 2000s, academic publications have seen increased coverage of university strategy according to the Scopus index. In 2015, at least fifteen institutions in the top 100 universities as ranked by the Times Higher Education World University Ranking in 2013–14 have comprehensive Strategy Maps (Han and Zhong 2015). However, strategy has not been a popular topic in Taiwanese literature. Most literature discussing internationalization in East Asia concentrates on national projects and governmental policies, given that there are 'close alignments in Asia between universities' and governmental goals' (Lin and Yang 2019). Chiang (2008) comments that there are only policies, proclamations and activities of internationalization of higher education in Taiwan. Strategy has not been formed (47).

Adopting a strategic internationalization approach can help universities build 'an effective conceptual process ... and maximiz[e] its efficacy and effectiveness to help the university achieve better quality and compete in the global market for favorable standings' (Han and Zhong 2015: 941). With the MOE encouraged the establishment of institutional research offices back in 2015, Hu (2017) also noted that there was an increasing number of research offices being established within higher education institutions that were reporting directly to the president or vice president.

Methodology

To capture the changes in Taiwanese higher education, including internationalization, it is necessary to address policies, laws and state-wide projects. Policy documents, governmental website announcements, news and academic papers all figure in the present study.

In addition, interviews bring in local-level voices from higher education institutions. The study includes five administrative heads of international affairs from different universities – they were drawn from national universities, private universities as well as universities of technology. The national universities were chosen from those which received grants from both ATUP and SPROUT, with a concern for geographical diversity. Only one university of technology and six private universities were included in ATUP, and the funding was aimed at only one research centre in the universities. The selection standard for universities of technology and private universities was different. Invitations were sent out to those with a stronger focus on internationalization, and the first to respond to the invitation was included in the case study.

In sum, three of the universities selected, Universities A, B and C, all are national universities. All three have received funding through both ATUP and SPROUT to encourage internationalization. They are all research-focused, comprehensive universities. University D is a small-scale private university and has a Catholic origin, with internationalization being listed as one of its core developments. University E is a national university of technology with a focus on industrial education.

Administration staff also joined the interview at University B and E, while the head of international office was the only interviewee at Universities A, C and D. Out of the total eight interviewees, five were female and three were male. Out of the five heads of international affairs, three had held their position for a year or less, but all were scholars who had been actively promoting internationalization on campus for a considerable amount of time beforehand. The interviews lasted from thirty to sixty minutes.

The interviews were conducted in a semi-structured format. Questions were mostly centred on two topics: institutional strategy towards internationalization, and whether the growing attention in society towards national identity has influenced higher education institutions and their internationalization processes. The five interviews were conducted between July 2020 and September 2020. In order to understand the universities' internationalization strategies, interviewees were asked three questions derived from Mintzberg's 1987 discussion on the definition of strategy. The first question was designed to ascertain the 'Plan' aspect of strategy, a simple, straightforward question asking them to describe their university's internationalization strategy. Second, the interviewees were asked to provide 'keywords' to describe their institution's strategy, in order to bring out 'Purpose'. The third question asked interviewees what they felt was unique about their institution's experience of internationalization, in order to understand the 'Position' aspect. Following the strategy-related questions, representatives from the institutions were asked about their Covid-19 countermeasures, and about how and responses to it had affected higher education, in general in relation to internationalization and specifically in relation to international cooperation. Lastly, interviewees were asked about the relationship between internationalization of higher education and national identity, and whether the sociopolitical changes since 2019 had impacted on this topic.

Findings

Institutional Strategy

When asked about their internationalization strategy, most interviewees provided answers related to the substantial inter-institutional cooperation or programmes they have been implementing. Their answers were similar. They all addressed strategy according to the definition of 'Pattern': 'consistency in behaviour, whether intended or not' (Mintzberg 1987: 13). University A mentioned that internationalization strategy is always a part of, and operates in order to support, institutional development goals. Of the five schools, only University C had a strategy office within the university management structure. That office leans towards the role of organizer for institutional development, rather than being an internationalization-focused independent entity. University C was also the only university surveyed whose Office of International Affairs website listed 'core values' and used them as a guideline to direct future development so as to mitigate influence from changes in leadership.

None of the interviewees mentioned a more value-based approach, such as 'Perspective' or 'Positioning'. Most sounded as if their current strategy was derived from past actions, matching what Mintzberg called 'Pattern produced Perspective' where the repetition of a series of actions creates an unintended pattern that then forms institutional perspective.

Universities A, B and C all mentioned that the earlier internationalization development during ATUP focused too much on quantifiable elements ('numbers'). Each claimed that though their institution was able to grow bilateral agreements – the number of students sent abroad or the number of foreign students on campus – the actual impact that these 'improved scores' represented was limited. All had turned to valuing the quality of internationalization and investing more into substantial cooperation programmes rather than into easily quantified memorandums of understanding. Universities B, C and E elaborated on detailed double/joint degree programmes. University A provided an example where they co-researched disaster prevention with scholars from more than three countries. This research then led to engineering projects as well as to a co-founded course module.

Students seem to be at the centre of internationalization. All five universities brought up students in their interviews, yet intriguingly their foci were vastly different. University A discussed how they provided local students with administrative internships, allowing them to practice the skills they had learnt, while at the same time facilitating the internationalization of the institution. University B focused on the quality of life and rights of foreign students, but also viewed their alumni as a crucial link in internationalization cooperation. University C emphasized recruitment and how to acquaint foreign students with the culture and campus, maximizing their experience in Taiwan as well as promoting learning, research and potential employment. University D enhanced at-home internationalization. While providing the students with chances for overseas exchange and internships, they also worked on infrastructure and projects on campus to deepen interactions between the local students and exchange students. University E ran many problem-based learning projects and brought students from country to country, studying and prototyping in different labs with in-depth involvement from business enterprises. Naturally, many student activities were consistent from school to school, but the answers indicated differentiation related to aims.

The same finding of broader similarities with specific differences continued into the way the universities described their internationalization goals. Most cited their past activities in support of a general mission statement rather than laying out specific future goals. University A, the one university that had a goal-oriented definition of internationalization, called their internationalization mission 'solving global problems' with partners. University B stated that no one could ultimately know what constituted internationalization, but by implementing internationalization cooperation, projects and programmes, and adjusting them as needed, they have achieved good results. University D had not yet thought about it, but repeating their student-focus, stated that their university would be a platform for interaction and communication between Taiwan and the rest of the world. University E, with its strong industrial connections, stated out that cultivating students, skills and bringing them together with international industry was one of their goals. All of the national universities (A, B and C) stressed their research-intensive status in the internationalization process; but in reference to their past actions, they do not have a definitional understanding of internationalization.

Common difficulties also emerged. Universities C, D and E all found it difficult to support their foreign students, given the strict regulation of post-graduation work visas. Universities C and E pointed out that, with protectionism-based policies, it was hard to recruit foreign talents. Education and work opportunities were not linked up. University D raised the issue of difficulty in launching new degree-granting courses online and recruiting non-degree students who wish to learn Mandarin.

Cross-office communication was a shared difficulty. Universities A, D and E all mentioned cases where anything related to English was seen as a task only the Office of International Affairs should handle. The lack of team support made it difficult to promote internationalization. Much time was wasted on internal negotiations.

Administrators played an interesting though hidden role in internationalization. All five universities mentioned the participation of international administrators during their interview. University A used 'empowerment' as a keyword specifically in reference to empowering administrators and stressed the importance of open communication as well as 'decision support' from the experienced administrators. When empowered, these people would proactively propose better, more on-ground measures in projects. University B noted that policy implementers (i.e. administrators) were every bit as important as leaders, stressing that without capable team members, a lot of the policies would not be realized as speedily. Universities C, D and E agreed that the key to sustainability comes from the administrators. In Taiwan, administrative offices are managed by appointed scholars from different backgrounds, but the history and experience of these offices are often passed down through the administrative staff. Out of the five interviews, two (Universities B and E) had an administrative staff member present during the interview. For Universities A and B, the staff had prepared a summary of meeting materials beforehand.

Covid-19 and National Identity in Higher Education

Covid-19 had brought about changes to the way higher education operates. In Taiwan, universities are responsible for student health, campus security and members' well-being. The MOE published guidelines regarding Covid-19 for higher education institutions on 31 March 2020 in order to regulate the conditions and the countermeasures to be taken (FICHET 2020). Higher education institutions reacted rapidly in the beginning, with many closing their campus to external visitors and requiring all students and faculty members measure their temperatures daily at the building entrances. Lectures with more than a hundred people were either broken into smaller classes or moved online.

Taiwanese universities were also asked to take turns sending representatives to pick up students who were entering Taiwan. The institutions had been deemed responsible for the commute from airport to quarantine accommodations. If universities missed first contact with a student at the airport, they were subject to punishment by the MOE. University B commented that without leadership, especially from the president, who wasn't previously a part of the traditional administrative system, this speed of response would have been nearly impossible. To University D, social media, especially communication software, was central to information sharing. With both the school's leadership and its administrators involved in group chats, implementation and delivery was almost immediate once decisions are made. University A further emphasized that the response and action from experienced administrators had played a crucial role in effectiveness.

The pandemic had prompted innovative internationalization activities even while international mobility declined. University D had launched a series of virtual courses with credits specially for the incoming exchange students unable to travel, ranging from culture and language to basic courses on engineering. University B cooperated with its sister schools, and it enrolled degree students from a list of US universities to study for a year or a semester in Taiwan, acting as their 'temporary boarding school'. This allowed students who could not travel back to their home schools to continue their education without delay. Facilities such as libraries, sport centres and student activities were all open to those temporary degree students as well, providing a full university experience for scholars from around the globe. Through these new forms of cooperation, we see the value that Taiwanese institutions of higher learning place on education beyond national borders. This can be considered another demonstration of the Confucian spirit underpinning Taiwanese society.

The Covid-19 travel ban prevented many Chinese students from returning to Taiwan for their studies. Most flights between China and Taiwan were halted starting in February and were only reopened after October under restrictive terms. Political tensions had also prevented students from travelling across the strait, when Taiwan and China had disagreements over what university titles were appropriate to put on travel documents. The Chinese government objected to the term 'National' being used by Taiwanese universities. China announced in April that it would 'pause degree students' return to Taiwan in 2020' (MOE 2020), and Taiwan waited until August to allow students from China entry to the country.

China is an unavoidable topic when discussing Taiwan's national identity. However, most interviewees did not find that their internationalization had been affected by the vast change in the Taiwanese public's view of its own national identity in recent times. Certain incidents were reported, including visas to travel to China being cancelled at the last minute (University C), publication affiliations altered without notification (Universities A and E) and obstructions to overseas recruitment events (University E), but most international interactions and activities did not see many changes. University C observed that the larger changes came from the pandemic and not political disputes. Universities A and B both believed that education and politics should be separated, but while University A only mentioned this concept in theory, University B called for equal rights of education for Chinese students. This can be interpreted in two, distinct and mutually exclusive ways, either a pro-China mentality that urges better rights for Chinese students in order to draw Taiwan closer to China, or the assumption that China is a separate country, and that by removing special regulations that only apply to Chinese students, these students can be treated as an objective third party like other foreign students. This type of non-committal vagary is a hallmark of Taiwanese politics, though again, both interpretations are in line with Confucian philosophy.

A special case occurred in 2019 when some Taiwanese universities published announcements offering to take students from Hong Kong. When asked about the decision-making process, Universities B and D replied that all parties agreed on the importance of students continuing their studies, and the consensus had built quickly. Universities A and C had sister schools in Hong Kong, so the aid progressed naturally. University B also received sister universities' inquiry about the possibility of transferring their incoming foreign exchange students to Taiwan. This close communication not only shows that, in almost all circumstances, educational values in Taiwan transcend borders, but also today's internationalization of higher education has become deeply rooted.

Conclusions

Through almost two decades, the internationalization of higher education in Taiwan has progressed with national support and government attention. Efforts have moved from a focus on international ranking to the promotion of egalitarianism and a diversity of research fields. Higher education institutions are now required to seek connections with their local communities and industries, which in turn builds local awareness of higher education, which then leads to both internationalization at home and a stronger voice for Taiwanese identity. The research demonstrates that despite an increasing Taiwanese national identity, the higher education sector has retained Confucian values and agrees that education should be a human right to be prioritized above international disputes.

Many higher education institutions in Taiwan develop their internationalization strategy based on past behaviour, and they have a practical interpretation of the concept rather than a set of clear definitions and long-term goals. While many scholars have emphasized a more balanced and effective internationalization strategy for the broader higher education sector as well as for individual universities, the research shows a need for more cross-office integration within universities based on the institutional research offices' development plans, allowing resources to be applied in a way that maximizes effect and growth. The interviews also brought out a less visible node in internationalization, the silent administrators. The talk of empowerment and the act of inviting them to either join or prepare for the interviews shows a trust in their professional service, though in literature this group is hardly ever addressed. It will be important for future research to look into the implementation side of internationalization, including the role and effect of administration within higher education institutions.

With government supervision gradually increasing, there seemed to be an underlying anxiety in the academy about political influence on higher education. Academic autonomy had been, and will continue to be, a delicate issue. On the other hand, governance at the institutional level had proven effective at countering the impact of the global pandemic. With advanced technology, communication was more timely and less hierarchical. Decisions were speedy and unburdened by bureaucratic procedures, and they were implemented almost immediately. Even as the pandemic created difficulties in the academic world and blocked travel opportunities, some international activities have seen innovations that had strengthened the network of global universities and had helped to develop an international academic community that was more cooperative and interactive online. At-home internationalization, a topic that has been nearly ignored in Taiwan, is now being explored, and it is reasonable to believe that future research will lead to an expanded discussion on this topic.

Geopolitics and Internationalization of Higher Education in Vietnam

Ly Thi Tran, Huong Le Thanh Phan and Huyen Bui

Introduction

Internationalization of higher education is regarded as a powerful vehicle for transforming higher education. The growing globalization and regionalization of economies and societies coupled with both the local needs and global demands have shifted internationalization from an ad hoc and fragmented practice to a more strategic approach, and from a marginalized to a central position (De Wit 2020). In a broader sense, internationalization is an ongoing process entailing 'international', referred to as building relationships among nations, cultures and societies at a global scale (Knight 2015). Despite the aspired narrative of fostering mutual understandings, regional and global ties, peace and solidarity in various discussions, in practice internationalization of higher education has been geared more towards an increasingly commercial orientation, especially in Anglophone countries like Australia, Canada, New Zealand, the UK and the United States. Internationalization of higher education has been positioned as a mechanism to generate revenues for host institutions and countries through the act of international recruitment. Within a transactional higher education model of internationalization, international students, who are the key actors in the process of internationalization, have been regarded as a commodity in a transactional higher education model of internationalization (Tran 2020).

Internationalization of higher education and both the international ties that it aspires to foster in ideology and the commercial business that internationalization in many countries entails in practice have been increasingly subject to global crises such as pandemics, global financial crises, natural disasters and geopolitics. Among these turbulences, geopolitics is strongly shaping the international education space.

The recent rise of the far-right parties in several European countries, the Brexit saga and the Trump administration have changed the global political landscape and influenced internationalization agendas and practices in higher education. The political movement driven by pro-nationalism or national protectionism, anti-immigration, anti-globalization, anti-multiculturalism and the rise of China and some middle powers create a 'new world order' and begin a fundamental period of change of international higher education (Altbach and de Wit 2017; Hsieh 2020; Tran 2020). The new world order has been marked with China's rising power, challenging the traditional notion of a US-dominated order, and at the same time, the growth of India has the potential to balance China's regional influence. In addition, various emerging middle powers like South Korea, Iran and Brazil are opening up a multipolar world system. In East Asia, geopolitics and aspirations to exercise soft power through the establishment of education hubs for the region also play a prominent role in shaping the directions, policies and practices of higher education internationalization (see below for detailed discussion). However, there is a lack of understanding of the geopolitical characters and challenges facing higher education internationalization in the East Asian region. This chapter responds to this gap and focuses on the geopolitical conflicts and their impacts on higher education internationalization agendas and practices in Vietnam, which is seen as one of the most dynamic economies in East Asia.

The chapter begins by providing an overview of the geopolitics of international education. It next discusses international geopolitical influences in Vietnam and their effects on Vietnamese international education prior to Đổi Mới (Economic and Social Reform), which marks the country's shift from a centrally planned subsidized socialist economy to a socialist-oriented multiple-sectored market economy. It analyses how prevailing headwinds shaped the internationalization of higher education in Vietnam during the country's long history of resistances to foreign incursions. It then discusses international education and geopolitics in Vietnam post-Đổi Mới wherein the renewed significance of higher education has heightened the role of internationalization as a strategic vehicle to revamp the higher education system and to project the country outward through forging international cooperation.

The Geopolitics of International Education

The development of internationalization of higher education cannot be seen as detached from political contexts because 'every relationship of "hegemony" is necessarily an educational relationship' that takes place not only within a nation but also in the international space and across various fields (Gramsci 2000: 348). Blessinger and Cozza (2017) reported three waves of globalization that have driven the development of higher education internationalization: (1) The first wave occurred between around 1870 and 1914 where internationalization of higher education was mainly a marginal activity and was treated in isolation; (2) The second wave was highlighted by the resurgence of globalization after the Second World War with internationalization of higher education as a tool for developed countries to promote democratic values and human rights, improve cross-cultural relations and world peace, and enhance global economic growth and political stability; (3) The third wave occurred from about 1980 to the present, characterized by a growing participation in the global trade from developing countries, the failure of colonial regimes and the advances in international communication, transportation and scientific technologies. In this third wave, the focus of higher education internationalization is around increasing the recruitment of international students, creating new ways to deliver and export education, forming international partnerships and enhancing institutional reputation and ranking. Especially, the period between 2010 and 2020 has seen not only a surge in the number of international students but also a growing increase in transnational education including branch campuses, articulation arrangement, franchise operation and online programme delivery (De Wit 2020).

The interplay between internationalization of higher education and geopolitics has been observed around the globe as internationalization of higher education is often viewed as part of a nation's 'soft power' influence (Altbach and de Wit 2017). In Asia, international education has also been used as a political power that drives nations' agendas. A study into the development of three key educational hubs in Asia, namely Malaysia, Singapore, and Hong Kong, pointed out that although the models and the conceptions of education hubs are different in these three countries, there is a strong desire to increase the country's geopolitical influence through taking leadership position in higher education (Lee 2015). In some countries, governments often use internationalization as a tool to serve their domestic purposes, resulting in political controversies that can hinder and shape internationalization efforts (Bamberger et al. 2019). For example, in Taiwan, international education has been used as a tool for different political purposes under different ruling governments including serving as a vehicle to maintain Chinese culture and values and promote Chinese solidarity by the Chinese Nationalist Party government or a mechanism to advocate for Taiwan's independence from China by the Democratic Progressive Party (Hsieh 2020).

China is among the few countries in East Asia that strategically use internationalization of higher education as a mechanism to reinforce and strengthen soft power. China's Belt and Road Initiative launched in 2013 aims at strengthening China's economic leadership by connecting China with more than sixty-five countries through the land and sea routes linking Eurasia (Peters 2020). This ambitious economic initiative has been seen as a strategic tool for China to increase its influence in East and Southeast Asia as a geopolitical competition with the United States (Flint and Zhu 2019). Higher education has been used by the Chinese government to serve this political purpose through an Education Action Plan that establishes a ministerial-provincial joint platform for the Belt and Road Initiative, provides Silk Road Scholarship programmes and increases substantial investment in research (Peters 2020). The implementation of the Belt and Road Initiative has also contributed to the expansion of Chinese education in overseas markets along the route (Gong 2020). Internationalization of higher education as a political tool has also been manifested in the country's implementation of the 'bring-in' (*qing jin lai zhan lue*) strategy that attracts international students to China and supports its positioning as a regional education hub (Cheng 2009). The period between 1995 and 2015 saw a ten-fold increase in the number of international students enrolled in universities in China (Wen and Hu 2019). In 2018, there were 492,185 international students studying in China for both degree courses and short-term mobility programs, of whom almost 60 per cent were from Asia (MOE 2019). In addition, China has fostered the development of transnational education including expanding partnerships with foreign universities (Yang 2008) and setting up off-shore campuses in Laos, Malaysia, Thailand and Japan (He and Wilkins 2018).

The process of enhancing China's soft power in a target region often comprises three steps: identifying a region for influence and increasing investment, usually in infrastructure or new market; fostering the signing and the execution of different bilateral agreements; and sustaining this influence using cultural diplomacy (Hall 2017). The creation of Confucius Institutes, co-founded universities and language schools and the provisions of scholarships for local students to study in China are among the strategies used to increase local students' awareness and participation in Chinese language and culture (Hall 2017). By 2017, there were 516 Confucius Institutes and 1,076 Confucius Classrooms in primary and secondary schools in 142 countries and regions globally (Haban News 2017). In the United States, by the end of 2015, Confucius Institutes and Confucius

Classrooms were set up in almost all states (Luqiu and McCarthy 2019). Unlike the British Council, the Alliance Française and the Goethe Institute of Germany that are all located outside university campuses, Confucius Institutes' curricular programming often exists within an autonomous unit inside host universities (Luqiu and McCarthy 2019). The growth of Confucius Institutes has recently triggered nation states' concern that these are under significant control and influence by the Chinese government and are used to promote its political interests abroad. This concern has led to an increased scrutiny of Confucius Institutes in a range of countries, including in Australia and the United States (Marklein 2020; Ren and Wilhelm 2020).

The geopolitical tensions between China and some major destinations of Chinese international students including Australia and the United States have been intensified during the Covid-19 pandemic. The outbreak of the disease and the unprecedented geopolitical tensions between the United States and China have triggered a war of words and threatened the educational relations between the two countries after decades of fruitful multifaceted cooperation (Marginson and Yang 2020). Following Washington's warning that some Chinese students are Beijing's proxies who are trying to 'conduct economic espionage, orchestrate pro-China views and monitor other Chinese students on American campuses' (Feng 2020: para 6), Chinese national students in the United States have been a subject of an ongoing scrutiny and placed under pressure. But the new Biden administration has the potential to create a better sense of security and inclusion for prospective international students, as compared to the Trump one, thereby likely helping the United States regain its destination attraction.

In the same vein, the escalating geopolitical tensions between China and Australia amid the Covid-19 pandemic have caused damages to international education in both countries. In retaliation for the Australian government's response to the issues of Hong Kong Security Law, Taiwan and South China Sea and calls for an independent investigation into the origins of the Covid-19 outbreak, China warned Chinese students from travelling to Australia citing threats of increasing racial attacks, violence and discriminations that target Chinese students (Kuo and Murphy 2020). Subsequently, education agents in China threatened to divert thousands of Chinese students to the UK if Australia did not change their political position (Bagshaw, Hunter and Liu 2020). While there has been heightened Covid-19 related racism against people of Asian background and Chinese students in particular in Australia as well as in other parts of the world during the pandemic (Human Rights Watch 2020), the Chinese government has singled out Australia. China's response is considered as 'an implicit warning to other major destination countries if they do not cooperate with China on matters related to Hong Kong, Taiwan, independent investigations into the origins of Covid-19 and its recent escalation in the South China Sea' (Tran 2020: 1). As a result of such politicization of international education, a study into motivations for overseas study conducted by Zhang (2020) reveals that Chinese students were reported to take the Chinese government's warning about coming to Australia seriously and only less than half of them planned to return to their study in Australia. In this context, the UK has recorded an increase by 9 per cent in the number of non-EU international students to the UK as a result of global politics, employment opportunities and perceived education quality (Mittelmeier, Lim and Lomer 2020).

Geopolitics and Internationalization of Higher Education in Vietnam

Geopolitics has been a major force in shaping the directions, policies and practices of higher education internationalization in Vietnam given the country's history of warfare and long-lasting struggles to gain national independence, maintain peace and seek regional and world integration. In Vietnam, internationalization of higher education is not used as a tool to exercise soft power in the region like its neighbouring country China. Rather, it is regarded as a vehicle to build international relationships and regional ties and to foster both national and international solidarity within a broader agenda to defend its national independence and support its development and prosperity.

The following sections will discuss the interplay between geopolitics and internationalization of higher education in Vietnam prior to and after the country's social and economic reform, Đổi Mới, which is a milestone marking the social and economic transformations of the country.

Prior to Đổi Mới (until 1986)

International education is indeed not new to Vietnam. During the country's history of resistance to major foreign incursions and occupations by China, France, Japan and the United States, Vietnamese higher education reflected the foreign imprint to some extent. During the periods when Vietnam was dominated, controlled or colonized, international education in Vietnam was largely imposed to serve the dominators' purposes rather than deliberately practised at the country's will.

The earliest dimensions of international education were related to Vietnam's neighbouring geographical location to China and the long-standing Chinese domination over the country. During the Chinese invasion, an unequivocal form of internationalization was student mobility, through which elite Vietnamese scholars crossed borders to China for examinations and learning (Tran, Le and Nguyen 2014). Internationalization was also manifested in the infusion of Chinese mechanisms and philosophy, notably Confucianism, as part of the Chinese invader's policy of assimilating Vietnam. First established in the eleventh century, Confucian academies posed a significant influence over Vietnamese society for almost nine centuries (Anh and Hayden 2017). Vietnam's first higher education institution, the Quốc Tử Giám, essentially resembled the Chinese style and operated for ten centuries despite several nationalization attempts by the Vietnamese kings (Ngo 2016). The Chinese influences had long-term effects on Vietnamese educational philosophy and the education system (Welch 2010); some remain noticeable in the Vietnamese ways of teaching and learning today, for example, incontestable knowledge and rote learning. However, throughout over 1000 years of Chinese domination, Vietnam was able to leave its own identity imprint by creatively Vietnamizing many Confucian ideologies and values to suit its sociocultural conditions (Tran and Marginson 2018; Tran, Marginson and Nguyen 2014; Welch 2010).

In the mid-1990s, Vietnamese higher education underwent tremendous transformations (Ngo 2016), radically oriented by the abrupt changes in geopolitics and the political upheavals of the country. Within just four decades between 1945 and 1986, the country went through two resistance wars against the French (1945–54) and the Americans (1954–75), the North-South division and then reunification, two wars against the Khmer Rouge (1978) and China's incursion (1979), the difficult socioeconomic situation in the aftermath of the wars and under the embargo imposed by Western countries (Ngo 2016). These political turbulences warranted an eventful period for international education with fast changes in the areas of mobility, institutional structure and foreign language learning.

Under the French domination, scholar and student mobility was a prevalent element of international education which comprised two distinctive streams serving different purposes (Tran, Marginson and Nguyen 2014). The first stream was the outbound mobility of Vietnamese young men to France, initiated by the French colonizer with the expectation that these people would become knowledgeable about French civilization and serve colonial imperatives. However, the process was proved counterproductive since many of those intellectuals became progressive-minded and actively promoted nationalism (Tran, Marginson and Nguyen 2014). This resulted in the second stream, a 'massive and organized mobility' (Ngo 2016: 446) of Vietnamese students to Japan in the *Đông Du* (Go East) movement initiated by those nationalists, notably Phan Bội Châu, an exemplary nationalist educated under the French's colonial regime. In terms of institutional structure, a Western-styled education system was imposed to educate officials for colonial purposes. In terms of language policy, the French language was chosen to be the official language for education and administration. For the first time in the history of Vietnamese higher education, the Confucianism system was replaced by the Westernized one, corresponding to the changes in the country's geopolitics.

During the anti-American war, Vietnam was divided and so was its higher education system. After 1956, the north of Vietnam, pursuing socialist construction, abandoned the French model and adopted the Soviet model where all institutions were public and highly specialized in monodisciplinary terms. The main international education activity in the north was student and scholar mobility to the 'brother' socialist countries, including the Union of Soviet Socialist Republics, the German Democratic Republic, Poland and Hungry, with support from these foreign governments. In the south, Vietnamese higher education followed the American model in all aspects of institutional structure, governance, curriculum as well as the diversification of education providers and models (Tran, Marginson and Nguyen 2014). Mobility continued to be a prevalent dimension of international education, enabled by the scholarships from the United States as part of the US government's strategy of 'winning the hearts and minds of the people (Tran, Marginson and Nguyen 2014: 132).

Language policies across different periods also reflect the geopolitics of international education in Vietnam. Foreign language policies and trends in Vietnam have always 'reflected historical events and been a barometer of waxing and waning relationships with other powers' (Wright 2002: 243). Although most foreign language learning, if not all, is essentially associated with geopolitics and/ or geoeconomics, the interesting aspect of foreign language learning in Vietnam, according to Wright (2002), was the 'abruptness of the changes and the very evident cause-effect relationships' (243), particularly during the four eventful decades from 1945 to 1986 mentioned above. The foreign language in use was heavily associated with the political, diplomatic relations between Vietnam and other countries in light of the ideological differences and the embargo imposed by Western countries at the time. More specifically, during the anti-American war, English was considered the language of enemy and mainly studied for the military and diplomatic purposes against the United States (Hoang 2010) while Chinese and Russian were widely popular since the country received much support from these two fellow socialist states. Nevertheless, since China's land invasion in the late 1970s and the collapse of the Soviet Union in the early 1990s, Chinese and Russian languages have lost their popularity in Vietnam. According to Pham (2014), after the country's reunification in 1975, all foreign languages were awarded a low status. As Wright (2002) argues, 'the ideological division of the world and the isolation of Vietnam, gravitating in turn to one or another of the factions of the Communist world, limited the international networks in which the Vietnamese were involved and restricted both the desire and the need for foreign language acquisition' (225). It was only after the Đổi Mới that the status of foreign languages changed dramatically in accordance with the country's socioeconomic development (Pham 2014).

Post-Đổi Mới (1986 Onwards)

From a war-ravaged country at the brink of economic and social crises in 1986, Vietnam has undergone a profound transformation in terms of both economic growth and its regional and international integration over the last few decades. This was largely attributed to the government's momentous decision to initiate Đổi Mới. The new economic regime aims at developing a multisectoral market economy under state management while maintaining the socialist orientation. Walking the fine line between the two political socioeconomic doctrines – capitalism and socialism – characterizes Vietnam's redefined national identity and reconstructed national image in the world's geopolitical landscape. The political orientation of Vietnam is well reflected in Vietnam's higher education policies after Đổi Mới and its approach to internationalization in higher education contributes to the development of the market-oriented economy (Tran, Marginson and Nguyen 2014) and the retention of the socialist ideology (Welch 2011).

In the late twentieth century, the geopolitics of global higher education witnessed dramatic changes as globalization opened up a new era where not only the worldwide market but also worldwide culture, communications, information and knowledge head towards a single world community (Marginson and Wende 2007). Higher education is not immune to changes, among which is the commodification of higher education endorsed by international agencies such as the World Bank, the International Monetary Fund, the World Trade Organization (WTO), the Asian Development Bank and the Association of Southeast Asian Nations (ASEAN) who have 'tirelessly promoted neo-liberal initiatives' (Majhanovich 2014: 170). Neoliberalism, at its core, advocates a free-market mechanism that eliminates state intervention (Block, Gray and Holborow 2012), thus entailing deregulation, privatization and decentralization throughout higher education systems worldwide.

After a decade of economic failure due to the ravages of wars and the isolation of Vietnam from most countries in the world, the Đổi Mới policy that opened the country to the outside world and liberalized its sociopolitical life was 'a watershed in the modern history of Vietnam' (Ngo 2016: 446). Thanks to Đổi Mới, Vietnam's economy has developed vigorously, for example, with an impressive GDP growth of 6.8 per cent in 2019 and exports expanding by 8 per cent, nearly four times faster than the world average (World Bank 2019). Remarkably geared towards international integration, Vietnam has now joined various regional and international organizations, notably the ASEAN since 1995 and WTO since 2007.

However, despite the remarkable economic growth in a short period post-Đổi Mới, the country is still struggling to cater for the 'tough demands on higher education and human resource development to supply human capital advanced enough to function in a global market' (Brooks 2010: 10). According to a World Bank report by Bodewig et al. (2014), around 80 per cent of employers in high-skilled job sectors found Vietnamese applicants lacked the knowledge and skills needed. While skilled labour and technological capability increasingly become 'the touchstones of competitiveness in an open and integrated world environment' (World Bank 2012: 1), Vietnam's higher education sector remains out of tune with the demands of the growing economic and cultural integration at regional and global levels (Pham and Fry 2004). As Tran and Marginson (2014) remark, much of the higher education curriculum has not kept pace with education reforms in other countries and the international currents of knowledge and technologies.

Amid such geopolitical changes and the tough demand for uplifting education quality, the government of Vietnam has undertaken numerous strategies for reforming the higher education system. According to Tran, Marginson and Nguyen (2014), Vietnamese higher education reforms post-Đổi Mới have centred on three fundamental policies: democratization, diversification and socialization which, in the Vietnamese discourse, refers to the shift of a significant proportion of national education costs from the government to families and society (Do 2014). These policies subtly conformed to neoliberal ideology and global forces and were associated with the commodification of higher education from a public good to private good (Tran, Marginson and Nguyen 2014). To reap the most benefits of globalization, the government also placed emphasis on internationalization as a way to tackle the problem of 'a system in transition' (Ngo 2016: 451). For Vietnam, internationalization of higher education has been primarily a means of overhauling its higher education sector, boosting human capacity building, upgrading institutional ranking and integrating more deeply into the global world.

As stated in the National Strategy for Education Development for Vietnam 2011–20 (The Government of Vietnam 2012b), international cooperation and outbound mobility are strongly emphasized in order to obtain knowledge and skills from abroad (Ziguras and Pham 2017). With the government's funding of over 6000 billion VND (approximately USD300 million), Project 322 and Project 911 have sent more than 7000 lecturers and students in key higher education institutions to study in postgraduate programmes overseas (Tran, Marginson and Nguyen 2014; Tuoi tre 2017). Since Vietnam has now had diplomatic relations with over 180 countries in all continents and enjoyed normal relations with all major powers (Ministry of Foreign Affairs 2020), more scholarships from foreign governments are available for Vietnamese students, and study destinations have been extended beyond the communist world. The current outbound mobility is shaped by Vietnam's foreign diplomacy agenda. Particularly, students are encouraged to study in Asian and Western countries that have bilateral relations with Vietnam (C. H. Nguyen 2018). The United Nations Educational, Social and Cultural Organization's (UNESCO) data show that the top destinations for Vietnamese students include Japan, the United States, Australia, South Korea and France (UNESCO 2021). According to Education Minister Phung Xuan Nha, there were around 170,000 Vietnamese students studying overseas in 2018 (BMI 2020), three times higher than that in 2011 (Ngo 2016). This number placed the country in the top ten biggest provider country of international students for major destination countries (Tram 2019) and is expected to continue increasing in the coming years.

Inbound mobility, however, has not grown as strongly. In 2008, there were only 3362 international students in Vietnam (UNESCO 2010), mostly from Asia Pacific countries including China, Laos, Cambodia, Thailand, Japan and Korea (Pham 2011). In addition to the close geographical proximity between Vietnam and these countries, various macro-level influencing factors included the development status of both the economy and higher education system, capacity, policies and bureaucratic framework (Tran, Marginson, Do et al. 2014). Being cognizant of the values of student inbound mobility in gaining regional and international recognition for social and political development purposes, in March 2011 the Ministry of Education and Training (MOET) loosened the top-down requirements for international student recruitment, allowing individual universities to establish their own enrolment criteria (Pham 2011). In addition, English-medium instruction was officially approved in 2012 (H. T. Nguyen 2018) as a result of the Vietnamese government's enthusiastic promotion through various policies on foreign cooperation and investment in education (The Government of Vietnam 2008, 2012a). These favourable measures contributed to increasing the population of international students in Vietnam. With 455 ongoing foreign-direct-investment projects in the field of education in 2020, Vietnam is hosting 21,000 international students and interns at both undergraduate and postgraduate levels (Le 2020), a growing proportion of whom are from developed countries. The development of joint educational programmes where English is employed as the medium of instruction is regarded as a key internationalization-at-home strategy for bridging the quality gap between Vietnamese education and that of other countries in the world.

In addition, Vietnam is promoting itself as an attractive destination for overseas students to study under short-term mobility and internship programmes. Vietnam is among the top five destinations for short-term mobility for Australian students who are funded by the Australian government through its signature programme of student mobility and public diplomacy, the New Colombo Plan. There were 3612 Australian students studying and/or taking internships in Vietnam through the New Colombo Plan between 2014 and 2019 (Australian government 2020). Attracting overseas students to Vietnam via short-term mobility and internship programmes has been regarded by the Vietnamese government and universities as a strategic tool to internationalize higher education, boost international ranking and foster bilateral relationships with other countries. This positive development, among others, in the internationalization landscape would benefit Vietnam's ultimate goal of global integration since international students in developing countries, including Vietnam, are regarded as 'actors of public diplomacy assisting with the realization of country-to-country connections and as vehicles to increase and humanize their industry links and transnational university partnerships' (Tran and Bui 2021: 439).

Apart from student mobility, internationalization in Vietnam is also characterized by the mobility of teachers, scholars and different modes of international cooperation, for example, international exchange projects and research collaboration. These activities aim to facilitate policy borrowing, advance the country's research capacity and promote the mobility of transnational research and technology (Tran and Marginson 2018). At the institutional level, universities proactively seek to broaden their international networks to build educational partnerships. Between 2016 and 2017, Vietnamese higher education institutions welcomed 3214 foreign lecturers and scholars to their campuses to give lectures and conduct research, which was an increase of 14 per cent from the previous year (Daidoanket News 2017). Such vibrancy marks a new stage in which international education has escalated in both scale and scope (Tran, Marginson and Nguyen 2014) and the country has shifted from being merely an importer of international education to being a partner in educational cooperation. However, national research output remains still largely dependent on collaborative research (Nhan and Le 2019) since the lead authors of 77 per cent of the publications between 1996 and 2013 were foreign researchers (Manh 2015, cited in Nhan and Le 2019).

The geopolitics of international education in Vietnam could also be examined in relation to the country's collaboration with foreign partners in establishing international branch campuses. Over the past three decades, the Vietnamese government has been more active in creating the mechanisms for high-profile universities and investors overseas to establish international branch campuses and foreign representative education offices in Vietnam (Hoang, Tran and Pham 2018). This move closely aligns with the government's 2005 policy on expanding and enhancing the effectiveness of international cooperation in education, which was aimed at uplifting the higher education system. A milestone for transnational education in Vietnam was the issue of Decree No. 18/2001/ND-CP in 2001, regulating the establishment and operation of foreign educational and cultural institutions. This decree paved the way for the establishment of the first foreign university brand campus, the Royal Melbourne Institute of Technology (or RMIT Vietnam), in 2002 and the subsequent development of other foreign brands as well as numerous joint and twinning programmes. The first fully foreign-owned university RMIT Vietnam was followed by British University Vietnam and international campuses established by Thailand's Asian Institute of Technology (AIT), US Roger Williams University campus, the Chamber of Commerce and Industry of Paris (CCIP), the International College of IT and Management and Swinburne's recent location in Hanoi and forthcoming one in Ho Chi Minh city.

Following Decree No. 18/2001/ND-CP, Decree No. 73/2012/ ND-CP, issued in September 2012, was considered as a detailed regulatory framework in foreign investment, joint ventures with Vietnamese entities and cooperation with foreign universities in developing international branch campuses in line with its commitment to the General Agreement on Trade in Services (GATS) (Vietnamese Government 2012a). Foreign countries and institutions are motivated to establish branch campuses or joint and twinning programmes in Vietnam for not only educational and commercial gains but also for diplomatic purposes. Expanding the delivery of their programmes in Vietnam is considered as a vehicle to forge institution-to-institution and country-to-country connections and strengthen their international standing. For Vietnam, the establishment of international branch campuses and joint programmes is seen to support the inflow of international curriculum, knowledge and research development into Vietnam, as well as to provide Vietnamese students with international education experiences at home. International collaborations in education also contribute to building Vietnam's bilateral and multilateral relationships with other countries and facilitates its desire to integrate into the region and the world.

However, international campuses and programmes in Vietnam are only established in some major cities, such as Ho Chi Minh City, Hanoi and Da Nang, and serve a small number of elite Vietnamese families and students who can afford the relatively high tuition fees and access to internationally delivered education onshore. In addition, Hoang, Tran and Pham (2018) argued that internationalization at home in Vietnam is predominantly based on foreign curriculum borrowing. One typical representative is the Advanced Programmes project (*chương trình tiên tiến*) commonly known as the Vietnamese government's signature initiative of internationalizing the higher education curriculum. By employing English as the medium of instruction and importing the curriculum of the top 200 universities in the world, the aim of the advanced programmes is to contribute to the 'fundamental and comprehensive renovation of Vietnam's higher education' (MOET 2008) and ultimately enhance the country's competitiveness in the globalized market. Legitimated by the Government's Resolution Number 14/2005/NQ-CP that explicitly encourages the importation of world renown universities' curricula, the advanced programmes borrowed not only the content but also all other aspects of the foreign curricula such as course design, teaching methodologies and assessment (Tran, Phan and Marginson 2018). However, to conform with MOET's centralized higher education curriculum framework (Tran, Le and Nguyen 2014), courses on national political values and ethics – including Marxist-Leninist philosophy, Ho Chi Minh ideology and military training – were incorporated into the advanced programmes' curriculum (Duong 2009). This inclusion is a clear evidence of how internationalization is influenced by the political orientation of the country, that is, internationalization within socialist frame and under the Communist principles.

Tedesco, Opertti and Amadio (2014) state that the curriculum is a reflection of 'political and societal agreement about the what, why, and how of education for the desired society of the future' (528). The internationalized curriculum, such as the advanced programmes' curriculum, is not ideology free. On the one hand, internationalized programmes are a means to project the country outward. On the other hand, they can be considered the Vietnamese government's efforts to 'domesticate elite higher education' (Koch 2014: 47) that is bringing Western education to their students with an infusion of the socialist identity through political indoctrination. There has been a close relation between internationalization and geopolitics and the country's political orientation. The continued promotion of Marxist-Leninist and Ho Chi Minh thought as part of the government's socialist-retaining goals arguably added pressure to Vietnam's reforms towards a neoliberal economy. However, it is equally arguable that reservation of a distinctive national identity is much needed in the context where internationalization has been criticized as 'a form of soft imperialism' (Marginson 1999: 19) or Westernization that entails an imbalance in the power relationship between the global North and global South.

Conclusion

This chapter has provided an overview of the geopolitics of international education and discussed the interplay between geopolitics and internationalization of higher education in Vietnam. Prior to Đổi Mới, international education in Vietnam, especially outbound student mobility, was heavily influenced by geopolitics and the political orientations of the country. In particular, Vietnam is a unique case in the history of student mobility where its outbound-sponsored student mobility to France in the early 1900s was counterproductive to the sponsoring government's intended goal underpinning the programme. The original purpose of providing Vietnamese scholars with mobility experiences and an exposure to French civilization to reinforce the colonial imperatives failed, as the international experience helped expand their minds and enabled them to become activists of nationalism. The mobility programme helped lead to the collapse of the French rule in Indo-China. This case is an example of how a mobility programme was politicalized and mobile students were positioned as actors of political agendas. It also shows how mobile students and scholars can exercise agency and act to achieve their political goals, which might be contradictory to the receiving country's wish. The Vietnamese student mobility scheme to France during the French colonization in Indo-China also indicates the complex relationship between geopolitics and international education. Not only did different actors from the sending and receiving countries attach different meanings to international education, they engaged in it in contrasting ways and used it to serve different purposes. For the colonizer government, student mobility was a strategic means to reinforce the colonization regime in Vietnam and Indo-China but it turned out to become a powerful force to enable scholars of the colonized country to form nationalist ideology that led to the liberation of their country from colonization.

Between the 1960s and 1970s, outbound student mobility in Vietnam was shaped by the country's political division. Russia and Eastern Europe were the key destinations for students from northern Vietnam while the United States was chosen by those from southern Vietnam (London 2010). After periods of being under the American embargo and being isolated from the world after the Vietnam war, Đổi Mới as an economic and social reform and open-door policy brought fresh air to the country. The Vietnamese government has prioritized the internationalization of higher education as a mechanism to support the open-door aim of Đổi Mới and boost the country's international integration. The Strategy for Education Development for Vietnam 2011–20 refers to expansion and enhancement of international cooperation in education as one of the key pillars for the overall development of Vietnamese education. International education has helped the country realize its political and diplomatic agendas, contributing to fostering multilateral relationships and international ties for Vietnam after the long period of warfare. In addition, the increased emphasis on international cooperation has enabled Vietnamese universities to accelerate their transnational partnerships, programmes, models, student mobility and research collaboration with foreign partners within the socialist frame and under the communist principles. International cooperation has facilitated internationalization at home and English-medium instruction programmes to enable the curriculum to catch up with regional and world developments and improve graduate employability.

The analysis in this chapter shows the difference of the approach to internationalization of higher education with Vietnamese characteristics which was in line with the country's resistance against colonization during the French rule and supported its international integration agenda after periods of warfare, as opposed to the transactional characteristics that dominate internationalization of higher education in many Anglophone countries. It shows that overall, during wartime, internationalization of higher education was closely related to the political agendas of the nation to fight against foreign incursions. After the war, international cooperation has become a primary dimension of internationalization of higher education in Vietnam to boost the quality of Vietnamese universities, foster international ties and facilitate the country's integration into the world.

Part Three

International Mobility and Academic Migration

人

Chinese meaning:

Human, person (people, personality), manpower, mortal, artificial, someone else, adult

Japanese meaning:

Human, person (people, personality), manpower, mortal, artificial, someone else, adult

Korean meaning:

Human, person (people, personality), manpower, mortal, artificial, someone else, adult

Vietnamese meaning:

Human, person (people, personality), manpower, mortal, artificial

10

Agency of International Student-Migrants in Japan

Thomas Brotherhood

Introduction

The relationship between international student mobility and international migration is increasingly significant in the Japanese context. The Japanese government has shown an extended commitment to internationalizing its universities to increase their competitiveness as measured in global rankings, and as a 'lifeline' for an ailing higher education sector struggling with a lack of resources and democratic ageing (Yonezawa 2020). For the past forty years, the policies designed to catalyse this internationalization have prioritized the attraction of foreign-born students (Ota 2018) and, as a consequence, international students are now the single largest group of foreign nationals in Japan (Ministry of Justice 2019). Critically, recent reforms to migration policy have opened new and attractive pathways for international students to remain in Japan after their graduation, thereby cementing a dedicated migration pathway for foreign students into the country's migration control regime (Brotherhood 2020; Hamaguchi 2019). As a result, Japanese universities could now be described as 'intermediary organizations' playing a critical role in the management of Japan's most powerful migration flow (Liu-Farrer and Tran 2019; Van Den Broek, Harvey and Groutsis 2015).

This recognition of universities' 'intermediary' position between international students and a life in Japan reflects a broader recognition of this phenomena in the international literature. Indeed, Japan is among the latest to seek to capitalize on the potential of student-migration. The so-called education-migration nexus (Robertson 2013) was first noted in Australia in the late 1990s, when the country explicitly pivoted its skilled migration strategy to prioritize the attraction and retention of foreign students. By being the first country to earnestly commit to 'picking winners' in this way, Australia repositioned its universities in the international education market, laying the foundation for rapid expansion of the number of international students in Australia and its stock of skilled migrants. Indeed, by 2002, roughly half of all skilled migration applications came from international students (Hawthorne 2005). In recognition of Australia's success, similar strategies have been employed in other contexts. This was first evident in other major English-speaking countries with advanced higher education systems such as the UK, Canada and New Zealand (Chiou 2017; Kim and Sondhi 2015), but has more recently emerged in non-English speaking contexts countries, such as France and Japan. The success and spread of this education-migration model of attracting skilled workers have drastic implications for both higher education and broader migration control systems, with some arguing that international education and migration 'have increasingly become entangled – even to the point where it appears both have merged' (Baas 2019: 223). Universities and nation states are increasingly reliant on international student flows to balance the books of higher education provision, afford status and prestige in the global higher education marketplace, and provide a steady flow of skilled workers to ensure success in the twenty-first century's 'race for talent' (Chatterjee 2015: 544).

In recognition of both the importance of student migration flows and our limited understanding of these flows' internal dynamics, academic attention is increasingly applied to the education-migration nexus. Some have sought to chart the scale and form of global flows of student-migrants, providing a valuable record of the growing significance of student migration worldwide (Abbott and Silles 2016). Others have looked at the reasons why flows of students may emerge into or between particular contexts, and how regulatory conditions such as the availability of post-study work visas can drastically influence potential international students' choice of study destination (Geddie 2015). Finally, some have concentrated on understanding the political and institutional appetites that influence these regulatory conditions (Lomer 2017).

Here, I offer a novel supplement to these systemic perspectives on the education-migration nexus in Japan, foregrounding individual student-migrants' experiences as the fundamental unit of analysis and seeking to foreground the role of individual agency in guiding their student-migration trajectories. I investigate the role of agency in the education-migration nexus in two ways. First, I draw on sociological theory to delineate different ways in which agency can manifest through the flow of time, as individuals draw on the past, present and future to guide their desires and actions. Second, to convey the complexities and dynamism of agency, I employ narrative analysis and present a series of composite vignettes that portray 'truthful' accounts of the journey from 'student' to 'migrant' in the context of Japan. These vignettes not only provide in-depth insight into the experience of migrating to Japan via higher education, drawing solely on the words of the student-migrants themselves, but also illustrate the diverse and dynamic development and practice of agency in the education-migration nexus.

Japan as a Space of Student Migration

It is important to ground this discussion in an understanding of Japan, in particular, as a space of student migration. To do so, it is useful to look to the historical origins of present-day flows of students and migrants to Japan. In the post-war period, the Japanese government sought to rebuild their national image and soft power in the region by investing heavily in international education scholarships and exchanges as a part of its Overseas Development Assistance strategy, a pattern of investment that continued through to the end of the turn of the millennium (Yonezawa 2008). This resulted in the development of sizeable and persistent flows of international students to Japan from across East and Southeast Asia, though they were not actively encouraged to remain in Japan post-study. Concurrently, Japan's labour migration programmes looked to these same national communities, with various trainee programmes offering primarily Southeast Asian nationals the opportunity to travel to Japan for job training and short-term employment (Yamanaka 1993). However, as criticisms of these programmes grew and Japan's labour needs evolved from un- and low-skilled labour throughout the twentieth century to highly skilled and 'global human resources' in the twenty-first century, patterns of migration also had to evolve.

While the 'Overseas Development Assistance' imperative remains important in Japanese higher education, evident in ongoing investment in scholarships for students from low- and middle-income countries, it now intersects – sometimes awkwardly – with concerted attempts to attract and retain international students. Today, Japan plays host to two functionally distinct groups of international students, only one of which is associated with migration at the level of policy. Those coming to Japan self-funded or on scholarship programmes from the Ministry of Education, Culture, Sports, Science and Technology (MEXT) are encouraged and supported to stay post-study and seek employment, but those on Overseas Development Assistance scholarships offered by Japan International Cooperation Agency are mandated to return to their home countries after their graduation (MEXT 1983; The Prime Minister of Japan and His Cabinet 2014; Yonezawa 2008). In effect, two international students in the same classroom could have very different post-study prospects by virtue of their source of funding though, of course, these individuals' desires and priorities may not necessarily align with their treatment in policy. However, we have little sense of the effect to which individual desire and agency interacts with the established patterns of post-study opportunity in the Japanese context.

Migrant Agency and Narrative Inquiry

Engaging empirically with the role of individual agency promises to significantly develop our understanding of the education-migration nexus. This is partially because research to date has not placed agency as the 'explicit focus of theoretical and empirical investigation' (Tran and Vu 2018: 167) and, as a result, we lack evidence of the influence of individuals' desires and actions on their individual trajectories, and how the aggregation of individual agency may contribute to the emergence and sustenance of student migration pathways between particular contexts. Engaging empirically with agency is also important because of the extended or 'processual' nature of student migration trajectories (Carlson 2013). People may begin to think about studying abroad early in their youth, before engaging in a course of study that spans a number of years before their graduation and potential entry to the workforce. Throughout, they are constantly evaluating their desires and actions in response to rapidly changing circumstances and their own personal growth. Therefore, while acknowledging the significance of the systemic factors described above, it is clear that individuals exert a degree of control over their trajectories, and hence we must pay close attention to their desires and actions if we are to understand the education-migration nexus.

As a result of these complex temporal dynamics, seeking to understand the role of agency in student migration trajectories requires a theoretical framework for agency that is sensitive to the flow of time. Emirbayer and Mische (1998) provide such a framework. Their 'chordal triad' model of agency distinguishes between three distinct but overlapping elements of agency that reflect the influence of the past, present and future, respectively. The element of agency that draws directly on the past – which the authors describe as 'iterational' – describes the way in which past experiences or precedents may guide individuals' desires and actions. For instance, the tendency for people to 'follow in the footsteps' of their role models is an example of the potential influence of precedent on decision making. The element of agency situated in the present – 'practical-evaluation' in the authors' terms – concerns the way in which individuals pass judgement on their personal situation and social milieu. The results of this judgement may influence their desires and actions. For example, someone may come to the sudden realization that they are dissatisfied with their current circumstances and resolve to change their job, house or course of study as a result. Finally, the element of agency directed towards the future – the 'projective' element – concerns individuals' imagination as a way to understand and evaluate their opportunities and possibilities. We are all familiar with the question: 'where do I want to be in five years?' The process of answering this question, and its influence on our actions in the present, illustrates the significance of this element of agency.

Emirbayer and Mische (1998) argue that these three elements of agency offer a powerful lens to understand agency at two temporal scales. First, it helps us to understand the significance and nature of agency at a specific time. At any given moment, the three elements of agency combine to reflect an individual's general agentic orientation. All three are likely to be present to varying degrees, but one element may emerge as a dominant and have a particularly powerful influence over the individual's desires and actions. Second, this model of agency provides the tools to understand the development and dynamism of individual agency over time. By engaging longitudinally with individuals, the model provides the tools to see how the flow of time and changing circumstances may be met with different agentive orientations.

The strengths of Emirbayer and Mische's model for understanding agency over time correspond to the requirements of this study, which seeks to examine agency throughout student migration journeys of individuals. However, analysis of this type requires a specific form and depth of data to be feasible. The data must capture detailed descriptions of individuals' reflections on specific events and decisions, and must also capture this data over time. Narrative inquiry offers a solution to these empirical challenges.

Narrative methods have a number of advantages over other methods of qualitative data as they take advantage of the human tendency to make stories of their experiences. Storytelling is often described as the 'primary scheme by means of which human existence is rendered meaningful' (Polkinghorne 1988: 1). Humans possess the ability to share our stories in forms that follow established patterns of 'long-standing literary or oral traditions ... [that] contain many cycles and re-cycles of basic narrative structures' (Labov and Waletzky 1967: 12). Polkinghorne (1995) identifies how a 'plot' is a powerful window into understanding the 'relational significance' of events and actions within participants' narratives. Plot is the inherent structure of narrative (Carr 1986), which ties together a series of events 'into an organized whole', identifying the sequence of events that contribute to the overall narrative (Polkinghorne 1995: 7). This sequencing of events into a coherent story inherently helps in the identification of the meaning of each event, and the significance of each event emerges from their relationship to other events in the story. To illustrate how the relational significance of events within a plot underpin meaning in narrative texts, Polkinghorne gives the example of the six-word story 'the king died; the prince cried'. Though perhaps emotive as isolated events, when combined into a plot 'the prince's crying appears as a response to his father's death ... and provides a context for understanding the crying' (Polkinghorne 1995: 7). In addition, Labov and Waletzky (1967) also argue that narrative has an 'evaluative' property, through which the narrator communicates the meaning that they attribute to the events being described 'by establishing some point of personal involvement' (Cortazzi 1993: 44). Furthermore, extended narratives are particularly powerful in preserving stories as told by participants, and in so doing, preserving the situatedness of experience and social action (Polkinghorne 1995).

By taking advantage of these salient features of storytelling, narrative inquiry can help researchers to develop shared understandings of the significance of individual experiences which may be restricted or prevented by more structured forms of qualitative interview. Narrative methods are less vulnerable to inadvertent manipulation of participants' responses by the research process. Narrative methods typically seek to avoid the substantive input of the researcher to mitigate the influence of the researcher on the narratives provided. This, it is argued, allows participants a more authentic method of expression than a structured interview, often leading to more grounded responses from participants (Wengraf 2001). Indeed, the free-associative method of conducting interviews that is common in the induction of participants' narratives avoids 'constraining respondents by the assumptions embedded in interview questions' (Dwyer, Davis and Emerald 2017: 13). Furthermore, narrative data provide 'high context knowledge' that is fundamentally drawn from the lives of individuals. While narratives can form the basis for synoptic or composite vignettes or illustrative stories that portray the social realities of particular social groups, as is the case in this study, these vignettes are built upon individuals' experience in context, and the 'complex relations between ideology and culture, self and society' that they reveal (Amos Hatch and Wisniewski 1995: 117). Finally, narratives offer a way to contextualize high-order theoretical concepts in the everyday actions of individuals, thereby making them 'especially meaningful and accessible' to social researchers and the readers of published research (Amos Hatch and Wisniewski 1995: 118).

For these reasons, extended narratives are not only a particularly rich source of data in social research, but they also correspond to the empirical requirements of this study. As described above, one of the key concerns of this study is understanding the development and practice of agency among individual student-migrants, and particularly its evolution through the flow of time. Indeed, Emirbayer and Mische assert that engaging with agency empirically requires both the data collected and subsequent analysis to be 'situated within the flow of time' (1998: 963). Narrative methods provide such data, as they are sensitive to both temporality and the context of individual actions due to the diachronic nature of the data collected which 'contain temporal information about the sequential relationship of events … [and] include reference as to when and why actions were taken and the intended results of the actions' (Polkinghorne 1995: 12). Thus, while many qualitative methods are adept at providing data that describe at length the contexts of action, narrative inquiry provides a greater degree of temporal acuity upon which development and practice of agency, and the influence of this agency on participants' actions, can be interpreted.

Research Methods

Drawing on the theoretical and methodological insights described above, in this study I sought to develop a series of composite narrative vignettes that illustrate the variable development and practice of agency in the education-migration nexus. The results of this study consist of four composite vignettes which are presented and interpreted below. The first vignette illustrates the significance of past experiences and precedent in influencing student-migrants' desires and actions. The second vignette shows the significance of judgement in the present, by highlighting how participants' reflections on their current circumstances influenced their desires and actions. The third vignette captures the importance of imagination by focusing on how participants used projection to the future to guide their desires and actions. The fourth 'mixed' vignette shows how movement between different agentive orientations is a common feature of student-migrants' trajectories and may explain changes in direction. It should be noted here that the first three vignettes which aim to illustrate the role of a particular element of agency are not intended to, in isolation, accurately represent any individual's narrative. A stoic commitment to one particular agentive orientation was not evident in participants' narratives. Rather, the final 'mixed' vignette is a closer reflection of any one individual's narrative as dynamism of agentive orientations was the norm as participants' orientations changed in response to their changing circumstances over time.

The composite vignettes were constructed as follows. Sixteen degree-mobile international students in their final year of study in Japan were recruited to take part in the study. They were then interviewed via the Biographical-Narrative Interpretive Method, which uses two interviews to develop a comprehensive biography of each participant in their own words and allows for in-depth reflections on a particular event or transition. In this case, the transition in question was their student migration journey. The first 'entry' interview took place during the participants' final year of study, and it used an open-ended free associative interview technique to facilitate the telling of a comprehensive biographical narrative. The second 'exit' interview took place around nine months after the participants had graduated. After opening with further open-ended questioning, the second portion of the interview included some targeted semi-structured questioning intended to invoke reflection on the period between interviews and particular topics of interest from the 'entry' interview itself. Interviews took place in English or Japanese according to the preferences of individuals, and at a time and location arranged according to their convenience. All 'entry' interviews were conducted face-to-face at the participants' universities, typically in cafes, restaurants or unused study spaces. Participants who remained in Japan post-study were also interviewed face-to-face in the 'exit' interviews, while those who moved abroad were interviewed online. All data were audio recorded[1] before being transcribed and analysed in the original language. Only direct quotations to be included in written outputs from the study were eventually translated into English using an adapted back-translation method proposed by Jones et al. (2001) that draws on group discussion with native speakers.

Initial data analysis of interview transcripts consisted of mutually informing thematic and structural coding, which is typical of narrative analysis. Thematic analysis of the trajectories of participants was used to identify important life events and decisions. Further structural coding of participants' subconscious

---

[1] With the exception of one participant who requested I take extended field notes, rather than audio record the interview.

storytelling techniques and non-verbal communication provided insights into the meaning that participants attributed to these life events. These two tracks of coding were used in parallel to provide an 'objective history' of the trajectories of each individual participant that could then be analysed and interpreted in light of the significance afforded to particular events by the participant (Wengraf 2001: 144). Finally, I subsequently conducted a third deductive track of coding using Emirbayer and Mische's iterational, practical-evaluative and projective elements of agency as top-level nodes, under which examples of particular orientations from the text were coded. All interviews were coded using NVivo versions 11 and 12.

Composite vignettes were constructed using a method adapted from Willis (2019). In her article, Willis describes the advantages and complexities of creating composite vignettes, but reflects on the fact that research using this technique rarely provides a comprehensive account of how the vignettes were created. In response, she offers a detailed and transparent account of her creative process that clarifies the link between interview transcripts and final narratives vignettes. Willis's process can be summarized as follows:

1. In reporting the results of vignette-based research, there should be clarity of which participants' narratives contributed to the creation of which vignettes.
2. Researchers should provide confirmation that all quotations came directly from interview transcripts.
3. All details, such as locations and paraphrasing, should be taken directly from source interviews.
4. Researchers should 'avoid imposing any judgment on the interviewees' experiences and opinions [or] assuming motivations or feelings. Any comments of this nature … are taken directly from interviewees' (adapted from Willis 2019: 475).

I was guided by this process. In my case, all of the vignettes draw freely from all participants' narratives and both the 'entry' and 'exit' interviews, thereby reflecting the aim of this study to offer generic reflections on the development and practice of agency in the education-migration nexus, rather than develop categorizations of different types of actors according to their agentive processes. The vignettes are built using only direct quotations and details provided from interview participants for their substantive content. Subtle modifications ensured that, grammatically speaking, the vignettes read as a coherent story from an individual told in the past tense and which, as far as possible, covers the entire student migration journey.

Finally, all judgements and opinions included in the vignettes are taken directly from participants' narratives. The resulting vignettes provide a comprehensive overview of the variety of experiences and opinions described by participants, while also offering direct insight into the development and practice of different elements of agency and their influence on trajectories.

Findings and Discussion

In this section, I present the findings of this study in the form of four composite vignettes, composed solely from the words of interviewees. Following each vignette, I consider how they reflect the nature and significance of a particular orientations throughout student-migration journeys, and how these orientations may inform individuals' action.

Drawing on the Past

> I don't remember exactly why I wanted to study abroad, but my parents had graduated overseas. I was also raised in a very bilingual environment, and all of my classmates and peers came from very similar backgrounds; they were returnees. I think that has everything to do with my present trajectory. Growing up in that kind of household, studying abroad was a given, though I wasn't particularly interested in it, personally. It's not really a matter of choice. It's just one of those things that you do; the 'successful route'. The timing and location of my study abroad just occurred due to chance. My brother studied abroad first, and he told me: 'you have the chance to enlarge your connections around the world, it must be time for you to study and work abroad'. That made me look for opportunities. I checked a few countries, and my main opportunity was Japan, therefore I came here. In fact, there was a symposium between a Japanese university and my university, and my supervisor told me to go. Also, my family insisted.
>
> Now that I've graduated, the reason I returned home is that a lot of people around me follow that route. Study abroad, then go home, that's the overwhelming impression I have. Very few international students stay to work. Also, in my country, we feel the need to stay with our parents. When I talked to my cousin about getting a job, that was the first question they asked, 'what are you going to do with your parents?' Anyway, I knew that, finally, it is my duty, and I must go back. Maybe right after graduating, maybe in two years, but I have to go back.
>
> So, I returned to my home country, and re-entered my old job in the same position. Just regular life. I think this is normal. Most parents, they want to see

their son or daughter doing something stable, you know? They don't want me to be a rich person, they want to see a stable person. Anyway, I'm happy because I could receive a degree from a foreign country. People value that experience; I feel it's more valued if you've done different things in different countries than just doing one thing at home.

The above vignette illustrates the significance of past experience, important people in life and shared understandings of appropriate social conduct in influencing student-migrants' desires and actions. Participants recognized the significance of their upbringing, particularly in their decision to study abroad. Many shared the perception that studying abroad was expected of them, as the natural progression for someone from their background. This perception held even in some cases where the individual participants were unenthusiastic about the opportunity to study abroad or return to their home country after graduating, but chose to do so in response to social pressure to follow a 'successful' or accepted pathway of action. Participants frequently and repeatedly referred to the influence of family members – whether it be their parents, grandparents, siblings, aunts, uncles or cousins – as well as close friends and colleagues on their decisions. In some cases, participants were directly following the precedent of others who were important to the participants which provided a model trajectory of action that they, too, could pursue. In other cases, advice or expectations from such people who mattered in their life seemed to be the crucial factor. This points to the evidence of the significance of shared understandings of appropriate social conduct. Whether it be the recognition and pursuit of a common trajectory of action, such as returning home after studying abroad in Japan or the acknowledgement that a particular trajectory of action is expected of them, such as the need to look after their parents, this vignette shows how an understanding of social expectations can exert a powerful influence on student-migrants' desires and actions. When viewed holistically, this vignette illustrates how decisions can be powerfully influenced by factors outside of personal experience and student-migrants' immediate environment, and the way in which the decisions of individual student-migrants are not necessarily their own.

Judgement in the Present

Most of my learning here hasn't been through the programme itself, or my job, but rather through interactions with the Japanese society. When I was a student, I was just preparing myself for life post-study. I interpret it that way. My

Japanese friends, they treat me differently now. It's like 'you are *shakaijin*[2] now'. They started saying that 'Now you are an adult, you have more responsibilities.' I think I've been successful to an extent, but it's far from perfect. I have more personal responsibility, and I was able to get some financial independence and I'm making a fist of living alone, but there is a particular culture, a particular set of rules that are difficult for me. I'm doing my best to come to terms with it, but some things I just can't comprehend. I guess the tricky part, now that I'm past the transition, is that now this is the evaluation period for seeing if Japan is a place where I could settle, long-term. Europe and America are countries that welcome migrants, but Japan is not accustomed to migration issues. It's mostly composed of only Japanese people. I will always be a foreigner; I think that will not change in our lifetime.

So, do I want to live here? I wouldn't say it that directly. I think as a migrant you want to feel welcome, that you are not invisible and that you have a voice of some sort in society, that you're acknowledged as part of the fabric of society. I got very mixed messages; I think Japan is getting to the point where it might have to slowly renegotiate how it positions itself vis-à-vis the rest of the world but is it my battle to fight? There is part of Japan that I don't like, but Japan is my second home. On the whole, I want to say that it has worked out. I came here to evaluate it, and we'll see. It's not like, 'I'm already done, I can just live in Japan'; every day is like seeing something new, discovering something new, so it's still uncertain. I've committed to staying for two years, more or less, and if it doesn't work out, I will pivot out and maybe switch geographies again.

This vignette illustrates the significance of participants' judgements of their present circumstances and their changing position in Japanese society. Specifically, it reveals how a recognition of problems, tensions and conflicts is central to an individual's understanding of their circumstances and opportunities, and their related ability to understand these problems, tensions and conflicts influences their responses in action. Emirbayer and Mische (1998) refer to the recognition of the challenges of the present as 'problematization'. This is evident in the above vignette in the recognition that, despite remaining in Japan post-study and finding employment, many participants argued that their position in Japanese society remained unresolved. On the one hand, through their transition to the workforce and becoming as *shakaijin* they had become fully fledged members of society. On the other hand, participants

---

[2] *Shakaijin* is a term used to refer to a working adult, which carries nuances of having become a fully fledged member of society. The term is usually only attributed to people with a full-time job and evokes contrast to the term *gakusei,* meaning 'student'.

understood that the 'tricky part' of their student migration journey extended well beyond the post-study transition, and that their incorporation into the 'particular culture, a particular set of rules' that govern Japanese society was complicated by the fact that they would 'always be a foreigner' in the eyes of native Japanese people.

Emirbayer and Mische go on to explain that, having recognized problematic and unresolved features of their social milieu, individuals go on to 'characterize' these problems in terms of broader social movements. In this case, the ongoing problems and tensions surrounding participants' integration into Japanese society post-study was 'characterized' within the context of Japan's historical aversion to migrants. Direct reference to this aversion was common within the narratives, and sometimes emphasized by comparisons to other contexts that, as participants felt, were more 'accustomed' to accepting and welcoming migrant populations. These statements reflect a normative judgement of Japan as a place to settle post-study, wherein student-migrants must seek a balance between their sense of opportunity and excitement around living and working in Japan, and the lingering concern that they may be 'invisible' or not 'acknowledged as part of the fabric of society'. The unresolved nature of this relationship appears not only as a vivid reflection of participants' everyday experiences in Japan, but also as a powerful influencing factor on their decision to either 'settle' in Japan long-term or seek other opportunities abroad.

Imagination of the Future

> I'm the type of person that's always planning, thinking of the future. Even in primary school, I dreamed of studying abroad. Then, maybe from age ten to fourteen, I started to like and then love Japan, so I started to plan how to come and study here. My dream was to come here, that was the first part. The second part was to live in Japan, and stay living in Japan. So I made a plan A, plan B, plan C. I was preparing everything to go there, and thought about the contingencies, just in case. Even after the disaster of 2011, my family asked, 'are you sure you want to go to Japan?' It was such a strong dream; I didn't want to go anywhere else. I applied six times for the scholarship. That specific scholarship was the best plan to guarantee that I could stay after graduating, so I just kept trying and trying.

> Fundamentally, I was happy to study in a developed country. I chose to study here in Japan not only to change my life, but to have the opportunity to choose the things I really want in future. Also, in a sense, it was hypothesis testing to see

if a life in Japan would be viable. It was a low-risk way to try it. If everything fails, rocks fall, I could go somewhere else.

From now, it's really hard to say what will happen. I am okay with adapting to life here, but I'm also keeping my options open. If I want to do a Ph.D. in the Netherlands of Germany, it is possible. Maybe I can go to the US, maybe Australia or something like Canada. Maybe Singapore? Actually, I want to go to London or England; it's a huge country and I want to learn how the global company grows there. In ten years, I want to become at least the manager of a brand's office in London. Maybe after twenty years, I want to make my own company.

This vignette illustrates the significance of imagination throughout student-migrants' trajectories. First, the changing target of projection reflects student-migrants' changing temporal horizons. Narratives revealed that some participants began to imagine studying and living abroad as early as primary school, developing both dreams of a future abroad and plans in their pursuit. During studies, the focus of imagination turned to the immediate post-study environment, and the best opportunities that awaited them after their graduation. Finally, post-study, participants began to look to myriad possible futures with wildly varying goals and timescales. Evidently, the target of the imagination shifts throughout an extended trajectory, such as the education-migration nexus, but the influence of imagination on action was evident throughout, indicating the persistent influence of an imagined future on present actions.

This vignette reveals how various types of action can be linked to the imaginative element of agency. Participants engaged in what Emirbayer and Mische (1998) call 'hypothesization', developing images of possible futures and playfully imagining where they might fit within them. This often took the form of distant imagination of various mobility trajectories, but was also evident in more considered and extended narrations of specific pathways of action. Similarly, the participants provided extended narratives of their specific plans for how they might pursue particular pathways of action that they had come to value. This was not always limited to a specific plan, but often ran to several linked contingencies numbered or lettered according to their preferences. Finally, the participants imagined how these plans may resolve themselves in the fullness of time and how these imagined resolutions influenced their decision regarding whether a particular path of action was worth pursuing at all.

A further important feature of narratives was what Emirbayer and Mische (1998) refer to as 'experiential enactment', where individuals experiment with possible trajectories in low-risk ways to gain insights into the probable outcomes of a particular course of action. Some described the very act of studying abroad as a 'low risk' way to experience life in Japan before committing to living and working there in the long term. For others, the immediate post-study job was not described as an end in itself, but rather as a way to prolong their time in Japan while 'keeping ... options open' to either remain in Japan or move elsewhere. In either case, a short-term commitment to Japan was seen not only as a means to both experience and enjoy life in the country, but also as a way to reduce uncertainty around a more prolonged stay.

Mixed

> It would have been so different if I studied at a university at home. Just go to class every day, you don't really need to think about anything, just follow the route like everyone is doing. But I don't necessarily go places just because I know people there, I don't try to just walk in others' footsteps. I prefer to do what I want to do, instead of what people are telling me I should do. That feeling got stronger after I came to Japan. I had wanted to be a civil servant because that's a stable job. But now I want something more challenging, where I can try different things. Once I got away from that discourse, that sense of what other people do, I was opened to new ideas.
>
> Since coming to Japan my whole sense of values, my view of the world has changed. I used to think 'I just want to fly', and prioritized my freedom over everything. I didn't have any distant goals. But now I'm not satisfied with my life; I need to grow up. I started thinking more long term. Before, I thought maybe two years ahead, but now I'm thinking ten years, fifteen years, twenty years in the future. It's a big change. After all, the world is just so damn huge.
>
> Of course, wherever I go, I will continue my relationship with Japan. Even as a student A, I've been working and B, I came with the intent of seeing whether or not this is a place where I want to stay. I was assessing it as a potential migrant. But I don't know what's going to happen in the future, so I'm going to do my best now to open as many options as I can, so I won't have any regrets in future.

This 'mixed' vignette illustrates the dynamism of agency evident in participants' changing desires and actions, showing evidence of all three elements of agency and the circumstances that lead to a transition between them. In this sense, it is a 'truer' reflection of any one individual's narrative, as changes in participants' desires, priorities and actions in response to changing circumstances and their own personal development was the norm.

An important example of changing orientations is evident in the opening paragraph, which illustrates how an anti-iterational sensibility may lead participants to discount or actively avoid pursuing established courses of action – thereby foregoing the influence of the past – and becoming more imaginative and judgemental in its place. Within this anti-iterational sensibility, participants were fully aware of the past, recognizing the courses of action that had been modelled by other important people or were socioculturally valued among their peers. However, rather than follow these examples, they instead made the decision to consciously avoid them and open themselves up to new ideas and alternatives. This is indicative of a conscious decision to value imagination of the future over the instructive influence of the past. Similarly, the evolution of participants' imagination was not only influenced by their changing temporal horizon, but by their satisfaction with their personal growth and position within society. The realization that one's position in society is unresolved or unsatisfying caused some participants to seek to understand the source of this dissatisfaction, thereby interrogating their evolving relationship with Japan as a place to reside.

Importantly, the vignette reveals how changes in agentive orientations may influence trajectories. A move away from iterational thinking was the catalyst for some participants' decision to come to Japan in the first place, while for others it laid a foundation for them to extend their stay post-study. Alternatively, participants who became more judgemental about their position within Japanese society developed a critical sensibility with regards to Japan itself and their place within it. Some found they were unable to reconcile the tensions inherent to their relationship with Japan and returned to their home country. Others found that they could reconcile these tensions and were happy to commit for at least the short-term.

Concluding Remarks

These vignettes provide novel insights into the development and practice of agency in the education-migration nexus. They show how each element of agency can have a powerful influence on individuals' actions, alerting them to opportunities and providing various tools to negotiate the challenges and tensions that they encounter en route. Furthermore, the vignettes illustrate the dynamic and changeable nature of agency in response to changing contexts and the simultaneous personal growth experienced by participants. Importantly, these findings are expressed in easily digestible narrative accounts, which effectively condense the essence of more than hundreds of pages of interview transcripts into a format that should be instructive and revealing for both social researchers and higher education practitioners. Specifically, practitioners should develop an understanding that agency, and the attendant desires and actions of individual student-migrants, must be understood as multifaceted and dynamic. While it is tempting to understand and manage international students as a uniform population, each student brings with them to Japan immeasurably complex personal and cultural histories that exert a powerful influence on their trajectories. I argue that, if we seek to better understand and manage flows of student-migrants through Japanese higher education institutions, we must be alert and responsive to these differences and not seek to flatten them for the purposes of administrative convenience.

This study represents only a preliminary foray into the study of agency in the education-migration nexus. While it provides powerful insights into various forms of agency that are evident in international students' trajectories, and the propensity for their agency to evolve and change dynamically throughout their journey, this study has only begun to tap into the potential of intensive research of this nature. Further research into the role of agency in guiding student-migrants' journeys, using a combination of narrative and alternative research methods, promises to further deepen our understanding of the internal dynamics of the education-migration nexus to the benefit of both universities and individuals.

11

Motivations and Work Roles of International Faculty in China

Futao Huang

Introduction

Since the 1990s, various important drivers have facilitated the international mobility of scientists, researchers and faculty members across nations and regions (OECD 2015). In some countries and regions, the main rationale of mobility relates to diplomacy or cultural development (Knight 2004). In others, the aim is to attract talents from other countries to support domestic knowledge economies (Woldegiyorgis, Proctor and de Wit 2018). As an integral part of the cross-border mobility of academics and scientists, it is generally agreed that recruiting international talents, including faculty members, from other countries or regions is considered as an effective way to enhance global competitiveness and to improve academic excellence of national higher education and research (Morano-Foadi 2005; Kim and Locke 2010). In East and Southeast Asia, countries like China, Japan, Korea, Malaysia, and Singapore share this perspective (OECD 2001). In these countries, hiring international faculty has played an increasingly important role in facilitating the internationalization of higher education, building up world-class universities as well as levelling quality and global competitiveness in the national higher education and research systems, especially since the early 2000s (Hazelkorn 2016).

Compared to much research on the international mobility of academics and scientists, and on recruiting inbound international faculty members in Western countries like the United States, the UK, some EU countries, and even Japan (Huang, Finkelstein and Rostan 2014; Altbach and Yudkevich 2017; Brotherhood, Hammond and Kim 2020), there has been less research on inbound international faculty in Chinese universities. Among the existing research, some researchers analyse how the Chinese government created and implemented strategies to attract international talents from other countries, especially advanced Western countries (Cao 2004; Chu 2013; Kim 2017). Kim's research (2015) describes foreign instructors' reasons for migrating to mainland China in addition to their academic activities and the difficulties they face in their Chinese universities, based on interviews with forty-one non-Chinese university instructors teaching in Beijing. Wu and Huang (2018) explore the main characteristics and motivations of international faculty in several case universities in Shanghai by discipline, age, gender and other characteristics. Larbi and Ashraf (2020), drawing on interviews with international academics in Beijing, investigate how international academics VIEW Chinese academia as either resourceful or restrictive for their academic careers and the challenges that international academics face in relation to mobility. However, little is known of full-time international faculty's motivations to work in China, and their work roles in China, whether based on quantitative or qualitative analyses.

This chapter discusses the main characteristics of full-time international faculty in several Chinese universities (excluding faculty hired as language teachers), focusing on their motivations for entering and working in China as well as on their work roles. Both quantitative and qualitative research methods are used. First, the chapter briefly reviews previous research. Second, it outlines key changes that have occurred in relation to international faculty in China, from a historical perspective, and discusses recent strategies relating to attracting international faculty to China. Third, it describes the demographic profiles, motivations and work roles of international faculty in Chinese universities based on findings from a survey and semi-structured interviews. The study concludes with an overall summary of why international faculty move to work in China and what they do after entering the country.

In this chapter, international faculty are defined as full-time faculty members who are non-Chinese citizens or foreign passport holders. This differs from definitions based on place of birth (foreign-born) or education (foreign-educated) as used in the United States and Australia. The term *Waiji Jiaoshi* in Chinese is similar to 'international faculty' in English. It normally refers to all teachers with foreign nationalities or citizenships who are hired in kindergartens, schools and higher education institutions in China. In the chapter, international faculty includes *Waiji Jiaoshi* at higher education institutions (note that most of this group are, however, usually language teachers who are not included in the study); faculty members who are hired in professional departments, colleges or schools; and high-level talents with foreign passports who are mainly concerned with research and writing up papers in Chinese universities.

International Faculty in China

Context

In the late nineteenth century, when the Qing Dynasty attempted to establish a modern higher education system, many international or foreign experts and academics were invited to come to China (Altbach and Selvaratnam 1989). Between the early twentieth century and the late 1920s, various Christian missionary groups established fourteen mission universities in China. Many Western faculty and administrators worked in these Western-style universities (Ng 2006, 2019). After the People's Republic of China was established in 1949, the new government invited thousands of Soviet educators and specialists in various fields to come to China. Although all of them returned by July 1960 following the outbreak of Sino-Soviet ideological conflict, they made a remarkable contribution to China's socialist construction, by restructuring China's higher education system and training university staff (Shen 2009).

As part of the culture revolution from 1966 to 1976, a great revolution also occurred in higher education. As China attempted to search for a totally new 'Chinese way' in higher education and research, and emphasized the contribution of higher education to proletarian politics and ideologies, and to solving particular problem in the Chinese society, the inward transmission of nearly all systematic Western knowledge in humanities and social sciences was blocked, and there were no real international exchange activities with either the former Soviet Union or the United States and other Western countries. The hostility between China and the United States from 1949 onwards, and the ideological and political conflicts with the former Soviet Union after the late 1950s, meant that in China it was almost impossible to educate and train domestic academics and scientists who understood Western developments in science and technology and had advanced knowledge. Because China lacked high-level talents or internationally recognized scholars in science and technology, when the reform and open-door policy was implemented from 1978 onwards, there was an urgent need to attract high-level overseas talents, including international scholars, to work in China. The early stage of internationalization of China's higher education from 1978 to 1992 was primarily concerned with dispatching students, scholars and faculty members abroad to learn advanced studies and conduct high-level research, inviting foreign scholars and experts to China, and the practice of teaching and learning foreign languages, especially the English language. As the English language becomes one of the university-wide subjects, international faculty, especially those from English-speaking countries, were hired at Chinese universities as language teachers. Their numbers expanded rapidly with the massification of China's higher education from the late 1990s onwards (Huang 2003).

After 1995, the emergence and development of transnational higher education institutions and programmes (*Zhongwai Hezuo Banxue* in Chinese, meaning co-operation between China and foreign countries in the operation or management of higher education institutions and educational programmes) generated the need for a large number of international faculty to work in China, in relation to educational programmes for domestic students that were provided either in branch campuses of foreign universities in collaboration with China's universities or within China's universities where joint programmes were provided in cooperation with institutions from the United States, Australia, the UK, Canada, France, Norway and Singapore. These faculty differed from the international faculty exclusively engaged in teaching foreign language for domestic undergraduate students. The fields of study offered in the branch campuses of foreign universities, and joint programmes inside Chinese universities, that became the task of international faculty (MOE 1998) included international finance, international accounting, computing, marketing, secretarial studies, fashion design, commercial English, practical English and other fields. With rapid growth in the number of both branch campuses of foreign universities and Sino-foreign jointly operated educational programmes in China, the number of international faculty working in these branch campuses and joint programmes expanded quickly. Some were directly dispatched by the foreign partner or home universities to Chinese campuses, while others were hired by the Sino-foreign jointly collaborative universities or branch campuses. For example, the University of Nottingham Ningbo China (UNNC) was the first Sino-foreign university, established in 2004. It now has an international community of approximately 8000 students and faculty members from about sixty countries. Many of its faculty members are world authorities in their fields (UNNC 2020).

With the outflow of Chinese scholars, faculty members and students abroad increased markedly from the early 1980s. The Chinese government, since the early 1990s, has made various efforts to attract overseas Chinese scholars, especially high-level young researchers or scientists undertaking research in cutting-edge fields of science and technology in advanced Western countries, to return and work in China (Zweig 2006; Welch and Hao 2013). Later, some of these so-called talents-attracting programmes also began to recruit non-Chinese nationals. As early as 1994, Chinese Academy of Sciences developed the Hundred Talents Programs to recruit skilled professionals from abroad. Although the main purpose of the programme was to attract young Chinese scholars who obtained their degrees in science and technology from advanced Western countries or had experience of conducting research in these countries, in 2011 it also began to attract high-level talents with foreign nationality and citizenship. According to Bai (2014), president of Chinese Academy of Sciences, by 2013, a total of 2145 high-level scholars had been attracted to work in China. Over 90 per cent came from the United States or European countries. Nearly one-third of them previously worked in either global top 100 universities or in fifty-nine internationally recognized research institutes. Soon after the implementation of the Hundred Talents Program, other national-level programmes were launched by the central-level ministries and departments to attract both overseas Chinese scholars and foreign scholars to work in China. Major programmes include the Changjiang Scholars Program of 1998, the Thousand Talents Plan of 2008, Recruitment Programs of Young Global Experts of 2011, and the Ten Thousand Talents Plan of 2012 (Peters and Besley 2018). Some globally renowned academics are given the title of Changjiang Scholar. For example, Michael Herzfeld, a professor in the anthropology department of Harvard University, was appointed to be a Changjiang Scholar at the beginning of 2015 (Byju and Levine 2015).

There are no publicly available data of how may international scholars or scientists have been recruited to come to China through all these programmes together, but by the mid-2017, the Thousand Talents Plan had attracted 381 foreigners (Jia 2018). Among these foreign scholars, some are world-famous scientists. For example, it has been reported that Professor Charles Lieber, a prominent Harvard University chemist and nanotechnology pioneer, was recruited to work in Wuhan University of Technology through the Thousand Talents Plan (Subbaraman 2020). In relation to the recruitment of high-level talents from abroad, the significance of the 985 Project in 1998 and the Double World-Class Project in 2017 cannot be overestimated. These projects have aimed at improving the quality of China's higher education and research, lifting the global competitiveness of China's higher education, building world-class universities and establishing disciplines that are globally first-class. Similar to the

985 Project but much more ambitious, the key goal of the Double World-Class Project in 2017 is to build forty-two world-class universities and approximately 456 world-class disciplines in ninety-five universities by mid-century. Hiring global talents is considered to be one of the most effective and quickest ways to achieve the goal (Huang 2017). In addition to these national-level programmes aimed at recruiting high-level talents from foreign countries, the central government expects local authorities and individual universities, especially research-intensive universities, to hire more international faculty members who conduct research and teach graduate programmes in professional fields. The Shanghai local government has several supportive policies designed to attract increased numbers of high-level international talents to work in Shanghai (Shanghai Administration of Foreign Experts Affairs (2021).

As a result, a large number of universities have developed their own strategies, job positions and salary systems so as to attract international faculty to help them fulfil their missions. Top universities like Peking and Tsinghua, and Shanghai Jiaotong, hope that by attracting top international faculty members, they will enhance the standard of their academic faculty, their internationalization, their global reputation and their standing in major global university ranking systems (Huang 2015). Even non-research universities, including local public institutions, hope that by employing high-level international faculty members they will better incorporate the international dimension into their university-wide curricula, build their research capacity and level, form international academic networks and especially train graduate students and young academics. Moreover, as mentioned earlier, the emergence and expansion of Sino-foreign collaborative programmes and universities in China has continued to generate increasing numbers of international faculty members.

Recruiting international faculty members from abroad is only one part of China's ambitious plans to attract high-level talents from foreign countries. Without a doubt, the changing goals of internationalization of China's higher education, and the other factors discussed above – especially the programmes and strategies developed at the levels of local authorities and individual universities – have facilitated a rapid rise in the number of international high-level talents, including faculty members, to work in China. However, certain issues have emerged. For example, given national policies relating to migration, including the adoption of the Green Card (Permanent Residence Card) System in 2004 (Wang and Liu 2014), given China's social welfare systems and given the relatively low level of internationalization of many Chinese cities compared to Singapore and even Japan, these recruitment programmes have not been able

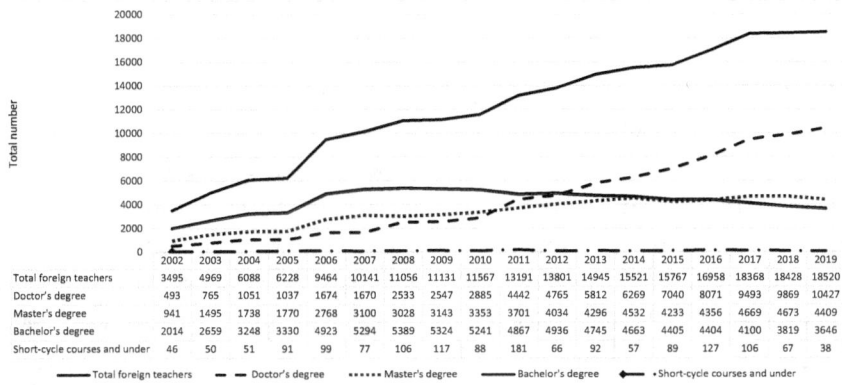

Figure 11.1 Changes in Foreign Teachers at Chinese Higher Education Institutions. *Source:* MOE (2019, 教育统计数据 [Educational Statistics]), http://www.moe.gov.cn/s78/A03/moe_560/jytjsj_2019/ (in Chinese).

to permanently attract the return of many of the best and brightest Chinese students, and the entry of international scholars, beyond the length of their overseas research and study stint (Cao 2008).

Further, as the majority of research-intensive and leading universities are located in big cities and coastal areas, a large proportion of the international scholars and faculty members are hired at leading universities and branch campuses of foreign universities that tend to be located in wealthier places in China. There is a net inflow of high-level talents from abroad into good universities and economically developed areas, while the northeastern and midwestern regions have difficulties in attracting these talents (Zhou, Guo and Liu 2018). This is one reason why this study focuses only on international faculty members hired at research-intensive universities, local public universities in the big cities and Sino-foreign jointly collaborative universities.

Growth of Foreign Teachers

There are no available national statistics of all international faculty members working in China. Partial data are available, for some faculty only.

The Ministry of Education issues a national table of foreign teachers (*Waiji jiaoshi* in Chinese) who are hired at Chinese higher education institutions every year (Figure 11.1). All university students in China are required to learn the English language as one compulsory subject and the number of language teachers is relatively easy to gather at a national level. These foreign teachers are hired as a result of the work of the national-level agency that is specifically in charge of inviting and recruiting international faculty members to come to China and work in Chinese higher education institutions on a fixed term basis. As a large number of these faculty are employed at Chinese higher education institutions as language teachers, the phrase 'foreign teacher' is mostly used as an official title for them. This is one category of the various academics, experts and scientists who move from foreign countries to work in China temporarily, for periods ranging from more than one year to less than one month. Those who are hired by individual higher education institutions based on various projects or college or faculty-wide budgets are not included in Figure 11.1. These foreign teachers only constitute one part of all the international faculty members who are hired at Chinese higher education institutions. In most cases, they are not considered to be full-time faculty members, let alone tenured faculty members.

In addition to that group, there are many full-time international faculty who are not primarily engaged in teaching foreign languages for Chinese students, but employed as faculty members or researchers in professional faculties, colleges or schools. These include those invited and employed in individual universities and research institutes as specially hired professors as well as scientists who work on various national projects and institutional projects. Unfortunately, summative data for this second group are not publicly available.

As shown in Figure 11.1, the number of foreign teachers at Chinese universities has expanded rapidly, growing from 3495 in 2002 to 18,520 in 2019, a five-fold increase over the period. Not only did the size of the foreign teacher workforce grow, but also the number of foreign teachers with doctoral degrees increased steadily. In 2002, the largest number of foreign teachers was those with bachelor degrees (2014), followed by those with master's degrees (941) and those with doctoral degrees (493). By 2019, those with doctoral degrees (10,427) had become the largest group, followed by those with master's degrees (4409) and those with bachelors (3646). This suggests that China has made good progress in attracting and hiring foreign teachers, based on the quality of academic degrees held.

Research Design and Methods

The study summarized in this chapter addresses the following two broad research questions.

1. Why did international faculty come to work in Chinese universities?
2. What roles were they expected to play in their current universities?

In order to deal with these questions, the study uses relevant data from a survey of full-time international faculty at twelve Chinese universities which was carried out from July to August 2017. The list of the target population was created based on the websites and other publicly available sources of international faculty who worked in Chinese universities. The study includes four research universities, six local public universities and two Sino-foreign jointly collaborative universities located in big cities such as Beijing, Shanghai and Hangzhou. By looking at the homepages and other publicly available sources of information on approximately 14,800 full-time faculty in these universities, the study team collected the profiles of 855 faculty who were considered as international faculty on the basis of name and personal experiences. The data on their personal, educational and professional characteristics, especially the nationalities or citizenships of these faculty members, were confirmed and checked for correctness via emails and other social media.

In July 2017, on the basis of the information collected as detailed above, the research team sent emails to 365 international faculty in these twelve universities, in English, with a link to an online survey questionnaire and an invitation to recipients to participate in the survey. In September 2017, after excluding the number of part-time international faculty answering to the survey, the research team received thirty-eight valid responses (response rate 10.4 per cent) from full-time faculty with foreign citizenship and nationalities. The main characteristics of these full-time international faculty in the twelve universities are presented in Table 11.1.

In terms of nationality, international faculty from English-speaking countries made up the largest proportion of the total. By discipline, the largest group were from humanities and social sciences.

The fuller study, of which this study in China is one part, is an international and comparative research project focusing on the identities, motivations and work roles of full-time international faculty in universities offering four-year programmes in several countries: the United States, the UK, Australia, the Netherlands, China, South Korea and Singapore, and also the Hong Kong Special Administrative Region (SAR) of China. In the case countries, a common survey questionnaire and interview guideline were used. The main objective of the survey of international faculty was to obtain a better understanding of the actual situation of these international faculty. In the case of China, specifically, it aimed

Table 11.1 Characteristics of International Faculty Survey Respondents

Gender	Male	32 (86%)
	Female	5 (14%)
Nationality	United States	13 (35%)
	UK	6 (16%)
	France	4 (11%)
	Germany	4 (11%)
	Australia	2 (%)
	Canada	1 (3%)
	Others	7 (19%)
Degree	Bachelor	28 (30%)
	Master	24 (26%)
	Doctoral degree	31 (34%)
	Post-doctoral degree	9 (10%)
Academic rank	Professor/Research professor	10 (27%)
	Specially appointed professor	1 (3%)
	Associate professor/Associate research professor	13 (35%)
	Lecturer/Assistant professor	9 (24%)
	Other (please specify)	4 (11%)
Discipline	Teacher training and education science	2 (5%)
	Humanities and arts	10 (27%)
	Social and behavioural sciences	4 (11%)
	Business and administration, economics	5 (14%)
	Law	3 (8%)
	Life sciences	2 (5%)
	Physical sciences, mathematics	6 (16%)
	Computer sciences	1 (3%)
	Engineering, manufacturing and construction, architecture	2 (5%)
	Other (please specify)	2 (6%)
Employment situation	Permanently employed (tenured)	11 (30%)
	Continuously employed (no pre-set term, but no guarantee of permanence)	4 (11%)
	Fixed-term employment with permanent/continuous employment prospects (tenure-track)	10 (27%)
	Fixed-term employment without permanent/continuous employment prospects	12 (32%)

Source: Based on Huang's investigation in 2017.

at identifying their career paths, living and working conditions, academic life and work, their roles, duties and responsibilities, and the challenges facing them.

As shown in the sections that follow, the motivations of the international faculty in China were shaped by academic or professional factors, cultural factors, economic factors, political factors and others. In relation to their expected roles, these related to engagement in international activities, teaching and research activities, faculty development activities and others. It is hoped that this research provides a comprehensive description of faculty motivations to work in China and the roles they expect, or are expected, to play.

As mentioned earlier, the study also undertook semi-structured interviews with a dozen international academics from different countries, working at different universities in China, before their profiles were gathered and analysed. These interviews were carried out in English with a common interview guideline, and they focused on the faculty's personal background, motivations of coming to China, their work roles, the challenges they face as well as their career expectations and prospect of an academic career. Each interview lasted for about forty to sixty minutes, depending on interviewees' convenience. All except two of the interviews were recorded and coded. The main characteristics of interviewees are described in Table 11.2. As indicated in Table 11.1, over

Table 11.2 Profiles of International Faculty Interviewees

University	Location	Institutional type	Interviewees
Q	Beijing	Research university	Professor A from Canada in School of Humanities
			Professor B from the UK in School of Medical Sciences
X	Southeast	Local public university	Associate professor from the United States in School of Engineering
S	Shanghai	Research university	Professor from the United States in School of Mechanics
D	Northeast	Research university	Professor from the United States in School of Material Science
J	Northeast	Research university	Professor from the UK in School of Sciences
H	Central China	Local public university	Professor from the United States in School of Life Sciences
N	East China	Sino-foreign collaborative university	Associate professor from the UK in School of Business

Source: Based on Huang's interviews in 2015–16.

half of all international faculty come from the United States and the UK, and this study used the findings only from interviews with faculty members from English-speaking countries.

In analysing the findings from the semi-structured interviews to gain a comprehensive understanding of participants' interpretations of their expected roles in China's universities, the team members read all relevant transcripts of interviews and became familiar with their main ideas and key points. The team members also reviewed and defined major themes, and conceptualized key themes in relation to the research questions. The team developed an overall sense of the structure of all analysed data, which is presented below using interviewees' comments and observations to illustrate this structure.

Results of Survey and Interviews

Motivations to Work in China Based on the Survey

As Table 11.3 shows, if 'Comparatively important' and 'Strongly important' are combined, twenty-nine of international faculty stated that they came to work to China for both academic or professional reasons. This is followed by those who answered with 'fondness for Chinese life and culture' (twenty-five), and those with 'Difficulty of finding employment in home country' (thirteen). In contrast, neither the economic reason 'Better living conditions than home country' nor 'Family reason is important for them to work in China' were important, because only eight respondents admitted each of these two factors.

We also asked international faculty to rate the importance of several factors to their work life in China; a question similar to the one about their motivation to work in Chinese universities. As Table 11.4 reveals, combining 'Comparatively important' and 'Strongly important', all mentioned 'interesting work', suggesting that this is the most important factor affecting their work life in China. This is followed by 'Personal independence in research' (thirty-six), and 'Personal independence in teaching' (thirty-four). Only twenty-eight of them noted 'Salary', which was ranked to be the fifth important factor among all the eight factors listed in the questionnaire. Apparently, the academic or professional reason and interesting work are the most decisive factors attracting and affect them to work in China.

With regard to the methods used by their current university to recruit international faculty, the data from the survey indicate that the largest number of

Table 11.3 International Faculty's Motivation to Work in Chinese Universities

Item	Strongly disagree	Comparatively disagree	Neutral	Comparatively agree	Strongly agree	Average
Academic or professional reasons	1	1	6	7	22	4.3
Fondness for Chinese life and culture	5	2	15	10	5	3.22
Difficulty of finding employment in home country	12	7	5	9	4	2.62
Better living conditions than home country	11	12	6	8	0	2.3
Family reason	14	4	11	5	3	2.43
Political reasons	22	7	8	0	0	1.62
By chance	12	1	12	9	3	2.73
Other	10	0	24	2	1	2.57

Note: Survey question: Why have your decided to teach/do research at a university in China?' ('1→5' indicates 'Strongly disagree → Strongly agree').
Source: Based on Huang's investigation in 2017.

Table 11.4 Factors Affecting International Faculty's Work Life in China

Item	Strongly unimportant	Comparatively unimportant	Average	Comparatively important	Strongly important
Salary	0	2	8	19	9
Job security	1	1	11	17	8
Career opportunities	1	4	6	21	6
Institutional prestige	1	4	11	15	7
Opportunities to learn and enhance competences	0	1	7	18	12
Personal independence in teaching	0	0	4	16	18
Personal independence in research	0	0	2	13	23
Interesting work	0	0	0	10	28

Note: Survey question: How do you rate the importance of the following factors to your work life? ('1→5' indicates 'Strongly unimportant →Strongly important').
Source: Based on Huang's investigation in 2017.

them (twenty-two) applied directly to their current university through public or international advertisement for the post, followed by those who applied for their current post through personal contact (fifteen) and those who were employed through an intermediate agency (three).

Data on Motivations from the Interviews

As suggested in the following findings, from interviews with all the participants in Table 11.2, it seems that almost all of the interviewees emphasized academic and professional reasons for working in their current universities. Those reasons included favourable research conditions, intensive research grant, personal support, the provision of advanced equipment and laboratories, the possibility of undertaking of long-term research and especially the capacity to concentrate on research without many teaching duties. For example, the professor at J University provided a typical answer.

> I found working in the current university is more exciting and productive compared to my previous affiliation in UK. I do not have to worry about research funding, facilities or supportive systems here. You just do research as you wish based on the contract. I take a great deal of pleasure from my academic and professional life here. (Professor at J University)

Self-actualization was one more factor affecting the decision of some to migrate to China. Some mentioned that it was possible to realize their ambitious dream and academic goals and also apply their knowledge and experience in Chinese universities. In a major sense, this can also be understood to be relating to academic or professional motivation.

> I used to work in a top research centre of environment science in a European country. I was a junior research assistant there and worked very hard. My research was not so evaluated as I expected. Perhaps it is because I was not graduated from that European country. But in current university, I am highly respected despite my young age. I am tutoring young doctoral and academics here in how to publish good papers, and even involved in faculty development activities. (Associate professor at N University)

Different from many Western countries, international faculty in Chinese universities also include some overseas Chinese scholars who changed their nationalities after going to foreign countries. In the study, there is one China-born faculty who changed his nationality to the American and returned to his university of graduation as a specially appointed professor. According to him, the most important reason for him to work in his current university is to contribute to the university in which he learnt a lot while he was a college student. His goal is to make his home university more internationally competitive and more internationally accepted. Similarly, his motivation to work in China is driven by academic or professional reasons.

> I graduated from this university about twenty-five years ago. I should contribute to my home university with my academic reputation and international networking in return to my beloved professors here, I suppose. (Professor A at Q University)

Some mentioned higher salaries and better treatment which they received from Chinese universities, through both national programmes and the universities that employed the faculty.

> As I am invited to work here based on a talent-attracting project, my salary is much higher than my Chinese colleagues. Besides, I have been allocated additional research grant and other research allowances, as well as a good team working for my project. I am quite satisfied with working and employment situation here. (Professor at S University)

Expected Work Roles Based on the Survey

As mentioned earlier, as in other East Asian countries like Japan and South Korea, international faculty are broadly divided into two types. One type refers to language teachers, who are outside the target population of the survey in this study, and the other refers to non-language teachers affiliated to professional colleges or faculties within their universities.

Table 11.5 presents the data concerning to what extent international faculty consider themselves to be exposed to the various expectations by their universities. In total, the largest number of them respond that they are expected to enhance the international reputation of their current universities (3.81, combining both 'Comparatively high' and 'To a very high extent'), followed by those yielding high research productivity (3.62), being active in carrying out international activities (3.24), bridging the linkage of their current universities and universities of their home countries (2.65), organizing faculty development activities in their current universities (2.76), recruiting more international students (2.65), undertaking any activities which cannot be accomplished by my Chinese colleagues here (2.65) and teaching language programmes for students

Table 11.5 International Faculty's Expected Roles in Their University

Item	Not at all	Comparatively low	Average	Comparatively high	To a very high extent	Average
Undertaking any activities which cannot be accomplished by my Chinese colleagues here	9	6	12	9	1	2.65
Teaching language programmes for students	20	8	2	4	3	1.97
Bridging the linkage of my current university and universities in my home country	9	9	6	12	1	2.65
Recruiting more international students	10	7	9	8	3	2.65
Helping enhance the international reputation of my current university	3	0	9	14	11	3.81
Organizing faculty development activities in my current university	7	9	9	10	2	2.76
Yielding high research productivity	5	3	3	16	10	3.62
Being active in carrying out international activities	6	2	12	11	6	3.24
Other	7	1	25	1	3	2.78

Note: Survey question: To what extent do you consider yourself to be exposed to the following expectations by your institution? ('1→5' indicates 'Not at all →To a very high extent').

Source: Based on Huang's investigation in 2017.

(1.97). Obviously, from the perspective of international faculty, they are hired to enhance the international reputation of Chinese universities through their research activities. In addition, they are expected to be primarily involved in international activities, but the fewest number of them are expected to teach language programmes for students.

Expected Roles Based on the Interviews

In relation to their expected roles, despite differences in degree and expression, it seems that no fundamental differences can be found between the interviewees' answers and the results from the survey. None mentioned being asked to recruit more international students for their departments, colleges or schools within their affiliations, or only to teach language programmes for students, especially undergraduate students. Most of them emphasized that they were hired to concentrate on research. Most noted that the universities seem to expect high research productivity from faculty; this was consistent with the results from the survey.

> I do not have teaching responsibility neither am I asked to attend any committees. What I am asked to do is just to conduct research and to publish research papers in SCI journals. (Professor B at Q University)

Some of them mentioned that they were invited to be leaders of one key discipline or laboratory at a national or international level.

> I am asked to lead a national-level key discipline and form a team. My team is expected to produce graduates with international competitiveness and especially to publish research articles in journals indexed by the *Web of Science* such as *Science* and *Nature*. (Professor at S University from the United States)

One of the interviewees said that he was asked to manage a domestic faculty. Previous studies suggest that that is a rare case in the role played by international faculty in most countries.

> I am executive dean of this college. I am supervising two doctoral students. But my major duty is to run this college modelled on my home university in the United States. (Professor at H Universit)

Further, some of them are expected to foster and mentor young academics.

> I am mainly concerning with supervising doctoral students and mentoring young academics here. I also teach them how to write English research papers

and how to publish research outputs in internationally peer-reviewed journals. (Associate professor at X University)

In contrast with the situation of language teachers, it appears that the most interviewees' primary roles and responsibilities were engaging in the enhancement of the research quality of their current affiliations through work on publications in indexed journals, supervision of doctoral students and mentoring of young faculty.

Discussion

Impacted by the massification of Chinese higher education, and the increased emphasis on the importance of teaching and learning of English and other foreign languages on Chinese campuses, the number of international faculty hired as language teachers underwent a major expansion in the past thirty years. Since the late 1990s, strategies to hire a new type of international faculty, non-language teachers, have developed, at both national and institutional levels. This has facilitated the recruitment of international faculty, who are expected to meet specific requirements in particular fields of study, to achieve goals of internationalization and to enhance the global competitiveness and academic excellence of Chinese universities.

Clearly, the characteristics of international faculty as reported in this survey are different from those of international faculty providing foreign language programmes for undergraduate students in Chinese universities. For example, a majority of the former are male with doctoral degrees, associate professors and US citizens. The largest number of them were associated with the humanities and social sciences, and a majority of them were hired as tenured and tenure-tracking faculty members. Despite the very limited number of valid respondents, the study depicts a category of international faculty who were additional to the category of language teachers, and also distinct from the category of specially appointed professors who are mostly involved in supervising Chinese doctoral students and young academics, and work as principal investigator in national-level key laboratories, supported by programmes such as the Thousand Talents Plan and the Changjiang Scholars Programme.

In relation to their motivations for coming to Chinese universities, both the results of the survey and interviews suggest that academic and professional reasons are the most important. These include the availability of adequate research funding, favourable working conditions and the possibility of self-actualization. These points are consistent not only with recent research by Huang (2018a) who found that academic and professional factors are the two key drivers for international faculty working in Japanese four-year universities, but also largely with research by Janger and Nowotny (2016). These researchers found that 'attractive jobs satisfy researchers' "taste for science" and increase their expected scientific productivity, responding to both intrinsic and extrinsic motivations' (1672). Also, salaries, research funding and working with stimulating peers matter when faculty move from home country to foreign countries. Further, the findings of the present study are partly consistent with Kim's finding (2015) which notes that many foreign professors moved to China as their last resort for various reasons, including fulfilling research purposes and advancing their careers. These findings were based on the interviews with forty-one foreign academics working in Beijing.

In relation to their expected work roles, because the study concentrates on the analysis of non-language full-time faculty working in universities, mostly research universities, it is not difficult to understand why most of these faculty are expected to produce research papers and enhance the international reputation of their current universities. This is a fundamental difference in their expected roles, when compared with those of language teachers. From the global and comparative perspective, they are different not only from foreign-born and foreign-educated faculty in the US universities, who are more academically productive than domestic faculty (Kim, Wolf-Wendel and Twombly 2011), but also different from most international faculty in Japanese universities, who are hired so as to carry out duties and undertake activities which cannot be accomplished by Japanese faculty (Huang 2018b).

Conclusions

The main findings of this study are as follows. First, the most striking characteristics of non-language teachers with foreign nationality in Chinese universities have been presented, although some of these characteristics are shared with international faculty in other countries. Second, the survey and interviews demonstrate clearly that the most important factors influencing international faculty to work in Chinese universities are academic or professional, rather than the prospect of better salaries. Third, international faculty are treated differently from language teachers and also somewhat differently from domestic faculty in relation to salaries, working conditions, workload and roles; they are expected to play different roles from those of the language teachers. A new type of international faculty has been gradually forming and expanding among faculty in Chinese higher education institutions. It is likely that the formation and growth of this new type of international faculty has led and will continue to lead to a wide variety of international faculty who are hired in Chinese universities.

The limitations of this research are obvious. First, the number of valid responses from the survey is too small and can hardly provide a comprehensive portrait of international faculty in Chinese universities. Second, as part-time and language teachers are not included in the study, it is unclear as to what extent the main findings from the study apply to those other type of international faculty who are mainly concerned with teaching language programmes in China. Third, it is desirable to develop a deeper and more detailed analysis of the characteristics of international faculty by considering variables such as age, gender and form of employment, an analysis that can account for the impact of these variables on their motivations and expected roles. Finally, a more comprehensive study of the division of labour and work roles between international faculty and domestic faculty, and the impact of institutional context, academic discipline, age, gender and academic rank is sorely needed.

12

The Covid-19 Pandemic and International Higher Education in East Asia

Ka Ho Mok

Introduction

The internationalization of education is facing an unprecedented challenge because the world is presently confronted with the Covid-19 pandemic. Prior to the current global health crisis, increasing concerns were raised about the value and benefits of international education to different social groups. Critics of the internationalization of education emphasized that international student mobility only favours the elites in society, disadvantaging groups with limited socioeconomic status (Mok, Wang and Neubauer 2020). In view of the Covid-19 pandemic, some leading scholars in the field of international higher education believe that a broad-based global crisis for higher education is emerging, of which one major consequence is the intensifying inequality after the post-pandemic period (Marinoni and de Wit 2020). Although Mok and Marginson anticipated a potential paradigm shift from West to East when students choose their overseas learning destinations (Mok 2020; Marginson 2020a), other scholars have considered that the future of globalization may be called into question.

Issues related to the impact of Covid-19 include international student mobility, international collaboration in terms of research and academic programmes and higher education financing of those institutions with heavy reliance on international students as major funding sources (Neubauer 2020; Tilak 2020; Welch 2020; Facer 2020; Montgomery and Watermeyer 2021). This chapter is presented in the context of the Covid-19 pandemic to critically examine (1) how international students evaluate their learning being affected by the sudden outbreak of this health crisis and (2) how Chinese students assess the impact of the Covid-19 pandemic on their future overseas study plans. The chapter also discusses how geopolitical and socio-psychological factors will affect future international higher education, particularly how the deteriorating diplomatic relations between China and the West will affect the future of international higher education in East Asia. Special attention is also given to examining whether and how the enhanced regional cooperation framework between Association of Southeast Asian Nations (ASEAN) and the 'Big Three' (i.e. China, Japan and South Korea) plus Australia and New Zealand could promote considerable intra-regional student mobility in East and Southeast Asia.

Impact of Geopolitics and Stigmatization on Future International Education

Notwithstanding debates on the value of international education favouring the elite but disadvantaging the less-fortunate socioeconomic groups across the world (Mok, Wang and Neubauer 2020; Altbach and de Wit 2020), students from Asia, particularly from China, India and some East Asian countries, have constituted the major sources of international students to popular destinations for study overseas based in the UK, the United States, Canada and Australia. Over the past two decades, the number of Chinese students studying overseas has increased from 39,000 in 2000 to 662,120 in 2018 (Li, Fang and Sun 2020).

Figure 12.1 clearly shows an increasing trend of Chinese students going overseas for international learning. Similar upward trends are found in Australia, one of the university systems attracting and admitting a significant number of international students from Asia, particularly from China and India (see Table 12.1).

Taking Australia as an example, the majority of the universities have been reliant on international students as one of the major sources of income, and Chinese students constitute approximately 33 per cent of overseas students in Australian higher education, while the majority of the international students are from Asia (see Table 12.1). Figure 12.2 presents the trends of steady increase in the past decade of Chinese students pursuing international education in preferred institutions in traditional Western societies, such as the United States, the UK, Canada, Australia, New Zealand and other European countries. However, a few Asian cities/regions have also attracted some Chinese international students.

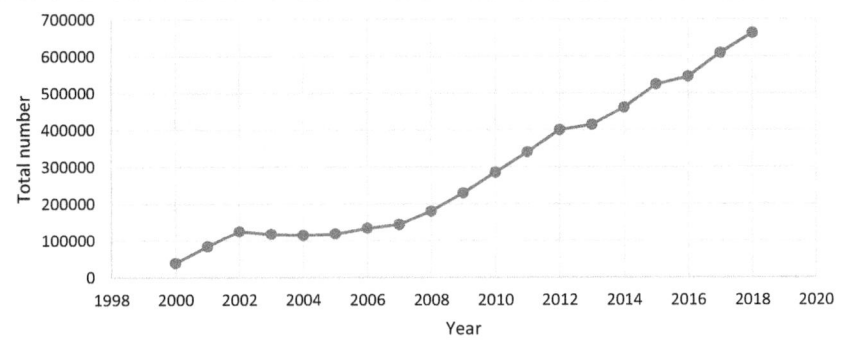

Figure 12.1 Total Number of Chinese Tertiary Students Studying Overseas, 2000–20. *Source:* UNESCO Institute of Statistics (2020); Education: Inbound internationally mobile students by country of origin, students from China, both sexes.

Nonetheless, with the emergence of anti-China politics and anti-Chinese sentiments being orchestrated by some liberal economies in the last few years, partially resulting from the trade war between the United States and China, coupled with the worsening diplomatic relations between China and the West 'dramatized' by the Covid-19 pandemic, the following discussion will critically examine whether and how the changing geopolitics between China and the major powers in the West would affect international education. Recent research has suggested that the future of international higher education is dependent upon the geopolitical conflicts between China and the United States. As a superpower since the end of the Second World War, the United States is made anxious by the emergence of China, which may challenge American hegemony (Tunsio 2018). The recent trade war between the United States and China clearly shows the superpower rivalry between the two giant economies (Dupont 2020). The power struggle between the two countries is escalating regardless of the current pandemic, and this would certainly pose a challenge for the future development of higher education, especially when higher education is becoming one of the arenas of great power politics (Song 2017).

Against the context of great power politics, the containment strategies adopted by the United States and its allies have moved beyond geopolitical conflicts, territorial disputes and trade (Riddervold and Rosen 2018; Dupont 2020). Higher education has become another domain for competition, particularly given China's global promotion of 'soft power' through supporting the establishment of Confucian Institutes globally (He et al. 2020). The unfriendly policies adopted by liberal

Table 12.1 Top Five Sources of International Students in Australian Higher Education, 2013–19

		2013	2014	2015	2016	2017	2018	2019
China	enrolments	85,724	89,087	96,768	112,505	133,542	152,534	164,458
	% of total	37.2%	35.7%	35.6%	36.8%	38.3%	38.3%	37.3%
India	enrolments	16,653	26,237	35,135	44,311	54,012	71,668	90,333
	% of total	7.2%	10.5%	12.9%	14.5%	15.5%	18.0%	20.5%
Nepal	enrolments	8,005	10,144	12,176	15,123	21,339	28,120	34,403
	% of total	3.5%	4.1%	4.5%	5.0%	6.1%	7.1%	7.8%
Malaysia	enrolments	14,962	14,348	14,395	14,586	14,647	13,982	13,080
	% of total	6.5%	5.8%	5.3%	4.8%	4.2%	3.5%	3.0%
all other countries	enrolments	96,658	101,065	104,697	110,048	116,271	121,936	128,107
	% of total	41.9%	40.5%	38.5%	36.0%	33.3%	30.6%	29.0%
total	enrolments	230,719	249,350	271,641	305,306	349,083	398,123	440,995
	% of total	100.0%	100.0%	100.0%	100.0%	100.0%	100.0%	100.0%

Source: Author, adapted from Welch (2020).

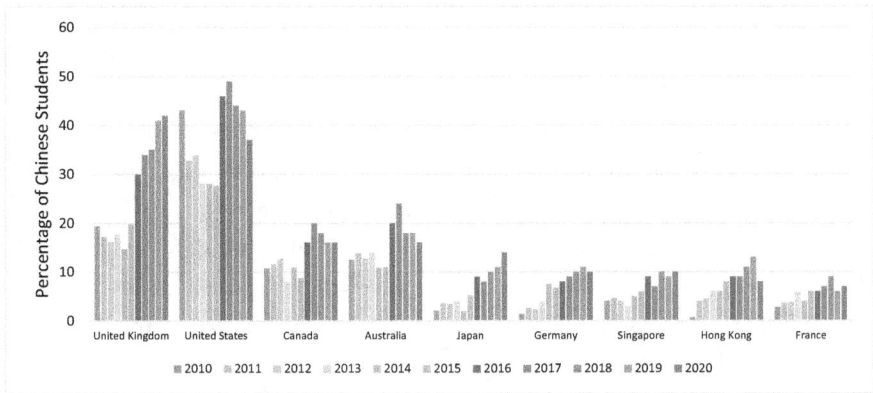

Figure 12.2 Chinese Students' Preferred Destinations for Studying Abroad, 2010–20. *Source:* Author, using data for 2010–15 from the *Report on the Intent of Chinese Students to Study Abroad* (Eic Education, 2010–15); data for 2016–20 generated from *Report on Chinese Students' Overseas Study* (New Oriental Education).

economies in the West, such as Australia and the United States, when dealing with Chinese researchers and students have been the result of fear that some of these students and researchers would act as spies for the Chinese government. The tense relationships between the Chinese government and its Australian and American counterparts should have affected the choices of Chinese students when planning for studying overseas (Marginson 2020a; Welch 2020; Mok 2020).

Marginson (2020b: 1) explained that 'COVID-19 has hit at a time of worsening geopolitical rivalry, the weakening of multilateral institutions, an implosion of national politics and an increase in state control'. Despite these trends, he noted that the public good model in academia remained relatively strong and the levels of US-China collaboration in science and higher education is still remarkably high. In relation to the pandemic and higher education, Marginson highlighted the situation in the UK.

> In response, universities in the UK decided to continue offering face-to-face classes in 2020–21 academic year, and enrolment numbers have, indeed, stayed up, at least for now… the big worry was what might happen to revenue, to the bottom line, in what is a market-based system where institutions survive partly on international student fees. UCL – the country's third-largest research university – gets £300 million, or 20.2% of its income from non-EU student fees. (Marginson 2020b: 1)

Anthony Welch, a professor of education based in the University of Sydney, highlighted the challenges faced by universities in Australia, and he argued that except for the Group of Eight, which are the country's top-tier universities, all other universities, particularly the regional ones, would face severe financial difficulties in view of the declining number of international students. Since the diplomatic relation between China and Australia worsened, the Chinese government has repeatedly discouraged Mainland students from going to Australia to study. Welch indicated that given the impact of the Covid-19 pandemic, together with the unsatisfying China-Australia relationship, the future of higher education in Australia is anticipated to become bleak. Universities in Australia have begun to face funding cuts, redundancies, positions being withhold and capital projects being stopped (Welch 2020).

The situations portrayed by Welch and Marginson vividly reveal the worries confronting some major higher education systems which are heavily reliant on international students as a major source of incomes. Most importantly, the future of international higher education, particularly student mobility patterns, can be significantly affected by the geopolitical factors, although we cannot strictly offer scientific measures.

Apart from the impact generated by the changing geopolitical factors, we must also consider international students' well-being and learning experiences during the Covid-19 pandemic when analysing the future of international higher education. Since the outbreak of the Covid-19 pandemic, Chinese international students have faced *double stigmatization*. Qi, Wang and Dai (2020) explained that the 'double stigmatization' that Chinese students experienced when studying overseas is as follows: 'first, they have been discriminated against by the "Chinese virus" stigma whilst they were overseas in the early stage of the pandemic. Second, they have been targeted in multiple ways by the anti-China politics triggered by the coronavirus' (1). Before the Covid-19 pandemic, Chinese students were extremely keen on attending traditional Western countries to study, the most popular choices being the United States, the UK, Canada, Australia and New Zealand, while Asian countries or regions, such as Japan, South Korea, Hong Kong, Singapore and Taiwan, also received a few Chinese students. The preceding research on Chinese students' choices of destinations for overseas learning has suggested a potential shift from Western countries to Asian countries/region. Although we have no systematic research findings supporting the potential paradigm shift previously highlighted, we should not disregard the significant but negative impact of the 'anti-China politics and anti-Chinese sentiments' commonly found in traditional Western liberal economies on Chinese students' choices when planning to study overseas.

Qi, Wang and Dai (2020) indicated that:

Since April 2 [2020], over 410 reports of COVID-19-related racism have been documented in Australia. In the Australian COVID-19 racism Incident Report Survey, 15 per cent of 410 respondents identified themselves as international students, of whom 80 per cent were from China. Considering that more than 165,000 Chinese students currently study in Australia, this report indicates strong anti-China and Chinese sentiments there. With the deepening of the tension between the Five-eye Alliance and China, and different queries about China's way of handling the pandemic in the early stage, Chinese students seemed to bear the brunt of such conflicts. (3)

Moving beyond Australia, no difficulty is noted in finding similar anti-China politics and anti-Chinese sentiments across traditional Western destinations preferred by Chinese students for studying overseas. Prior to the conclusion of the US presidential elections in 2020, we can easily find the 'Blame China for Gaining Votes Campaign' in the United States. Former US president Donald Trump implemented several unprecedented anti-Chinese international education policies, including banning some of China's postgraduate students from staying in the United States after their graduation, accusing them of stealing intellectual property from the United States and having links with the People's Republic of China (PRC) military, among others. One report has indicated that at least 3000 Chinese students would have been affected by incidents related to such anti-Chinese sentiments (Wong and Barnes 2020). Xu et al. (2021: 51) showed that '[w]ith the number of cases outside China surpassing that in China, stigmatisation was imposed by some Chinese onto Africans in China'. Xu and the research team (2021) also explore how various factors 'such as the fear of infection, food and mask culture, political ideology and racism have affected the stigmatisation of different victim groups' (51).

The point that deserves attention in this study is that some Chinese students have experienced double stigmatization and *triple stigmatization* while studying overseas during the Covid-19 pandemic. Given an extremely strong determination to combat the pandemic, the Chinese government has adopted highly stringent and restrictive measures to prevent Chinese international students attempting to return to China after completing their studies overseas. With media reports of 'imported cases' often associated with student returnees, there has been another form of anti-Chinese international student returnees' sentiments emerging in the country. Striving for 'Covid-19-free' status, these returnees undoubtedly experience another form of stigmatization for being guarded against as potential/actual carriers and spreaders of Covid-19. When coming home, their experiences of strict border control measures, stringent public health preventive practices being imposed on quarantine and the resulting socio-psychological pressures would have affected their future in pursuing international education (McCarthy 2020). They may recall triple stigmatization, and such a 'discrimination' would deter them from considering overseas learning in the near future.

Sharing different conceptions and adopting diverse public health and Covid-19 preventive measures, high individualization and low social responsibility associated with the majority of the universities based in the West have contributed to the increase in infection cases and associated deaths. Institutions based in East Asia have adopted more stringent health preventative measures to combat the current global health crisis compared with their Western counterparts. Given an increase in infection cases confronting numerous universities in the West, we witnessed the lockdown of major cities and university campuses (Marginson 2020a). The closure of national borders has adversely affected student mobility and international higher education. Taking the UK as an example, although the country could still maintain an increase in international students in the 2020–1 academic year, the failure of the UK government to manage the Covid-19 pandemic again led to calls for the closure of numerous university campuses in October 2020, immediately after the commencement of the new academic year. When the academic term in the UK commenced in October 2020, numerous higher education institutions (HEIs) in the country had planned to offer online and face-to-face instructions. However, the increasing Covid-19 infection cases prevented the universities to return to face-to-face instruction. In view of the increasing infection cases in Europe, UK and the US, and Australia's ban on inward travel, Marginson expected international student mobility to take at least five years to recover, with significant regional differences. In a recent webinar hosted by Lingnan University in Hong Kong in October 2020, Marginson remarked that 'in East Asia student mobility has been growing for 15 years and will now grow a little bit faster' (2020b: 1).

The preceding discussions have set out the broad political economy context for the following analysis of two major surveys closely examining international students' evaluation of their well-being and learning experiences during the Covid-19 pandemic, and a survey focusing on how Chinese and Hong Kong nationals assess the impact of the health crisis on their study overseas plans. Two specific research questions were addressed in this research:

1. Would the growing anxiety emerging from the negative socio-psychological experiences resulting from the stigmatization and discrimination during their overseas learning deter Chinese students from studying overseas?
2. Would the intense relations between China and the major powers in the West affect Chinese students' overseas study plans? The following discussions will answer the two questions from the socio-psychological and geopolitical aspects.

Covid-19 Pandemic and International Student Experiences

The Covid-19 pandemic came so suddenly that many international students across the globe had not made any preparations from the financial, physical and even psychological dimensions. What is commonly found among international students studying overseas is anxiety and frustration during the global health crisis, specifically when they were not well informed with sufficient information on the pandemic and the related preventive measures (Amoah and Mok 2020; Teter and Wang 2020; Zhai and Du 2020). With strong intention to explore the impact of the Covid-19 pandemic on student well-being and learning, a survey was conducted by the research team of Lingnan University to explore the knowledge and experiences of international/non-local higher education students regarding the Covid-19 pandemic and the impact on their well-being. The survey was conducted online by using the Qualtrics ^{XM} survey system from 12 April 2020 to 1 May 2020. A convenience and snowball sampling approach was adopted to recruit participants globally. For international/non-local students, the study primarily involved students who were not citizens or permanent residents of the countries/regions where they are currently studying.

The survey involved responses from 583 students who responded to the questionnaire from six continents: Africa, Asia, Oceania (Australia), Europe, North America and South America. The respondents studied in twenty-six countries/regions. They studied in all types of academic fields broadly relating to the social sciences, the arts, humanities and physical sciences. The average age of the respondents was twenty-six years and the majority (54 per cent) were females. Research postgraduates (46 per cent) dominated the sample. The majority (46 per cent) of the respondents did not receive any form of financial assistance (i.e. scholarships). At the time of the survey, the majority (61 per cent) were still in the countries/regions where they are studying.

Major Findings

Main Sources of Covid-19 Information

The source of information for international students are diverse, with the main ones being new media, social media and social networks (e.g. family and friends). Although universities were also a regular source of information, they were certainly not the main channel providing students with updated news related to the Covid-19 pandemic (see Figure 12.3).

Knowledge of Covid-19

The respondents were generally conversant with the nature of Covid-19. However, their knowledge of where and how to seek help for Covid-19-related problems in the various countries/regions where they are studying was comparatively low (see Figure 12.4). A Wilcoxon Signed Ranks Test on the students' knowledge of the different aspects of Covid-19 showed a significant difference between each of the knowledge areas and their knowledge on where and how to seek help for Covid-19 (Table 12.2). This result indicates a need for additional support to students to improve their help-seeking attitudes and abilities in the countries where they study.

Feeling at Risk and Loneliness

The survey showed that the majority (47.5 per cent) of international students globally felt at risk to the Covid-19 pandemic. Given their immigration status in the various countries/regions where they study, they would apparently require

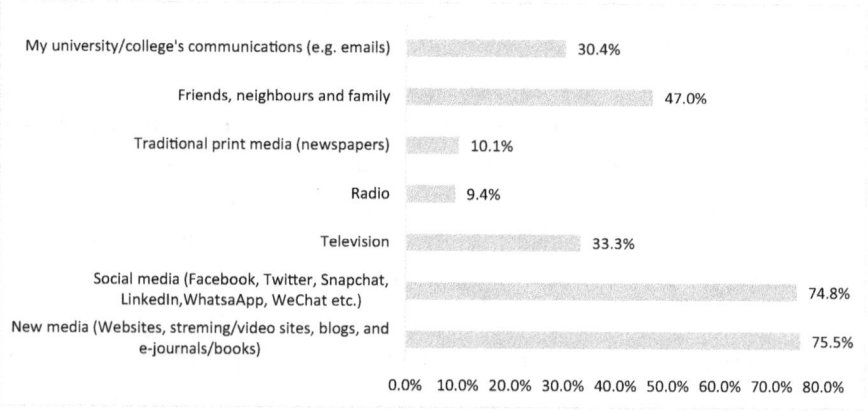

Figure 12.3 Sources of Information about Covid-19.
Source: Author, from Lingnan University survey.

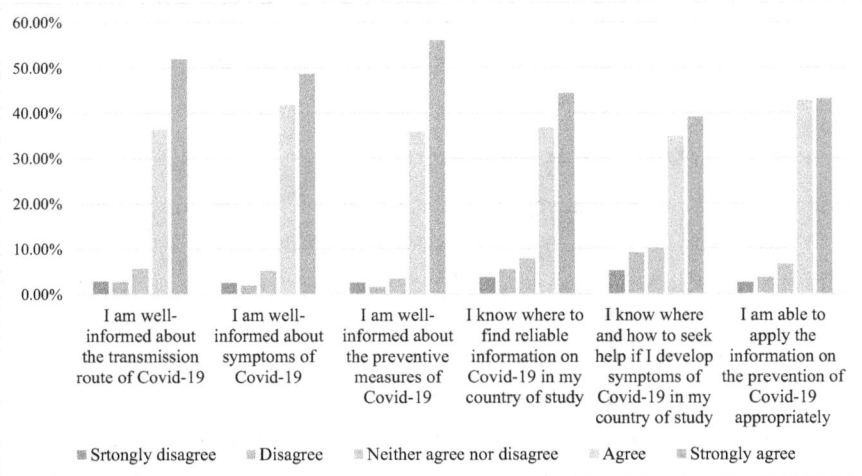

Figure 12.4 Knowledge of Covid-19.
Source: Author, from Lingnan University survey.

Table 12.2 Wilcoxon Signed Ranks Test of the Differences among the Various Knowledge Areas of Covid-19

	I am well-informed about the transmission routes of Covid-	I am well-informed about the symptoms of Covid-19	I am well-informed about the preventive measures of Covid-19	I am able to apply the information on the prevention of Covid-19 appropriately	I know where to find reliable information on the Covid-19 in my country of study
Z	−7.510	−7.636	−9.735	−6.114	−4.65
Asymp. Sig. (2-tailed)	0.000	0.000	0.000	0.000	0.000

Note: Bonferroni adjustment p-value criteria: 0.05/5 = 0.01.

additional support to deal with the pandemic. The high-risk perception relatively correlated with the extent to which the students felt worried with Covid-19, with approximately 71.7 per cent expressing worry. One major source of worry was their concern for their families when they were still overseas, and away from their homes after being locked down.

A troubling issue among the students was a clear sign of loneliness, as 45.2 per cent of them felt lonely during the pandemic. On the academic front, the majority of the students felt that the Covid-19 pandemic has caused a major disruption of their academic activities, with the survey indicating that as many as 89.6 per cent considered the effects from moderate to extremely large.

Covid-19 and Impact on Student Learning

In view of the apparent challenges to the academic activities of the respondents, the research team invited the respondents to evaluate how Covid-19 had affected their learning. The response was relatively mixed, with as many as 49.6 per cent of those responding to the question expressing slight to extreme satisfaction with current teaching and supervision arrangements by their institutions. Despite the uncertain conditions caused by the pandemic, the majority (57.4 per cent) of the students felt relatively satisfied with their life under the current circumstances. Most importantly, international students interviewed in the survey remained extremely positive amid the global health crisis. Despite their worries and the resulting loneliness, numerous respondents (83.8 per cent) were keen to return and study in their current institutions.

Placing the preceding studies into comparative perspective, every international student would undoubtedly have received the same level of support during the global health crisis. Although modern technology could maintain a considerable level of engagement with students through the online platform for teaching and learning, research related to students' evaluations of online learning provide strong evidence suggesting the limitations of having online learning as the only medium of teaching and learning (Xiong, Jiang and Mok 2020). Bush argued that 'excessive reliance on remote teaching and learning leads to an impoverished model, with students missing out on the wider benefits of global learning, including cultural gains' (2020: 13). Even though the adoption of online teaching and learning could maintain a certain level of student and staff interactions, we must note that students would have diverse learning experiences, particularly when some countries/regions have not developed adequate infrastructure to facilitate online learning (Baber 2021). 'If we look throughout the Asian region though, not all university students may be in the same situation – some of them may not even have internet access, let alone laptops or tablets' (Cham 2020: 4).

Taking the case of the Philippines as an example, Simbulan (2020) assessed that arrangements for online teaching and learning 'became unsustainable and some universities had to suspend remote or online classes because the uneven socioeconomic status of students affected their access to these modalities of learning'. A similar problem has been noted also in Malaysia, and Wan

(2020: 21) revealed that 'access to the internet throughout the country remains a challenge, especially for those in rural areas. Even those with internet access outside of campus may not have the bandwidth and speed to adequately support online learning'. The challenges related to internet access are obvious in Asia, enabling us to easily imagine that internet access is also a challenge to many countries/regions in Africa and South America (Teter and Wang 2020; Adotey 2020). Altbach and de Wit (2020) correctly suggested that the failure to offer a strong infrastructure to create a learning environment conducive for student learning would lead to a bleak future for poor countries. Critical reflections upon adopting online teaching and learning as the only or primary mode of instruction lead to the following question: Are we ready for post-Covid-19 educational practice? (e.g. Korkmaz and Toraman 2020; Mok, Xiong and Hamzah 2021).

Covid-19 Pandemic, Student Well-being Assessment and Overseas Learning

The preceding findings on international students' assessment of their well-being across twenty-six countries/regions have set out a relevant context for examining how Chinese students conceive plans for international education in the post-Covid-19 era. A survey conducted by the British Council in April 2020 shows that 39 per cent of Chinese students are unsure about cancelling their study plans. China is the largest source of international students in the UK, with 115,014 study visas issued to Chinese students in 2019, 45 per cent of which are international visas. When asked about their major concerns when conceiving their plans for overseas learning, the majority of the respondents overwhelmingly rated health and well-being (79 per cent), personal safety (87 per cent), finances (86 per cent) and application difficulties (70 per cent) as their major worries. However, the international media has reported several cases showing Asian students and residents experiencing discrimination or even assault when wearing face masks in the UK, Europe and Australia. These images would have affected Chinese students' plans and choices for international education. To understand how international students' well-being when confronting the Covid-19 pandemic would affect Chinese students' desire for overseas learning, the author of this chapter led a research team to conduct another study inviting university students in Hong Kong and Mainland China to assess their future overseas learning plans.

Covid-19: Impact on Chinese Students' Mobility

With reference to examining the impact of the Covid-19 pandemic on Chinese students' assessment of international education, the research team led by the author from Lingnan University distributed questionnaires to non-local students in Hong Kong and students in Mainland China, asking them to share their plans to study overseas after the global health crisis. The survey conducted by the research team has a broad policy implication if the interest of Chinese students choosing to study overseas has declined.

By mid-May 2020, the author and his research team had successfully reached out to approximately 2900 respondents and secured 2739 valid responses after data cleaning. Hong Kong, as an international metropolis, is also a popular choice for Mainland students. This survey on Chinese students' plans for overseas learning was conducted after another survey reporting citizens living conditions in the Greater Bay Area (GBA) in Guangdong Province indicated negative perceptions of Hong Kong early in April 2020. Witnessing the protests/social unrests responding to the Hong Kong government's attempts to introduce the Fugitive Offenders amendment bill in 2019, the GBA survey shows that people in Guangdong Province found Hong Kong to be no longer friendly, safe and well managed in terms of urban governance. These perceptions would inevitably affect Mainland Chinese students' preference to make Hong Kong as their destination for further studies. Whether people outside the city perceiving Hong Kong as performing well in social management, safety, tolerance and friendliness would have a direct impact on their decisions regarding studying and working in Hong Kong (Mok and Huang 2020).

The survey conducted in May 2020 on Chinese students' overseas study plans indicated that the majority of the respondents (84.4 per cent) chose NOT to study overseas, and only 16 per cent of the interviewees still had plans to study overseas when the global health crisis was over. When asked about their preferred destinations for overseas learning, several countries/regions were considerably popular. Among them, Hong Kong was identified as the second most popular place for further education, while the United States remained the most popular destination for overseas learning. One point that deserves particular attention is that many of the respondents preferred to study in Asian countries/regions; Japan and Taiwan are equally popular (both 10.8 per cent), while the UK is third (12.2 per cent) among the top five destinations. The less preferred countries were as follows: France (3.3 per cent), New Zealand (3.3 per cent), South Korea (3.04 per cent), Malaysia (0.94 per cent) and Italy (0.94 per cent).

Comparing the two major groups of respondents, those students who previously had overseas learning experiences or had enrolled in transnational education programmes through the Sino-foreign cooperative universities based in Mainland China showed additional interests to pursue higher degrees through international education. Among this cohort of students, their intentions for overseas learning were approximately 20 per cent more than the rest of the interviewees. Hong Kong was again chosen as the second most popular destination by students with overseas learning or transnational education experiences for further studies. The preceding findings are consistent with a recent research that examined how Chinese students who graduate from UK universities assess the relevance of overseas learning experiences to job acquisition/career development. The present survey again shows the perceived importance of international learning to Chinese students. However, will there be a paradigm shift from studying primarily in Western societies to the East, particularly in East Asia, with HEIs having received consistent international recognition in Asia?

To address the preceding question, the research team from Lingnan University conducted another small-scale survey asking Chinese students in the Mainland to review their overseas study plans when the global health crisis has become considerably stable in October 2020. Approximately 220 respondents shared their overseas study plans with us. When asked whether they still had overseas study plans, only 46 per cent were keen on studying overseas, while 54 per cent were not interested. For the top five destinations, the UK and the United States remained the most popular, followed by Hong Kong, Canada and Australia. When asked whether they would go for overseas learning after the Covid-19 pandemic, the responses were substantially positive, with 62 per cent indicating their interest and 38 per cent with no interest. For the preferred destinations, the top five were the UK, the United States, Australia, Germany and Hong Kong and Canada (tied). Evidently, Chinese students remain keen on international learning, although the survey sample is relatively small. When reflecting upon whether Asian universities would replace the traditionally preferred Western institutions for overseas study, only Hong Kong stands out from the preference list, while the rest of the top four remained the traditional countries that are popular among Chinese students (see Table 12.3).

The preceding findings on Chinese students' choice when planning their international education offers useful policy insights for HEIs globally, particularly where institutions of higher education have relied heavily on Chinese students as one of their major funding sources or incomes. For small cities developed as university towns across the UK, Europe, the United States and Australia, the

Table 12.3 The Most Popular Study Destinations for Chinese Students (Two-Round Comparison)

First round		Second round	
Countries/regions	Selected percentage (%)	Countries/regions	Selected percentage (%)
USA	17.1	UK	25.19
Hong Kong	13.3	USA	13.33
UK	12.18	Australia	10.37
Japan	10.8	Germany	9.63
Taiwan	10.8	Hong Kong	8.89
		Canada	8.89

Source: Lingnan University Research Team.

present surveys indicate that even these towns would welcome Chinese students to stay with them for international learning. However, whether they feel safe and secure would become major factors influencing these students' study plans. Most importantly, the future developments of international higher education will not be affected by the Covid-19 pandemic alone but also be significantly affected by the declining diplomatic relationship between China and some liberal economies in the West.

The major findings of the aforementioned surveys clearly present differences across cultures. On the bases of cultures that tend to emphasize social responsibility over individualism, the more effective response to the pandemic in East Asia means that the higher education situation in the region is considerably robust and stable. In view of the crisis management capability against the Covid-19 pandemic context, how Chinese and Asian students plan for their future overseas studies would become an important issue when examining the future of international higher education. Although US and UK institutions may rely on their reputations, Australia may struggle longer to recover, and HEIs in East Asia, such as those in Singapore and Hong Kong, may become more popular for Chinese students as destinations for overseas learning, particularly when these two city-states have highly ranked universities globally. Some of the challenges that higher education systems in the traditionally popular international study destinations in the West are currently facing, as well as their responses, will become institutionalized (Marginson 2020a).

Among the major challenges for institutions with strong intentions to win over international students is to adopt policies and measures supporting medically, physically, psychologically or financially vulnerable students studying overseas. All institutions with strong interests in recruiting international students should properly manage their desire for social interactions and cultural exposures. Offering only online learning and teaching for international students, and locking them down at hostels without carefully addressing their diverse learning needs, may deter them from choosing these institutions as their destinations for overseas learning (Mok et al. 2020). Having discussed the major findings of the two surveys presented, the following section examines whether the recently signed Regional Comprehensive Economic Partnership (RCEP) between the ASEAN and China, together with Japan, South Korea, Australia and New Zealand, will lead to a paradigm shift of Asian students choosing overseas studies within the Asian region than going to traditional Western countries for international learning.

Strengthened Regional Collaboration: Implications for East Asia

In the past decade, the Chinese government has made serious attempts to strengthen its relationships with neighbouring countries in East and Southeast Asia (Mok, Wang and Neubauer 2020). ICEF Monitor (2016) reported that China is using its relations with Southeast Asian countries to strengthen its education links and economic power in the region. In terms of student mobility, the Chinese government seeks to host many students from Southeast Asia. A report in 2016 indicated that the number of scholarships available to international students has increased by 500 per cent over the past ten years. This development has changed China's position as the third largest study destination in the world (Chan and Wu 2020). However, since the introduction of Belt and Road Initiative (BRI) as a global trade and investment strategy in 2013, the Chinese government has gone further to increase educational collaboration across ASEAN. The current tensions between the United States and China will affect international student mobility but to the advantage of HEIs in China. These strained relations, coupled with the Covid-19 control measures in China, will affect international higher education in the United States but provide an opportunity for Chinese universities to widen their increasing educational influence in Asia, particularly in Southeast and East Asia. Khanna (2019) argued that the United States and Europe's relations with Asian countries could weaken China's regional influence. Therefore, less interaction within Asia is important for China's influence.

Regardless of this assertion by Khanna (2019) and questions over the United States' involvement in Asia, China is further strategically cementing its position as an economic partner of Japan, South Korea, New Zealand, Australia and the ten members of ASEAN through the RCEP deal signed on 15 November 2020. Arguably, RCEP as a free trade agreement has a positive impact on 'China's image as a cooperative economic actor' (Lemert and Runde 2020). Performing a leading role in promoting RCEP, China will reap economically from RCEP's involvement and expand its industries in other countries. Against this political economy context, Monan (2020) argued that BRI supports developing countries to establish their own dual circulation development and should not be suspended as some development and political scholars are advocating.

Lemert and Runde (2020) analysed the impact of RCEP on China's positioning in the regional cooperation framework and indicated that 'RCEP also fits the China's "dual circulation" strategy, which pairs self-sufficiency driven by domestic consumption with supplemental international connections'. Given that China was excluded in the Trans-Pacific Partnership (TPP), the United States' withdrawal from TPP nearly four years ago has encouraged the former to move into that vacancy (Bradsher and Swanson 2020). Moreover, RCEP has provided China with an opportunity to reaffirm itself as a global leader through multilateralism, thereby increasing its dominant economic power in the Asia-Pacific region. Bradsher and Swanson (2020) explained that although RCEP is relatively limited in scope, it still plays a significant role in terms of trade deals. The RCEP deal is anticipated to provide significant growth by adding USD200 billion annually to the world economy by 2030, and USD19 billion to ASEAN's regional economy (ASEAN Today 2020). The following question should be answered from the geopolitical point of view: Could China, with RCEP, stop its reliance on overseas markets and technology affected by its rift with the United States? Damien O'Connor, trade minister of New Zealand, stated that education and primary industry sectors are among the major sectors to benefit from RCEP. Hence, Beijing would strategically target the 2.2 billion people in the region for trade and higher education development as well (RNZ News 2020).

Despite the aforementioned benefits, China could have benefited from India's involvement in RCEP and gained access to the latter's market if India had not pulled out of the negotiation of the RCEP deal in July 2020 (RNZ News 2020). During the RCEP deal meeting, Prime Minister Lee Hsien Loong of Singapore asserted that 'at a time when multilateralism is losing ground, and global growth is slowing, the RCEP shows Asian countries' support for open and connected supply chains, freer trade and closer interdependence' (ASEAN Today 2020).

RCEP shows that the US-China tensions do not dilute and destroy China's Asia-Pacific influence but uplift its image as a global leader, which is open for economic cooperation and trade. On the geopolitical level, RCEP could be a strategy by ASEAN and other RCEP members to support China in its dispute with the United States. Lemert and Runde (2020) correctly explained that the RCEP deal is 'China's first multilateral free trade agreement' that will usher them into a more open approach to global trade and increase market access in the Asia-Pacific region. Hence, this regional agreement could be interpreted as a game changer for economic cooperation and trade in the Asia-Pacific region. Accordingly, Petri and Plummer (2020) argued thus:

> The new agreements offset the effects of the trade war globally, but not for the US and China. The trade war between US and China makes RCEP especially valuable because it strengthens East Asian interdependence, raising trade amongst members by $428 billion and reducing trade amongst non-members by $48 billion.

Petri and Plummer (2020) believed that the United States and India are losers in terms of RCEP, but China, Japan and South Korea stand to yield large benefits from global national incomes by 2030, when 186 billion will be generated annually thereafter. The aforementioned study further argued that the pandemic threatens global interdependence, but deeper cooperation will help improve economic growth. By examining the impact of the newly assigned RCEP on higher education development, China would evidently ride over the Covid-19 pandemic to assert its regional and global leadership.

Beyond trade and economic development, a recent review of regional student mobility among different higher education systems in Asia has suggested the success of the ASEAN International Mobility for Students (AIMS) programme in promoting student mobility across different Asian countries. Between globalization and a decoupled Covid-19 world, regional student mobility has become and will become even more popular among Asian students, particularly when the unprecedented global health crisis has locked down numerous university systems in the West, leaving limited choices for Asian students when planning for overseas learning (Yeong 2020). Nomura (2020) analysed the recent student mobility across Asia and found there is success in establishing a sustainable student mobility platform between Japan and Southeast Asia, with steady increase of student exchanges. Dong Seok Seo and Hyeon Joo Kim (2020) analysed the recent development trend of student mobility between South Korea and ASEAN countries, and they argued that 'cooperation with diverse countries has led to the valuable opportunity to learn good practices of foreign education systems as well as to share ours (Korean education) with other countries' (2020: 11). The cultural exchange between South Korea and its ASEAN counterparts has enhanced the former's 'soft power', particularly when the existing curriculum combines with 'Korea's attractive pop culture'. Well before the recent RCEP agreement, ASEAN has led the way in repositioning Southeast Asia as a hub for international education and student mobility (Dang 2017).

The following question should be answered in analysing the future mobility trends of Chinese students or Asian students, who constitute the major sources of international students to major universities and HEIs traditionally based in Europe, the UK, North America, Australia and New Zealand. In the light of the referred regional cooperation frameworks enhanced by ASEAN and the Big Three, together with Australia and New Zealand in the Pacific: Would Chinese and Asian students engage in intra-regional mobility and learning? In the context of the Covid-19 pandemic, scholars have begun to analyse how the pandemic would affect international student mobility. Bothwell (2020) argued that the pandemic may lead to an increase in student mobility within Asia. As such, countries such as China and Malaysia will become major competitors to English-speaking countries, particularly the UK, the United States and Australia, because both countries have established transnational higher education programmes through branch campuses established by overseas universities (specifically from the traditionally preferred universities in the West) (Mok 2020). Marginson (2020a) noted that East Asia will become a regional hub for international students and higher education after the pandemic.

According to a recent QS Report, prospective Asian students may prefer pursuing studies in intra-regional universities. Malaysia, Singapore and the Philippines could be popular destinations for Chinese students when making their overseas study plans because these countries offer courses in English. One possible reason accounting for the increasing interest of Chinese or Asian students to pursue education in these countries is related to minimal pressure for applicants in terms of English requirements, given that universities in these countries may require international students commanding functional proficiency of English, which is the primary tool for cross-cultural communication (Nott 2020). Placing their specific concerns over safety, health and well-being as well as the quality of education, coupled with the reduced pressure for English proficiency, a potential 'shift away from Western dominance towards a greater variety and diversity in international education' is anticipated (Qi, Wang and Dai 2020: 5–6). We should also note that the increase in international students has decreased significantly in the last five years (Bennell 2019). Hawkins (2017) cited in Mok, Wang and Neubauer (2020) mentioned that China has the highest percentage of East Asian student mobility. Our discussion on and analysis of the Chinese and Hong Kong students' preferred destinations for overseas study also shows Asian universities stand out as Chinese students' preference compared with their Western counterparts during the Covid-19 pandemic (see also Mok et al. 2020).

If we consider the previously discussed socio-psychological factors when Chinese and Asian students recall their negative experiences and being discriminated and stigmatized when practising distancing amid the Covid crisis, we may well anticipate a declining number of these students going to study destinations associated with strong discrimination against students practising different public health preventive measures amid the global health crisis. We should also note that more parents in China and Asia would prefer enrolling in transnational higher education programmes through the 'joint-venture', having the international education experiences through the branch campuses established by leading universities in the West operating in Asia located in Singapore, Malaysia, Mainland China and Hong Kong. Such a trend is also reported by recent research, which has revealed the increasing interest of Chinese students enrolling in transnational higher education offered in the mainland by Sino-foreign cooperative universities, such as Xi'an Jiaotong-Liverpool University, University of Nottingham (Ningbo Campus) or other branch campuses operating in China through the cooperation between institutions from Hong Kong and their Mainland counterparts (Feng 2020; Mok, Ke and Tian 2021).

Capturing the opportunity for regional cooperation, 'countries within a region as culturally diverse as ASEAN stand to benefit greatly from student mobility programmes, such as AIMS, which provide a potentially powerful platform for bridging these cultures' (Gopinathan, Naidu and Yeong 2020: 29). With the recent RECP deal signed between China and ASEAN countries, New Zealand and Australia, China will seriously use the regional cooperation framework to strengthen its relationships with the member-countries to promote trade and the economy and also cultural and education exchange. Such actions would certainly break the difficulty for global student exchange when many national borders in the West remain closed because of the Covid-19 pandemic. Deepening regionalization more seriously, China would be able to consolidate its regional leadership in the coming years. With serious engagements with its Asian neighbours for deep collaborations, China would be able to develop a stronger regional collaborative platform, similar to the European Union, to counterbalance the challenges orchestrated by the United States and its allies.

Conclusion

The present chapter critically reflected upon two streams of research recently completed amid the Covid-19 pandemic. The findings and analysis have significant implications for future developments of higher education in Asia and the rest of the world. Well before the present health crisis, people have begun to question the value of the internationalization of higher education. The Covid-19 pandemic has fundamentally challenged the 'normal operations' of HEIs across the globe. Most people had taken student mobility and online learning for granted before Covid-19.

The above analysis clearly poses challenges for educators in higher education to search for ways to better manage student learning and protect international students when they study overseas. Specifically, for higher education systems, which have relied heavily upon international students as major sources of funding/income, they must devise measures appropriate for enhancing student learning and protect international students' well-being (Mok 2020). New university governance and additional collaboration across different higher education systems should be promoted to co-manage the uncertain future of higher education amid the Covid-19 pandemic (Fry et al. 2020).

Acknowledgements

The author would like to thank his research team from Lingnan University in Hong Kong for the support in conducting the surveys presented in this chapter. Special thanks go to Dr Padmore Amoah, Dr Weiyan Xiong, Ms Guoguo Ke and Mr Francis Arthur-Holmes. Part of the materials presented in this chapter is the revised and adapted version of previous research published online as media reports (see Amoah and Mok 2020; Mok 2020). The author is also grateful to Lingnan University for offering internal research grants to support the two surveys completed during the Covid-19 pandemic in 2020.

References

Chapter 1

Chen, K.-H. (2010), *Asia as Method: Toward Deimperialization*, Durham, NC: Duke University Press.

Chou, C. P. (2014), 'The SSCI Syndrome in Taiwan's Academia', *Education Policy Analysis Archives*, 22: 1–17.

Feng, Y. (1946/2020), *Xi Nan Lian He Da Xue Ji Nian Bei Wen* [Essay for the Commemorative Stele of the National Southwestern Associated University], https://www.tsinghua.edu.cn/info/1661/56243.htm.

Hall, S. (1992), 'The West and the Rest: Discourse and Power', in S. Hall and B. Gieben, eds, *Formations of Modernity*, 275–332, Cambridge: Polity Press.

Han, S., and X. Xu (2019), 'How Far Has the State "Stepped Back": An Exploratory Study of the Changing Governance of Higher Education in China (1978–2018)', *Higher Education*, 78 (5): 931–46.

Holcombe, C. (2011), *A History of East Asia: From the Origins of Civilization to the Twenty-First Century*, Cambridge: Cambridge University Press.

Jacques, M. (2012), *When China Rules the World: The End of the Western World and the Birth of a New Global Order*, London: Penguin.

Lee, J. T. (2015), 'Soft Power and Cultural Diplomacy: Emerging Education Hubs in Asia', *Comparative Education*, 51 (3): 353–74.

Leiden University (2020), 'CWTS Leiden Ranking', https://www.leidenranking.com/ranking/2020/list.

Li, J. (2012), *Cultural Foundations of Learning: East and West*, Cambridge: Cambridge University Press.

Li, Y. (2016), '"Publish SCI Papers or No Degree": Practices of Chinese Doctoral Supervisors in Response to the Publication Pressure on Science Students', *Asia Pacific Journal of Education*, 36 (4): 545–58.

Liu, W., G. Hu, L. Tang and Y. Wang (2015), 'China's Global Growth in Social Science Research: Uncovering Evidence from Bibliometric Analyses of SSCI Publications (1978–2013)', *Journal of Informetrics*, 9: 555–69.

Lu, Y., and G. Jover (2019), 'An Anthropocosmic View: What Confucian Traditions Can Teach Us about the Past and Future of Chinese Higher Education', *Higher Education*, 77 (3): 423–36.

Marginson, S. (2011), 'Higher Education in East Asia and Singapore: Rise of the Confucian Model', *Higher Education*, 61 (5): 587–611.

Marginson, S. (2013), 'Emerging Higher Education in the Post-Confucian Heritage Zone', in D. Araya and P. Marber, eds, *Higher Education in the Global Age*, 89–112, New York: Routledge.

Marginson, S. (2018), 'National/Global Synergy in the Development of Higher Education and Science in China since 1978', *Frontiers of Education in China*, 13 (4): 486–512.

Marginson, S. (2020), 'The Relentless Price of High Individualism in the Pandemic', *Higher Education Research and Development*, 39 (7): 1392–5.

Marginson, S. (2021), '"All Things Are in Flux": China in Global Science', *Higher Education*, https://doi.org/10.1007/s10734-021-00712-9.

Marginson, S., and X. Xu (2021), 'Moving Beyond Centre-Periphery in Science: Towards an Ecology of Knowledge', Centre for Global Higher Education Working Paper No. 63, Oxford: ESRC/OFSRE Centre for Global Higher Education, Department of Education, University of Oxford, https://www.researchcghe.org/perch/resources/publications/working-paper-63.pdf.

Marginson, S., and L. Yang (2021), 'Individual and Collective Outcomes of Higher Education: A Comparison of Anglo-American and Chinese Approaches', *Globalisation, Societies and Education*, https://doi.org/10.1080/14767724.2021.1932436.

MOE (Ministry of Education, People's Republic of China) (2020), *Guanyu Pochu Gaoxiao Zhexueshehuikexueyanjiu Pingjia Zhong 'Wei Lunwen' Buliangdaoxiang De Ruo Gan Yi Jian* [Opinions on Eliminating the Unhealthy 'Paper-Only' Orientation in the Evaluation of Humanities and Social Sciences Research in Higher Education Institutions], http://www.moe.gov.cn/srcsite/A13/moe_2557/s3103/202012/t20201215_505588.html.

MOE (Ministry of Education, People's Republic of China) and Ministry of Science and Technology (2020), *Guanyu Guifan Gaodengxuexiao SCI Lunwen Xiangguanzhibiao Shiyong Shuli Zhengque Pingjiadaoxiang De Ruogan Yijian* [Opinions on Regulating the Use of SCI Indicators by Higher Education Institutions and Establishing the Correct Evaluation Orientations], http://www.moe.gov.cn/srcsite/A16/moe_784/202002/t20200223_423334.html.

Mok, K. H. (2003), 'Similar Trends, Diverse Agendas: Higher Education Reforms in East Asia', *Globalisation, Societies and Education*, 1 (2): 201–21.

Nature Index (2021), 'Nature Index', https://www.natureindex.com.

NSB (National Science Board) (2020), 'Science and Engineering Indicators', https://ncses.nsf.gov/pubs/nsb20201.

OECD (Organisation for Economic Co-operation and Development) (2019), *PISA Results 2018, Volume 1: What Students Know and Can Do*, Paris: OECD.

OECD (Organisation for Economic Co-operation and Development) (2021), 'Main Science and Technology Indicators', https://stats.oecd.org/Index.aspx?DataSetCode=MSTI_PUB.

Ortega y Gasset, J. (1949), 'El Problema de China. Un Libro de Bertrand Russell' [The Problem of China. A Book by Bertrand Russell], in J. Ortega y Gasset, ed., *Goethe Desde Dentro y Otros Ensayos* [Goethe from Within and Other Essays], 2nd edition, 157–62, Revista de Occidente.

Pieterse, J. (2018), *Multipolar Globalization: Emerging Economies and Development*, London: Routledge.

Said, E. (1977), *Orientalism*, London: Penguin.

Santos, B. de S. (2014), *Epistemologies of the South: Justice against Epistemicide*, Boulder, CO: Paradigm Publishers.

Shahjahan, R., and K. Edwards (2021), 'Whiteness as Futurity and Globalization of Higher Education', *Higher Education*, https://doi.org/10.1007/s10734-021-00702-x.

Shin, J. C., B. M. Kehm and G. A. Jones, eds. (2018), *Doctoral Education for the Knowledge Society: Convergence or Divergence in National Approaches?* Cham: Springer.

Shin, K.-Y. (2007), 'Globalization and the National Social Science in the Discourse on the SSCI in South Korea', *Korean Social Science Journal*, 34 (1): 93–116.

Takeuchi, Y. (1961), 'Asia as Method', in R. F. Calichman, ed., *What Is Modernity? Writings of Takeuchi Yoshimi*, 149–65, New York: Columbia University Press.

Tight, M. (2019), 'Mass Higher Education and Massification', *Higher Education Policy*, 32 (1): 93–108.

Trow, M. (1973), *Problems in the Transition from Elite to Mass Higher Education*, Berkeley, CA: Carnegie Commission on Higher Education.

Tu, W.-M. (1985), *Confucian Thought: Selfhood as Creative Transformation*, Albany: SUNY Press.

UASR (University Alliance of the Silk Road) (2021), 'University Alliance of the Silk Road (UASR)', http://uasr.xjtu.edu.cn/index.htm.

UNESCO (United Nations Educational, Social and Cultural Organization) (2021), 'Institute of Statistics', http://data.uis.unesco.org.

Wang, H., Q. Wang and N. Liu (2011), 'Building World-Class Universities in China: Shanghai Jiao Tong University', in P. Altbach and J. Salmi, eds, *The Road to Academic Excellence: The Making of World-Class Universities*, 33–62, Washington: World Bank.

Welch, A., and J. Hao (2013), 'Returnees and Diaspora as Source of Innovation in Chinese Higher Education', *Frontiers of Education in China*, 8 (2): 214–38.

World Bank (2021), 'Indicators', https://data.worldbank.org/indicator.

Xu, X. (2020), 'China "Goes Out" in a Centre-Periphery World: Incentivizing International Publications in the Humanities and Social Sciences', *Higher Education*, 80 (1): 157–72.

Xu, X. (2021a), 'A Policy Trajectory Analysis of the Internationalisation of Chinese Humanities and Social Sciences Research (1978–2020)', *International Journal of Educational Development*, https://doi.org/10.1016/j.ijedudev.2021.102425.

Xu, X. (2021b). 'Epistemic Diversity and Cross-Cultural Comparative Research: Ontology, Challenges, and Outcomes', *Globalisation, Societies and Education*, https://doi.org/10.1080/14767724.2021.1932438.

Yang, R. (2019), 'Riddled with Gaping Wounds: A Methodological Critique of Comparative and International Studies in Education: Views of a Professor', in L. E. Suter, E. Smith and B. D. Denman, eds, *The SAGE Handbook of Comparative Studies in Education*, 63–78, London: Sage.

Yonezawa, A., and F. Huang (2018), 'Towards Universal Access amid Demographic Decline: High Participation Higher Education in Japan', in B. Cantwell, S. Marginson and A. Smolentseva, eds, *High Participation Systems of Higher Education*, 418–38, Oxford: Oxford University Press.

Chapter 2

Aquarone, F., L. Nehéz-Posony, P. R. Anwar, S. Salam, E. Koutsouri, M. Kim, S. Suh, T. Mayomi, J. Pilarska, E. Houghton and Y. Boodai (2020), '*We Are Trying to Do Things Differently*': *The Challenges of Relationships and Recognition in Higher Education*, The Centre for Public Policy Research (CPPR), King's College London, London: Premier Print Group.

Braun, V., V. Clarke, G. Terry and N. Hayfield (2018), 'Thematic Analysis', in P. Liamputtong, ed., *Handbook of Research Methods in Health and Social Sciences*, 843–60, Singapore: Springer.

Buissink, N., P. Diamond, J. Hallas, J. Swann and A. D. Sciascia (2017), 'Challenging a Measured University from an Indigenous Perspective: Placing "Manaaki" at the Heart of Our Professional Development Programme', *Higher Education Research and Development*, 36 (3): 569–82.

Cho, Y. K. (2002), 'A Study on Development of I-Consciousness-We-Consciousness Scale and Validity: Relationships between I-Consciousness-We Consciousness and Individuality-Relatedness, Psychosocial Maturity, and Interpersonal Problems', Doctoral thesis, Korea University, Seoul.

Choi, S. J., and J. J. Lee (1999), 'The Psychological Interior and Social-Cultural Functions of Korean Cheong', *Korean Journal of Social and Personality Psychology*, 13 (1): 219–34.

Choi, S. J., J. Y. Kim and B. K. Kim (2000), 'The Structural Relationship among Cheong, and Its Actions and Functions', *Korean Journal of Social and Personality Psychology*, 14 (1): 203–22.

Chung, C. K., and S. Cho (1997), *Significance of 'Jeong' in Korean Culture and Psychotherapy*, Torrance, CA: Harbor-UCLA Medical Center, http://www.prcp.org/publications/sig.pdf.

Hazelkorn, E., and A. Gibson (2019), 'Public Goods and Public Policy: What Is Public Good, and Who and What Decides?', *Higher Education*, 78 (2): 257–71.

Jeong, K. W. (2018), 'Democracy and Autonomy of University', *Public Law Journal*, 19 (1): 83–107.

KEDI Statistics (2020), https://kess.kedi.re.kr/index.

Ko, M. S. (2010), 'A Study on the Human Being with Cheong as the Ideal of Moral Person', *Journal of Ethics Education Studies*, 22: 131–56.

Ko, M. S. (2014), 'The Establishment of Ethic of Cheong (정): Focused on the Relation with Ethic of Caring', *The Korean Journal of Philosophy of Education*, 36 (2): 1–29.

Kwak, B. S., M. S. Jin, E. G. Kim and S. J. Lee (2010), *Educational Development in Korea: Strengths and Implications for Educational Reform*, Beijing: Ministry of Education, Science and Technology.

Lee, K. T. (1994a), *Korean Emotional Structure 2*, Seoul: Shinwonbook.

Lee, S. W. (1994b), 'The Structure of Interpersonal Relation and "Jung" Feeling in Korea', *Hanyang Education Review*, 1 (1): 95–125.

Lim, T. K. (1993), *Communicational Base of Korean Relationship: Chaemyun, Jeong, and Nunchi (Korean)*, Korea Media Research Autumn Conference.

Liu, X., and W. Ma, eds (2018), *Confucianism Reconsidered: Insights for American and Chinese Education in the Twenty-First Century*, Albany: SUNY Press.

Marginson, S. (2011), 'Higher Education and Public Good', *Higher Education Quarterly*, 65 (4): 411–33.

Marginson, S. (2017), 'The Public Good Created by Higher Education Institutions in Russia', *Вопросы образования*, 3.

Marginson, S. (2019), 'Limitations of Human Capital Theory', *Studies in Higher Education*, 44 (2): 287–301.

Marginson, S. (2020), 'Public and Common Goods: Key Concepts in Mapping the Contributions of Higher Education', in C. Callender, W. Locke and S. Marginson, eds, *Changing Higher Education for a Changing World*, 249–64, London: Bloomsbury.

Marginson, S., and L. Yang (2020), 'Higher Education and Public Good in East and West', Centre for Global Higher Education Research Findings 5, Oxford: ESRC/OFSRE Centre for Global Higher Education, Department of Education, University of Oxford.

Mayumi, K. (2018), 'A Study on the Teaching Method of Korean Emotion "Cheong(情)" – Focused on the Korean Language Expressions Related to Korean Culture, "Cheong(情)"', Master's thesis, Busan University of Foreign Studies, Busan.

Mignolo, W. D. (2011), *The Darker Side of Western Modernity: Global Futures, Decolonial Options*, Durham, NC: Duke University Press.

Owen-Smith, J. (2018), *Research Universities and the Public Good: Discovery for an Uncertain Future*, Stanford, CA: Stanford University Press.

Papadimitriou, A., and M. Boboc (2021), 'Introduction: Examining Higher Education Institutions Public Mission Initiatives Through the Lens of Organizational Perspective', in A. Papadimitriou and M. Boboc, eds, *Re-envisioning Higher Education's Public Mission*, 1–14, Cham: Palgrave Macmillan.

Park, J. H. (2015), 'An Analysis of Change Process in Higher Education Policy from the Perspective of Educational Accountability', *Journal of Politics of Education*, 22 (4): 87–140.

Reid, D. W., E. J. Dalton, K. Laderoute, F. K. Doell and T. Nguyen (2006), 'Therapeutically Induced Changes in Couple Identity: The Role of We-Ness and Interpersonal Processing in Relationship Satisfaction', *Genetic, Social, and General Psychology Monographs*, 132 (3): 241–84.

Rider, S., M. A. Peters, M. Hyvönen and T. Besley (2020), 'Welcome to the World Class University: Introduction', in S. Rider, M. A. Peters, M. Hyvönen and T. Besley, eds, *World Class Universities: A Contested Concept*, 1–8, Singapore: Springer.

Shin, J. C., and H. B. Park (2007), 'Diverse Types of Governmental Interventions in Higher Education', *Journal of Educational Administration*, 25 (4): 315–39.

Silova, I., J. Rappleye and E. Auld (2020), 'Beyond the Western Horizon: Rethinking Education, Values, and Policy Transfer', in G. Fan and T. Popkewitz, eds, *Handbook of Education Policy Studies*, 3–29. Singapore: Springer.

Stein, S. (2020), 'Pluralizing Possibilities for Global Learning in Western Higher Education', in D. Bourne, ed., *The Bloomsbury Handbook of Global Education and Learning*, 63–75, London: Bloomsbury.

Takayama, K., A. Sriprakash and R. Connell (2017), 'Toward a Postcolonial Comparative and International Education', *Comparative Education Review*, 61 (S1): S1–S24.

Waghid, Y. (2020), 'Towards an Ubuntu Philosophy of Higher Education in Africa', *Studies in Philosophy and Education*, 39 (3): 299–308.

Yang, I. (2006), '*Jeong* Exchange and Collective Leadership in Korean Organizations', *Asia Pacific Journal of Management*, 23: 283–98.

Yoon K. (2016), 'The Local Sociality and Emotion of *Jeong* in Koreans' Media Practices', in S. S. Lim and C. Soriano, eds, *Asian Perspectives on Digital Culture: Emerging Phenomena, Enduring Concepts*, 85–99, London: Routledge.

Yu, J. H. (2015), 'A Study on the Possibility of Global Acceptance of "*Cheong*", the Korean Emotional-Culture-DNA – Focusing on K-Drama', *Contents Culture*, 6: 11–58.

Zajda, J. (2020), 'Research on Globalisation and Neo-Liberalism in Higher Education', in J. Zadja, ed., *Globalisation, Ideology and Neo-Liberal Higher Education Reforms*, 151–61, Dordrecht: Springer.

Chapter 3

Bayer, P., and J. Urpelainen (2013), 'Funding Global Public Goods: The Dark Side of Multilateralism', *Review of Policy Research*, 30 (2): 160–89.

Beck, U. (2016), 'Varieties of Second Modernity and the Cosmopolitan Vision', *Theory, Culture & Society*, 33 (7–8): 257–70.

Beine, M., F. Docquier and H. Rapoport (2008), 'Brain Drain and Human Capital Formation in Developing Countries: Winners and Losers', *Economic Journal*, 118 (528): 631–52.

Bodde, D. (1957), *China's Cultural Tradition, What and Whither?*, New York: Holt, Rinehart and Winston.

Boni, A., and M. Walker (2013), *Human Development and Capabilities: Re-imagining the University of the Twenty-first Century*, Abingdon: Routledge.

Calhoun, C. (2006), 'The University and the Public Good', *Thesis Eleven*, 84 (1): 7–43.

Callahan, W. A. (2004), 'Remembering the Future: Utopia, Empire and Harmony in 21st Century International Theory', *European Journal of International Relations*, 10 (4): 569–601.

Callahan, W. A. (2008), 'Chinese Visions of World Order: Post-Hegemonic or a New Hegemony?', *International Studies Review*, 10 (4): 749–61.

Callahan, W. A., and E. Barabantseva (2011), *China Orders the World: Normative Soft Power and Foreign Policy*, Washington, DC: Woodrow Wilson Center Press.

Carnoy, M., I. Froumin, P. K. Loyalka and J. B. Tilak (2014), 'The Concept of Public Goods, the State, and Higher Education Finance: A View from the BRICs', *Higher Education*, 68 (3): 359–78.

Cheng, K., and R. Yang (2015), 'A Cultural Value in Crisis: Education as Public Good in China', in O. Filippakou and G. L. Williams, eds, *Higher Education as a Public Good: Critical Perspectives on Theory, Policy and Practice*, 127–39, New York: Peter Lang.

Chernilo, D. (2006), 'Social Theory's Methodological Nationalism: Myth and Reality', *European Journal of Social Theory*, 9 (1): 5–22.

Chirot, D., and T. D. Hall (1982), 'World-System Theory', *Annual Review of Sociology*, 8 (1): 81–106.

Collins, C. S. (2016), 'Public Good in Asian Higher Education', in C. Collins, M. N. N. Lee, J. N. Hawkins and D. E. Neubauer, eds, *The Palgrave Handbook of Asia Pacific Higher Education*, 89–99, New York: Palgrave Macmillan.

Davies, I., and G. Pike (2010), 'Global Citizenship Education: Challenges and Possibilities', in R. Lewin, ed., *The Handbook of Practice and Research in Study Abroad*, 83–100, New York: Routledge.

Deneulin, S., and N. Townsend (2007), 'Public Goods, Global Public Goods and the Common Good', *International Journal of Social Economics*, 34 (1/2): 19–36.

Duara, P. (2017), 'The Chinese World Order and Planetary Sustainability', in B. Wang, ed., *Chinese Visions of World Order: Tianxia, Culture, and World Politics*, 65–85, Durham, NC, and London: Duke University Press.

Earley, P. C., and C. B. Gibson (1998), 'Taking Stock in Our Progress on Individualism-Collectivism: 100 Years of Solidarity and Community', *Journal of Management*, 24 (3): 265–304.

Fairbank, J. K. (1968), *The Chinese World Order: Traditional China's Foreign Relations*, Cambridge, MA: Harvard University Press.

Fang, K. (2003), 'Heer Butong: Zuowei Yizhong Wenhuaguan De Yiyi He Jiazhi' [Harmony and Diversity], *Zhongguo shehui kexueyuan yanjiushengyuan xuebao* [Journal of Graduate School of Chinese Academy of Social Sciences], 1: 26–33.

Fei, X. (2015), *Globalization and Self-Cultural Awareness*, Heidelberg: Springer.

Fougner, T. (2006), 'The State, International Competitiveness and Neoliberal Globalisation: Is There a Future Beyond "the Competition State?"', *Review of International Studies*, 32 (1): 165–85.

Gernet, J. (1996), *A History of Chinese Civilization*, Cambridge: Cambridge University Press.

Griffiths, T. G., and R. F. Arnove (2015), 'World Culture in the Capitalist World-System in Transition', *Globalisation, Societies and Education*, 13 (1): 88–108.

Han, S.-J., Y.-H. Shim and Y.-D. Park (2016), 'Cosmopolitan Sociology and Confucian Worldview: Beck's Theory in East Asia', *Theory, Culture & Society*, 33 (7–8): 281–90.

Huang, C. (2010), 'East Asian Conceptions of the Public and Private Realms', in K.-P. Yu, J. Tao and P. J. Ivanhoe, eds, *Taking Confucian Ethics Seriously: Contemporary Theories and Applications*, 73–98. Albany: SUNY Press.

Jarvis, P. (2002), 'Globalisation, Citizenship and the Education of Adults in Contemporary European Society', *Compare: A Journal of Comparative and International Education*, 32 (1): 5–19.

Kivelä, A. (2012), 'From Immanuel Kant to Jahann Gottlieb Fichte: Concept of Education and German Idealism', in P. Siljander, A. Kivelä and A. Sutinen, eds, *Theories of Bildung and Growth: Connections and Controversies between Continental Educational Thinking and American Pragmatism*', 59–86, Rotterdam: Sense Publisher.

Liang, S. (1990), *Zhongguo Wenhua Yaoyi* [Main Ideas of Chinese Culture], Volume 3, Jinan: Shandong Renmin Chubanshe [Shandong People's Press].

Locatelli, R. (2017), 'Education as a Public and Common Good: Revisiting the Role of the State in a Context of Growing Marketization', PhD dissertation, University of Bergamo, Bergamo.

Lu, Y., and G. Jover (2019), 'An Anthropocosmic View: What Confucian Traditions Can Teach Us about the Past and Future of Chinese Higher Education', *Higher Education*, 77: 423–36.

Marginson, S. (2018a), 'Public/Private in Higher Education: A Synthesis of Economic and Political Approaches', *Studies in Higher Education*, 42 (2): 322–37.

Marginson, S. (2018b), 'World Higher Education under Conditions of National/Global Disequilibria', Oxford: ESRC/OFSRE Centre for Global Higher Education, Department of Education, University of Oxford.

Marginson, S. (2019), 'Limitations of Human Capital Theory', *Studies in Higher Education*, 44 (2): 287–301.

Marginson, S. (2020), '*Shengshengbuxi De Huoyan: Quanqiu Kexue Zhong De hongguo*' [Everliving Fire: China in Global Science], *Beijing Daxue Jiaoyu Pinglun* [Peking University Education Review], 18 (4): 2–33.

Marginson, S., and L. Yang (2020a), 'China Meets Anglo-America on the New Silk Road: A Comparison of State, Society, Self and Higher Education', in M. C. van der Wende, W. C. Kirby, N. C. Liu and S. Marginson, eds, *China and Europe on the New Silk Road: Connecting Universities across Eurasia*, 255–83, Oxford: Oxford University Press.

Marginson, S., and L. Yang (2020b), 'The Role of Higher Education in Generating "Public" and "Common" Goods: A Comparison of Sinic and Anglo-American Political Cultures', Centre for Global Higher Education Working Paper No. 52, Oxford: ESRC/OFSRE Centre for Global Higher Education, Department of Education, University of Oxford.

McGrath, M. (2020), 'Climate Change: US Formally Withdraws from Paris Agreement', *BBC*, 4 November, https://www.bbc.co.uk/news/science-environment-54797743 (accessed 26 April 2021).

Palfreyman, D. (2007), 'Is Academic Freedom under Threat in UK and US Higher Education?', *Education and the Law*, 19 (1): 19–40.

Qi, H., and D. Shen (2015), 'Chinese Traditional World Citizenship Thoughts and Its Impact on the Cultivation of Chinese World Citizenship Awareness', *Citizenship Studies*, 19 (3-4): 267–84.

Reisen, H., M. Soto and T. Weithöner (2008), 'Financing Global and Regional Public Goods through ODA: Analysis and Evidence from the OECD Creditor Reporting System', in T. Addison and G. Mavrotas, eds, *Development Finance in the Global Economy*, 124–50, New York: Palgrave Macmillan.

Rosemont Jr, H. (2015), *Against Individualism: A Confucian Rethinking of the Foundations of Morality, Politics, Family, and Religion*, London: Lexington Books.

Samuelson, P. A. (1954), 'The Pure Theory of Public Expenditure', *Review of Economics and Statistics*, 36 (4): 387–9.

Sen, A. (1999), *Development as Freedom*, Oxford: Oxford University Press.

Stiglitz, J. E. (1999), 'Knowledge as a Global Public Goods', in I. Kaul, I. Grunberg and M. Stern, eds, *Global Public Goods: International Cooperation in the 21st Century*, 308–25, Oxford: Oxford University Press.

Szadkowski, K. (2019), 'The Common in Higher Education: A Conceptual Approach', *Higher Education*, 78: 241–55.

Taylor, I. (2014), 'Distributive Justice and Global Public Goods', DPhil dissertation, University of Oxford, Oxford.

Tian, L., and N. C. Liu (2018), 'Local and Global Public Good Contributions of Higher Education in China', Centre for Global Higher Education Working Paper No. 37, Oxford: ESRC/OFSRE Centre for Global Higher Education, Department of Education, University of Oxford.

Traianou, A. (2015), 'The Erosion of Academic Freedom in the UK Higher Education', *Ethics in Science and Environmental Politics*, 15: 39–47.

UNESCO (United Nations Educational, Social and Cultural Organization) (2015), *Rethinking Education: Towards a Global Common Good?*, Paris: UNESCO.

Verbik, L., and V. Lasanowski (2007), 'International Student Mobility: Patterns and Trends', *World Education News and Reviews*, 20 (10): 1–16.

Viggiano, T., A. I. LópezDamián, E. Morales Vázquez and J. S. Levin (2018), 'The Others: Equitable Access, International Students, and the Community College', *Journal of Studies in International Education*, 22 (1): 71–85.

Wang, B. (2017), 'Introduction', in B. Wang, ed., *Chinese Visions of World Order: Tianxia, Culture, and World Politics*, 1–24, Durham, NC, and London: Duke University Press.

Wang, H. (2003), *China's New Order: Society, Politics, and Economy in Transition*, Cambridge, MA: Harvard University Press.

Woodfield, S., R. Middlehurst, J. Fielden and H. Forland (2009), 'Universities and International Higher Education Partnerships: Making a Difference', https://eprints.kingston.ac.uk/id/eprint/19777/ (accessed 26 April 2021).

Xu, J. (2017), *Jiaguo Tianxia* [Family, Nation and All under Heaven], Shanghai: Shanghai Renmin Chubanshe [Shanghai People's Publishing].

Xu, Z. (2018), ' "Jiaguo Tianxia": Zhongguo Yu Shijie De Heping Gongchu' [Family, State, and *Tianxia*: China and the World in Peace] *Wen, Shi, Zhe* [Literature, History, and Philosophy], 1: 14–19.

Yan, X. (2011), 'Xunzi's Interstate Political Philosophy and Its Message for Today', E. Ryden (trans.), in D. A. Bell and S. Zhe, eds, *Ancient Chinese Thought, Modern Chinese Power*, 70–106, Princeton and Oxford: Princeton University Press.

Zhang, D. (1996), *Zhang Dainian Quanji*, Volume 1 [The Collection of Works of Zhang Dainian], Shijiazhuang: Hebei Renmin Chubanshe [Hebei Remin Publishing].

Zhao, T. (2006), 'Rethinking Empire from a Chinese Concept "All-Under-Heaven" (tian-xia)', *Social Identities*, 12 (1): 29–41.

Zhao, T. (2009), 'A Political World Philosophy in Terms of All-Under-Heaven (tian-xia)', *Diogenes*, 56 (5): 5–18.

Zhao, T. (2011), *Tianxia Tixi: Shijie Zhidu Zhexue Daolun* [The Tianxia System: An Introduction to the Philosophy of World Institution], Beijing: Zhongguo Renmin Daxue Chubanshe [Renmin University Press].

Zhu, X., and Z. Lv ([1175] 2001). *Jinsi Lu* [Reflections on Things at Hand], Jinan: Shangdong Youyi Chubanshe [Shandong Friendship Publishing House].

Chapter 4

Alviar-Martin, T., and M. C. Baildon, eds (2021). *Research on Global Citizenship Education in Asia Conceptions, Perceptions, and Practice*, Charlotte, NC: Information Age Publishing.

Cheng, H. (2019), 'A Critical Review of Chinese Theoretical Research on Moral Education since 2000', *ECNU Review of Education*, 2 (4): 561–80.

Davies, I., L. C. Ho, D. Kiwan, C. L. Peck, A. Peterson, E. Sant and Y. Waghid, eds (2018). *The Palgrave Handbook of Global Citizenship and Education*, London: Palgrave Macmillan.

DeVoto, M. (2017, 8 September). *Polyphony. Encyclopedia Britannica*, https://www.britannica.com/art/polyphony-music.

Fairbrother, G. P. (2014), 'The Chinese Paternalistic State and Moral Education', in Z. Z. Kennedy, K. J., Fairbrother and G. F., Zhao, eds, *Citizenship Education in China Preparing Citizens for the 'Chinese Century'*, 11–26, New York: Routledge.

Fu, J. (2019), 'Online Citizenship Learning of Chinese Young People', in H. Peterson, A. Stahl and G. Soong, eds, *The Palgrave Handbook of Citizenship and Education*, 1–13, Cham: Springer.

Han, S. M., and X. Xu (2019), 'How Far Has the State "Stepped Back": An Exploratory Study of the Changing Governance of Higher Education in China (1978–2018)', *Higher Education*, 78: 931–46.

Hayhoe, R. (2020), 'Reflections', *China Quarterly*, 244: 1160–7.

Hua, X. (2020), 'Gaoxiao Quanqiu Gongmin Jiaoyu de Kecheng Shezhi Yanjiu – Yi Liangsuo Benke Daxue Wei Lie' [A Comparison of the Curriculum of University Global Citizenship Education between Two Universities], *Journal of Hubei University of Education*, 37 (5): 75–9.

Huineng Lu J., Y. Wang and P. J. Ivanhoe (2009), *Readings from the Lu-Wang School of Neo-Confucianism*, Indianapolis: Hackett.

Jiang, K., and Y. J. Xu (2014), 'Paradoxes of Civic and Political Education in China's Higher Education Institutions', in Z. Z. Kerry, J. Fairbrother and G. Zhao, eds, *Citizenship Education in China: Preparing Citizens for the 'Chinese Century'*, 66–84, London: Routledge.

Jiang, M. (2017), *Dongya Guoji Lijie Jiaoyu de Zhengce yu Lilun* [Policies and Theories of Education for International Understanding in East Asia], Beijing: Gaodeng Jiaoyu Chuban She [Higher Education Press].

Law, W. W. (2006), 'Citizenship, Citizenship Education, and the State in China in a Global Age', *Cambridge Journal of Education*, 36 (4): 597–628.

Law, W.-W. (2011), 'Citizenship and Citizenship Education in a Global Age: Politics, Policies, and Practices in China', New York: Peter Lang.

Law, W.-W. (2013). 'Globalization, National Identity, and Citizenship Education: China's Search for Modernization and a Modern Chinese Citizenry', *Frontiers of Education in China*, 8 (4): 596–627.

Liu, B. C., and W. Zhang (2018), 'Wenhua Chongtu Yu Linian Mihe "Yi Dai Yi Lu" Beijing Xia Xin Xing Shijie Gongmin Jiaoyu Chuyi' [Cultural Conflict and Ideas Bridging – New World Citizenship Education under the Background of "One Belt, One Road"], *Tsinghua Journal of Education*, 39 (4): 56–63.

Ning, R., and D. A. Palmer (2020), 'Ethics of the Heart: Moral Breakdown and the Aporia of Chinese Volunteers', *Current Anthropology*, 61 (4): 395–417.

Pan, S. Y. (2011), 'Multileveled Citizenship and Citizenship Education: Experiences of Students in China's Beijing', *Citizenship Studies*, 15 (2): 283–306.

Parmenter, L. (2011), 'Power and Place in the Discourse of Global Citizenship Education', *Globalisation, Societies and Education*, 9 (3–4): 367–80.

Peng, J. (2009), 'Zouyi Zhongguo Daxue Peiyang Shijiegongmin Zhi Neihan' [Discussion About Cosmopolitan Cultivation by China's Colleges], *Journal of Sichuan Normal University (Social Science)*, 36 (3): 4–9.

Print, M., and C. B. Tan, eds (2015), *Educating 'Good' Citizens in a Globalising World for the Twenty-First Century*, Rotterdam: Sense Publishers.

Qi, H., and D. Shen (2015), 'Chinese Traditional World Citizenship Thoughts and Its Impact on the Cultivation of Chinese World Citizenship Awareness', *Citizenship Studies*, 19 (3–4): 267–84.

Reddy, S. (2018), 'Going Global: Internationally Mobile Young People as Caring Citizens in Higher Education', *Area*, September: 1–9.

Shi, Z. Y. (2018), 'Kongzi "Ren" De Sixiang Jiqi Dangdai Jiaoyu Yiyi' [Confucius's Concept of 'Ren' and Its Application in Modern Education], *Educational Research*, 4: 127–34.

Singh, M., and J. Qi (2013), 'Research Summary 21st Century International-Mindedness: An Exploratory Study of Its Conceptualization and Assessment', International Baccalaureate, https://www.ibo.org/globalassets/publications/ib-research/singhqiibreport27julyfinalversion.pdf.

Song, G. (2016), 'Shifting Global Citizenship Education: Broadening Citizenship Education through Global Events in China', *Asian Journal of Education*, 17: 81–105.

Song, Q. (2018), *Shijie Gongmin Jiaoyu Sichao Yanjiu* [The Research on World Citizenship Education's Ideological Trend], Beijing: Zhongguo Shehui Kexue Chuban She [China Social Sciences Press].

Song, Q. (2020), 'Ruhe Peiyang Daai Dade Da Qinghuai' [How to Cultivate a Great Love, Strong Morals and All-Embracing Feelings], http://www.cssn.cn/ddzg/ddzg_ldjs/ddzg_wh/202006/t20200625_5147773.shtml?COLLCC=1267981995&

Song, Q., and C. Rao (2018), 'Zhaoyan Quanqiu Gongtong Liyi: "Shijie Gongmin" Jiaoyu De Guoji Yanjiu Xin Qushi' [Focus on Global Common Good: The New International Research Trend on World Citizenship Education], *Xiandai Jiaoyu Guanli*, 2: 106–11.

Sriprakash, A., M. Singh and J. Qi (2014), 'A Comparative Study of International-Mindedness in the Diploma Programme in Australia, China, and India', International Baccalaureate, https://www.ibo.org/globalassets/publications/ib-research/dp/international-mindedness-final-report.pdf.

Tan, C. (2019), 'An Ethical Foundation for Global Citizenship Education: A Neo-Confucian Perspective', *Journal of Beliefs and Values*, 41 (4): 446–57.

UNESCO (United Nations Educational, Social and Cultural Organization) (2015), 'Global Citizenship Education: Topics and Learning Objectives', http://www.unesco.org/open-access/terms-use-ccbysa-en.

Veg, S. (2019). *Minjian: The Rise of China's Grassroots Intellectuals*, New York: Columbia University Press.

Wan, M. Z. (2005), 'Duoyuan Wenhua Beijing Zhong De Quanqiu Jiaoyu Yu Shijie Gongmin Peiyang' [Global Education in the Backdrop of Multiculturalism and Cultivation of Global Citizens], *Xibei Shifan Daxue Xuebao* [Journal of Northwest Normal University], 8 (1) 99–100.

Wan, Z. (2019), 'The Relationship between Science and Religion in Kang Youwei's Confucianism', Doctoral thesis, University of Oxford, Oxford.

Wang, B. (2017), *Chinese Visions of World Order: Tianxia, Culture, and World Politics*, Durham, NC: Duke University Press.

Wang, C. (2019), 'Service-Learning in Rural China', https://www.anthropology-news.org/index.php/2019/07/12/service-learning-in-rural-china/.

Wang, H. Y., and M. H. Wu (2011), 'Lun "Duoyuan Wenhua Zhuyi" Shiyu Xia De Shijie Gongmin Jiaoyu' [On Global Citizenship Education in Perspective of 'Multiculturalism'], *Journal of Research on Education for Ethnic Minorities*, 22 (1): 5–9.

Wang, L. P. (2019), 'Possibility of Global Citizenship Education in China: A Secondary School Curriculum Perspective', *Universidad, Escuela Y Sociedad*, 6: 126–43.

Wang, W. L., and J. Wang (2016), 'Meiguo Duoyuan Wenhua Gongmin Jiaoyu Ji Dui Wo Guo Gongmin Jioayu De Qishi' [Multicultural Citizenship Education in American and Implication for National Minority Education in Our Country], *Contemporary Education and Culture*, 8 (1): 13–19.

Wu, X. (2020), 'Houzhimin Zhuyi Shiyu Xia Dui Quanqiu Gongmin Jiaoyu De Pipan Yu Fansi' [Critical Reflections on Global Citizenship Education from the Postcolonial Perspective], *International and Comparative Education*, 9 (368): 90–6.

Xu, J. Y. (2020), 'Goujian Renlei Mingyun Gongtongti – Rujia "Xiu Shen" Sixiangxia Quanqiu Gongmin Jiaoyu De Zhongguo Luoji [Building a Community for the Shared Future of Mankind – Chinese Logic of Global Citizenship Education Under Confucian Notions of 'Self-Cultivation'], *Education Exploration*, 10 (334): 63–6.

Yang, L. (2020), 'Similarities and Differences between Notions of Public in the Sinic and Liberal Anglo-American Traditions, and the Implications for Higher Education', Doctoral thesis, Department of Education, University of Oxford, Oxford.

Yang, X. (2017), 'Zouxiang "Shijie Gongmin" – Lun Zuowei Shijiegongmin Jiaoyu De Waiyu Jiaoyu' [Towards the Global Citizen – On the Foreign Language Education in the Framework of Global Citizenship Education], Doctoral thesis, Northeast Normal University, China National Knowledge Infrastructure (CNKI).

Zhang, C. (2016), 'Cultural Citizenship and Its Implications for Citizenship Education: Chinese University Students' Civic Experience in Relation to Mass Media and the University Citizenship Curriculum', Doctoral thesis, University of Glasgow, Glasgow.

Zhang, C., and C. Fagan (2016), 'Examining the Role of Ideological and Political Education on University Students' Civic Perceptions and Civic Participation in Mainland China: Some Hints from Contemporary Citizenship Theory', *Citizenship, Social and Economics Education*, 15 (2): 117–42.

Zhao, Z. (2013), 'The Shaping of Citizenship Education in a Chinese Context', *Frontiers of Education in China*, 8 (1): 105–22.

Zhong, M., and W. O. Lee (2008), 'Citizenship Curriculum in China: A Shifting Discourse towards Chinese Democracy, Law Education and Psychological Health', in K. J. Grossman, D. L. Lee and W. O. Kennedy, eds, *Citizenship Curriculum in Asia and the Pacific*, 61–73, Dordrecht: Springer.

Zhou, X. Y. (2019), *Quanqiu Gongmin Jiaoyu Huayu Yanjiu* [A Study of Global Citizenship Education Discourses], Shanghai: East China Normal University.

Chapter 5

Altbach, P. G. (2009), 'Peripheries and Centres: Research Universities in Developing Countries', *Asia Pacific Education Review*, 10 (1): 15–27.

Altbach, P. G., and J. Knight (2007), 'The Internationalisation of Higher Education: Motivations and Realities', *Journal of Studies in International Education*, 11 (3/4): 290–305.

Clark, B. R. (1986), *The Higher Education System: Academic Organization in Cross-National Perspective*, Berkeley: University of California Press.

Gu, J. M., and A. S. Liu (2011), 'Shi Jie Yi Liu Da Xue De Jia Zhi Zhui Qiu' [The Pursuit of World-Class Universities], *Jiao Yu Fa Zhan Yan Jiu* [Exploring Education Development], 17: 54–7.

Hu, D. X. (2019), 'Wo Guo Shi Jie Yi Liu Da Xue Jian She De Zhi Du Luo Ji Yu Lu Jing Xuan Ze' [The System Logic and Path of the Building of World-Class Universities in China], *Fu Dan Jiao Yu Lun Tan* [Fudan Education Forum], 17 (3): 74–80.

Huang, F. T. (2017), 'Shen Me Shi Lung Jie Yi Liu Da Xue De Ben Ke Jiao Yu' [What Is the Undergraduate Education of World-Class Universities], *Gao Deng Jiao Yu Yan Jiu* [Journal of Higher Education], 38 (8): 1–9.

Hüther, O., and G. Krücken (2018), *Higher Education in Germany: Recent Developments in an International Perspective*, Berlin: Springer.

Kim, D., Q. Song, J. Liu, Q. Liu and A. Grimm (2018), 'Building World Class Universities in China: Exploring Faculty's Perceptions, Interpretations of and Struggles with Global Forces in Higher Education', *Compare: A Journal of Comparative and International Education*, 48 (1): 92–109.

Knight, J. (2004), 'Internationalisation Remodelled: Definition, Approaches, and Rationale', *Journal of Studies in International Education*, 8 (1): 5–31.

Lewis, D. R., and J. Hearn (2003), *The Public Research University: Serving the Public Good in New Times*, Maryland: University Press of America.

Li, J. (2020), *Comprehensive Global Competence for World-Class Universities in China*, Singapore: Springer.

Liu, N. C. (2009), 'Building up World-Class Universities: A Comparison', Presentation in 2008–2009, Research Institute for Higher Education, Hiroshima University.

Locatelli, R. (2018), 'Higher Education as a Public and Common Good', Lecture delivered at the CGHE, UCL, London, 8 February, http://www.researchcghe.org/perch/resources/higher-education-as-a-public-and-common-good-rl-08-feb.-seminar.pdf (accessed 1 January 2020).

Lockwood, G. (2011), 'Management and Resources', in W. Rüegg, ed., *A History of the University in Europe, Volume 4, Universities since 1945*, 124–61, Cambridge: Cambridge University Press.

Lu, X. Z., and L. Yang (2018), 'Shuang Yi Liu Jian She De Zhong Guo Te Se Yu Shi Jie Yi Liu' [The Chinese and World-Class Characteristics of the Double First-Class Construction], *Guo Jia Jiao Yu Xing Zheng Xue Yuan Xue* Bao [Journal of National Academy of Education Administration], 9: 20–27.

Ma, W. H. (2013), 'The Global Research and the "World-Class" Universities', in J. C. Shin and B. M. Kehm, eds, *Institutionalization of World-Class University in Global Competition*, 33–44, Dordrecht, Heidelberg, New York and London: Springer.

Ma, W. H. (2014), 'Quan Qiu Hua, Quan Qiu Can Yu He Shi Jie Yi Liu Da Xue Jian She Ying Guan Zhu De Wen Ti' [Globalisation, Global Engagement and Issues in the Building of World-Class Universities], *Hua zhong shifan da xue due bao: Ren wen she hui ke xue ban* [Journal of Huazhong Normal University: Humanities and Social Science] 53 (2): 148–58.

March, J. G. (1993, *Primer on Decision Making: How Decisions Happen*, New York: Free Press.

Marginson, S. (2011), 'Global Perspectives and Strategies of Asia-Pacific Research Universities', in N. C. Liu, Q. Wang and Y. Cheng, eds, *Paths to a World-Class University: Lessons from Practices and Experiences*, 3–28, Rotterdam: Sense Publishers.

Marginson, S. (2013), 'Different Roads to a Shared Goal: Political and Cultural Variation in World-Class Universities', in Q. Wang, Y. Cheng and N. C. Liu, eds, *Building World-Class Universities: Different Approaches to a Shared Goal*, 13–33, Rotterdam: Brill Sense Publishers.

Marginson, S. (2019), 'Global Cooperation and National Competition in the World-Class University Sector', in Y. Wu, Q. Wang and N. C. Liu, eds, *World-Class Universities: Towards a Global Common Good and Seeking National and Institutional Contributions*, 13–53, Rotterdam: Brill Sense Publishers.

Mohrman, K. (2005), 'World-Class Universities and Chinese Higher Education Reform', *International Higher Education*, 39: 22–3.

Morrow, R. A., and C. A. Torres (2000), 'The State, Globalisation and Education Policy', in N. C. Burbules and C. A. Torres, eds, *Globalisation and Education: Critical Perspectives*, 27–56, London: Routledge.

Qiu, Y. (2019), 'Confident Tsinghua University Is More Open: A Speech on the 108th Anniversary of Tsinghua University', Tsinghua University, 26 April, 2019, http://www.wenming.cn/wmxy/yw_01/201904/t20190426_5094275.shtml.

Reichert, S. (2009), 'Institutional Diversity in European Higher Education. Tensions and Challenges for Policy Makers and Institutional Leaders', European University Association, https://eua.eu/downloads/publications/institutional%20diversity%20in%20european%20higher%20education%20%20tensions%20and%20challenges.pdf (accessed 13 July 2019).

Rodriguez-Pomeda, J., and F. Casani (2016), 'Legitimating the World-Class University Concept Through the Discourse of Elite Universities' Presidents', *Higher Education Research & Development*, 35 (6): 1269–83.

Salmi, J. (2009), *The Challenge of Establishing World-Class Universities*, Washington, DC: World Bank Publications.

Shin, J. C. (2013), 'The World-Class University: Concept and Policy Initiatives', in J. C. Shin and B. M. Kehm, eds, *Institutionalization of World-Class University in Global Competition*, 17–32, Dordrecht, Heidelberg, New York and London: Springer.

Soliman, S., J. Anchor and D. Taylor (2019), 'The International Strategies of Universities: Deliberate or Emergent?', *Studies in Higher Education*, 44 (8): 1413–24.

Sporn, B., and M. C. van der Wende (2020), 'The New Silk Road and the "Idea of the University"', in M. C. van der Wende, W. C. Kirby, N. C. Liu and S. Marginson, eds, *The New Silk Road: Connecting Universities between China and Europe*, 331–60, Oxford: Oxford University Press.

Tian, L. (2019), 'World-Class Universities: A Dual Identity Related to Global Common Good(s)', in Y. Wu, Q. Wang and N. C. Liu, eds, *World-Class Universities: Towards a Global Common Good and Seeking National and Institutional Contribution*, 93–113, Rotterdam: Brill Sense Publishers.

Tian, L., and N. C. Liu (2019), 'Rethinking Higher Education in China as a Common Good', *Higher Education*, 77 (4): 623–40.

Tian, L., and N. C. Liu (2020), 'The Role of World-Class and Other Research Universities in Contributing to the New Silk Road Initiative', in M. C. van der Wende, W. C. Kirby, N. C. Liu and S. Marginson, eds, *The New Silk Road: Connecting Universities between China and Europe*, 312–30, Oxford: Oxford University Press.

Tian, L., and N. C. Liu (forthcoming), 'Globalising as World-Class Universities' Special Function or Unique Mission', in N. C. Liu, Y. Wu and Q. Wang, eds, *World-Class Universities: Global Trends and Institutional Models*, Rotterdam: Brill Sense Publishers.

UNESCO (United Nations Educational, Social and Cultural Organization) (2015), 'Rethinking Education: Towards a Global Common Good', UNESCO, http://unesdoc.unesco.org/images/0023/002325/232555e.pdf.

UNESCO (United Nations Educational, Social and Cultural Organization) (2019), 'Towards a UNESCO Recommendation on Open Science', UNESCO, https://en.unesco.org/sites/default/files/open_science_brochure_en.pdf.

Vaira, M. (2004), 'Globalisation and Higher Education Organizational Change: A Framework for Analysis', *Higher Education*, 48 (4): 483–510.

van der Wende, M. C. (2019), 'World-Class Universities' Contribution to an Open Society: Chinese Universities on a Mission?', in Y. Wu, Q. Wang and N. C. Li, eds, *World-class Universities: Towards a Global Common Good and Seeking National and Institutional Contributions*, 189–214, Rotterdam: Brill Sense Publishers.

van der Wende, M. C., W. C. Kirby, N. C. Liu and S. Marginson (2020), *The New Silk Road: Connecting Universities between China and Europe*, Oxford: Oxford University Press.

Wang, Q., Y. Cheng, Y. and N. C. Liu (2013), *Building World-Class Universities: Different Approaches to a Shared Goal*, Rotterdam: Brill Sense.

Wang, Z. J., and W. T. Lan (2019), 'Xin Shi Dai Yi Liu Da Xue De Nei Han Tan Xi' [An Analysis on the Connotation of World-Class Universities in the New Era], *Xian Dai Jiao Yu Guan Li* [Modern Education Management], 8: 1–7.

Wolfensberger, M. V. (2015), *Talent Development in European Higher Education*, Cham: Springer International Publishing.

Yang, J. L. (2018), 'Ze Ren, Shi Ming, Zuo Wei: Xin Shi Dai Yi Liu Da Xue Jian She De Tan Suo Yu Shi Jian' [Responsibility, Mission and Deeds: An Exploration of the Building of World-Class Universities in the New Era], *Xue Wei Yu Yan Jiu Sheng Jiao Yu* [Academic Degrees and Graduate Education], (9): 1–5.

Yang, L. L. (2017), 'The Public Role of Higher Learning in Imperial China', Centre for Global Higher Education Working Paper, https://www.researchcghe.org/perch/resources/publications/wp28.pdf.

Chapter 6

Acharya, A. (2012), 'Comparative Regionalism: A Field Whose Time Has Come?' *International Spectator*, 47 (1): 3–15.

Becher, T., and P. Trowler (2001), *Academic Tribes and Territories: Intellectual Enquiry and the Culture of Disciplines*, 2nd edition, Open University Press.

Börzel, T. A. (2016), 'Theorizing Regionalism', in T. A. Borzel and T. Risse, eds, *The Oxford Handbook of Comparative Regionalism*, July: 1–30. Oxford: Oxford University Press.

Breaden, J. (2018), *Articulating Asia in Japanese Higher Education*, London: Routledge.

Byun, K., and S. Um (2014), 'The Regionalization of Higher Education in Northeast Asia', in A. Yonezawa, Y. Kitamura, A. Meerman and K. Kuroda, eds, *Emerging International Dimensions in East Asian Higher Education*, 121–43, Dordrecht: Springer.

Cabanda, E., E. S. Tan and M.-H. Chou (2019), 'Higher Education Regionalism in Asia: What Implications for Europe?', *European Journal of Higher Education*, 9 (1); 87–101.

Chao, R. Y. (2014), 'Pathways to an East Asian Higher Education Area: A Comparative Analysis of East Asian and European Regionalization Processes', *Higher Education*, 68 (4): 559–75.

Checkel, J. T. (2006), 'Constructivism and EU Politics', in K. E. Jorgenson, M. Pollack and B. Rosamund, eds, *Handbook of European Union Politics*, London: Sage.

Chen, S., and Y. Shimizu (2017), 'Regionalizing Higher Education in East Asia: The Asia Education Leader Course as a Specific but Distinctive Case', *Kyoiku Nettowakusenta Nenpo* [Education Network Center Annual Report], 17, 13–21.

Chou, M.-H., and P. Ravinet (2016), 'The Emergent Terrains of "Higher Education Regionalism": How and Why Higher Education Is an Interesting Case for Comparative Regionalism', *European Journal of Higher Education*, 6 (June): 1–17.

Chou, M.-H., and P. Ravinet (2017). 'Higher Education Regionalism in Europe and Southeast Asia: Comparing Policy Ideas', *Policy and Society*, 36 (January), 1–17.

CSTI (Council for Science, Technology and Innovation) (2015), 'About the Council for Science, Technology and Innovation'.

Cummings, W. K. (2014), 'Asian Research: The Role of Universities', in A. Yonezawa, Y. Kitamura, A. Meerman and K. Kuroda, eds, *Emerging International Dimensions in East Asian Higher Education*: 35–54, Dordrecht: Springer.

Hammond, C. D. (2019), 'Dynamics of Higher Education Research Collaboration and Regional Integration in Northeast Asia: A Study of the A3 Foresight Program', *Higher Education*, 78 (4): 653–68.

Hawkins, J. N., K. H. Mok and D. E. Neubauer (2012), 'The Dynamics of Regionalization in Contemporary Asia-Pacific Higher Education', in J. N. Hawkins, K. H. Mok and D. E. Neubauer, eds, *Higher Education Regionalization in Asia Pacific: Implications for Governance, Citizenship and University Transformation*, 191–205, Palgrave Macmillan.

Hay, C. (2011), 'Ideas and the Construction of Interests', in D. Beland and R. H. Cox, eds, *Ideas and Politics in Social Science Research*, 45–66, Oxford University Press.

Hou, A. Y.-C., C. Hill, K. H.-J. Chen, S. Tsai and V. Chen (2017). 'A Comparative Study of Student Mobility Programs in SEAMEO-RIHED, UMAP, and Campus Asia', *Higher Education Evaluation and Development*, 11 (1): 12–24.

JSPS (Japan Society for the Promotion of Science) (2015), 'A3 Foresight Program FY2017, Call for Proposals <Molecular Imaging-Based Precision Medicine>', https://www.jsps.go.jp/english/e-foresight/data/Callforproposals.pdf.

Katzenstein, P. J. (2005), *A World of Regions: Asia and Europe in the American Imperium*, Ithaca, NY: Cornell University Press.

Knight, J. (2016), 'Regionalization of Higher Education in Asia: Functional, Organizational, and Political Approaches', in C. S. Collins, M. M. N. Lee, J. N.

Hawkins and D. E. Neubauer, eds, *The Palgrave Handbook of Asia Pacific Higher Education*, Basingstoke: Palgrave Macmillan.
Kuroda, K. (2016), 'International Student Mobility: Asia as the Next Higher Education Destination', NAFSA 2016 Annual Conference.
Kuroda, K., T. Yuki and K. Kang (2010). 'Cross-Border Higher Education for Regional Integration: Analysis of the JICA-RI Survey on Leading Universities in East Asia', in *Analysis of Cross-Border Higher Education for Regional Integration and Labor Market in East Asia*, 26, https://www.jica.go.jp/jica-ri/publication/workingpaper/cross-border_higher_education_for_regional_integrationanalysis_of_the_jica-ri_survey_on_leading_univ.html.
Kyung, E. Y. (2015), 'Challenges and Possibilities of Regional Collaboration in East Asian Higher Education', Doctoral thesis, University of Melbourne, Melbourne.
Marginson, S. (2011), 'Higher Education in East Asia and Singapore: The Rise of the Confucian Model', *Higher Education*, 61 (5): 587–611.
MEXT (Ministry of Education, Culture, Sports, Science and Technology) (2016), CAMPUS Asia Program Overview, N. D., http://www.mext.go.jp/component/english/__icsFiles/afieldfile/2017/09/13/1395541_001.pdf.
Mok, K. H. (2012), 'Cooperation and Competition in Tango: Transnationalization of Higher Education and the Emergence of Regulatory Regionalism in Asia', in J. N. Hawkins, K. H. Mok and D. E. Neubauer, eds, *Higher Education Regionalization in Asia Pacific: Implications for Governance, Citizenship and University Transformation*, 137–60, New York: Palgrave Macmillan.
NIAD-QE (2019), CAMPUS Asia Monitoring + Joint Monitoring Report.
Ozga, J., and B. Lingard (2007), 'Globalisation, Education Policy and Politics', in B. Lingard and J. Ozga, eds, *The RoutledgeFalmer Reader in Education Policy and Politics*, London: Routledge.
Robertson, S. L., M. L. Azevedo and R. Dale (2016), 'Higher Education, the EU and the Cultural Political Economy of Regionalism', in S. L. Robertson, K. Olds, R. Dale and Q. A. Dang, eds, *Global Regionalisms and Higher Education: Projects, Processes, Politics*, 24–48, Cheltenham: Edward Elgar.
Robertson, S. L., R. Dale, K. Olds and Q. A. Dang (2016), 'Introduction: Global Regionalism and Higher Education', in S. L. Robertson, R. Dale, K. Olds and Q. A. Dang, eds, *Global Regionalisms and Higher Education: Projects, Processes, Politics*, 1–23, Cheltenham: Edward Elgar.
Rosamond, B. (2005), 'The Uniting of Europe and the Foundation of EU Studies: Revisiting the Neofunctionalism of Ernst B. Haas', *Journal of European Public Policy*, 12 (2): 237–54.
Schmidt, V. A. (2008), 'Discursive Institutionalism: The Explanatory Power of Ideas and Discourse', *Annual Review of Political Science*, 11 (1): 303–26.
Schmidt, V. A. (2010), 'Reconciling Ideas and Institutions through Discursive Institutionalism', in D. Beland and R. H. Cox, eds, *Ideas and Politics in Social Science Research*, 45–66, Oxford: Oxford University Press.

Schmidt, V. A. (2015), 'Discursive Institutionalism: Understanding Policy in Context', in F. Fischer, D. Torgerson, A. Durnova and M. Orsini, eds, *Handbook of Critical Policy Studies*, 171–89, Cheltenham: Edward Elgar.

Schmitter, P. C. (2005), 'Ernst B. Haas and the Legacy of Neofunctionalism', *Journal of European Public Policy*, 12 (2): 255–72.

Sugimura, M. (2012), 'Possibility of East Asian Integration through the Regional Networks and Universities' Cooperation in Higher Education', *Asian Education and Development Studies*, 1 (1): 85–95.

Yonezawa, A., and A. Meerman (2012), 'Japanese Higher Education and Multilateral Initiatives in East Asia', in J. N. Hawkins, K. H. Mok and D. E. Neubauer, eds, *Higher Education Regionalization in Asia Pacific: Implications for Governance, Citizenship and University Transformation*, 67–78, New York: Palgrave Macmillan.

Chapter 7

Alatas, S. F. (2003), 'Academic Dependency and the Global Division of Labour in the Social Sciences', *Current Sociology*, 51 (6): 599–613.

Central Committee of the Chinese Communist Party (2017), *Guanyu Jiakuai Goujian Zhongguo Tese Zhexue Shehuikexue De Yijian* [Opinions on Accelerating the Construction of Philosophy and Social Sciences with Chinese Characteristics], http://www.gov.cn/zhengce/2017-05/16/content_5194467.htm.

Chen, H., and Y. Bu (2019), 'Anthropocosmic Vision, Time, and Nature: Reconnecting Humanity and Nature', *Educational Philosophy and Theory*, 51 (11): 1130–40.

Chen, K.-H. (2010), *Asia as Method: Toward Deimperialization*. Durham, NC: Duke University Press.

Coleman, J. S. (1994), *Foundations of Social Theory*, Cambridge: Harvard University Press.

Connell, R. (2007), *Southern Theory: Social Science and the Global Dynamics of Knowledge*, Cambridge: Polity Press.

Dang, S. (2005), 'Meiguo Biaozhun Neng Chengwei Zhongguo Renwensheke Chengguo De Zuigao Biaozhun Ma? – Yi SSCI Weili' [Can American Standards Set the Highest Evaluation Benchmark for Chinese Social Sciences? – Take SSCI as an Example], *Social Sciences Forum*, 4: 62–72.

Dübgen, F. (2020), 'Scientific Ghettos and Beyond. Epistemic Injustice in Academia and Its Effects on Researching Poverty', in V. Beck, H. Hahn and R. Lepenies, eds, *Dimensions of Poverty: Measurement, Epistemic Injustices, Activism*, 77–95, Cham: Springer.

Evans, K. (2007), 'Concepts of Bounded Agency in Education, Work, and the Personal Lives of Young Adults', *International Journal of Psychology*, 42 (2): 85–93.

Fumasoli, T., and J. Huisman (2013), 'Strategic Agency and System Diversity: Conceptualizing Institutional Positioning in Higher Education', *Minerva*, 51 (2): 155–69.

Gao, C. (1995), 'Lun "Tian Ren He Yi" Guan De Jiben Yiyun Ji Jiazhi' [The Meaning and Value of the Idea of 'Tian Ren He Yi'], *Philosophical Research*, 6: 22–8.

Gao, X. (Andy), and Y. Zheng (2018), '"Heavy Mountains" for Chinese Humanities and Social Science Academics in the Quest for World-Class Universities', *Compare: A Journal of Comparative and International Education*, 50 (4): 554–72.

Giddens, A. (1984), *The Constitution of Society: Outline of the Theory of Structuration*, Cambridge: Polity Press.

Hayhoe, R. (1993), 'Chinese Universities and the Social Sciences', *Minerva*, 31 (4): 478–503.

Held, D., A. McGrew, D. Goldblatt and J. Perraton (1999), *Global Transformations: Politics, Economics and Culture*, Cambridge: Polity Press.

Jiang, X. (2012), 'Rationality and Moral Agency – A Study of Xunzi's Philosophy', *Journal of East-West Thought*, 2 (2): 95–106.

Larivière, V., Y. Gingras and E. Archambault (2006), 'Canadian Collaboration Networks: A Comparative Analysis of the Natural Sciences, Social Sciences and the Humanities', *Scientometrics*, 68 (3): 519–33.

Liu, K. (2018), 'Social Sciences, Humanities and Liberal Arts: China and the West', *European Review*, 26 (2): 241–61.

Ma, J., and Y. Cai (2021), 'Innovations in an Institutionalised Higher Education System: The Role of Embedded Agency', *Higher Education*, https://doi.org/10.1007/s10734-021-00679-7.

Marginson, S. (2018), 'National/Global Synergy in the Development of Higher Education and Science in China since 1978', *Frontiers of Education in China*, 13 (4): 486–512.

Marginson, S. (2021), 'Heterogeneous Systems and Common Objects: The Relation between Global and National Science', Centre for Global Higher Education Special Report, April, https://www.researchcghe.org/perch/resources/publications/cghe-special-report-april-2021.pdf.

Marginson, S., and G. Rhoades (2002), 'Beyond National States, Markets, and Systems of Higher Education: A Glonacal Agency Heuristic', *Higher Education*, 43 (3): 281–309.

Marginson, S., and X. Xu (2021), 'Moving Beyond Centre-Periphery Science: Towards an Ecology of Knowledge', Centre for Global Higher Education Working Paper No. 63, https://www.researchcghe.org/perch/resources/publications/working-paper-63.pdf.

Ministry of Education (2011), *Jiaoyubu Guanyu Shenru Tuijin Gaodengxuexiao Zhexueshehuikexue Fanrong Fazhan De Yijian* [Opinions on Further and Vigorous Development of Philosophy and Social Sciences in Higher Education Institutions], http://www.gov.cn/jrzg/2011-11/13/content_1992063.htm.

National Planning Committee of Philosophy and Social Sciences (2006), *Guojia Zhexueshehuikexue Yanjiu Shi Yi Wu (2006-2010 Nian) Guihua* [The National 11th

Five-year Plan for Philosophy and Social Sciences Research (2006–2010)], http://www.npopss-cn.gov.cn/GB/219555/219556/14587978.html.

OECD (Organisation for Economic Co-operation and Development) (2020), *Gross Domestic Spending on R&D*, http://www.oecd-ilibrary.org/industry-and-services/gross-domestic-spending-on-r-d/indicator/english_d8b068b4-en.

Phillipson, R. (1992), *Linguistic Imperialism*, Oxford: Oxford University Press.

Qian, M. (1990), 'Zhongguo Wenhua Dui Renlei Weilai Keyou De Gong Xian' [Possible Contributions of Chinese Culture to the Future of Humankind], *United Daily*, 26 September.

Saldaña, J. (2013), *The Coding Manual for Qualitative Researchers*, 3rd edition, London: Sage.

Santos, B. de S. (2014), *Epistemologies of the South: Justice against Epistemicide*, Boulder, CO: Paradigm Publishers.

Sen, A. (1999a), *Development as Freedom*, Oxford: Oxford University Press.

Sen, A. (1999b), 'Global Justice: Beyond International Equity', in I. Kaul, I. Grunberg and M. Stern, eds, *Global Public Goods: International Cooperation in the 21st century*, 116–25, Oxford: Oxford University Press.

Sen, A. (2006), *Identity and Violence: The Illusion of Destiny*, London: Penguin.

Tlostanova, M. V., and W. D. Mignolo (2012), 'Learning to Unlearn: Decolonial Reflections from Eurasia and the Americas', in *Learning to Unlearn Decolonial Reflections from Eurasia and the Americas* (Issue April), Columbus: Ohio State University Press.

Tu, W. (1999), Interview with Tu Wei-ming, *Philosophy Now*, https://philosophynow.org/issues/23/Interview_with_Tu_Wei-ming.

US National Science Foundation (2020), 'The State of U.S. Science and Engineering 2020', https://ncses.nsf.gov/indicators.

Wagner, C. S. (2009), *The New Invisible College: Science for Development*, Washington, DC: Brookings Institution Press.

Weidemann, D. (2010), 'Challenges of International Collaboration', in M. Kuhn and D. Weidemann, eds, *Internationalization of the Social Sciences Asia – Latin America – Middle East – Africa – Eurasia*, 353–78, Berlin: Verlag.

Xu, X. (2018), 'Incentives for International Publications in the Humanities and Social Sciences: An Exploratory Study of Chinese Universities', Doctoral thesis, Department of Education, University of Oxford, Oxford.

Xu, X. (2021a), 'Epistemic Diversity and Cross-Cultural Comparative Research: Ontology, Challenges, and Outcomes', *Globalisation, Societies and Education*, https://doi.org/10.1080/14767724.2021.1932438.

Xu, X. (2021b), 'A Policy Trajectory Analysis of the Internationalisation of Chinese Humanities and Social Sciences Research (1978–2020)', *International Journal of Educational Development*, https://doi.org/10.1016/j.ijedudev.2021.102425.

Yang, R., M. Xie and W. Wen (2019), 'Pilgrimage to the West: Modern Transformations of Chinese Intellectual Formation in Social Sciences', *Higher Education*, 77 (5): 815–29.
Zhao, T. (2016), *Tianxia De Dangdaixing: Shijie Zhixu De Shijian Yu Xiangxiang* [A Possible World of the All-Under-Heaven System: The World Order in the Past and for the Future], Beijing: China CITIC Press.

Chapter 8

Anderson, B. (1983), Imagined Communities: Reflections on the Origin and Spread of Nationalism, London: Verso.
The Central News Agency (2018), '166 Yi Gaojiao Shengeng Mingdan Chulu: Jin Si Xiao Fuzhu Da 'Guojibei', Youshi Zhong Ligong, Qing Renwen?' [List for 16.6 Billion SPROUT Funding Announced, Only Four Universities Are Funded to the International League, Is It Again Valuing Science and Ignoring Social Science?], *The News Lens*, 23 February, https://www.thenewslens.com/article/89772.
Chan, D. K. K., and W. Y. W. Lo (2008), 'University restructuring in East Asia: Trends, Challenges and Prospects', *Policy Futures in Education*, 6 (5): 641–52.
Chiang, L-C. (2008), 'Song Celue Benzhi ji Zhixingli Fansi Taiwan Gardeng Jiaoyu Guojihua Zhi Xiankuang' [Rethinking the State of the Art of Internationalization of Higher Education in Taiwan from the Nature of Strategy and Execution], *Educational Resources and Research*, 83: 47–70.
Connor, W. (1994), *Ethnonationalism: The Quest for Understanding*, Princeton: Princeton University Press.
Dahbour, O. (2002), 'National Identity: An Argument for the Strict Definition', *Public Affairs Quarterly*, 16 (1): 17–37.
Election Study Center, National Chengchi University (2020), 'Changes in the Taiwanese/Chinese Identity of Taiwanese as Tracked in Survey by the Election Study Center, National Chengchi University (1992～2020.06)', https://esc.nccu.edu.tw/PageDoc/Detail?fid=7804&id=6960.
Fu, Y.-C., D. P. Baker and L. Zhang (2020), 'Engineering a World Class University? The Impact of Taiwan's World Class University Project on Scientific Productivity', *Higher Education Policy*, 33 (3): 555–70.
The Foundation for International Cooperation in Higher Education of Taiwan (FICHET) (2020), 'Jiaoyubu COVID-19 Fangyi Cuoshi: Tingke Biaozhun, Shouke Yanlian Yu Yuanju Jiaoxue Duice' [MOE Covid-19 Guideline: School Suspension, Off-line Courses Preparation, and Online Learning Measures], *Xin Nanxiang Rencai Peiyu Jihua* [New Southbound Talent Cultivation Programme], 30 April, https://www.edunsbp.moe.gov.tw/news1964.html.

Fu, Y. Z., and M. C. Chin (2020), 'The Dilemma and Opportunity in the Accountability System of Taiwan Higher Education: The Application of Agency Theory', *Journal of Educational Research and Development*, 16 (3): 1–30.

Hammond, C. D. (2016), 'Internationalisation, Nationalism, and Global Competitiveness: A Comparison of Approaches to Higher Education in China and Japan', *Asia Pacific Education Review*, 17 (4): 555–66.

Han, S., and Z. Zhong (2015), 'Strategy Maps in University Management: A Comparative Study', *Educational Management Administration and Leadership*, 43 (6): 939–53.

Hsueh, J. C. (2018), 'Gaojiao Shengeng Jihua Jieguo Chulu: Taida Yusuan Dakan Jin Si Xiao Lieru Guojibei Daxue' [SPROUT Result: NTU Funding Cut and Only Four Universities Are Developing Internationalization?]. *The C Media*, 23 February, https://www.cmmedia.com.tw/home/articles/8550.

Hou, A. Y. C., C. Hill, Z. Hu and L. Lin (2020), 'What Is Driving Taiwan Government for Policy Change in Higher Education after the Year of 2016 – In Search of Egalitarianism or Pursuit of Academic Excellence?' *Studies in Higher Education*, https://doi.org/10.1080/03075079.2020.1744126.

Hu, Y.-S. (2017), 'Daxue Jianli Shuju Qudong Jiaoyu Juece De Chuangxin Wenhua' [Universities Should Build Innovation Culture that Uses Data to Drive Education Decisions], *Evaluation Bimonthly*, 5 May, http://epaper.heeact.edu.tw/archive/2017/05/01/6754.aspx.

IMF (International Monetary Fund) (2020), 'GDP, Current Prices', https://www.imf.org/external/datamapper/NGDPD@WEO/WEOWORLD.

Lai, C. (2020), 'A Case Study of Recent Social Movements in Hong Kong and Taiwan', *Global Taiwan*, August, https://globaltaiwan.org/wp-content/uploads/2020/08/GTI-A-Case-Study-of-Recent-Social-Movements-in-Hong-Kong-and-Taiwan-Aug-2020-final-2.pdf.

Law, W. (1996), 'Fortress State, Cultural Continuities and Economic Change: Higher Education in Mainland China and Taiwan', *Comparative Education*, 32 (3): 377–93.

Law, W.-W. (2002), 'Education Reform in Taiwan: A Search for a "National" Identity through Democratization and Taiwanisation', *Compare: A Journal of Comparative and International Education*, 21 (1): 61–81.

Lee, J. W-S. and B.-J. Fwu (2017), 'Quanqiu Shiye Zaidihua de Xiaowu Yanjiu: Yi Guoli Taiwan Daxue Jingyan Weili' [Think Globally and Act Locally: National Taiwan University's Experience of Institutional Research], *Journal of Research in Education Sciences*, 62 (4): 1–25.

Lin, W., and R. Yang (2019), 'To Borrow or to Mix? A Cultural Approach to Observing Taiwan's Higher Education', *Higher Education Forum*, 16: 143–59.

Lo, W. Y. W. (2020), 'A Year of Change for Hong Kong: From East-Meets-West to East-Clashes-with-West', *Higher Education Research and Development*, 39 (7): 1362–6, https://doi.org/10.1080/07294360.2020.1824210.

Lo, W. Y. W., and A. Y.-C. Hou (2020), 'A Farewell to Internationalisation? Striking a Balance between Global Ambition and Local Needs in Higher Education in Taiwan', *Higher Education*, 80 (3): 497–510.

Marginson, S., and G. Rhoades (2002), 'Beyond National States, Markets, and Systems of Higher Education: A Glonacal Agency Heuristic', *Higher Education*, 43 (3): 281–309.

MOE (Ministry of Education, Republic of China (Taiwan)) (2019), About the Project: SPROUT, https://sprout.moe.edu.tw/SproutWeb/Home/Index/en.

MOE (Ministry of Education, People's Republic of China) (2020), Jiaoyubu: Zanting 2020 Nian Lusheng Futai Jiudu Shidian Gongzuo [Ministry of Education: 2020 Mainland Student Study in Taiwan Project Paused], http://www.moe.gov.cn/jyb_xwfb/gzdt_gzdt/s5987/202004/t20200409_441791.html.

MOE (Ministry of Education, Republic of China (Taiwan)) (n.d.), 'Fazhan Guoji Yiliu Daxue Ji Dingjian Yanjiu Zhongxin Jihua/Maixiang Dingjian Daxue Jihua' [Develop International Universities and Top Research Centres Program/Aim for the Top University Programme], https://ws.moe.edu.tw/Download.ashx?u=C099358C81D4876CB9232B8E83EAD7A4C0AF2F715242CFFDD315456B1402B431EB1AD2F45E2601605AA01B1C78937B74A8E2F5B03BA2B04451391B4F3E8364EC&n=E3818BD1DFF394E10D01BAB9EB40A12910FE395EEED83BF36CC83500BEA7B76C440C5BC878F88852.

Mintzberg, H. (1987), 'The Strategy Concept I: Five Ps for Strategy', *Management Review*, 30 (1): 11–24.

Mok, K. H. (2002), 'From Nationalisation to Marketisation: Changing Governance in Taiwan's Higher-Education System', *Governance*, 15 (2): 137–59.

Mok, K. H., and K. M. Yu, eds (2013), *Internationalization of Higher Education in East Asia: Trends of Student Mobility and Impact on Education Governance*, Abingdon: Routledge.

Muyard, F. (2018), 'The Role of Democracy in the Rise of the Taiwanese National Identity', in J. Sullivan and C.-Y. Lee, ed., *New Era in Democratic Taiwan: Trajectories and Turning Points in Politics*, 35–59. Routledge.

Shin, J. C., and G. Harman (2009), 'New Challenges for Higher Education: Global and Asia-Pacific Perspectives', *Asia Pacific Education Review*, 10 (1): 1–13.

Shreeve, R. L. (2020), 'Globalisation or Westernisation? The Influence of Global University Rankings in the Context of the Republic of China (Taiwan)', *Compare: A Journal of Comparative and International Education*, 50 (6): 922–7.

Song, M.-M., and H.-H. Tai (2007), 'Taiwan's Responses to Globalisation: Internationalisation and Questing for World Class Universities', *Asia Pacific Journal of Education*, 27 (3): 323–40.

Sullivan, J., and C.-Y. Lee (2018), 'Introduction', in J. Sullivan and C.-Y. Lee, eds, *New Era in Democratic Taiwan: Trajectories and Turning Points in Politics*, 1–9, Routledge.

Tian, M.-S. (2019), 'Taida Zhuanan Xiezhu Jin 600 Zaigang Xuesheng Jiuxue, Buwen Beijing Quan Shourong' [NTU Special Project Assists Almost 600 Students in Hong

Kong to Enroll Regardless of Their Backgrounds], *Common Wealth Magazine*, 21 November, https://www.cw.com.tw/article/5097800.

Weng, F.-Y. (1999), 'The Implementation of Equality of Educational Opportunities in Taiwan in the Early 1990s: A Post-Fordist Perspective', *Comparative Education*, 47: 28–54.

Wu, N. D. (1996), 'Liberalism, Ethnic Identity and Taiwanese Nationalism', *Taiwan Political Science Review*, 1: 5–39.

Wu, P. S. (2020), 'Gaojiao Zhanwang. Daxue Kan Shengeng Jingfei/Youde Ren Bi Guowang Pingjun Youde You Liangjihua' [Higher Education Vision: Universities' View on SPROUT Funding, Some Found It More Even Than the Past while Some Worry about Polarization], *Liberty Times Net*, 9 November, https://talk.ltn.com.tw/article/paper/1411387.

Yang, J. C. C. (2019), 'The Shaping of Academic Culture in Higher Education in Taiwan', in A. Jun and C. Collins, eds, *Higher Education and Belief Systems in the Asia Pacific Region*, 15–24, Dordrecht: Springer.

Chapter 9

Altbach, P. G., and H. de Wit (2017). 'Trump and the Coming Revolution in Higher Education Internationalization', *International Higher Education*, 89: 3–5.

Anh, L. T. K., and M. Hayden (2017), 'The Road Ahead for the Higher Education Sector in Vietnam', *Journal of International and Comparative Education*, 6 (1): 77–89.

Australian Government (2020), 'Vietnam Country Brief', Canberra: DFAT.

Bagshaw, E., F. Hunter and S. Liu (2020), ' "Chinese Students Will Not Go There": Beijing Education Agents Warn Australia', https://www.smh.com.au/politics/federal/chinese-students-will-not-go-there-beijing-education-agents-warn-australia-20200610-p55151.html.

Bamberger, A., P. Morris, Y. Weinreb and M. Yemini (2019), 'Hyperpoliticised Internationalisation in a Pariah University: An Israeli Institution in the Occupied West Bank', *International Journal of Educational Development*, 66: 119–28.

Blessinger, P., and B. Cozza (2017), 'The Case for Internationalisation of Higher Education', *University World News*, https://www.universityworldnews.com/post.php?story=20171010115112828.

Block, D., J. Gray and M. Holborow (2012), *Neoliberalism and Applied Linguistics*, London: Routledge.

BMI (2020), 'The Outbound Student Recruitment Market in Vietnam', https://bmiglobaled.com/Market-Reports/Vietnam/student-recruitment.

Bodewig, C., R. Badiani-Magnusson, K. Macdonald, D. Newhouse and J. Rutkowski (2014), *Skilling Up Vietnam Preparing the Workforce for a Modern Market Economy*, Washington, DC: World Bank, http://documents1.worldbank.org/

curated/en/283651468321297015/pdf/888950PUB0Box30lso0829400June172014.pdf.

Brooks, T. (2010), 'Innovation Education: Problems and Prospects in Governance and Management of the Vietnamese Higher Education System', http://digitalcollections.sit.edu/isp_collection/874.

Cheng, X. (2009), 'Education: The Intellectual Base of China's Soft Power', in M. Li, ed., *Soft Power: China's Emerging Strategy in International Politics*, 103–23, Washington, DC: Lexington Books.

Daidoanket News (2017), 'Hội nhập quốc tế trong giáo dục đại học: Những bước chuyển mình' [International Integration in Higher Education: Transformation Steps], http://daidoanket.vn/xa-hoi/hoi-nhap-quoc-te-tronggiao-duc-dai-hoc-nhung-buoc-chuyen-minh-tintuc378051.

De Wit, H. (2020), 'Internationalization of Higher Education', *Journal of International Students*, 10 (1): i–iv.

Do, H. (2014), 'Towards more Flexible Organization', in L. T. Tran, S. Marginson, H. Do, Q. Do, T. Le, N. Nguyen, T. Vu, T. Pham and H. Nguyen, *Higher Education in Vietnam: Flexibility, Mobility and Practicality in the Global Knowledge Economy*, 54–85, Basingstoke: Palgrave Macmillan.

Duong, T. H. H. (2009), 'The Modernization of the National Higher Education of Vietnam, 1990s–Present: American Universities, a Resource and Recourse', Doctoral thesis, St. John's University, New York.

Feng, Z. (2020), 'Being a Chinese Student in the US: "Neither the US nor China Wants Us" ', https://www.bbc.com/news/world-us-canada-53573289.

Flint, C., and C. Zhu (2019), 'The Geopolitics of Connectivity, Cooperation, and Hegemonic Competition: The Belt and Road Initiative', *Geoforum*, 99: 95–101.

Gong, S., W. Huo, M. Wu, Y. Huang, J. Gong and D. Wang (2020) 'The Impact of the Belt and Road Initiative on the Expansion of China's Higher Education in Overseas Markets along the Route', *Thunderbird International Business Review*, 62 (3): 263–77.

The Government of Vietnam (2008), Decision No. 1400/QD-TTg on 'Teaching and Learning Foreign Languages in the National Education System, Period 2008–2020', Hanoi: Vietnamese Government.

The Government of Vietnam (2012a), 7 Decree No. 73/2012/ ND-CP on 'Foreign Investment and Cooperation in Education', 26 September, Hanoi: Vietnamese Government.

The Government of Vietnam (2012b), 'National Strategy for Educational Development 2011–2020', Hanoi: Vietnamese Government.

Gramsci, A. (2000), *The Gramsci Reader: Selected Writings, 1916–1935*, New York: New York University Press.

Haban News (2017), 'Five Years of Sheer Endeavour: What Data Says about Confucius Institutes (2012–2017)', http://english.hanban.org/article/2017-10/26/content_703508.htm.

Hall, I. (2017), 'What China's Soft Power Means for European Universities', *University World News*, https://www.universityworldnews.com/post.php?story=20171025102935623.

He, L., and S. Wilkins (2018), 'The Return of China's Soft Power in South East Asia: An Analysis of the International Branch Campuses Established by Three Chinese Universities', *Higher Education Policy*, 32: 321–37.

Hoang, L., L. Tran and H. H. Pham (2018), 'Vietnamese Government Policies and Practices in Internationalisation of Higher Education', in L. T. Tran and S. Marginson, eds, *Internationalisation in Vietnamese Higher Education*, 19–42, Springer.

Hoang, V. V. (2010), 'The Current Situation and Issues of the Teaching of English in Vietnam', 立命館言語文化研究 [Ritsumeikan University's Institute for Teaching and Learning Journal], 22 (1): 7–18.

Hsieh, C. C. (2020), 'Internationalization of Higher Education in the Crucible: Linking National Identity and Policy in the Age of Globalization', *International Journal of Educational Development*, 78: 1–12.

Human Rights Watch (2020), 'Australia Events of 2020', 25 June, https://www.hrw.org/world-report/2021/country-chapters/australia.

Knight, J. (2015), 'Updated Definition of Internationalization', *International Higher Education*, 33: 2–3.

Koch, N. (2014), 'The Shifting Geopolitics of Higher Education: Inter/nationalizing Elite Universities in Kazakhstan, Saudi Arabia, and Beyond', *Geoforum*, 56: 46–54.

Kuo, L., and K. Murphy (2020), 'China Warns Students to Reconsider Travel to Australia for Study', *The Guardian*, https://www.theguardian.com/world/2020/jun/09/china-warns-students-to-reconsider-travel-to-australia-for-study.

Le, T. N. (2020), 'Điểm đến mới của sinh viên quốc tế' [International Students' New Destination], Báo Thời Nay, https://nhandan.com.vn/baothoinay-xahoi-songtre/diem-den-moi-cua-sinh-vien-quoc-te-579589.

Lee, J. T. (2015), 'The Regional Dimension of Education Hubs: Leading and Brokering Geopolitics', *Higher Education Policy*, 28 (1): 69–89.

London, J. D. (2010), 'Globalization and the Governance of Education in Viet Nam', *Asia-Pacific Journal of Education*, 30 (4): 361–79.

Luqiu, L. R., and J. D. McCarthy (2019), 'Confucius Institutes: The Successful Stealth "Soft Power" Penetration of American Universities', *Journal of Higher Education*, 90 (4): 620–43.

Majhanovich, S. (2014), 'Neo-Liberalism, Globalization, Language Policy and Practice Issues in the Asia-Pacific Region', *Asia Pacific Journal of Education*, 34 (2): 168–83.

Manh, H. D. (2015), 'Scientific Publications in Vietnam as Seen from Scopus during 1996–2013', *Scientometrics,* 105 (1), 83–95.

Marginson, S. (1999), 'After Globalization: Emerging Politics of Education', *Journal of Education Policy*, 14 (1): 19–31.

Marginson, S., and M. v. d. Wende (2007), *Globalisation and Higher Education*, OECD Education Working Paper No. 8, http://dx.doi.org/10.1787/173831738240.

Marginson, S., and L. Yang (2020), 'Higher Education and Public Good in East and West', Centre for Global Higher Education Research Findings 5, Oxford: ESRC/OFSRE Centre for Global Higher Education, Department of Education, University of Oxford..

Marklein, M. B. (2020), 'Trump Moves to Ramp up Scrutiny of Confucius Institutes', *University World News*, https://www.universityworldnews.com/post.php?story=20200830091037652.

MOE (Ministry of Education, People's Republic of China) (2019), 'Statistical Report on International Students in China for 2018', http://en.moe.gov.cn/news/press_releases/201904/t20190418_378586.html#:~:text=Figures%20show%20that%20in%202018,or%200.62%25%20compared%20to%202017.

Ministry of Foreign Affairs (2020), 'General Information about Countries and Regions', http://www.mofahcm.gov.vn/mofa/cn_vakv/.

Mittelmeier, J., M. A. Lim and S. Lomer (2020), 'Why International Students Are Choosing the UK – Despite Coronavirus', *The Conversation*, https://theconversation.com/why-international-students-are-choosing-the-uk-despite-coronavirus-147064.

MOET (Ministry of Education and Training) (2008), 'Project for Training by Advanced Curricula in Some Vietnamese Universities: Period 2008–2015', Hanoi: MOET.

Ngo, T. L. (2016), 'Higher Education Internationalization in Vietnam: Unintended Socio-Political Impacts of Joint Programs Seen as Special Free Academic Zones', Paper presented at the meeting on the Contribution of Social Sciences and Humanities on Socioeconomic Development, https://dulieu.itrithuc.vn/dataset/fb3d23d1-ed4d-411b-8e24-c30f936d93d8/resource/054ae38e-e4c6-4584-bbc9-4e04bbfb4802/download/12-ngo-tu-lap-_phuong-sua.pdf.

Nguyen, C. H. (2018), 'Historical Trends of Vietnamese International Student Mobility'. in L. T. Tran and S. Marginson, eds, *Internationalisation in Vietnamese Higher Education*, 141–59, Cham: Springer.

Nguyen, H. T. (2018), 'English-Medium-Instruction Management: The Missing Piece in the Internationalisation Puzzle of Vietnamese Higher Education', in L. T. Tran and S. Marginson, eds, *Internationalisation in Vietnamese Higher Education*, 119–37, Cham: Springer.

Nhan T. T., and K. A. T. Le (2019), 'Internationalisation of Higher Education in Vietnam', in C. Nguyen and M. Shah, eds, *Quality Assurance in Vietnamese Higher Education*, 25–58, Cham: Palgrave Macmillan.

Peters, M. A. (2020) 'China's Belt and Road Initiative: Reshaping Global Higher Education', *Educational Philosophy and Theory*, 52 (6): 586–92.

Pham, H. (2011), 'Vietnam: Struggling to Attract International Students', *University World News*, https://www.universityworldnews.com/post.php?story=2011121617161637.

Pham, L. H., and G. W. Fry (2004), 'Education and Economic, Political, and Social Change in Vietnam', *Educational Research for Policy and Practice*, 3 (3): 199–222.

Pham, N. T. (2014), 'Foreign Language Policy', in L. T. Tran, S. Marginson, H. Do, Q. Do, T. Le, N. Nguyen, T. Vu, T. Pham and H. Nguyen, eds, *Higher Education in Vietnam: Flexibility, Mobility and Practicality in the Global Knowledge Economy*, 169–85, Basingstoke: Palgrave Macmillan.

Ren, Y., and B. Wilhelm (2020), 'Trump's Attacks on China's Soft Power Extend to the Confucius Institutes', *World Politics Review*, 25 August, https://www.worldpoliticsreview.com/trend-lines/29002/trump-s-attacks-on-china-s-soft-power-extend-to-the-confucius-institutes.

Tedesco, J. C., R. Opertti and M. Amadio (2014), 'The Curriculum Debate: Why It Is Important Today', *Prospects*, 44 (4): 527–46.

Tram, B. (2019), 'Chi 3 tỉ USD mỗi năm, du học sinh Việt Nam đến nước nào?' [Spending 3 billion USD Per Year, Which Country Do Vietnamese Students Go to?] https://forbesvietnam.com.vn/tin-cap-nhat/chi-3-ti-usd-moi-nam-du-hoc-sinh-viet-nam-den-nuoc-nao-8274.html.

Tran, L. T. (2020), 'How to Secure Recovery of International Student Mobility', *University World News*, 20 June, https://www.universityworldnews.com/post.php?story=20200620071618800.

Tran, L. T., and H. Bui (2021), 'Public Diplomacy and Social Impact of Australian Student Mobility to the Indo-Pacific: Host Countries' Perspectives on Hosting New Colombo Plan Students', *Journal of Studies in International Education,* 25 (4): 425–42..

Tran, T. L., and S. Marginson (2014), 'Education for Flexibility, Practicality and Mobility', in L. T. Tran, S. Marginson, H. Do, Q. Do, T. Le, N. Nguyen, T. Vu, T. Pham and H. Nguyen, *Higher Education in Vietnam: Flexibility, Mobility and Practicality in the Global Knowledge Economy*, 3–25, Basingstoke: Palgrave Macmillan.

Tran, L. T., and S. Marginson (2018), 'Internationalisation of Vietnamese Higher Education: An Overview', in L. Tran and S. Marginson, eds, *Internationalisation of Vietnamese Higher Education*, 1–16, Dordrecht: Springer.

Tran, L., T. Le and N. Nguyen (2014), 'Curriculum and Pedagogy', in L. T. Tran, S. Marginson, H. Do, Q. Do, T. Le, N. Nguyen, T. Vu, T. Pham and H. Nguyen, *Higher Education in Vietnam: Flexibility, Mobility and Practicality in the Global Knowledge Economy*, 86–107, Basingstoke: Palgrave Macmillan.

Tran, T. L., S. Marginson and N. Nguyen (2014), 'Internationalization', in L. T. Tran, S. Marginson, H. Do, Q. Do, T. Le, N. Nguyen, T. Vu, T. Pham and H. Nguyen, *Higher Education in Vietnam: Flexibility, Mobility and Practicality in the Global Knowledge Economy*, 127–51, Basingstoke: Palgrave Macmillan.

Tran, L. T., L. T. H. Phan and S. Marginson (2018), 'The "Advanced Programmes" in Vietnam: Internationalising the Curriculum or Importing the "Best Curriculum" of the West?' in L. T. Tran and S. Marginson, eds, *Internationalisation of Vietnamese Higher Education*, 55–76, Dordrecht: Springer.

Tran, L., S. Marginson, H. Do, Q. Do, T. Le, N. Nguyen, T. Vu, T. Pham and H. Nguyen (2014), *Higher Education in Vietnam: Flexibility, Mobility and Practicality in the Global Knowledge Economy*, New York: Palgrave Macmillan.

Tuoi tre (2017), 'Đề án 911 không đạt mục tiêu, Bộ GD-ĐT ra đề án mới?' [Project 911 Did Not Meet the Objectives, the Ministry of Education and Training Launched a New Project?] https://tuoitre.vn/de-an-911-khong-dat-muc-tieu-bo-gd-dt-ra-de-an-moi-20171113085028796.htm.

UNESCO (United Nations Educational, Social and Cultural Organization) (2010), 'Global Education Digest, 2010: Comparing Education Statistics across the World', https://unesdoc.unesco.org/ark:/48223/pf0000189433.

UNESCO (United Nations Educational, Social and Cultural Organization) (2021), 'Data on Student Mobility', http://uis.unesco.org/en/uis-student-flow.

Welch, A. (2010), 'Internationalisation of Vietnamese Higher Education: Retrospect and Prospect', in G. Harman, M. Hayden and T. N. Pham, eds, *Reforming Higher Education in Vietnam*, 197–213, Dordrecht: Springer.

Welch, A. (2011), 'Ho Chi Minh Meets the Market: Public and Private Higher Education in Viet Nam', in A. Welch, ed., *Higher Education in Southeast Asia: Blurring Borders, Changing Balance*, London: Taylor & Francis.

Wen, W., and D. Hu (2019), 'The Emergence of a Regional Education Hub: Rationales of International Students' Choice of China as the Study Destination', *Journal of Studies in International Education*, 23 (3): 303–25.

World Bank (2012), 'Putting Higher Education to Work: Skills and Research for Growth in East Asia', https://openknowledge.worldbank.org/handle/10986/2364.

World Bank (2019), 'Vietnam's Economy Expanded by 6.8 Percent in 2019 but Reforms Are Needed to Unleash the Potential of Capital Markets', Press Release, https://www.worldbank.org/en/news/press-release/2019/12/17/vietnams-economy-expanded-by-68-percent-in-2019-but-reforms-are-needed-to-unleash-the-potential-of-capital-markets.

Wright, S. (2002), 'Language Education and Foreign Relations in Vietnam', in J. Tollefson, ed., *Language Policies in Education: Critical Issues*, 225–44, Mahwah, NJ: Lawrence Erlbaum Associates.

Yang, R. (2008), 'Transnational Higher Education in China: Contexts, Characteristics and Concerns', *Australian Journal of Education*, 52 (3): 272–86.

Zhang, M. Y. (2020), 'Students in China Heed Their Government's Warnings against Studying in Australia – Less Than Half Plan to Come Back', https://www.sbs.com.au/news/students-in-china-heed-their-government-s-warnings-against-studying-in-australia-less-than-half-plan-to-come-back.

Ziguras, C., and A. Pham (2017), 'Internationalization of Higher Education in Vietnam: Moving Towards Interdependence', in H. De Wit, J. Gacel-Avila, E. Jones and N. Jooste, eds, *The Globalization of Internationalization*, 131–41, Florence: Taylor and Francis.

Chapter 10

Abbott, A., and M. Silles (2016), 'Determinants of International Student Migration', *The World Economy*, 39 (5): 621–35.

Amos Hatch, J., and R. Wisniewski, eds (1995), *Life History and Narrative*, London: Falmer Press.

Baas, M. (2019), 'The Education-Migration Industry: International Students, Migration Policy and the Question of Skills', *International Migration*, 57 (3): 222–34.

Brotherhood, T. (2020), 'Considering Agency in the Education-Migration Nexus: A Temporal Analysis of Structure-Agency Relations with Student-Migrants', Doctoral thesis, Department of Education, University of Oxford, Oxford.

Carlson, S. (2013), 'Becoming a Mobile Student – A Processual Perspective on German Degree Student Mobility', *Population, Space and Place*, 19 (2): 168–80.

Carr, D. (1986), *Time, Narrative, and History*, Bloomington: University of Indiana Press.

Chatterjee, S. (2015), 'Skills to Build the Nation: The Ideology of "Canadian Experience" and Nationalism in Global Knowledge Regime', *Ethnicities*, 15 (4): 544–67.

Chiou, B. (2017), 'Two-Step Migration: A Comparison of Australia's and New Zealand's Policy Development between 1998 and 2010', *Asian and Pacific Migration Journal*, 26 (1): 84–107.

Cortazzi, M. (1993), *Narrative Analysis*, Abingdon: Routledge.

Dwyer, R., I. Davis and E. Emerald, eds (2017), *Narrative Research in Practice: Stories from the Field*, Singapore: Springer.

Emirbayer, M., and A. Mische (1998), 'What Is Agency?' *American Journal of Sociology*, 103 (4): 962–1023.

Geddie, K. (2015), 'Policy Mobilities in the Race for Talent: Competitive State Strategies in International Student Mobility', *Transactions of the Institute of British Geographers*, 40 (2): 235–48.

Hamaguchi, K. (2019), 'How Have Japanese Policies Changed in Accepting Foreign Workers?', *Japan Labour Issues*, 3 (14), https://www.jil.go.jp/english/profile/hamaguchi.html.

Hawthorne, L. (2005), ' "Picking Winners": The Recent Transformation of Australia's Skilled Migration Policy', *International Migration Review*, 39 (3): 663–96.

Jones, P., J. Lee, L. Phillips, X. Zhang and K. Jaceldo (2001), 'An Adaptation of Brislin's Translation Model for Cross-Cultural Research', *Nursing Research*, 50 (5): 300–4.

Kim, A. H., and G. Sondhi, G. (2015), *Bridging the Literature on Education Migration*, No. 3, http://ir.lib.uwo.ca/cgi/viewcontent.cgi?article=1016andcontext=pclc.

Labov, W., and J. Waletzky (1967), 'Narrative Analysis: Oral Versions of Personal Experience', in J. Helm, ed., *Proceedings of the 1966 Annual Spring Meeting of the American Ethnological Society*, Seattle and London: University of Washington Press.

Liu-Farrer, G., and A. H. Tran (2019), 'Bridging the Institutional Gaps: International Education as a Migration Industry', *International Migration*, 57 (3): 235–49.

Lomer, S. (2017), *Recruiting International Students in Higher Education: Representations and Rationales in British Policy*, London: Palgrave Macmillan.

Ministry of Justice. (2019), Table 4 Applicant of the Certificate of Eligibility (Immigration Control Act Enforcement Regulation Annex Table 4) | Immigration Bureau of Japan Website, http://www.immi-moj.go.jp/english/tetuduki/kanri/shyorui/Table4.html.

MEXT (Ministry of Education, Culture, Sports, Science and Technology) (1983), *Committee for the International Student Policy toward the 21st Century*. Tokyo: MEXT.

Ota, H. (2018), 'Internationalization of Higher Education: Global Trends and Japan's Challenges', *Educational Studies in Japan: International Yearbook*, 12 (12): 91–105.

Polkinghorne, D. (1988), *Narrative Knowing and the Human Sciences*, Albany: State University of New York Press.

Polkinghorne, D. (1995), 'Narrative Configuration in Qualitative Analysis', in J. Amos Hatch and R. Wisniewski, eds, *Life History and Narrative*, London: Falmer Press.

The Prime Minister and His Cabinet (2014), *Japan Revitalization Strategy 2014*, https://www.kantei.go.jp/jp/singi/keizaisaisei/pdf/honbunEN.pdf.

Robertson, S. (2013), *Transnational Student-Migrants and the State*, London: Palgrave Macmillan.

Tran, L. T., and T. T. P. Vu (2018), '"Agency in Mobility": Towards a Conceptualisation of International Student Agency in Transnational Mobility', *Educational Review*, 70 (2): 167–87.

Van Den Broek, D., W. S. Harvey and D. Groutsis (2015), 'Commercial Migration Intermediaries and the Segmentation of Skilled Migrant Employment', *Work, Employment and Society*: 1–21.

Wengraf, T. (2001), *Qualitative Research Interviewing: Biographic Narrative and Semi-Structured Methods*, London: Sage.

Willis, R. (2019), 'The Use of Composite Narratives to Present Interview Findings', *Qualitative Research*, 19 (4): 471–80.

Yamanaka, K. (1993), 'New Immigration Policy and Unskilled Foreign Workers in Japan', *Pacific Affairs*, 66 (1): 72–90.

Yonezawa, A. (2008), 'Facing Crisis: Soft Power and Japanese Education in a Global Context', in W. Yasushi and D. McDonnell, eds, *Soft Power Superpowers: Cultural and National Assets of Japan and the United States*, 54–74, New York: M. E. Sharpe.

Yonezawa, A. (2020), 'Challenges of the Japanese Higher Education amidst Population Decline and Globalization', *Globalisation, Societies and Education*, 18 (1): 43–52.

Chapter 11

Altbach, P. G., and V. Selvaratnam, eds (1989), *From Dependence to Autonomy: The Development of Asian Universities*, Dordrecht: Kluwer Academic.

Altbach, P. G., and M. Yudkevich (2017), 'Twenty-first Century Mobility: The Role of International Faculty', *International Higher Education*, 90: 8–10.

Bai, C. (2014), '"Bai Ren Ji Hua": Er Shi Nian Huigu Yu Sikao' [A Review of and Considerations on the Hundred Talents Programme], *Guangmin Daily*, 20 November, https://epaper.gmw.cn/gmrb/html/2014-11/20/nw.D110000gmrb_20141120_1-16.htm?div=-1.

Brotherhood, T., C. D. Hammond and Y. Kim (2020), 'Towards an Actor-Centered Typology of Internationalization: A Study of Junior International Faculty in Japanese Universities', *High Education*, 79 (3): 497–514.

Byju, A., and D. Levine (2015), 'Anthropology Professor Named Changjiang Scholar', *The Crimson*, https://www.thecrimson.com/article/2015/2/23/herzelf-named-chiangjiang-scholar/.

Cao, C. (2004), 'China's Efforts at Turning "Brain Drain" into "Brain Gain"', *Report No. 216*, 1 November, National University of Singapore, Singapore.

Cao, C. (2008), 'China's Brain Drain and Brain Gain: Why Government Policies Have Failed to Attract First-Rate Talent to Return?', *Asian Population Studies*, 4, 331–45.

Chu, L. (2013), 'Looking to China for Scientific Careers', *Science Magazine*, 15 November.

Hazelkorn, E., ed. (2016), *Global Rankings and the Geopolitics of Higher Education: Understanding the Influence and Impact of Rankings on Higher Education, Policy and Society*, London: Routledge.

Huang, F. (2003) 'Policy and Practice of Internationalization of Higher Education in China', *Journal of Studies in International Education*, 7 (3): 225–40.

Huang, F. (2015), 'Building the World-Class Research Universities: A Case Study of China', *Higher Education*, 70 (2): 203–15.

Huang, F. (2017), 'Double World-class Project Has More Ambitious Aims', *University World News*, 29 September.

Huang, F. (2018a), 'International Faculty at Japanese Universities: Profiles and Motivations', *Higher Education Quarterly*, 72 (3): 237–49.

Huang, F. (2018b), 'International Faculty at Japanese Universities: Their Demographic Characteristics and Work Roles', *Asia Pacific Education Review*, 19 (2): 263–72.

Huang, F., M. J. Finkelstein and M. Rostan, eds (2014), *The Internationalisation of the Academy: Changes, Realities and Prospects* (The Changing Academy – The Changing Academic Profession in International Comparative Perspective), Volume 10, Dordrecht: Springer.

Janger, J., and K. Nowotny (2016), 'Job Choice in Academia', *Research Policy*, 45: 1672–83.

Jia, H. (2018), 'How to Find a Job in China?', *Nature*, 553 (S4–S7), https://doi.org/10.1038/d41586-018-00537-0.

Kim, D., L. Wolf-Wendel and S. Twombly (2011), 'International Faculty: Experiences of Academic Life, Productivity in U.S. Universities', *Journal of Higher Education*, 82 (6): 720–47.

Kim, E. (2015), 'International Professors in China: Prestige Maintenance and Making Sense of Teaching Abroad', *Current Sociology*, 63 (4): 604–20.

Kim, H. (2017), 'The Higher Education Policy of Global Experts Recruitment Program: Focused on China', *Current Business and Economics Driven Discourse and Education: Perspectives from Around the World BCES Conference Books 2017*, Volume 15, 151–8, Sofia: Bulgarian Comparative Education Society.

Kim, T., and W. Locke (2010), *Transnational Academic Mobility and the Academic Profession*, London: Open University.

Knight, J. (2004), 'Internationalization Remodeled: Definition, Approaches, and Rationales', *Journal of Studies in International Education*, 8 (1): 5–31.

Larbi, F. O., and M. A. Ashraf (2020), 'International Academic Mobility in Chinese Academia: Opportunities and Challenges', *International Migration*, 58 (3): 148–62.

MOE (Ministry of Education, People's Republic of China) (1998), 'Gaodeng Yuanxiao Zhong De Zhongwaihezuobanxue De Huigu Yu Sikao' [An Overview and Thoughts of Transnational Higher Education], *China Higher Education*, 10: 43.

MOE (Ministry of Education, People's Republic of China) (2019), 'Jiaoyu Tongji Shuju' [Educational Statistics], http://www.moe.gov.cn/s78/A03/moe_560/jytjsj_2019/.

Morano-Foadi, S. (2005), 'Scientific Mobility, Career Progression, and Excellence in the European Research Area', *International Migration*, 43 (5): 133–62.

Ng, P. T. M. (2006), *Jidu Zongjiao Yu Zhongguo Daxue Jiaoyu* [Christianity and University Education in China]. Beijing, China: China Social Sciences Press.

Ng, P. T.M. (2019), 'Resurgence of the Study of China's Christian Higher Education since 1980s', *Frontiers of Education in China*, 14: 364–86.

OECD (Organisation for Economic Co-operation and Development) (2001), *International Mobility of the Highly Skilled*, Paris: OECD.

OECD (Organisation for Economic Co-operation and Development) (2015), *Which Factors Influence the International Mobility of Research Scientists?* Paris: OECD.

Peters, M. A., and T. Besley (2018), 'China's Double First-Class University Strategy: 双一流', *Educational Philosophy and Theory*, 50 (12): 1075–9.

Shanghai Administration of Foreign Experts Affairs (2021), 'Dali Xiyin Waiguo Rencai Deng Youguan Tongzhi' [Notice of Further Attracting Foreign Talents], http://stcsm.sh.gov.cn/zwgk/tzgs/zhtz/20210301/dd53b0806f614968890b6a1ecb84a199.html.

Shen, Z. (2009), ed. *Sulian Zhuanjia Zai Zhongguo (1948–1960)* [The Soviet Experts in China 1948–1960], Beijing: Xinhua Publishing House.

Subbaraman, N. (2020), 'Harvard Chemistry Chief's Arrest over China Links Shocks Researchers', *Nature*, 3 February, https://doi.org/10.1038/d41586-020-00291-2.

UNNC (2020), *An International University in China: Facts*, https://www.nottingham.edu.cn/en/about/who-we-are.aspx.

Wang, H., and G. Liu (2014), *Zhongguo Guojiyimin Baogao, 2014* [Annual Report on Chinese International Migration, 2014], Beijing: Social Sciences Academic Press.

Welch, A., and J. Hao (2013), 'Returnees and Diaspora as Source of Innovation in Chinese Higher Education', *Frontier of Education in China*, 8 (2): 214–38.

Woldegiyorgis, A. A., D. Proctor and H. de Wit (2018), 'Internationalization of Research: Key Considerations and Concerns', *Journal of Studies in International Education*, 22 (2): 161–76.

Wu, X., and Huang, H. (2018), 'International Faculty in China: Case Studies of Four Leading Universities in Shanghai', *Asia Pacific Education Review*, 19: 253–62.

Zhou, Y., Y. Guo and Y. Liu (2018), 'High-Level Talent Flow and Its Influence on Regional Unbalanced Development in China', *Applied Geography*, 91, 89–98.

Zweig, D. (2006), 'Competing for Talent: China's Strategies to Reverse the Brain Drain', *International Labour Review*, 145 (1–2): 65–90.

Chapter 12

Adotey, S.K. (2020), 'What Will Higher Education in Africa Look Like after COVID-19?', *World Economic Forum*, https://www.weforum.org/agenda/2020/06/higher-education-africa-covid19-coronavirus-digital-online/.

Altbach, P., and H. de Wit (2020), 'Post Pandemic Outlook for HE Is Bleakest for the Poorest', *University World News*, 4 April, https://www.universityworldnews.com/post.php?story=20200402152914362.

Amoah, P., and K. H. Mok (2020), 'The COVID-19 Pandemic and Internationalisation of Higher Education: International Students' Knowledge, Experiences, and Wellbeing', https://www.hepi.ac.uk/2020/06/13/weekend-reading-the-covid-19-pandemic-and-internationalisation-of-higher-education-international-students-knowledge-experiences-and-wellbeing/.

ASEAN Today (2020), 'RCEP: Record Trade Deal Shows Value of Southeast Asian Leadership amid US-China Spat', https://www.aseantoday.com/2020/11/rcep-record-trade-deal-shows-value-of-southeast-asian-leadership-amid-us-china-spat/.

Baber, H. (2021), 'Social Interaction and Effectiveness of the Online Learning – A Moderating Role of Maintaining Social Distance during the Pandemic COVID-19', *Asian Education and Development Studies*, https://doi.org/10.1108/AEDS-09-2020-0209.

Bennell, P. (2019), 'Transnational Higher Education in the United Kingdom: An Up-Date', *International Journal of Educational Development*, 67: 29–40.

Bothwell, E. (2020), 'Asia "May Compete with UK" on International Students Post-Covid', *Times Higher Education*, https://www.timeshighereducation.com/news/asia-may-compete-uk-international-students-post-covid.

Bradsher, K., and A. Swanson (2020), 'China-Led Trade Pact Is Signed, in Challenge to U.S.', *New York Times*, 15 November, https://www.nytimes.com/2020/11/15/business/china-trade-rcep.html.

Bush, T. (2020), 'Life under Lockdown in Higher Education: Insights from a Global University', *HESB*, 8 (June): 12–14, https://headfoundation.org/2020/06/02/hesb-issue-8/.

Cham, T. S. (2020), 'E-learning and Higher Education in the Pre- and Post-COVID-19 Situation', *HESB*, 8 (June): 2–4, https://headfoundation.org/2020/06/02/hesb-issue-8/.

Chan, W. K., and X. Wu (2020). 'Promoting Governance Model Through International Higher Education: Examining International Student Mobility in China between 2003 and 2016', *Higher Education Policy*, 33: 511–30.

Dang, Q. A. (2017), 'Regionalising Higher Education for Repositioning Southeast Asia', *Oxford Review of Education*, 43 (4): 417–32.

Dupont, A. (2020), 'Mitigating the Cold War: Managing US-China Trade, Tech and Geopolitical Conflict', Analysis Paper No 8, Sydney: The Center for Independent Studies.

Facer, K. (2020), 'Beyond Business as Usual: Higher Education in the Face of Climate Change', HEPI Debate Paper No. 24, https://www.hepi.ac.uk/2020/12/10/beyond-business-as-usual-higher-education-in-the-era-of-climate-change/.

Feng, J. Y. (2020), 'How COVID-19 Has and Hasn't Changed Chinese Students' Plans for International Education', https://supchina.com/2020/11/09/how-covid-19-has-and-hasnt-changed-chinese-studnets-plans-for-international-education/.

Fry C. V., X. Cai, Y. Zhang and C. S. Wagner (2020), 'Consolidation in a Crisis: Patterns of International Collaboration in Early COVID-19 Research', *PLoS ONE*, 15 (7): e0236307.

Gopinathan, S., V. Naidu and L. H. Yeong (2020), 'The Big Picture: Student Mobility, Internationalisation and the "New Normal"', *HESB*, 9 (October): 29–31, https://headfoundation.org/2020/10/16/hesb-issue-9/.

He, Y. M., Y. L. Pei, B. Ran, J. Kang and Y. T. Song (2020), 'Analysis on the Higher Education Sustainability in China Based on the Comparison between Universities in China and America', *Sustainability*, 12 (2): 573.

ICEF Monitor (2016), 'Education and the Exercise of Soft Power in China', https://monitor.icef.com/2016/01/education-and-the-exercise-of-soft-power-in-china/.

Khanna, P. (2019), 'Washington Is Dismissing China's Belt and Road. That's a Huge Strategic Mistake', https://www.politico.com/magazine/story/2019/04/30/washington-is-dismissing-chinas-belt-and-road-thats-a-huge-strategic-mistake-226759.

Korkmaz, G., and C. Toraman (2020), 'Are We Ready for the Post-COVID-19 Educational Practice? An Investigation into What Educators Think as to Online Learning', *International Journal of Technology in Education and Science*, 4 (4): 293–309.

Lemert, A., and E. Runde (2020), 'Asia-Pacific Trade Deal RCEP Is Signed; Xi Signals Potential Interest in CPTPP', *Lawfare*, https://www.lawfareblog.com/asia-pacific-trade-deal-rcep-signed-xi-signals-potential-interest-cptpp.

Li, B. Q., Q. Fang and L. Sun (2020), 'Will Chinese Students Study Abroad Post-COVID-19?' https://www.eastasianforum.org/2020/07/11/will-chinese-students-study-abroad-post-covid-19/.

Marginson, S. (2020a), 'The Relentless Price of High Individualism in the Pandemic', *Higher Education Research and Development*, 39 (7): 1392–5.

Marginson, S. (2020b), 'The World Is Changing: Higher Education and the COVID-19 Pandemic', Paper presented at the Global Higher Education Webinar Series, 29 September, Lingnan University.

Marinoni, G., and H. de Wit (2020), 'A Severe Risk of Growing Inequality between Universities', *University World News*, 8 June, https://www.universityworldnews.com/post.php?story=20200608154051 40.

McCarthy, S. (2020), 'Coronavirus: Chinese Students Battle Rising Tide of Prejudice in US but Fear They May Not Be Welcomed Home', *South China Morning Post*, 14 April, https://www.scmp.com/news/china/article/3079877/coronavirus-means-chinese-students-battle-rising-tide-prejudice-us-fear.

Mok, K. H. (2020), 'Will Chinese Students Still Want to Study Abroad Post COVID-19?', *University World News*, 4 July, https://www.universityworldnews.com/post.php?story=20200703155021111.

Mok, K. H., and G. H. Huang (2020), 'Greater Bay Area Mainland Residents' Evaluation of COVID-19 Prevention and City Impression of Hong Kong and Macau', April 2020, https://scholars.ln.edu.hk/en/publications/greater-bay-area-mainland-residents-evaluation-of-covid-19-preven.

Mok, K. H., G. G. Ke and T. Tian (2021), 'China's Responses to Globalisation and Higher Education Reforms: Challenges and Policy Implications', in P. Mattei ed., *Oxford Handbook of Globalization and Higher Education*, Oxford: Oxford University Press.

Mok, K. H., Z. Wang and D. Neubauer, D. (2020), 'Contesting Globalisation and Implications for Higher Education in the Asia-Pacific Region: Challenges and Prospects', *Higher Education Policy*, 33 (3): 397–411.

Mok, K. H., W. Y. Xiong, G. G. Ke and J. Cheung (2020), 'Impact of COVID-19 Pandemic on International Higher Education and Student Mobility: Student Perspectives from Mainland China and Hong Kong', *International Journal of Educational Research*, https://doi.org/10.1016/j.ijer.2020.101718.

Mok, K. H., W. Y. Xiong and A. R. Hamzah (2021), 'The COVID-19 Pandemic's Disruption on University Teaching and Learning and Competence Cultivation: Student Evaluation of Online Learning Experiences in Hong Kong', *International Journal of Chinese Education*, 10(1): 1–20.

Monan, Z. (2020), 'Don't Misunderstand Dual Circulation. China US Focus', 27 October, https://www.chinausfocus.com/finance-economy/dont-misunderstand-dual-circulation.

Montgomery, C., and R. Watermeyer (2021), 'Finding Leadership and Direction in International Higher Education in the Context of Covid 19: Transitioning Forms of Internationalisation?', Paper presented at the Webinar for Education and Development in Asia, co-organized by Lingnan University, University of Bath and University of Durham, 26 February, hosted online.

Neubauer, D. (2020), 'Financing Higher Education in a Post-COVID Era', Paper presented at the CHER 2020 Conference, 13 November, Lingnan University.

Nomura, N. (2020), 'A New Dimension of Student Mobility between Japan and Southeast Asia through the AIMS Programme', HESB, 9 (October): 5–9, https://headfoundation.org/2020/10/16/hesb-issue-9/.

Nott, W. (2020), 'Asian Students Increasingly Likely to Study within Asia – QS Report', https://thepienews.com/news/qs-report-asian-students-increasingly-likely.

Petri, P. A., and M. G. Plummer (2020), 'East Asia Decouples from the United States: Trade War, COVID-19, and East Asia's New Trade Blocs', Peterson Institute for International Economics Working Paper, https://www.piie.com/system/files/documents/wp20-9.pdf.

Qi, Y., S. L. Wang and C. J. Dai (2020), 'Chinese Students Abroad during the COVID Crisis: Challenges and Opportunities', https://www.21global.ucsb.edu/global-e/september-2020/chinese-students-abroad-during-covid-crisis-challenges-and-opportunities.

Riddervold, M., and G. Rosen (2018), 'Unified in Response to Rising Powers? China, Russia and EU-US Relations', *Journal of European Integration*, 40 (5): 555–70.

RNZ News (2020), 'Opposition as NZ Joins World's Largest Free Trade Agreement', https://www.rnz.co.nz/news/national/430670/opposition-as-nz-joins-world-s-largest-free-trade-agreement.

Seo, D. S., and H. J. Kim (2020), 'The Impact of the AIMS Programme on International Higher Education: Student Mobility between the Republic of Korea and the ASEAN Region', *HESB*, 9 (October): 10–13, https://headfoundation.org/2020/10/16/hesb-issue-9/.

Simbulan, N. P. (2020), 'The Philippines: COVID-19 and Its Impact on Higher Education in the Philippines', *HESB*, 8 (October): 15–18, https://headfoundation.org/2020/06/02/hesb-issue-8/.

Song, J. (2017), 'The Manifestation of China's Soft Power Agenda in American Higher Education: The Case of the Confucius Institute Project in America', Doctoral thesis, University of California, California.

Teter, W., and L. B. Wang (2020), 'COVID-19 and UNESCO: Monitoring the Impact on People and Places for Relevant Higher Education', *HESB*, 8 (June): 9–11, https://headfoundation.org/2020/06/02/hesb-issue-8/.

Tilak, J. B. (2020), 'Reimagining Higher Education and Research during post-COVID-19', Paper presented at the CHER 2020 Conference, 13 November 2020, Lingnan University.

Tunsjo, O. (2018), *The Return of Bipolarity in World Politics: China, the United States and Geostructural Realism*, New York: Columbia University Press.

UNESCO Institute of Statistics (2020). http://data.uis.unesco.org/.

Wan, C. D. (2020), 'Malaysia: An Unexpected Disruption to Teaching and Learning', *HESB*, 8 (June): 19-21, https://headfoundation.org/2020/06/02/hesb-issue-8/.

Welch, A. (2020), 'The COVID-19 Crisis in Australian Higher Education', Paper presented at the Global Higher Education Webinar Series, 12 October, Lingnan University.

Wong, E., and Barnes, J. E. (2020), 'U.S. to Expel Chinese Graduate Students with Ties to China's Military Schools', https://.nytimes.com.com/2020/05/28/us/politics/china-hong-kong-trump.stu.

Xiong, W. Y., J. Jiang and K. H. Mok (2020), 'Hong Kong University Students' Online Learning Experiences under the Covid-19 Pandemic', *Higher Education Policy Institute*, https://www.hepi.ac.uk/2020/08/03/hong-kong-university-students-online-learning-experiences-under-the-covid-19-pandemic/ (accessed 10 February 2021).

Xu, J., G. Sun, W. Cao, W. Fan, Z. Pan, Z. Yao and H. Li (2021), 'Stigma, Discrimination, and Hate Crimes in Chinese-Speaking World amid Covid-19 Pandemic', *Asian Journal of Criminology*, 16: 51–74.

Yeong, L. H. (2020), 'Between Globalisation and a Decoupled, COVID-19 World: Regional Student Mobility in ASEAN and the EU', *HESB* 9 (October): 2–4, https://headfoundation.org/2020/10/16/hesb-issue-9/.

Zhai, Y., and X. Du (2020), 'Mental Health Care for International Chinese Students Affected by the COVID-19 Outbreak', *Lancet Psychiatry*, 7 (4): e22.

Index

The specific category 'East Asia' does not appear in the index but its components, inclusions and associations permeate almost every page of the book, and much of the index.

211 Project, China 12, 135–6
985 Project, China 12 ,135–6

academic freedom and autonomy 73, 143–4, 214–17
accountability 13
Africa xv, 6, 36, 135, 231, 233, 237
agency and agency/structure xvi, 125–6, 130–5, 186–7, 188–91, 195–201
Anglo-American xv, 17, 51–2, 57, 61–3
Anglo-European *see under* Euro-American
Association of Southeast Asian Nations (ASEAN) 5, 111, 116, 174, 226, 241, 244, 245
Australia 20, 21, 24–5, 79, 91, 123, 165, 169, 170, 175, 185, 186, 198, 204, 206, 211, 212, 226, 229, 230, 231, 233, 237, 239–45
autonomy of universities 33, 140–2, 143–4, 149, 152, 162–3
A3 Foresight programme, Japan 108–27

Belt and Road Initiative 6, 67, 76, 98–9, 168, 241
bibliometric collections 15
biological and medical sciences 114–15
see also science output
Bologna process in Europe 109
Brain Korea 21 project 12
Brexit xvii
Buddhism 2, 72, 84, 139

Canada 9, 18, 20, 24–5, 165, 186, 198, 206, 212, 213, 226, 229, 230, 239, 240
Centre for Global Higher Education xiv, xv–xviii, xix, xx

China xix, 1, 4, 5, 6, 7, 8, 9, 10, 11, 12, 13, 14, 15, 16, 17, 22, 23, 24, 25, 26, 27, 36, 51–67, 69–84, 85–104, 107, 113–15, 123–5, 129–45, 153, 161–2, 166–70, 170–1, 173, 175, 203–23, 225–31, 225–46
Chinese civilization xx, 1, 10, 12, 154
Collective Action for the Mobility Program of University Students in Asia (CAMPUS Asia) 6, 107–27
collectivism 53–4
commercialization *see under* marketization
Communist Party of China (CPC or CCP) 2, 5, 73–4, 83
'Confucian Model' *see under* Post-Confucian Model
Confucianism 2, 3, 4, 35, 51–67, 72, 73, 75–6, 84, 101, 130–5, 139, 154, 171, 172
  Confucian individualism 54
  Confucian self-cultivation 3, 8, 10, 11, 132
  see also collectivism
Confucius Institutes 168–9, 227
Covid-19 pandemic 4, 148, 160–2, 225–46
cross-cultural and intercultural relations 28, 84–7, 130
  see also East/West encounter and engagement
Cultural political economy 110
culture and cultural factors 4, 12, 29, 96, 167, 171, 173
  in East Asia 1, 4–6, 27

Daoism 72, 84, 133, 139
de-Chinalization 5
de-Japanization 5

de-Westernization 5, 26
devolution in higher education 12
diasporic talent 15, 129, 207–8
discursive institutionalism 112–13
doctoral education 14–15
Doi Moi (Vietnam) 166, 170, 173–4, 180
Double First-Class programme, China 12, 97, 135–6

East/West encounter and engagement xix, 21–7, 27–8, 35
economic role of higher education 34, 61–2
economies in East Asia 6–8
efficiency in higher education 13
endogenization (indigenization) 4, 21–7, 28, 29–30
English language monoculture xix, 23
in research 23
 English-medium education 23, 98
 see also languages in higher education
equity and equality in higher education 13
Euro-American countries, agendas and culture xv, xix, xx, 1, 2, 4, 5, 6, 10, 11, 21–7, 78, 134, 137–9, 140, 142–3, 172, 180, 230
Europe and European countries not elsewhere included 8, 12, 15, 85–104, 119, 124, 129, 203, 226, 237, 238–41, 241
European Union and European regionalisation 6, 16, 17, 116, 246

Feng Youlan 1
funding of higher education 11, 12, 33, 97, 102–4, 147, 152
funding of research 15, 129
in higher education 15–16

geo-politics *see under* US-China conflict
global citizenship 29, 34, 65–6, 69–84
global equity 63
global public good and common good 29, 45, 50, 51–67, 85–104
 comparison between public and common good 88
global scale and globalization xiv, 78, 88, 137–9, 165, 167, 173–5, 225

global university rankings 45, 86, 149–51, 155, 162
glonacal 134–5, 147–8
governance in higher education xvii, 12–15, 152
government, role and nature of 3, 10, 35, 54, 57, 97, 115–17
 see also policy on higher education
government-university relations 33, 144, 149, 162–3
 see also autonomy of institutions, funding, policy in higher education
graduate employment xvi, xvii, 13, 174, 196
Greater Bay Area (China) 13, 238

Han dynasty 3–4
harmony without uniformity xix, 27, 76
higher education xiv
Higher Education SPROUT project, Taiwan 13, 150–1, 156
Hong Kong SAR 2, 3, 5, 6, 7, 8, 9, 12, 13, 14, 15, 16, 22, 23, 25, 26, 154–5, 167, 169, 211, 230, 232, 237–40, 245
humanities 29, 94, 118–20, 129–45, 151
Humboldt Model 94–6, 102

India xv, 2, 14, 79, 166, 226, 228
indigenization *see under* endogenization
Indonesia 2
institutional scale, activity, mission and identity 85–104, 120–1, 140–2, 155–6
international branch campuses 81–2, 177–8, 206
international faculty mobility 30, 177, 203–23
international migration 185–201, 203–23
international research collaboration 15, 87, 113, 119, 137, 225, 229
international student fees xv
international student mobility xiv, xvii, 15, 25–6, 29–30, 85, 98, 148, 158–9, 165, 167, 168, 171–2, 176–6, 179–80, 185–201, 207, 225–46
internationalization in higher education and research xvii, 22, 23, 29–30, 85–6, 89, 93, 98–9, 205–9

internationalization strategies in East Asia 11, 21–7
  in Japan 107–27
  in research in China 129–45
  in Taiwan 147–63
  in Vietnam 165–81

Japan 1, 3, 5, 6, 7, 8, 9, 11, 12, 14, 15, 16, 17, 18, 22, 23, 24, 25, 26, 36, 107–27, 129, 153, 168, 170, 172, 175, 185–201, 203, 218, 226, 230, 240, 242, 243
jeong 29, 33–50

knowledge 64, 129–45
  published knowledge 3
knowledge economy and knowledge society discourse 14, 116, 125–6
Korea *see under* North Korea, South Korea

Latin America xv, 2, 6
land grant universities (US) 95
languages in higher education 7, 8, 72, 137–8, 142–3, 149, 168–9, 172, 176, 180, 206, 209–10, 221, 244

Macau SAR 2, 3, 7, 8, 9, 12, 13, 14, 22, 23, 25, 26
Malaysia 25, 167, 168, 203, 228, 236–7, 238, 244, 245
management in higher education xvii, 12, 155, 157–60
marketization and market-based systems of higher education 33–4, 94, 99–100, 102–4, 149, 165, 175
Marxism and Marxist-Leninism 130, 140, 179
massification 13, 14
methodological nationalism 52, 58–9, 61
modernization 5, 10, 12
Mongolia 2, 7, 8, 11, 13, 14, 23, 24, 25, 44

narrative method of inquiry 189–91
national scale, activity and identity 130–40, 148, 152–5
  see also glonacal, methodological nationalism
nature 46–8, 133–4

New Zealand 9, 21, 25, 165, 186, 226, 230, 238, 241, 242, 244, 245
neoliberalism 46, 174
North (global North) 71, 76, 131, 179
North-South distinction xx
North Korea 4, 23

Organization for Economic Cooperation and Development (OECD) 8–10

participation in tertiary education xiv, 3, 7, 8, 11, 13, 33
Philippines 25, 236, 244
policy on higher education 10, 107–27, 136, 139–40, 147, 148–52, 156, 160–3, 166–70
  economic competitiveness through higher education and science 116–17, 125–6, 147, 203
  see also entries for specific countries
political culture 4, 10, 55–7, 61
polyvocality 70
populism in politics xvii
Post-Confucian Model of higher education development 10–12, 13
postcolonialism 78
private higher education xvi, 11, 12, 33, 49, 150, 151
Programme for International Student Assessment (PISA) 8–10
Projects 911 and 322, Vietnam 13
public good 4
  and higher education xvii, 11, 33–50, 51, 175, 229
  see also global public good and common good
public/private distinction 52–4, 61

Qin dynasty 3–4
Qing dynasty 153, 205
quality assurance 13

racism, racial discrimination and stigmatization 2, 139, 169, 230–1
regional scale, regionalization, regional cooperation and barriers to cooperation in East Asia 5–6, 21–7, 107–27, 135, 241–6
research and researchers 14, 89, 94

research collaboration *see under*
international collaboration in
research
see also science output, science,
technology, engineering and
mathematics disciplines, social
sciences, humanities

science output xiv, 3, 11, 14, 15, 16,
23, 107
in biological and medical
sciences 16, 17
high citation science 18–21
internationalization and
endogenization 26
in science, technology, engineering
and mathematics disciplines 16,
17–18, 21, 129
science, technology, engineering and
mathematics disciplines (STEM) 14,
94, 114–15, 118–20, 130, 151, 205
see also science output
Singapore xv, 3, 4, 5, 7, 8, 9, 11, 15, 16,
17, 18, 22, 24, 25, 203, 211, 230, 240,
242, 244, 245
Sino-American conflict *see
under* US-China conflict
Sino-Japanese war 1
social and economic inequality xvii
social mobility xvii
social sciences 16, 29, 94, 114–15,
118–20, 129–45, 151
soft power 166–70, 187, 227, 244
Southeast Asia xv, 2, 26
South (global South) 4, 131, 179
South Korea 2, 3, 4, 5, 6, 7, 8, 9, 11, 12,
13, 14, 15, 16, 17, 18, 22, 23, 24, 25,
26, 33–50, 107, 113–15, 123–5, 166,
175, 203, 211, 218, 226, 230, 238, 242,
243, 244
SPROUT project *see under* Higher
Education SPROUT project
state, nature and role of *see
under* government, role and nature
of; political culture
stratification in higher education
systems 149–50

student financing and tuition xvi, 93–4

Taiwan 2, 3, 4, 7, 8, 9, 11, 16, 17, 18,
22, 23, 24, 25, 147–63, 167–8, 169,
230, 240
teaching and learning in higher
education xvii, 150, 236–7
technologies in higher education xvii
tianxia 55–7, 66, 75
tianxia weigong 29, 51–67
Top Global University project, Japan 12
Trow, Martin 13
Trump, Donald (US President) xvii
Tsinghua University 1, 18, 19, 21, 86
tuition and tuition loans *see
under* student financing and tuition

United Kingdom (UK) xv, 14, 24, 25, 93,
97, 129, 170, 198, 203, 211, 212, 226,
229, 230, 232, 237, 238–41
United Nations Educational, Social and
Cultural Organization (UNESO),
60, 62, 71
United States of America (US) xv, xix, 2,
3, 4, 5, 11, 14, 15, 16, 18, 22, 24, 25,
26, 85–104, 117, 119, 129, 166, 170,
171, 172, 175, 180, 198, 203, 205,
211, 212, 226–31, 238–43
University Alliance of the Silk Road
(UASR) 6
US-China conflict 5, 169–70,
226–31, 241–3

Vietnam 2, 3, 4, 5, 7, 8, 11, 13, 14, 22, 24,
25, 26, 36, 44, 165–81
vocational education xvii

the West, Western, Westernization *see
under* Euro-America
white supremacy 2
world-class universities 3, 11, 12, 19–20,
21, 22, 27, 85–104, 203

Zhou Dynasty 3, 4, 139

www.ingramcontent.com/pod-product-compliance
Lightning Source LLC
Chambersburg PA
CBHW070750020526
44115CB00032B/1613